D0165921

The Interpreting Studies Reader

"At last, the seminal articles on interpreting have been compiled in a single volume. Many of them have been out of print, inaccessible, or unavailable in English until now. A must for every library, whether personal or institutional."

Holly Mikkelson, *International Interpretation Resource Center, USA*

The Interpreting Studies Reader is a comprehensive guide to the growing area of interpreting studies. Spanning the multiple and diverse approaches to interpreting, it draws together the key articles in the field and puts them in their thematic and social contexts. This is an authoritative and up-to-date overview of interpreting studies and the new directions the subject is taking in the twenty-first century.

Features include:

- an introductory essay reviewing the evolution of interpreting studies
- organization into seven thematic sections, each with an editors' introduction
- a comprehensive bibliography and suggestions for further reading.

The Interpreting Studies Reader is an invaluable introduction and reference for students, researchers and practitioners with an interest in this dynamic and fast-growing domain.

Extracts by: Bistra Alexieva, R. Bruce W. Anderson, Henri C. Barik, Susan Berk-Seligson, Ghelly V. Chernov, Ángela Collados Aís, Michael Cronin, Helle V. Dam, David Gerver, Daniel Gile, Frieda Goldman-Eisler, Basil Hatim & Ian Mason, Alfred Hermann, Hella Kirchhoff, Ingrid Kurz, Marianne Lederer, Barbara Moser-Mercer, Pierre Oléron & Hubert Nanpon, Eva Paneth, Fernando Poyatos, Cynthia B. Roy, Anne Schjoldager, Danica Seleskovitch, Robin Setton, Granville Tate & Graham H. Turner, Cecilia Wadensjö.

Franz Pöchhacker is Associate Professor of Interpreting Studies in the Department of Translation and Interpreting at the University of Vienna.

Miriam Shlesinger is Senior Lecturer in Translation and Interpreting Studies in the Department of Translation and Interpreting of Bar-Ilan University, Israel.

The Interpreting Studies Reader

Edited by

Franz Pöchhacker and
Miriam Shlesinger

Routledge
Taylor & Francis Group

LONDON AND NEW YORK

First published 2002
by Routledge
2 Park Square, Milton Park, Abingdon, Oxon OX14 4RN

Simultaneously published in the USA and Canada
by Routledge
711 Third Avenue, New York, NY 10017

Routledge is an imprint of the Taylor & Francis Group, an informa business

Typeset in Perpetua and Bell Gothic by RefineCatch Limited, Bungay, Suffolk

British Library Cataloguing in Publication Data
A catalogue record for this book is available from the British Library

Library of Congress Cataloging in Publication Data
The interpreting studies reader / [edited by] Franz Pöchhacker and Miriam Shlesinger.
    p.   cm.
    Includes bibliographical references and index.
    1. Translating and interpreting.   I. Pöchhacker, Franz.   II. Shlesinger, Miriam, 1947–

P306 .I57 2002
418′.02—dc21   2001050180

ISBN 10: 0-415-22477-2 (hbk)
ISBN 10: 0-415-22478-0 (pbk)

ISBN 13: 978-0-415-22477-2 (hbk)
ISBN 13: 978-0-415-22478-9 (pbk)

Contents

Preface

The idea of devoting a separate volume to Interpreting Studies, rather than relegating it to a subsection of Lawrence Venuti's *Translation Studies Reader*, was not immediately evident, but was readily espoused in consultations with Advisory Editor Mona Baker. The implementation of this project has been a collaborative effort from the start. Differences in our nationalities, academic orientations, languages, etc. have been of no consequence in the unfolding of a book which drew upon that which we share rather than that which sets us apart. We are grateful to Routledge for affording us the opportunity to engage in the long brainstorming sessions, the friendly battles and the magical epiphanies that occur when two individuals' thought processes are in perfect sync. We are grateful too for the opportunity to rediscover the rich and riveting literature that has come into being in a field that is often still thought of as a mere offshoot, and for the hours spent poring over it in an often painful struggle to stay within the confines of a single-volume selection.

In this project, we have had the good fortune to receive the encouragement, help and advice of numerous friends and colleagues, among them Barbara Ahrens, Jesús Baigorri, Mona Baker, Richard W. Bristin, Brian Butterworth, Stanislav Chernobylski, Terry Chesher, Hans W. Dechert, Edwin Gentzler, Daniel Gile, Klaus Kaindl, Ingrid Kurz, Sylvie Lambert, Kirsten Malmkjær, Ian Mason, Alexandre Mikheev, Barbara Moser-Mercer, Uldis Ozolins, Heidemarie Salevsky, Robin Setton, Graham H. Turner and Lawrence Venuti. Their contributions have included reviews of the initial proposal, bibliographical information and ingenious assistance with the detective work involved in tracking down some of the writers represented in this book, as well as hard-to-find materials.

We are also grateful to Louisa Semlyen, our editor, for embracing Mona Baker's proposal for a separate Reader on Interpreting Studies and for seeing this project through to its successful completion, and to her team at Routledge for making the process as efficient and frustration-free as possible.

And finally, our boundless thanks to Erika Pöchhacker and Moshe Shlesinger for their love and patience, and for their unselfish support throughout.

Franz Pöchhacker and Miriam Shlesinger
14 April 2001

Acknowledgments

We are indebted to the authors and copyright holders listed below for allowing us to reprint the materials that comprise this book. Where texts have been edited for reasons of space, we gratefully acknowledge authors' permission to use abridged versions of their work.

Bistra Alexieva, "A Typology of Interpreter-Mediated Events," *The Translator. Studies in Intercultural Communication* 3: 2 (1997): 153–74. Copyright © 1997 by St. Jerome Publishing (www.stjerome.co.uk). Reprinted by permission of the author and the publisher.

R. Bruce W. Anderson, "Perspectives on the Role of Interpreter," in Richard W. Brislin (ed.) *Translation: Applications and Research*, New York: Gardner Press, Inc., 1976, pp. 208–28. Copyright © 1976 by Gardner Press, Inc. Reprinted by permission of the author and the publisher.

Henri C. Barik, "Simultaneous Interpretation: Qualitative and Linguistic Data," *Language and Speech* 18: 2 (1975): 272–98. Copyright © 1975 by Kingston Press Ltd. Reprinted by permission of the author and the publisher.

Susan Berk-Seligson, "The Impact of Politeness in Witness Testimony: The Influence of the Court Interpreter," *Multilingua. Journal of Cross-Cultural and Interlanguage Communication* 7: 4 (1988): 411–39. Copyright © 1988 by Mouton de Gruyter. Reprinted by permission of the author and the publisher.

Ghelly V. Chernov, "Semantic Aspects of Psycholinguistic Research in Simultaneous Interpretation," *Language and Speech* 22: 3 (1979): 277–95. Copyright © 1979 by Kingston Press Ltd. Reprinted by permission of the author and the publisher.

Ángela Collados Aís, Excerpts from *La evaluación de la calidad en interpretación simultánea. La importancia de la comunicación no verbal* (pp. 81–3, 89–95, 169–89, 249–50), Peligros (Granada): Editorial Comares, 1998. Copyright © 1998 by Ángela Collados Aís. Reprinted in English translation by permission of the author and the publisher.

Michael Cronin, "The Empire Talks Back: Orality, Heteronomy and the Cultural Turn in Interpreting Studies," in Maria Tymoczko and Edwin Gentzler (eds) *Translation and Power*, Amherst, Massachusetts: University of Massachusetts Press,

2002. Copyright © 2002 by University of Massachusetts Press. Reprinted in abridged form by permission of the author and the publisher.

Helle V. Dam, "Lexical Similarity vs Lexical Dissimilarity in Consecutive Interpreting. A Product-oriented Study of Form-based vs Meaning-based Interpreting," *The Translator. Studies in Intercultural Communication* 4: 1 (1998): 49–68. Copyright © 1998 by St. Jerome Publishing (www.stjerome.co.uk). Reprinted by permission of the author and the publisher.

David Gerver, "The Effects of Source Language Presentation Rate on the Performance of Simultaneous Conference Interpreters," in Emerson Foulke (ed.) *Proceedings of the Second Louisville Conference on Rate and/or Frequency-Controlled Speech, October 22–24, 1969*, Louisville, Kentucky: Center for Rate-Controlled Recordings, University of Louisville, 1969, pp. 162–84. Reprinted by permission of the Estate of David Gerver (Prof. Elizabeth Gerver).

Daniel Gile, "Conference Interpreting as a Cognitive Management Problem," in Joseph H. Danks, Gregory M. Shreve, Stephen B. Fountain and Michael K. McBeath (eds) *Cognitive Processes in Translation and Interpreting*, Thousand Oaks, California: Sage Publications, 1997, pp. 196–214. Copyright © 1997 by Sage Publications, Inc. Reprinted by permission of the author and the publisher.

Frieda Goldman-Eisler, "Segmentation of Input in Simultaneous Translation," *Journal of Psycholinguistic Research* 1: 2 (1972): 127–40. Copyright © 1972 by Plenum Press. Reprinted by permission of the publisher.

Basil Hatim and Ian Mason, "Interpreting: A Text Linguistic Approach," Chapter 3 in *The Translator as Communicator*, London and New York: Routledge, 1997, pp. 36–60. Copyright © 1997 by Basil Hatim and Ian Mason. Reprinted by permission of the authors and the publisher.

Alfred Hermann, "Dolmetschen im Altertum. Ein Beitrag zur antiken Kulturgeschichte," in Karl Thieme, Alfred Hermann und Edgar Glässer, *Beiträge zur Geschichte des Dolmetschens*, München: Isar Verlag, 1956, pp. 25–59. Copyright © 1956 by Isar Verlag Dr. Günter Olzog. Reprinted in English translation by permission of Olzog Verlag.

Hella Kirchhoff, "Das Simultandolmetschen: Interdependenz der Variablen im Dolmetschprozeß, Dolmetschmodelle und Dolmetschstrategien," in Horst W. Drescher und Signe Scheffzek (eds) *Theorie und Praxis des Übersetzens und Dolmetschens*, Frankfurt am Main: Peter Lang, 1976, pp. 59–71. Copyright by Horst W. Drescher. Reprinted in English translation by permission of the author and Horst W. Drescher.

Ingrid Kurz, "Conference Interpretation: Expectations of Different User Groups," *The Interpreters' Newsletter* no. 5 (1993): 13–21. Copyright © 1993 by Università degli Studi di Trieste, Scuola Superiore di Lingue Moderne per Interpreti e Traduttori (Laura Gran and David Snelling). Reprinted by permission of the author and the publisher.

Marianne Lederer, "Simultaneous Interpretation – Units of Meaning and Other Features," in David Gerver and H. Wallace Sinaiko (eds) *Language Interpretation and Communication*, New York: Plenum Press, 1978, pp. 323–32. Copyright ©

1978 by Plenum Press. Reprinted by permission of the author and Kluwer Academic/Plenum Publishers.

Barbara Moser-Mercer, "Process Models in Simultaneous Interpretation," in Christa Hauenschild and Susanne Heizmann (eds) *Machine Translation and Translation Theory*, Berlin: Mouton de Gruyter, 1997, pp. 3–17. Copyright © 1997 by Walter de Gruyter & Co. Reprinted by permission of the author and the publisher.

Pierre Oléron and Hubert Nanpon, "Recherches sur la traduction simultanée," *Journal de Psychologie normale et pathologique* 62: 1 (1965): 73–94. Reprinted by permission of the Estate of Pierre Oléron (Mme. Geneviève Oléron).

Eva Paneth, Excerpt from "An Investigation into Conference Interpreting (with Special Reference to the Training of Interpreters)," (pp. 15–33), MA thesis, University of London, 1957. Reprinted by permission of the Estate of Eva Paneth (Dr Heinz Post).

Fernando Poyatos, "Nonverbal Communication in Simultaneous and Consecutive Interpretation: A Theoretical Model and New Perspectives," *TexTconTexT* 2: 2 (1987): 73–108. Copyright © 1987 by Julius Groos Verlag. Reprinted by permission of the author and the publisher.

Cynthia B. Roy, "The Problem with Definitions, Descriptions, and the Role Metaphors of Interpreters," *Journal of Interpretation* 6: 1 (1993): 127–54. Copyright © Registry of Interpreters for the Deaf. Reprinted by permission of the author and the publisher.

Anne Schjoldager, "An Exploratory Study of Translational Norms in Simultaneous Interpreting: Methodological Reflections," *Hermes. Journal of Linguistics* no. 14 (1995): 65–87. Copyright © 1995 by *Hermes. Journal of Linguistics*, published by the Aarhus School of Business, Faculty of Modern Languages (Jan Engberg). Reprinted by permission of the author and the publisher.

Danica Seleskovitch, Excerpts from *Langage, langues et mémoire. Étude de la prise de notes en interprétation consécutive* (pp. 56–67, 179–81), Paris: Lettres Modernes, 1975 (Coll. "Cahiers Champollion"). Reprinted in English translation by permission of the author and the publisher.

Robin Setton, "Meaning Assembly in Simultaneous Interpretation," *Interpreting. International Journal of Research and Practice in Interpreting* 3: 2 (1998): 163–99. Copyright © 1998 by John Benjamins Publishing Co. Reprinted by permission of the author and the publisher.

Granville Tate and Graham H. Turner, "The Code and the Culture: Sign Language Interpreting – In Search of the New Breed's Ethics," *Deaf Worlds* 13: 3 (1997): 27–34. Copyright © 1997 by Granville Tate and Graham H. Turner. Reprinted by permission of the authors and Forest Book Services.

Cecilia Wadensjö, "The Double Role of a Dialogue Interpreter," *Perspectives. Studies in Translatology* 1993 (1): 105–21. Copyright © 1993 by Museum Tusculanum Press, University of Copenhagen. Reprinted by permission of the author and the publisher.

INTRODUCTION

WHILE INTERPRETING AS a form of mediating across boundaries of language and culture has been instrumental in human communication since earliest times, its recognition as something to be studied and observed is relatively recent. In his Introduction to *The Translation Studies Reader*, Lawrence Venuti (2000) lists interpreting as an area of translation research whose "volume and degree of specialization demand separate coverage." The present collection is an attempt to provide such coverage, spanning the multiple approaches to the phenomenon of interpreting in all its diversity and complexity. The growing academization of the field – coupled with the search for effective ways of teaching it – and the rapidly expanding use of oral translation in its various forms have provided the impetus for a volume which affords the reader a panoramic view of research on interpreting in its cognitive, social and communicational dimensions.

As practitioners' interest in understanding and explaining their profession grows, it is also attracting the attention of researchers in more established disciplines. Indeed, these two groups – researchers within the profession and those beyond – sometimes in tandem but more often separately, have been producing a growing body of insights and findings. As a result, one can speak of a community of scholars and researchers, however diverse, which has made the study of interpreting into a (sub)discipline in its own right. Some of the most significant contributions to this emerging field of study are represented in *The Interpreting Studies Reader*, which is designed for anyone interested in finding out more about the past, present and future of Interpreting Studies, whether in the specific context of a university syllabus or in a more general tradition of scholarly inquiry.

In many respects, this Reader is unique. The closest thing to a broad overview of research on interpreting is more than twenty years old, and out of print. Notwithstanding its merits as a trailblazing multidisciplinary collection, the proceedings volume of the 1977 NATO Conference in Venice (Gerver and Sinaiko 1978) covers only the first decade or so of a fledgling area of research. Another compilation, Lambert and Moser-Mercer (1994), which also makes recourse to other disciplines, is primarily devoted to the simultaneous mode of conference interpreting. A landmark event designed to take stock of the rapidly growing field was the International Conference on Interpretation, which took place in Turku, Finland, in 1994 and resulted in two books, Tommola (1995) and Gambier *et al.* (1997). The former brings together papers and posters on diverse topics, and the latter reflects the interactive sessions devoted to the main strands in (conference) interpreting research, but neither volume offers the historical perspective and broad sweep aimed at in the present Reader. Other efforts towards capturing the state of the art have included, most notably, a monograph by Gile (1995a), who also guest-edited a special issue of *Target: International Journal of Translation Studies* (7:1, 1995), devoted to research on interpreting. This volume aspires, however, to be much more: to meet the basic requirements of an up-to-date, coherent and comprehensive anthology.

Many of the earlier papers on interpreting appeared in rather obscure and often inaccessible journals, and are difficult to track down. In providing a convenient representative sampling of the most significant writings on interpreting to date, including five which are appearing in English for the first time, the Reader aims at providing a sense of the broad scope of interpreting as a profession, and thus as an object of study, and reflecting the open-endedness and growth potential of the field.

A more specific description of the design and structure of the Reader will be given towards the end of this Introduction. First, however, let us try to define what interpreting is, in its various modes, modalities and applications. We will then present the discipline that aims at studying it, namely Interpreting Studies (IS), by reviewing its past and contemporary development as well as its relations with its parent discipline, Translation Studies (TS), and with other disciplines.

Interpreting defined

It was only in the course of the twentieth century that interpreting gained wide recognition as a profession (Bowen *et al.* 1995; *Interpreting* 4: 1, 1999). Yet interpreting must have been practiced when ancient peoples were driven into exile, when explorers had to transact business, and when slaves were being put to work for the colonizer. Cast into their role by dint of their knowledge of languages, early practitioners did not have access to structured training courses or to associations capable of establishing standards of practice and working conditions. It follows that a comprehensive definition of interpreting cannot be confined to its later professionalized forms, just as it cannot exclude any of the modes or settings in which it is practiced. Interpreting, usually in the simultaneous mode, is carried out at international conferences and symposia; it is also carried out, however, more often than not on an *ad hoc* basis, by the children of immigrants, by hospital cleaners, by trained and untrained signed-language interpreters, by tour guides and by countless others with widely varying levels of language and communication skills. Interpreting then can be defined most broadly as interlingual, intercultural oral or signed mediation, enabling communication between individuals or groups who do not share, or do not choose to use, the same language(s).

The word "interpret" is not without its problems, however: to the uninitiated, "interpreting" and "interpretation" sometimes evoke an imposition of meaning by someone who may expand, omit or otherwise filter the speaker's intention. Nor are the terminological difficulties confined to English. French, for instance, has two variants – *interprétation* and *interprétariat*, and the choice between them underlines the distinction between prestigious and less prestigious forms of the activity: *interprétariat*, probably patterned on *secrétariat*, has been applied rather disdainfully by conference interpreters to the work of the "interprète de liaison ou d'affaires, guide-interprète, secrétaire polyglotte, etc." (ESIT 2001). Yet, along with the professionalization of previously marginal domains, this self-same term has recently gained currency in the distinct, but by no means inferior, collocation *l'interprétariat communautaire* (Sauvêtre 2000). Whatever the language-specific lexical gridding (for a lexicographic analysis, cf. Mead 1999), and whatever the overtones assigned to the terms available, we use the term "interpreting" (rather than "interpretation") in the Reader to refer to the activity in all its ramifications, and "Interpreting Studies" as the name of the discipline.

Interpreting Studies

The name and nature of Interpreting Studies

James S Holmes, in his seminal 1972 paper on "The Name and Nature of Translation Studies" ([1972]/1988), proposes various sub-branches of Theoretical Translation Studies, and cites interpreting as an example of a "medium-restricted" form of human (versus machine) oral (versus written) translation. In other words, Holmes views interpreting as simply one of many objects of Translation Studies, and sees no need to designate it as a separate (sub)disciplinary entity.

Indeed, it was not until the 1990s that the term "Interpreting Studies" came into being. It was first used in a major international publication by Salevsky (1993a) after a presentation at the 8th Conference on Translation and Interpreting at Charles University, Prague, in October 1992 (Salevsky 1993b). A few weeks earlier, at the Translation Studies Congress in Vienna, Gile had delivered a keynote address on "Interpretation Studies" (Gile 1994). It appears that by 1992 both scholars had felt that the time was ripe for the study of interpreting to have a name of its own reflecting its emergence as a field of study in its own right. Prior to that, Gile had used "Interpretation Research and Theory (IRT)," later changed to "Interpretation Research (IR)" and, subsequently, to "Conference Interpretation Research (CIR)," whereas Salevsky, in a paper published in 1992, had posed the question: "*Dolmetschen – Objekt der Übersetzungs- oder Dolmetschwissenschaft?*" (Interpreting – Object of Translation or Interpreting Studies?).

The aims of IS are the same, *mutatis mutandis*, as those first put forth by Holmes in relation to its parent discipline, namely to describe the phenomenon of interpreting and interpretation(s) and to establish general explanatory and predictive principles (cf. Holmes [1972]/1988: 71). Like TS, moreover, IS has developed into a remarkably heterogeneous series of loosely connected paradigms. Attempts to provide a unifying description of the nature of IS are encumbered by this seeming lack of cohesiveness: the tools and methodologies used by interpreting scholars are as diverse as the theories and models that they apply. The object of IS is no less multi-faceted: a panoply of modes, modalities, settings, norms, institutional constraints and interactional constellations makes for fuzzy boundaries and a continual struggle to delineate the interpreting researcher's purview. Experts in IS have yet to agree, for example, whether court interpreting needs to be regarded as an area of community-based interpreting; whether media interpreting or diplomatic interpreting are special types of conference interpreting; or whether business and psychiatric interpreting should both be subsumed under liaison interpreting. Be that as it may, there seems to be enough common ground and research-oriented interaction to warrant a perception of the field as a single (sub)discipline.

IS in relation to TS and to other disciplines

If indeed IS is seen as a discipline within the broader framework of TS, one wonders to what extent the theoretical foundations of TS would necessarily apply to research on interpreting. Looking at the IS literature, one finds that very few authors draw upon the concepts and theories generated by translation scholars. The notion of equivalence is a case in point. While occupying a central position in the TS discourse for decades (cf. Venuti 2000: 121–2), it rarely figures in IS, where discussion has traditionally centered on notions like "errors," "omissions," "accuracy," "faithfulness," "fidelity" and "sense consistency with the original message." The same holds true for function-oriented accounts of translation such as Vermeer's (1978) *skopos* theory and Toury's (1980, 1995) concept of translational norms as a driving force in Descriptive Translation Studies. With very few exceptions, neither of these linchpins of modern translation theory has been incorporated into the mainstream of interpreting research. By the same token, very few TS scholars have actively engaged in interpreting research or even mentioned interpreting in their writings. On the whole, IS researchers have mostly been inspired by paradigms from other disciplines, especially psychology and linguistics.

It is quite revealing that the emergence of IS under its own disciplinary label should have coincided with the 1992 TS Congress on the theme "Translation Studies – an Interdiscipline" (Snell-Hornby *et al.* 1994). Indeed, leading representatives of IS, usually with a focus on conference interpreting, have stressed time and again that the scientific inquiry into this complex phenomenon requires the collaboration of researchers in established disciplines, in particular cognitive psychology and psycholinguistics and, to a lesser extent, linguistics and neuropsychology (cf. Gile 1995b: 18). While the paradigms of these disciplines, however varied, continue to feed into IS, the range of resources upon which it draws has been expanding. Specialists in such areas as sociolinguistics, discourse analysis, pragmatics, text linguistics, cross-cultural communication studies, forensic linguistics, artificial intelligence, neurophysiology and human engineering have been broadening and deepening the knowledge base of IS, and inspiring interpreting scholars to explore new insights and tools.

However, while this interaction does continue intermittently, it remains largely on the level of what Gile (1999: 41) has dubbed "doorstep interdisciplinarity." Elsewhere, Gile (2000: 89) notes that "close scrutiny shows that a large proportion of the interdisciplinary work is confined to base camp, with authors showing possible routes onwards but rarely venturing into the slopes." Among the many obstacles to sustained symbiotic relationships Gile discusses the difficulties of collecting authentic data; the problematics of experimentation (e.g. the reluctance of interpreters to serve as subjects in experimental studies, the challenge of controlling for all potential variables, issues of ecological validity); and the more fundamental problem of finding points of interface between the agendas of interpreting scholars and of those coming from other disciplines.

One of the more promising types of interdisciplinarity (cf. Gile 1995b) involves scholars, usually with a practitioner's background, who acquire considerable expertise in another discipline in the course of working towards a postgraduate degree. A case in point is Ruth Morris, a professional interpreter who spent two years in a law department to complete a PhD (1993) on court interpreting. The need to go so far afield also has to do with the dearth of translation and interpreting departments equipped to offer doctoral programs – as may be expected in view of the rather short history of IS as an academic pursuit.

The evolution of IS

For an activity to be perceived as a potential object of study, it must first be conceptualized as such. As its epistemological status takes shape, other factors may come into play to define its status in the real world. Whereas conference interpreting had coalesced into a recognized, albeit small profession by the 1930s, other types of interpreting such as those practiced in community settings did not undergo professionalization until much later. In either case, this stage of development creates the need for publications – often in the form of manuals or handbooks – which describe the practitioner's work and, more often than not, propose a set of dos and don'ts. In the case of conference interpreting, the earliest and best-known example is Herbert's (1952) *Interpreter's Handbook*. As its counterpart for signed-language interpreters, one might cite Quigley and Youngs's (1965) manual *Interpreting for Deaf People*. With the institutionalization of interpreting in various non-conference settings, the need for guidelines, codes of ethics, etc. was sometimes filled on a local, *ad hoc* basis; e.g. the *Manual for Interpreters and Clerks of Courts*, which appeared in the Federation of Malaya as early as the 1950s (Sia 1954).

It was not until the mid-1980s, however, that materials for spoken-language interpreting in community settings began to appear, independently of each other, in different places: Shackman's (1984) *Handbook on Working with, Employing and Training Community Interpreters* proved instrumental in defining the profession in the

UK, as did the *Cultural Interpreter Training Manual* (Cairncross 1989) in Canada and the handbook on *Working with Interpreters in Law, Health and Social Work* (Frey *et al.* 1990) in Australia. Similar publications for specific domains of community-based interpreting, most notably court interpreting, appeared – and continue to appear – in various countries, e.g. Jessnitzer (1982). All of these not only reflected an emerging field of practice but also played a formative role in promoting its professionalization, mainly by presenting their respective authors' recommendations to the next generation of practitioners.

It may also be said that in all three cases – conference, signed-language and (spoken-language) community interpreting – considerable time elapsed before the hands-on approach began to be complemented by a more research-oriented one. With the exception of an early inquiry by a Spanish psychologist (Sanz 1931) and a pioneering MA thesis by a young interpreter (Paneth 1957), the first scientific study of conference interpreting was not to appear until 1965, when Oléron and Nanpon published a paper on simultaneous interpreting in a French psychological journal. The same holds true for signed-language interpreting. The first more theoretical writings began to appear in the mid-1970s: Ingram (1974), for example, proposed a communication model for the interpreting process; Tweney and Hoemann (1976) summarized what little research had been done on signed languages, emphasized the need for linguistic and psycholinguistic knowledge, and called for research into the workings of "translation" between spoken and signed languages. Having evolved as a sub-domain only in the mid-1980s, community interpreting was not to become the object of sustained scientific inquiry until almost a decade later, spearheaded by Wadensjö's (1992) PhD thesis on interpreting in immigration hearings and medical encounters. Earlier work was widely dispersed and remains largely unknown, e.g. an LL.B. thesis by Teo (1983/84) on the role of court interpreters.

As a rule, doctoral dissertations, though often not widely available, have been crucial to the ongoing development of IS, as indeed for most fields of scientific inquiry. The first two in our field, Pinter (1969) and Barik (1969), were both completed four years after the study by Oléron and Nanpon (1965) cited above, and were soon followed by a third (Gerver 1971). All three were experimental studies by psychologists, and were devoted to simultaneous interpreting. A fourth dissertation in psychology, which drew on the newly emerging field of cognitive science, applied an existing information-processing model to simultaneous interpreting (B. Moser 1976). Some of the findings in these studies were published as journal articles in the early 1970s (e.g. Barik 1971, 1972, 1973, 1975; Gerver 1974a, 1974b) – and met with considerable skepticism on the part of professional conference interpreters (e.g. Bros-Brann 1975, for whom Barik's findings represented "pure unadulterated jabberwocky," p. 94, and who urged practitioners to take research into their own hands).

In fact, some of the most eminent representatives of the profession had started to do exactly that. In that same year, Danica Seleskovitch, one of the founders of AIIC (International Association of Conference Interpreters) and its long-time Executive Secretary, whose 1968 introduction to the profession is the most widely known of its kind, published a groundbreaking empirical study of consecutive interpreting, and was a driving force in creating the academic infrastructure at the École Superieure d'Interprètes et de Traducteurs (ESIT), which enabled others to follow suit. Among the first studies (on interpreting) carried out under her guidance and supervision were doctoral dissertations by Déjean le Féal (1978), García-Landa (1978) and Lederer (1978a), all of whom continued to contribute to the IS literature.

As the so-called "Paris School" was establishing "*traductologie*" ("*science de l'interprétation et de la traduction*") as a discipline in its own right, and as research on signed-language interpreting was also getting under way, interpreting was already being explored from the vantage points of linguistics and communication theory by the "Leipzig School" of translation research (Kade 1968; Kade and Cartellieri 1971), which was built on in West Germany by Kirchhoff (1976a, 1976b). Yet another contemporary research paradigm, that of Soviet psycholinguistics, was developing at the same time, epitomized by Chernov (1973, 1978). However limited the interaction among the various schools at the time, they were soon to become aware of each other's work, in no small measure thanks to a unique international gathering – the multidisciplinary 1977 NATO Symposium on *Language Interpretation and Communication* (Gerver and Sinaiko 1978). This event, however, also exposed the differences between the agendas of the two main participating groups, practicing interpreters and scientists from various other disciplines.

Following the NATO Conference, which had captured the buoyancy of interpreting research in the 1970s, the field seems to have lost some of its momentum; nonetheless, scholars in different places and paradigms did continue to carry out individual investigations (e.g. Goldman-Eisler 1980; Kopczyński 1980; Gile 1983, 1984; Lambert 1983; Mackintosh 1983; Stenzl 1983; Gerver *et al.* 1984). The fact that *Meta*, an international journal of translation, saw fit to dedicate a special issue to (spoken-language) interpreting in 1985, and that *Sign Language Studies* devoted one to signed-language interpreting in 1986 attests to the growing presence of research in the field. That same year, 1986, also saw the convening of the Trieste Symposium on *The Theoretical and Practical Aspects of Teaching Conference Interpretation* (Gran and Dodds 1989), reflecting a heightened interest in testing the prevailing pedagogical paradigms. Indeed, that conference appears to have ushered in what Gile (1994) called the "Renaissance" of research on interpreting. The shared aspiration to engage in closer cooperation and more effective networking, by such media as *The Interpreters' Newsletter* and the *IR(TI)N Bulletin*, helped reinforce the sense of community which was to forge IS into a discipline in the 1990s.

While conference interpreters were busy advancing their research endeavors, colleagues – if indeed they were viewed as such – in community interpreting were still grappling to establish themselves as a profession. Much of the early progress came about as the eventual result of legal provisions enacted to ensure that "language-handicapped" individuals enjoyed equal access to public services. In the US, for example, such legislation included the Vocational Rehabilitation Act Amendments of 1965, the Education for All Handicapped Children Act of 1975 and the Federal Court Interpreters Act of 1978, as well as laws passed by a number of states governing the use of interpreters in healthcare. Nevertheless, by the early 1990s, major research efforts were being published in these fields too, albeit by a small number of individuals, among them Berk-Seligson (1990a) on court interpreting, Cokely (1992) on signed-language interpreting, and Wadensjö (1992) on community interpreting. As in conference interpreting, so too here the convening of an international conference was a milestone: The *First International Conference on Interpreting in Legal, Health and Social Service Settings ("The Critical Link: Interpreters in the Community")*, held in Geneva Park, Canada, in 1995 (Carr *et al.* 1997), enabled colleagues in different regions and countries to share hitherto isolated findings and experiences, and served as a catalyst to networking and even to collaborative research. And so, with community-based interpreting coming into its own as an object of research, alongside the more firmly established domain of conference interpreting, we can safely begin to speak of the emergence of a broadly conceived discipline of IS.

IS as a discipline

Having reviewed the coalescence of IS through the 1990s, we would now like to profile the discipline in terms of its sociology, geographical distribution and institutional make-up. Given the pivotal role of international exchange, as illustrated above, we will place special emphasis on the exchange and pooling of information through international conferences and other forms of networking as well as publications in the field. We will also discuss the composition of the IS community, and ways in which the academic infrastructure comes to bear on the dynamics of the field.

Bearing in mind that as late as the mid-1990s IS could be described as a "(sub)-discipline in the making within a discipline in the making" (Shlesinger 1995: 9), research on interpreting was traditionally reported at general conferences on translation or Translation Studies, or in the framework of congresses in (applied) linguistics, most notably those of the International Association of Applied Linguistics (AILA). While this pattern continues, IS seems to have generated sufficient interest to warrant gatherings devoted solely to this field. The 1994 International Conference on Interpretation in Turku, Finland, was the first event to aim at a comprehensive stocktaking of research on interpreting across the entire spectrum of the object of study, even though the share of input on non-conference interpreting was rather limited – as reflected by the narrower title of the proceedings volume (Gambier *et al.* 1997).

The *Critical Link* Conference in Geneva Park, Canada, mentioned above could be seen as a counterpart to the Turku Conference in the evolution of research into community interpreting. The fact that this event was not a one-off effort but rather marked the launching of a tri-annual series, supported by a newsletter for continued networking, reflects a substantial degree of institutionalization of research on interpreting in community-based settings. Within this broad field, there are also meetings, usually on a more local basis, devoted to particular sub-domains – signed-language interpreting, court interpreting, healthcare interpreting, etc. – though their agendas are often more professional than research-oriented. In addition, the diversity of IS in general has given rise to specialist meetings designed around a particular theme, such as cognitive processing or quality assessment, or for a specific purpose, such as promoting interdisciplinary exchange (e.g. the 1997 and 2001 Ascona conferences) or research training (e.g. the 1997 seminar at Århus).

Conferences are but one of the ways in which a research community might develop a cohesive identity. No less important are bulletins and newsletters, both hardcopy and electronic, as well as mailing lists and discussion groups on the Internet. In IS such vehicles for networking have included the bulletin of the IRN (formerly IRTIN), an informal channel for disseminating information on conference interpreting research, initiated and maintained by Daniel Gile. Other networks, such as mailing lists on court and community interpreting, have tended to be more concerned with professional issues.

Less transient means of sharing theoretical insights and empirical findings in the scientific community include journals, monographs and proceedings. *The Interpreters' Newsletter*, which was set up in the wake of the 1986 Trieste Conference and soon turned into a full-fledged journal, was the first periodical devoted solely to interpreting research. Apart from special issues on interpreting in various TS journals (e.g. *Target* 7:1, 1995, *The Translator* 5:2, 1999), IS has seen the genesis of its own peer-reviewed journal, *Interpreting: International journal of research and practice in interpreting*, launched in 1996. The only other dedicated journal, though of very limited accessibility to the IS community at large, is that of the Japan Association of Interpretation Studies, *Tsûyaku Riron Kenkyû* (*Interpreting Research*). Another significant phenomenon, particularly for the literature on interpreting in community-based settings, consists of special issues of journals in other fields, such as *Deaf Worlds* 13:3 (1997), the *Journal of Health Care for the Poor and Underserved* 9, Suppl. (1998) and *Forensic Linguistics* 6:1 (1999).

As in most other fields, so too in IS, research momentum is largely fueled by the production of doctoral dissertations. While in the past these tended to remain largely inaccessible, the growing market for publications on interpreting has been conducive to their wider dissemination in book form (e.g. Collados Aís 1998; Kalina 1998; Wadensjö 1998; Metzger 1999; Setton 1999a; Roy 2000). These, together with IS-centered volumes published as individual and collective efforts, form the vital building blocks in a growing body of IS literature.

However important the role of conferences and publications, it goes without saying that research on interpreting, as on any field, could not exist without researchers, i.e. without the individuals who choose – whether for no longer than it takes to obtain a postgraduate degree or for the duration of their academic careers – to focus on interpreting as an object of study. As a rule, these individuals benefit from working within an academic environment in which they may acquire the necessary skills and tools, and receive guidance and support. The majority of researchers in IS are affiliated with university-level institutions for translator and interpreter training; however, in many of these the curriculum has been directed solely to the advancement of practical skills rather than academic inquiry. Notwithstanding, there has been a gradual increase in the number of programs which offer postgraduate studies. The challenge lies in strengthening the infrastructure: ensuring the acquisition of research skills as part of the curriculum, and providing for qualified supervision within the field. As in other disciplines, the dynamics of the research endeavor hinge on a variety of factors, which might be presented as the six Ms: Manpower, Motivation, Means, Materials, Methods and Market. Clearly, each of these prerequisites interacts with several or all of the others, and it is the complex interdependence among these sociological, economic and methodological factors that will determine the future of the field.

About this Reader

Fifty-odd years have elapsed since the earliest attempts at a systematic description of interpreting. By the turn of the millennium, the quantity and diversity of writings had grown to the point where no single volume could hope to cover the full breadth of research in IS. In what follows we will briefly describe the manner in which we dealt with this formidable challenge.

Selection

When setting the selection criteria for this anthology, we aimed at presenting as broad a spectrum as possible of the variegated field whose evolution is outlined above. While our foremost concern lay with doing justice to the scope of the work that has been done, we also tried, wherever possible, to include pieces which had hitherto been relatively inaccessible. In some cases, this had to do with the nature of the publications in which they appeared during the formative years of IS; many of the journals in other disciplines or even in TS have been discontinued, or are not readily available in most departments of translation and interpreting. By the same token, three papers and two excerpts from publications in languages other than English are being presented to the English-speaking readership for the first time.

As in most fields, research in IS comprises both theoretical and empirical endeavors, which build upon one another. Reflecting this interdependence, the present volume includes selections devoted to both conceptual analysis and observational or experimental investigations in a proportion which reflects the nature of the field. As regards the paradigms and methodological frameworks within which these investigations have been conducted, here again we have tried to mirror the variety of approaches, including translation theoretical, cognitive psychological, text linguistic and discourse analytical as well as sociolinguistic perspectives. In our effort to span the many forms which the object of study may take, we have included papers on both of the major modes of interpreting (simultaneous and consecutive) and language modalities (spoken and signed), as well as some of the many settings in which interpreters play a vital role in the interaction. On the whole, the work presented in this Reader reflects an emphasis on what Salevsky (1993a), in her map of IS inspired by Holmes ([1972]/1988), subsumed under the theoretical and descriptive rather than applied domains of IS. In other words, some rather significant areas of IS have been excluded, as explained below.

Apart from the fact that the Reader does not explicitly address the more fundamental epistemological issues (e.g. Gile 1990a; Salevsky 1993a; García-Landa 1995), the most conspicuous omission concerns the considerable body of pedagogically oriented literature. While there have been numerous pleas for closer examination of the relative effectiveness of different curricula and methods of teaching and assessment, and while a considerable number of descriptive studies has been reported (see, for example, Gran and Dodds 1989, as well as *The Interpreters' Newsletter*), there has been relatively little solid research in this direction. Another domain of applied IS which has not been accommodated in this volume relates to interpreters' working conditions and professional ecology. Research along these lines includes studies of physical and psychological stress (e.g. Tommola and Hyönä 1990; Klonowicz 1994; Moser-Mercer *et al.* 1998; Ezrachi *et al.* 2002); remote simultaneous interpreting (e.g. Kurz 2000); and technical aids and terminology (e.g. Gile 1987, Moser-Mercer 1992).

Another line of research not covered in our Reader is the neuropsychological/neurolinguistic paradigm, centering on the issue of cerebral lateralization in bilinguals (cf. Lambert and Moser-Mercer 1994: 237–355; Kurz 1995). Whatever its potential, this interdisciplinary avenue of investigation appears to have been difficult to sustain within IS, given its dependence on highly sophisticated infrastructure and research expertise (but see Tommola 1999). This also holds true for the work conducted by specialists in computer science and artificial intelligence, such as voice-to-voice machine translation (e.g. Jekat and Klein 1996; LuperFoy 1997), corpus-based NLP studies (e.g. Armstrong 1997) and computer modeling of the simultaneous interpreting process (e.g. Lonsdale 1997).

On the whole, then, our attempt to offer a representative sampling of significant research on interpreting since its inception reflects two main orientations: on the one hand, works which have long been regarded as comprising the foundations for IS, and on the other, those which point to research directions with high potential for the dynamic development of the discipline. The latter aspiration has been realized only to a more limited extent, since it was only in the late 1990s that the six Ms of research infrastructure mentioned above were becoming more available to the study of interpreting in legal, healthcare and social service settings, as well as the media. There is ample reason to believe that these widely disparate domains, together with some of those mentioned above, hold great promise for the future of IS and will warrant their inclusion in future anthologies.

Structure

Given the space limitations set by the publisher, our application of the selection criteria described above resulted in a sample of twenty-six texts, most of which had to be abridged. In an effort to ensure optimum coherence, we have organized the volume in seven parts: Parts 1 and 2 – "Breaking Ground" and "Laying Foundations" – comprise works which could be characterized as the "classics" of the research literature on conference interpreting, by such authors as Barik, Gerver and Seleskovitch. Part 3 – "Modeling the Process" – is devoted to what appears to be an overriding concern in conference interpreting research. "Broadening the View" is the motto of Part 4, which holds a central position, in more ways than one, and in which the context of interpreting is extended to include sociological and situational perspectives as well as the semiotic dimension of interaction and discourse in interpreting. Part 5 – "Observing the product and its effects" – addresses the phenomenon from the vantage points of discourse studies and pragmatics, while Part 6 – "Examining Expectations and Norms" – explores underlying patterns of interpreter performance and its reception by the user. Finally, in Part 7, the growing professionalization of interpreting in non-conference settings is reflected in research aimed at "(Re)Defining the Role" of interpreters in interaction. Framing the two dozen texts devoted to theoretical and empirical inquiry from a contemporary point of view are two stand-alone pieces: a seminal essay by Alfred Hermann on the early history of interpreting and Michael Cronin's forward-looking reflection on the object of study, culminating in an appeal for a "cultural turn in Interpreting Studies."

Each of the seven parts is preceded by an Introduction in which the unifying themes are discussed, and the individual pieces are contextualized. Particular emphasis is placed on the way in which these selections interrelate with similar or complementary work that could not be accommodated within the narrow confines of this volume. For all the thematic sections, suggestions for further reading can be found in the body of the Introductions; for Parts 5 and 7, additional references are provided. Every selection in turn is introduced by background information about the author and his or her work, including a list of related publications (Further reading). The Bibliography comprises all works cited in the editorial introductions (works cited by individual authors appear at the end of the repective chapters). A Name Index and a Subject Index are provided to assist the student and researcher in drawing together the many interweaving strands of the materials presented throughout the Reader.

Looking Back

WHILE THE EARLY history of interpreting did not draw widespread interest among interpreting scholars until late in the twentieth century, the pioneering publication on the topic, by Alfred Hermann (1904–67), is in fact one of the earliest scholarly works in the interpreting literature as a whole. Based on a lecture delivered at the "School of Foreign Studies and Interpreting" of the University of Mainz at Germersheim in 1955, Hermann's as well as two other historical essays (by K. Thieme and E. Glässer) made up the inaugural volume of the Interpreter School's monograph series, published in 1956 as *Beiträge zur Geschichte des Dolmetschens* (Contributions to the History of Interpreting).

Alfred Hermann had studied history and literature before embarking on a career as an Egyptologist in Berlin. In 1941, he was drafted into the German army and spent much of his service as an interpreter for Arabic in North Africa. Only in 1953 did he join the staff of the newly established F. J. Dölger Institute at the University of Bonn to work on an encyclopedic project on Antiquity and Christianity, to which he contributed some three dozen articles, including the one on "interpreting." Hermann was in his mid-fifties when he finally joined the University of Cologne. Only in 1965, two years before his death, was he appointed full professor of Egyptology.

Hermann's seminal thirty-page essay, originally entitled "Dolmetschen im Altertum. Ein Beitrag zur antiken Kulturgeschichte," covers both written and oral mediation and is richly documented by scholarly references. It is therefore being made available here in abridged form, translated into English by Ruth Morris.

Further reading: Bowen *et al.* 1995; Kurz 1985, 1986a, 1986b, 2001a.

Alfred Hermann

INTERPRETING IN ANTIQUITY

Translated by Ruth Morris

FROM THE FOURTH century BC onwards, we find increasingly clear
differentiation between groups of people in the Eastern Mediterranean area. In
different places and at different times, highly advanced civilizations came into being,
distinguished essentially by their languages. [. . .]

In Antiquity as in other eras, interlingual behaviour was determined by the
specific situation and, within it, by individual human decisions. On any particular
occasion, there would occur an encounter between two unequal levels of might, two
types of human beings as bearers of dissimilar power. One side's awareness that it
possessed the greater power – belonging to the "greater" country and people, or
having the "higher" ethos – must have constituted a temptation, from early on, to
view other people as being utterly inferior, and themselves as creation's crowning
glory.

I Ancient Egypt

Such was typically the case in Ancient Egypt, where the honorary title of "man/
human being" was only bestowed on its own people, foreign races being considered
wretched barbarians. In that self-assured world on the Nile, the path led upwards
from the "fully human" Egyptian via the different hierarchies of the civil servants and
priests, all the way to Pharaoh and the supreme deity in heaven. Such a view would
have meant harsh domination of any creature not provided for, or seen only as a
negative counterpart, in this world order. And in fact, the sequences of scenes
depicted in Egyptian temples and graves present us with foreigners – Nubians,
Libyans and Asiatics – only as prisoners or vassals obsequiously bringing tribute,
never as equal partners. The inscriptions which record the speeches delivered when
foreigners were received at court are not their actual words, translated from their

own languages. Rather, words were literally put in the mouths of the foreigners, words of entreaty for mercy, as thought out and put into stereotypical forms by the Egyptians. Thus, basically, any expression was always that of the Egyptians themselves.

Under such circumstances no real communication could take place when it came to talking to foreigners in everyday life, and the interpreter – that indispensable linguist – could not act as a genuine interlingual mediator. Starting at the end of the period of the Pyramids, we have knowledge of the title and activity of interpreters from a number of cases. Interpreters appear more and more frequently in the inscriptions of Aswan Elephantine, whose provincial ruler often bears the title "overseer of dragomans." The bilingual border area of the First Cataract, the Province of Elephantine, was the home not only of the interpreters who mediated between the resident Nubians and Egyptians, but also of most leaders of famed expeditions to Sudan, which were deemed a major challenge. Noteworthy examples include the expeditions of Harkhuf, "Prince of Elephantine, Prefect of Upper Egypt, Unique Friend of the King, Seal-Bearer of the Delta King and Overseer of Dragomans" under King Neferirka-Re (around 2500 BC). Harkhuf boasts emotionally of his own achievements.

Quite how unpacific such campaigns were is shown by the expedition of Pepinakht, known as Hekaib, who, as "Prince of Elephantine and Overseer of Dragomans," with his troops defeated two Nubian tribes before going on to become governor of the royal capital of Memphis. We learn from another man from Aswan called Sabni that his father died while on a trip to Nubia, and that he made another journey to bring the body back. In his account he boasts that he did not send "any desert guide, interpreter or Nubian" to the difficult region, instead going himself. Another area in which Egyptian interpreters appear as commercial negotiators is, typically, the copper-mining region of the Sinai Peninsula, home to speakers of a Semitic language. In an inscription about the Sinai expedition of a Temple superintendent during the time of King Neferirka-Re, the accompanying interpreters are listed next to miners and sailors. Interpreters also occur in connection with sailors on one of King Sahu-Re's large seagoing vessels, sailing to Byblos or Punt, as depicted by this pharaoh in his pyramidal temple. At the royal seat of Memphis, interpreters also appeared in other ways. If here a man is called "Overseer of Dragomans, Head of Missions, Keeper of the White Bull and Courtier," this shows that interpreting was important not only externally, on Egypt's borders and in foreign countries, but also in the central administration. The occasional linking of the titles of interpreter and doctor is undoubtedly based on the fact that the doctor spoke to the personified demon of disease as if addressing a wretched foreigner.[1]

The Egyptians did not leave further testimony about this oldest instance of interpreting in the history of the world. However, the title of interpreter and the corresponding hieroglyph do provide some additional information.[2] The single-consonant word ꜥ, formed with the glottal stop ꜥayin, would appear onomatopoeically to indicate a foreign language. The interpreter was thought of, rather disparagingly, as "the speaker of strange tongues." The character used shows an oddly shaped apron with strings which, from its yellow hue, would appear to be made not of linen, but of coarse sackcloth. This would seem to be the relic of an ancient human form of contact. Roman authors such as Mela, Pliny and Solinus write about the Serians, a legendary Asiatic people, as practicing the "silent trade" also observed between other peoples of marked cultural disparity. This "honest primitive people" exchanged their own products for goods deposited at a secluded location. While Pliny stresses that the Serians had hoarse voices and no trading language, Eusthatius reports that they indicated prices on sackcloth. What the Romans related about the Serians on the borders of civilization, the Egyptians of the era of the Pyramids appear to have experienced at the First Nile Cataract. Their word for interpreting is presumably an expression for overcoming a lack of linguistic understanding, and their hieroglyph for interpreter, the coarse apron, a reminder of primitive bartering.

While this evidence reflects rather simple arrangements rooted in ancient custom, the Egyptians also had more sophisticated methods for developing interlingual communication. Herodotus reports that Pharaoh Psammetichus (663–10 BC) handed over Egyptian boys to Hellenic settlers in the Nile Delta so that they would learn the Greek language. These, he suggests, were the first recruits to what was to become the class of interpreters. The foreign-language education of youth, here reported for the period of the first regular Egyptian–Greek relations, appears to have been an old custom in the land of the Nile. Starting in the Middle Kingdom, the sons of Nubian tribal rulers were brought together in one location to be educated as a kind of janissary guard [. . .]. Under Ramses II, young Asiatics underwent similar training in Fayoun.[3] Even if no specific reference is made here to language instruction, it goes without saying that it would be necessary to learn the Egyptian language in the process. What Herodotus considered particularly noteworthy about Psammetichus's educational policy was that, instead of having foreigners learn Egyptian, this king had Egyptians acquire a foreign language – a custom which was actually not entirely new. As we now know from the clay tablets found at Tel el Amarna, an international language of diplomats existed around 1400 BC, during the time of Amenophis III and IV. In the Egyptian Foreign Ministry, Akkadian – which had developed into this international language – could not have been used only by foreign employees, but must have been learned by Egyptians as well. If the Egyptians were making efforts to master a foreign language and script both in the fourteenth century and then again from the seventh century onwards, their reasons for doing so in these two periods were nonetheless very different. For the struggling state of the 26th Dynasty, connecting with the language of the rising power of the contemporary world was a forward-looking step; in contrast, in the self-assured New Kingdom, despite all its receptiveness to things foreign, there was still a prevailing conservative desire to prevent as far as possible the desecration of their own language and script with foreign contacts. Regardless of the preferred learning method for solving the language problem, however, the Egyptians always took steps to guard against incidents such as the one reported about Assurpanibal the Assyrian: on a visit to the court by a foreign envoy, no interpreter was to be found for his language.

[. . .]

II Greece/Rome

[. . .]

For the Greeks, the term "interpreter" or "translator" meant "*a person who acts like Hermes,*" a human being who performs one of this god's numerous activities (including linguistic ones). While the Greek concept emphasizes the divine and, to a lesser extent, the intellectual character, the Latin equivalent defines the down-to-earth situation of the person interpreting. Irrespective of whether the word "interpres" is derived from "inter-partes" or "inter-pretium," the term designates the human mediator positioned between two parties or values, performing far more diverse activities than simply providing linguistic mediation between parties transacting business. The basically divine character of the *hermeneus/interpres* is founded on inspiration. Over and above a linguistic mediator in the narrower sense, it makes him a prophet, seer and sage mediating between man and deity.

It was above all Plato who stressed the divine gift of *hermeneia*, which has the wise man interpret the dark words of enraptured seers. As the poet is thus the Hermeneus of the deity, so, at descending levels of mediation, the rhapsodist reciting him is a "hermeneus of hermeneuts." Even the common soothsayer would still be an "interpreter of the gods among mankind." Servius provides the Latin world with a similar explanation regarding the "*interpres* of divine and human beings": "Interpreter (interpres) means medium, for a person interpreting the gods and interpreting for people to whom he indicates the divine meaning, is called interpres." In this category he also includes the "soothsayer" or vaticinator. What is typical of the chronological scope of this universal view of interpreters is that, as late as AD *c*.600, Isidore of Seville said that the case of the linguistic interpreter came next to that of the interpreter between God and man. [. . .]

When it came to practical interpreting in interlingual communication in ancient times, the language problem varied. While the Greeks were in every way on a par with the Egyptians in terms of arrogance over the barbarians, considering their language to be the only one worthy of human beings from early colonization all the way up to Hellenism, the Roman Empire was mostly a bilingual state. *Utriusque linguae, utriusque orationis facultate,* i.e. having a mastery of Greek was one of the requirements of the educated Roman from the late Republic onwards. During the Imperial period, young children were often taught Greek as their first language, only learning Latin later on. The two languages were then given equal value in school lessons. Still, the aversion to Greek, well known from Cato's time on, found expression even in somebody so at home in that language as Cicero, who once remarked ironically that his compatriots were just like the Syrian slaves: the better their Greek, the more useless they were.

Generally speaking, matters were quite different among the Greeks. If at all, they studied Latin only for work in the administration of justice and government. Thus, for the individual Roman it was normally not difficult to communicate with Greeks, while the Greeks, for their part, almost always had to rely on interpreters.

When Greek envoys were granted an audience in the Roman Senate in earlier days, an interpreter had to be officially engaged, since a magistrate's law prohibited – for reasons of honour – replying to the Greeks in any language other than Latin. In the case of the celebrated reception of the Athenian deputation of philosophers in 154 BC, a Roman Senator called C. Acilius assumed the role of interpreter. From Sulla's time on, Greek was allowed. However, occasionally it was again prohibited in the Curia, such as on one occasion by Emperor Tiberius.

Interpreters were constantly needed in the administration, particularly for contacts with the non-classical peoples: the Egyptians, Syrians, Scythians, Germans, Celts, and so on. Sometimes they were paid for by the state, sometimes privately by the officials. As late as AD 400, the chancellery of the Interior Ministry, the Magister Officiorum, recorded interpreters for the barbaric languages, sometimes with diplomatic duties of their own. Pliny tells of 130 such interpreters in the region of Pontus, where 300 similar languages were spoken. The tombstones of several such men have been found in Rome. T. Flavius Arzachos, whose tombstone was in the Justinian Gardens, was presumably an African. Two interpreters erected a plaque to their teacher Domitius Heliodorus, probably an Oriental. Outside Rome, the presence of interpreters of the provincial administration is attested to by inscribed stones from the Budapest and Maastricht areas. Two interpreters in Moesia and Pannonia are called consular officials; the latter is called "interpreter of the Germans." From a Greek interpreter called Cn. Publicius Menander we learn that he was refused the dual nationality for which he had applied. A letter by Cicero shows what friendly ties could exist between Roman provincial officials and their interpreter. Full of praise for the loyalty and modesty of his "friend and interpreter," he emphatically lends his support to the latter's son. In another case, Cicero expresses himself very negatively about an interpreter in Sicily, reporting that he is used more as an intermediary for cheating and disgraceful deeds than as a linguistic mediator for Greek.

Certain individuals in ancient history are particularly celebrated as being linguistically proficient, or even as polyglots requiring no interpreters. Examples include Themistocles, because he spoke Persian, and Mithridates, who had complete mastery of the twenty-two languages of his multi-ethnic state. The people of Massilia – Marseilles – were praised for their trilingualism, speaking Latin, Greek and Gallic; similarly, the Sicilians spoke Greek, Latin and Punic. On the famous campaigns of the ancient world, those army commanders who were not so fluent always had interpreters with them. Thus Xenophon used a number of such interpreters in the course of the Anabasis to the Black Sea. In connection with Alexander the Great's expedition to Central Asia, reference is made to Persian, Hyrcanian, Sogdian and Indian interpreters. In the West, interpreters played a role during the Punic, Gallic and Jugurthine wars, being used not only by the Romans but also by the hostile tribal rulers. Although on any given occasion there is only a brief reference to the army interpreters, each instance nevertheless offers a new insight.

In the course of the Gauls' invasion of Italy in 390 BC, a Gallic ruler, according to Livy, had challenged a Roman to a duel through an interpreter. In Carthage, the value of the Greek interpreters rose when Hanno's treasonable ties with Dionysius of Sicily were discovered. It was to avoid such instances that the use of Greek without an interpreter had been prohibited. In the Second Punic War, one of Hannibal's soldiers offered himself as interpreter and peace negotiator with the Saguntians. In the same war, capitulation negotiations were conducted through interpreters: instances of such practices include Hannibal's negotiations with the inhabitants of Cannae, and Hanno's with those of Nola. When in 207 BC the Romans intercepted Hasdrubal's letters to Hannibal, which had been sent through their lines, interpreters immediately had to translate these for the Roman Senate. In 202 BC, in the peace negotiations between Scipio and Hannibal at Narragara, the two met unarmed, accompanied only by their interpreters. In Hannibal's mixed multiracial army, comprising Africans, Spaniards, Gauls and Italics, interpreters played a kind of steward's role. In the Jugurthine War (106–5 BC), reliable interpreters were required for Sulla's secret negotiations with King Bocchus of Mauretania for the handing over of Jugurtha. One Dabar was agreeable to both sides: despite the ambiguous business involved, he was called a "vir sanctus" – an honourable man. The assignment of interpreter Cn. Pompeius was less gratifying: he was sent by an officer of Caesar's to Ambiorix the Gaul with a request for mercy. The above examples should suffice to demonstrate the varied uses made of the army interpreter in ancient times.

III The Christian late classical period

[. . .]

Going beyond the traditional views of Hermeneus and the prophet, the first Christian scholar, Clemens of Alexandria, declared that God had no need of an interpreter in order to express His will.

[. . .]

More than theoretical considerations, what proved significant to Christianity was the practical example of interpreting and translating in the synagogue. Since Ezra made arrangements for the Torah to be rendered from the Hebrew text into Aramaic (the vernacular of the time) for the Jewish homecomers from exile, "targumim" came into being in the Holy Land. Initially they were not to be recorded, so that as spoken translations they would maintain their vitality. [. . .]

The language problem of the synagogue applied to Jesus' preaching too. When he expounded "Moses and the prophets" to the disciples, he could only have explained the Hebrew written text in Aramaic. Mark, the so-called "interpreter of Peter," thus produced a free translation by recording in writing a rendering of the Lord's words as he heard them from Peter's mouth, writing down in Greek what he had heard in Aramaic. [. . .]

Even after the Judaeo-Christians had left the synagogues, the problem of language in religious service cropped up time and time again. Greek became the church's language of worship, but from the third century on was increasingly incomprehensible to worshippers, and so the question arose as to whether it was possible to manage with similar "targumim," or whether a major change of language was required. Even after Latin generally became accepted as the ecclesiastical language of worship, some parts of the liturgy nevertheless remained in their Greek version, such as the "Hagios" in Gaul. Given the limits of the Roman Empire's Latinization in the area of worship as in daily life, the Roman Christians, like the Coptic, Syrian, Celtic and Germanic communities, sooner or later insisted that services be made accessible to them in their own language.

Before the occurrence of drastic language changes, such as the one carried out in Rome under Pope Damasus I, linguistic mediators were required at religious services. Evidence of their existence is available in both the East and the West. Epiphanius, listing the various ranks in the church hierarchy, refers to the "exorcists and interpreters from one to the (other) language," sandwiched between lectors and undertakers. Their rank was, therefore, rather low. According to the Acts of the martyrs St Prokop of Scythopolis, the latter's ascetic existence culminated in the activities of lector, exorcist and liturgical interpreter; the renunciation of glory and honours is thus a characteristic of the Christian rank of linguistic mediator. [. . .]

Similar to liturgical arrangements, the person versed in languages gained in importance when it came to spreading the faith among the heathen. According to apocryphal reports, which at least reflect the variety of possibilities, Apostle Thomas is said to have missionized among the Parthians, and Apostle Andreas among the Scythians, which presupposes that they overcame the attendant language problems. Writing about Johannes Chrysostomus, Theodoret reports that he appointed priests, deacons and lectors of the holy scriptures who spoke the language of the Aryan Scythians, i.e. the Goths. "Frequently he preached himself with the help of interpreters, who had mastery of both languages" and had others act accordingly. Athanasius, who, in addition to his own Greek tongue, also had both oral and written command of the Coptic language, would have faced the Anachoretes of the Egyptian desert, who could speak only Coptic. This is why the father of monasticism, St Anthony, had a number of interpreters with him, including one called Isaac, as well as a priest from Wadi Natrun by the name of Cronius. When Anthony wrote letters to Greeks, he had to dictate them in Coptic and then have them translated. The fact that interpreters were commonplace in Egypt even at confession can be inferred from a report that a Roman refused to accept one when making confession to St Pachomius.

[. . .]

At the official gatherings of the church leaders, the major councils, the use of Latin was limited, because these synods were initially held in the Greek-speaking part of the world, and the few guests from the West normally had a good command of the Greek language, in which negotiations were conducted. On the other hand, older fragments of council proceedings manuscripts more strongly suggest occasional negotiations in Latin than was previously assumed on the basis of the late Greek copies which obliterated Latin drafts. In the East, after Justinian, discussions were held exclusively in Greek, and the records were issued in Greek. This meant that the Latin reports which circulated in the West were private versions devoid of any official church sanction. However, at the Lateran Council held under Pope Martin I in AD 649, once more there was a linguistic problem, and interpreters were needed. Since the main topic was the condemnation of Monothelitism, the doctrine of Christ's *One Will*, and since the debate had been set in motion by Greek theologians such as Maximus Confessor, while most of the participants were Latin scholars, interpreters were needed. Thus as early as the second session, it was decided that the negotiations, held in Latin and recorded in shorthand, should immediately be translated into Greek. Consequently the anti-Monothelite Greek monks from Jerusalem and North Africa, who had fled to Rome and acted as linguistic mediators at this council, may be considered the oldest conference interpreters of the Western world.

Notes

1   In an ancient curse to ward off disease, the demons of disease are addressed as "Asiatic," "Negro," "slave," etc.

2   On the title of "interpreter," see A. H. Gardiner, "The Egyptian Word for 'Dragoman'," *Proceedings of the Society of Biblical Archeology* 37 (1915): 117–25 [. . .]. A. Wiedemann found the translation "interpreter" questionable (according to oral sources, including more recent ones such as Labib Habachi and Henry G. Fischer).

3   The Book of Daniel 1. 3–5 reports on the teaching of the Chaldean language to imprisoned Jewish youths at the court of Nebuchadnezar. [. . .]

Part 1

Breaking Ground

INTRODUCTION

IN THE 1950s, as conference interpreting, increasingly practiced in the simultaneous mode, was making great strides towards becoming a full-fledged profession – complete with university-level training, a professional organization and a code of ethics – it also began to attract interest as an object of scientific inquiry. Not surprisingly, among the first to discover its research potential was an inquisitive practitioner, who was to write the very first academic study on the subject (Paneth 1957). It was not until the mid-sixties that researchers in the field of psychology, intrigued by simultaneous interpreting as a challenge to prevailing theories on the limits of human processing capacity (cf. Broadbent 1952), also took it up as an object of research (e.g. Pinter 1969). The highly unusual task seemed to present them with material on several of the issues so prevalent in contemporary experimental research, such as divided attention, short- and long-term memory, interlingual word associations and response latencies. Psycholinguists too seized upon simultaneous interpreting as a means of testing their hypotheses concerning the role of input segmentation as well as hesitations and pauses in speech production.

An overriding theme pursued across the various paradigms was the role of temporal factors in the processing of language. Indeed, the lag between source-language input and target-language output was also a prominent topic in the "Investigation into Conference Interpreting," carried out as an MA thesis at the University of London by **Eva Paneth**. This first piece of degree-oriented academic writing on interpreting was mainly devoted to a systematic description of curricula and teaching methods as observed at a number of training institutions in Europe (Geneva, Saarbrücken, Paris, Munich, Heidelberg, Germersheim and Copenhagen). As documented in the appendix to her thesis, Paneth also collected a considerable amount of empirical data through the observation of interpreters' performance at authentic conferences. (Her assessment of the challenges confronting the would-be researcher are aptly captured in her own pithy comment: "Observing interpretation is much more tiring than doing the work" (p. 146)). Guided by her intuitions as a practitioner, she hypothesized about the time course of simultaneous interpreting, and suggested that "the avoidance of simultaneity is not a major concern of the interpreters" (Paneth 1957: 18, and in this volume). This conclusion was at odds with the direction initially taken in psychologically oriented studies (e.g. Goldman-Eisler 1967, 1968; Barik 1969, 1973) which rested on the assumption that the interpreter made maximum use of pauses in the original speech, so as to reduce the burden of listening and speaking simultaneously.

The extent to which two speech streams overlapped was also at the heart of the pioneering investigation of simultaneous interpreting by **Pierre Oléron** and **Hubert Nanpon** (1965, and in this volume). Their main achievement was to develop a method for obtaining precise measurements of the time delay (*décalage*) between the original and the interpreter's output. Acknowledging that simultaneous interpreting is in fact a highly complex operation, they chose to focus on its quantitative dimensions, noting that "Il est difficile d'évaluer la fidélité d'une traduction: c'est une matière où les elements qualitatifs, difficilement pondérables et variables selon les juges, jouent un rôle important" (1965: 88). Oléron's own autobiographical notes (1992: 153) refer to this particular study as "une sorte d'aberration [. . .] une sorte de contre-exemple par rapport aux recherches 'normales'," and reflect his belief that psychologists had not done any further work along these lines. We know, however, that this was not quite the case. The more elusive, qualitative dimensions of interpreting were soon to be tackled in psychologically oriented studies on the effect of external variables on interpreters' performance.

Without any doubt, the leading figure in this respect was **David Gerver**, whose 1971 doctoral dissertation can be regarded as the most comprehensive and influential piece of psychological investigation into simultaneous interpreting to this day. His experimental work on factors likely to affect the short-term memory capacity of the interpreter, such as list length and message structure, foreshadowed much later investigations into interpreters' performance on post-task recall tests (e.g. Lambert 1983, 1988) and working memory (e.g. Darò and Fabbro 1994; Padilla *et al*. 1995; Shlesinger 2000a), as did his experiments on the role of input intonation, prosodic stress and unfilled pauses (e.g. Williams 1995; Mazzetti 1999). His pioneering study on the effect of source-language presentation rate on simultaneous interpreters' performance (1969, and in this volume) has provided the underpinnings for any subsequent investigations of an issue that has always been of vital interest both to practitioners and to researchers (e.g. Darò 1990; Tommola and Laakso 1997). Taking issue with Welford's (1968) claim, based on the so-called single-channel hypothesis, that the ability to interpret simultaneously rests on learning to ignore the feedback from one's own voice, Gerver demonstrated that interpreters' monitoring of their own performance is intrinsic to the process, and that self-corrections decrease whenever the task becomes more demanding. In fact, this issue was later taken up by researchers who applied the delayed auditory feedback paradigm to the study of phonological interference in the interpreting process (e.g. Darò 1995; Darò *et al*. 1996; Fabbro and Darò 1995; Isham 2000) and self-monitoring among experts as opposed to novices (e.g. Moser-Mercer *et al*. 2000). In yet another experiment which bears on the issue of working conditions so crucial to the profession, particularly with regard to recent advances in teleconferencing, Gerver (1971, 1974a) investigated the effect of noise on simultaneous interpreters' performance. His suggestion to extend that type of research to "testing the comprehension by an audience of the translations produced under noisy conditions" (Gerver 1971: 114), which he himself implemented (Gerver 1972), anticipates work that was initiated only much later on the cognitive effect of interpretations on the listeners. Finally, it was also Gerver, drawing on findings from his wide-ranging experimental work, who formulated the first full information-processing model of simultaneous interpreting (see Part 3).

Some of the key issues in experimental psychology as studied by Gerver were also dealt with from a psycholinguistic vantage point by **Frieda Goldman-Eisler**, who saw the task of simultaneous interpreting as holding great potential for shedding light on the processes of speech comprehension and production. In the context of her work on spontaneous speech she focused on temporal factors, especially various types of hesitation phenomena, and came to hypothesize (1967, 1968) that pauses would afford the interpreter a particularly useful space in which to articulate the target-language discourse, thereby avoiding the added strain of concurrent listening and speaking. Apart from the issue of simultaneity between the input and the interpreter's speech, Goldman-Eisler was particularly interested in the linguistic determinants of the time that the interpreter allows to elapse between the point when a unit of discourse is sounded and the point at which it is reproduced in the target language, which she refers to as the ear–voice span (EVS). The EVS, which is variously measured in terms of time (seconds) or linguistic units (syllables, words, predicates), depends crucially on the interpreter's ability to store the incoming message before recoding it. This lag had been shown to be longer in interpreting than in a control task such as shadowing (Treisman 1965; Gerver 1969, and in this volume; see also L. Anderson 1994). In subsequent work on signed-language interpreting (Cokely 1986, 1992), the length of the EVS was found to interrelate closely with the number of errors, also referred to as "miscues," in the interpreter's output.

The nature of errors and the length of the time lags were two of the central themes in **Henri C. Barik's** "A Study of Simultaneous Interpretation" (1969), the first PhD thesis on interpreting by a non-interpreter. Being a very early contribution to the field, it is not surprising that Barik's work reflects some of its salient experimental-design problems. Most critically, his subjects were few in number and very heterogeneous, in terms of training and experience in interpreting as well as language profiles, and were required to interpret in both language directions. While considerable criticism has been leveled against Barik's methodology (e.g. Gerver 1976: 186; Stenzl 1983: 28; Gile 1991a: 163), it would be fair to say that the difficulties of devising an ecologically valid yet viable research design continue to plague and undermine experimental – and even observational – studies in IS (cf. Gile 1998). Whatever its drawbacks, however, various error typologies reminiscent of Barik's groundbreaking work have been productively applied in numerous studies ever since (e.g. Kopczyński 1980; Lambert 1983; Altman 1994; Falbo 1998). Among the temporal features studied by Barik (1969, 1973) were the speech-to-pause ratios in the source speeches and translations, and the differences between them. He also examined the synchronicity patterns between source and target versions and concluded that his findings appeared to corroborate Goldman-Eisler's (1967:128) suggestion that "intermittent silence between chunks of speech is . . . a very valuable commodity for the simultaneous translator," noting that "the T[ranslator] tries to use the S[peaker]'s pauses to good advantage for delivering his version, presumably in order to reduce the amount of time during which he must be engaged in the difficult task of speaking while S is also speaking" (1973:267). This issue was to be taken up again much later with the application of computer-assisted methods of speech signal analysis (e.g. Lee 1999a, 1999b; Yaghi 1994; Yagi 1999). In addition to such temporal issues and the analysis of errors in his subjects' outputs (Barik 1975, and in this volume), Barik (1975:293–4) also pointed to other avenues which remained to be explored in subsequent research, such as "the occasional reversal in translation of a set of structurally equivalent items" (e.g. Shlesinger 2000a; Wadensjö 1993, and in this volume) or the fact that "the T's speech is generally less smooth than 'natural' speech" (e.g. Shlesinger 1994).

Whether concerned chiefly with mental processes *per se* or with the specific task of simultaneous interpreting, the groundbreakers whose work is presented in this part focused attention on psychological and psycholinguistic issues which continue to occupy the attention of researchers in IS. These include both the methodological dilemmas of experimentation on interpreting in general and the conceptual complexity of analyzing the interpreter's output and performance. Indeed, in grappling for the first time with the qualitative dimensions of the task, these pioneering researchers paved the way for the significant line of quality-oriented studies that was to emerge in the 1980s and 1990s, and in which the early concern with correspondence at the lexical and structural levels was complemented by a fuller account of the situational, pragmatic and discourse-related factors involved (see Parts 5 and 6).

VIENNESE-BORN EVA PANETH (1914–96) settled in England in 1933, and was among the first to link empirical research with the hands-on experience of a professional interpreter. (Her career ran the gamut from international conferences to British Foreign Office assignments.) As a part-time graduate student at the University of London she undertook to learn more about the history of interpreting and the complex skills it entails. In her trailblazing MA thesis (1957), she presents her observations of both consecutive and simultaneous interpreting, along with pedagogical insights gleaned from her career as a teacher and trainer of (German-language) teachers. Her pilot study centered on the training of students in a skill which, in England at least, was being taught on an *ad hoc* basis only. Paneth, a harbinger of the systematization of interpreter training which was to gain momentum in the late 1960s, was keen on examining the desirability of establishing a training institute in the UK.

Along with its intrinsic importance as a seminal contribution to the field, Paneth's thesis is also a unique source of observations rarely found in academic work of this type today: "Interpreters insist that they must be allowed to smoke even when the audience is prohibited from it. There are other indications that their nerves are in the kind of state in which any additional strain would prove unbearable" (p. 146).

The excerpt presented here (from pp. 15–33 of her thesis) provides a broad sweep of the modes of interpreting, and anticipates many of the methodological quandaries which haunt and intrigue interpreting researchers to this day.

Further reading: Dodds and Katan 1997; Gile 1995c; Gran and Dodds 1989; Mackintosh 1995, 1999; Paneth 1962, 1984; Seleskovitch 1999.

Eva Paneth

AN INVESTIGATION INTO CONFERENCE INTERPRETING

FOR THE PURPOSE of this investigation, the term "interpreter" will be taken to mean a person who repeats a speech in a different language from that in which it is first pronounced, either simultaneously with, or consecutively to, the original speaker. At a later stage in this thesis we shall go into the functions which this definition rather surprisingly excludes.

Number of languages

The raw material to which the interpreter applies his techniques are words. In interpreting at least two languages are involved. The question arises whether it is best for an individual interpreter to confine himself to two or to try to obtain mastery of three or more. [. . .]

At the moment to ensure future employment a good command of two of the great European languages and knowledge of two subsidiary ones (for translation from but not into them) should be a pre-requisite before the more specific training in interpreting techniques is undertaken. [. . .]

In addition, for prestige and practical reasons it is absolutely essential that an interpreter should speak English and French, not necessarily professionally, but when addressed between sessions, on social occasions, when travelling. An interpreter, possibly sporting a badge of office, who cannot answer when a delegate asks him in English or French where the post office is, will not command the confidence essential for the exercise of his profession.

Mr. Kaminker is convinced that interpreters should only translate into their mother-tongue and that all their practice and studies should be conducted with this performance in view: they should work from a number of languages into one only, except in the few cases where it is impossible to tell which of the two is their mother tongue.

[. . .]

The languages are the interpreter's raw material, their transmutation his daily task. A description of the various techniques of conference interpretation is needed for an appreciation of the problems involved in the application of his skill. We shall therefore outline the characteristics of the techniques actually employed or likely to be employed in the near future. Fundamentally we have to deal with two ways of interpretation, simultaneous and consecutive, and their combinations and adaptations to various audiences.

Simultaneous interpretation

In simultaneous interpretation the audience can hear a translation of a speech while it is being delivered. The interpreters are placed in more or less sound-proof booths where they receive the speech through earphones; they transmit it in another language through microphones to wireless or telephone sets in the hall, which the audience can tune in to the booth (i.e. the language) of their choice. [. . .]

It is the details of the processes that happen in the interpreter, not the well-known ones in the wireless sets, that are being investigated.

As the description "simultaneous interpretation" indicates, it is usually assumed that the interpreter repeats in one language what he hears in another. Roughly speaking this is the case within the framework of a sentence or paragraph, but a closer observation of the actual correspondence between smaller groups of words reveals a different pattern. The interpreter says not what he hears, but what he has heard. This timing of the interpretation in relation to the original speech is illustrated in Figure 1.

The letters a, b, c, d, e, represent groups of words enunciated by the original speaker without appreciable pause between the words in one group. The groups a′, b′, c′, etc. represent their interpretation. Horizontal progress represents time.

Group a′ is moved to the right in relation to a, because observation has shown that in the most frequently practised type of interpretation the translation of a phrase follows its original enunciation with a considerable time lag.

This shift results in the overlapping in time of a′ with parts of b and means that the interpreter listens to parts of phrase b while still translating phrase a.

Two patterns emphasize these two points. The lines a, b, etc. have been connected with their interpretation. The resulting parallelograms show that a phrase and its interpretation are shifted in relation to each other in time; second the stippled rectangles, built up on that part of the interpretation which coincides with the act of listening, show the simultaneity of the translation of one phrase with the listening to another. The actual lag varies, but its mean value seems to be between 2 and 4 seconds, involving 15–21 words. According to the length of the phrases the overlap will vary. The interpretation of a long phrase, such as b, is often begun before its termination; shorter phrases such as c may in their entirety fit into a pause of the speaker's delivery; the translation of very long phrases such as b or d

The Timing of "Simultaneous" Interpretation

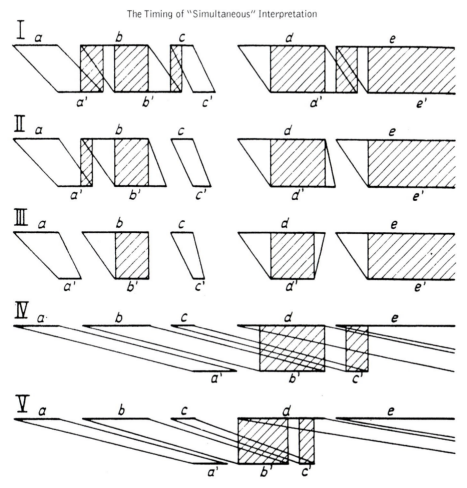

Figure 1   Five techniques are illustrated. Word groups in the original speech are represented by a, b, c, d, e. Their interpretation is shown as a′, b′, c′, d′, e′. The abscissa represents time.

may coincide partly with the end of its delivery and partly with the beginning of a new phrase.

It was further noted that the pauses made by speakers between groups of words are, on average, of considerable length and that the interpreters made the maximum use of them by speeding up their own delivery and thus fitting a great deal of the translation of a phrase into a period of rest, reducing the overlaps.

This pattern is shown in the second line of the diagram, where a speed-up of one quarter is assumed; this reduces the area of over-lap between listening and interpreting. With the not at all rare speakers whose pauses take nearly as long as their word groups, the interpreter can thus fit the translation into the interval. It seems to follow from the cases illustrated that by far the most frequent occurrence is the situation where the interpreter speaks one group of words while listening to part of the next and only for some of the time of his speaking is he not forced to perform two actions, as there is a pause in the delivery of his speaker. It was noted a number of times, however, that the interpreter managed to get the whole of his phrase into the speaker's pause.

But the avoidance of simultaneity is not a major concern of the interpreters. Those who speed up considerably more, e.g. by one half, as indicated in line III, do not necessarily make more use of the pauses for delivery. It may well be that in the general rhythm, they unconsciously fall in with the type of word-group/pause relationship set by the speaker. But it will be generally found that the interpretation of short word groups is more often left till the speaker has finished them, than that of longer ones. Thus the interpretation of group c is only begun after its delivery is completed. Yet the numerous very fast speakers among the interpreters, whose technique is illustrated here, finish nearly in step with their original: they squeeze a great deal more into the time while the original speaker delivers the last half of his long word group. Indeed the combination of early starts on long phrases with considerable acceleration in the delivery of the interpretation may result in the interpreter finishing a group before the speaker, as happens to group d in line III. This means that the interpreter has anticipated the likely conclusions of a cliché or grammatical construction. When the interpretation is thus much more compressed than is shown in II, the breathless haste with which the interpreter accompanies the speech is often quite noticeable.

The start of the interpreter's delivery has so far been placed comparatively near to the beginning of the speaker's word group, in illustration of a technique which Mr. A. Kaminker would call "am Wort kleben", as he says he does himself. It seems more likely, however, that it is the word-group, rather than the single word, to which he clings. He compares his technique with that of Rozan, which forms the basis of illustrations IV and V.

> (Jean-François Rozan) a l'habitude de courir, sans se hâter, au moins une, et souvent deux phrases derrière l'orateur. Comment le fait-il? Je n'en sais rien. Cela a été pour moi un mystère que j'ai depuis longtemps renoncé à éclaircir. Quant à moi, j'essaie de coller autant que possible à l'orateur, de sorte que cela devient un mot à mot.[1]

This extreme case of J.-F. Rozan, who is several "phrases" behind his original, means that he hears part of group d, which may belong to a subsequent sentence, while still enunciating groups of an earlier sentence.

The expression "phrase" in the French text is of course ambiguous. It seems to support our theory that in the majority of cases the interpretation takes place in word groups. When practised by Rozan, it probably means that he is as many "phrases" behind as are needed to complete the sentence, as only this gives him the "appui sur l'idée", discussed in his description of the simultaneous interpretation process. This pattern is illustrated in IV, where c is supposed to be the last group in a sentence. Therefore interpretation starts at the end of its delivery. In V it is additionally assumed that he makes, as most interpreters do, shorter pauses than his original between the groups of words in a sentence and speaks 25% faster. It is assumed that d and e are the initial word groups of a longer sentence to come; so their interpretation would not start within the time-frame of the illustration.

This results in Rozan's having longer continuous pauses than his colleagues for types I–III for intake only, as for instance after the enunciation of cc', which agrees very well with his claim to base his interpretation on a complete thought. He takes in a much larger whole than the interpreters of types I–III and will thus more frequently receive complete thoughts or, if they are not quite complete, have a more considerable portion of their configuration available on which to base his – unconscious – guess for the rest. The advantage of having the whole idea available for translation would also operate in the less favourable situation, not illustrated here, where d might represent an entire sentence which would then leave Rozan little or no pause after the later delivery of his previous one.

A great many fast talkers among the interpreters of this type who have a long time to spare between long sentences also sometimes use it for variation and elucidation.

With these extreme time-lags the correspondence between the "source" and the "target" word groups will presumably be less close. It must be assumed, as Rozan's interpretation is very much admired, that he delivers the same information as the speaker within the limits of single sentences or short sentence groups. [. . .] A comparison of the version of a speaker following pattern I with that of Rozan should be made from the point of view of contents, phrasing, style. This could only be done by a couple of observers analysing passages of the original and of the interpreter with a stop-watch and collecting data on the length of pauses as well, while another couple jotted down the pattern. Tape-recordings would be needed, as not enough observations could be made at a single hearing, and suspected divergences and interesting timings would have to be followed up. Further suggestions are made for such experiments in the section on psychological factors. But some points already observed are worth noting here.

Interpreters of the Rozan type – as far as time relation to the original text is concerned – will of course get away from the correspondence in word groups between the original and the translation. They do not necessarily even operate with the same clauses and the whole sentence structure may be different.

[. . .]

The configuration of the relationship between the interpretation and the original speech is naturally dependent on the two language patterns involved. It affects the corresponding of the phrases more than the whole sentence, although the general build-up of the language enters into it too, but it does not alter the fundamental point that the unit listened to and the unit delivered in the same time are usually not the same.

One ought also to investigate the speed of delivery that interpreters can comfortably reach, and how helpful fast output in the pauses can be to them when dealing with difficult texts. A great many interpreters are only happy when their quick delivery ensures them a great deal of time in hand for corrections or amplification. (For comparison: a normal-sounding good speech in French progressed at an average of 160 words per minute. How much faster can interpreters comfortably speak and how much does it ease the strain for them if they automatically do it?)

The technique illustrated in II, the "step-behind" one, seems to be by far the most frequent and was definitely observed to be applied in a very successful interpretation from French into English at Strasburg which was pleasant to listen to.

The essential step by step approach has been verified frequently by checking translations of phrases such as "nicht ganz unbeteiligt gewesen ist" ("played a certain part"); when in a list of countries the interpreter was two countries behind (!), and of course at the end of paragraphs or speeches.

To investigate the psychological background of the man who says what he hears in another language would be one problem; in the majority of "cases" of simultaneous interpretation we deal with the different one of the man who says one thing (remembered from the past) while listening to another. It is the average performer in the large majority of cases who sets up this puzzle. He seems to be more conscious of his speaking than of his listening, as in good and fluent performances corrections of clichés or slips ("Bestätungun/Bestätigungen") are frequently heard.

And they seem so conscious of *having* to interpret that they will correct satisfaction (for French "satisfaction") into "pleasure"; it is a very usual trick one's mind plays in such an atmosphere of interpretation – suggesting alternatives for everything that anybody says.

In addition to the varieties in the style of the performance of different interpreters, the styles of the speakers of course affect it too, e.g. when a German speaker produces his groups of words so staccato that all the interpreter has available to deal with are two or three words at a time.

[. . .]

Consecutive interpretation

The second type, the consecutive interpretation, can be a "travail ingrat" when everybody has understood the original, or realised that it was not worth listening to; when filling a real gap it is the most worthwhile and rewarding form of interpretation and far more than a stopgap – an artistic performance in itself. It can be the highest art when one personality lends all his knowledge, skill and style to the presentation of the thought of another.

Consecutive interpretation is not only done by professional interpreters; for commercial undertakings, scientific discussions or other conferences between homogeneous groups it can often be serviced by their own members; thus not only its highest flights but also the approaches to it deserve study. An analysis of the techniques might help specialists in finance, commercial matters, science and others who happen to speak a foreign language, to act as more efficient interpreters for their colleagues in their particular subject.

At all stages of proficiency the consecutive interpretation process involves listening to a speech and arrangements for its retention in notes and/or the memory and reproduction in another language after it is finished.

Listening is a more onerous part of the interpreter's work than is generally realised. [. . .] While he listens, he takes notes. In the initial stages the quality of the speech delivered seems to be enhanced by notes taken in the language in which it is to be read out. The interpreter should of course not pause – pause is a very rare thing in an interpreter's work altogether – if a French word for an English original does not occur to him at once, but continue in his note-taking. Most likely, when he is in the midst of his French recitation, the word will come automatically in the context; in any case a descriptive phrase could always be substituted. But on the whole beginners will give a better account of a speech which they already have in front of them in the language to be used; the knowledge that this is so increases their confidence in the delivery. Gradually, as practice increases, symbols will take the place of most notes and with really experienced interpreters it is impossible to tell in which language, if any, their notes and squiggles are taken down. [. . .]

A look at actual notes used in interpretation will introduce further points for discussion. Thanks to Mr. Ilg's kindness we can compare the notation for an interpretation into English with the French original text:

A la première session du Groupe de travail spécial chargé par la commission économique pour l'Europe de préparer le projet de convention, le Royaume-Uni a réservé sa position en ce qui concerne le projet adopté pour l'article 2 et il a, en même temps, proposé un autre texte pour cet article.

Le Groupe de travail a rejeté la proposition du Royaume-Uni pour diverses raisons, et notamment parce que cette proposition ne faisait qu'exonérer le transporteur de sa responsabilité dans certains cas ou les droits et les obligations des parties devaient être régis par la loi applicable au mode de transport considéré, sans donner à la victime du dommage d'autres recours contre le transporteur autre que le transporteur routier.

En droit anglais, cette objection ne presenterait guère d'importance car toute personne qui a un droit sur les marchandises peut exercer un recours contre un transporteur en cas d'avarie, même en l'absence d'un lien contractuel entre cette personne et le transporteur; toutefois, il a été indiqué qu'il pourrait ne pas être ainsi dans certains pays. Estimant toujours que le projet adopté à la première session du Groupe de travail n'est pas applicable, le Royaume-Uni a préparé un nouveau projet de texte pour l'article 2 (voir Annexe 2).

—[≠1, ℗ °]

UKP/ /σσ Rd φ
/cl σσ f, φ ó
+ free ¢ ≠ clfg

_____

Le nouveau texte entraîne certaines modifications a l'article 1, et il est plus simple que le texte primitivement proposé par le Royaume-Uni.

La proposition du Royaume-Uni tend à limiter le rôle du transporteur routier à l'etablissement d'un lien entre le client et l'autre transporteur, et à exonérer le transporteur routier de toute obligation née de l'utilisation de l'autre mode de transport.

These leaves from Mr. Ilg's pad clearly exemplify:

- the paucity of notes;
- the emphasis on ideas rather than on words;
- the mainly non-linguistic nature of the notation . . . symbolic rather than syntactical connections, no grammar;
- the "in-die-Augen-Springen" of the main subjects, e.g. Annex, English law, and of the attitudes of them, e.g. O.K.;
- the indifference to the language used, e.g. English "free", "no", "Rd", combined with French "que", av (avarie), and the German sign for paragraph, §;
- the reference back that saves a multitude of words: e.g. the line connecting mention of the "project" in the first and fourth paragraphs in the example (called by Mr. Rozan "la flèche de rappel");
- the function of the notes as aide-mémoire and not as text for the delivery of the interpreted speech.

[. . .]

The example before us demonstrates that the taking of these notes meant at the same time an assimilation of the text, an analysis of its contents and a transposition. [. . .]

As even a good rendering will easily appear longer than the original (especially to an audience semi-familiar with it) the interpreter usually has to make his speech shorter, by quicker delivery and occasional summarising. [. . .]

"Verhandlungsdolmetschen"

For the interpretation of – mostly commercial – negotiations the interpreter mediates between two partners only, practising a kind of consecutive interpretation in which he often is not able to take notes. The "interprètes de liaison" and military interpreters . . . belong to this group. This is also called "Verkehrs- oder Geschäftsdolmetschen". The "Betreuungsdolmetscher", "Fremdsprachige Reisebegleiter" or "Bader-Dolmetscher" has much the same function, the second partner being mostly waiters, custom officials etc.[2]

The exchange of short question and answer is also often characteristic of the work of the interpreter before a court of law. A case can be made for classifying interpreters who have to deal with cross-questioning in a special group. Here a precise knowledge of the subject, e.g. legal terms, is more important than an accomplished technique.

How important the terminology is, is shown by the fact that interpreters who have coped more or less satisfactorily with a longish speech at a scientific conference fail at question time. In a short question, unless the terms are precisely right and as normally used by the specialist, the interlocutor fails to realise what he is being asked. A special vocabulary is thus needed for the "gerichtlich beeidigte Dolmetscher" (there is no such class of beings in England) who works at the courts of law and has taken an oath that he will "faithfully" translate both documents and statements in the course of legal proceedings. Only in Denmark is there an official linguistic test ensuring that the interpreter has the necessary qualifications to implement such an oath.[3] [. . .]

"Chuchotage"

Interpretation for one listener only takes place when, during a conference involving a number of people, the interpreter sits behind his one client and whispers a translation to him; he is well advised to make copious use of a note-pad, for the illustration of relationships, figures, underlining of points etc., as writing disturbs the neighbours less than whispering, and good notes may serve as an "aide-mémoire" to the client and even as an explanation of points involved. How far the interpreter can go here in real interpretation and elucidation of the discussion, depends on the personal relationship established, which can be one of the most rewarding in the profession, because of the amount of help that can be given to an important negotiator by a really well-informed interpreter. [. . .]

Radio and theatre and film interpreters

Here the work is different in that these people usually work from a prepared text; as the interpreter is present at rehearsals, to note the cuts, business, and highlights, he has a kind of producer's copy . . . and, in so far as he merely reads this out aloud, these new "souffleurs" are not true interpreters, but only partake of the technique when they anticipate jokes (with explanation!), so that they should not be lost in the laughter of the rest of the audience.

Interpretation on the radio is sometimes of the same type . . . It does occur however, that we have true simultaneous interpretation on the wireless. [. . .]

Telephone interpretation

A very neat and obvious use of interpreters will be introduced in the near future by the German Post Office; it will soon be possible to insert a simultaneous interpreter into the line connecting a German subscriber with his interlocutor abroad; different exchanges will service various languages, Frankfurt, e.g., will take calls demanding

French interpretation.[4] [. . .] This service might easily be developed further, so that it should no more be necessary to displace interpreters for short conferences of a few hours. [. . .]

Writing interpreters

In conclusion I would advocate experiments with written interpretation on the illuminated disc some lecturers use for drawings, that are executed and projected during their discourse. Abbreviated statements of the theme being discussed, projected onto a screen in another language, might be a quick way in which linguists could help their colleagues at international conferences.

Notes

1   "Conférence de M. André Kaminker", *L'Interprète*, 1955, 4–5, p. 9.
2   Günther Haensch, "Dolmetschen – Einmal Anders", *L'Interprète*, 1947, 5, p. 2–3.
3   "Traducteurs-Interprètes assermentés au Danemark", *L'Interprète*, 1947, 2, p. 2.
4   Fredo Nestler, "Tel-Interpret. Begründung und Grundlagen eines deutschen Telefon-Dolmetschdienstes", *Lebende Sprachen*, 1957, 1, p. 21–3.

A **LEADING FRENCH** psychologist with a special interest in language and intellectual skills, it seems fitting that Pierre Oléron (1915–95) should have published the first scientific study of simultaneous interpreting based on authentic as well as experimental data. His pioneering work, done in collaboration with an assistant, Hubert Nanpon, was published in 1965 in the *Journal de Psychologie Normale et Pathologique*, where his very first publication (on intelligence tests for deaf children) had appeared in 1949. While Nanpon died early, Professor Oléron continued his distinguished career until well into the 1990s. He published over a dozen monographs, some of which were translated into several languages, and some 150 articles in scientific journals and books on a variety of subjects, including intelligence, language acquisition, deaf education, sign language and rhetoric. Nevertheless, and despite the great effort obviously invested into his pioneering work on simultaneous interpreting, Oléron never took up the subject again.

The paper by Oléron and Nanpon, originally entitled "Recherches sur la traduction simultanée" was first presented at the 17th International Congress of Psychology held in Washington in 1963, and is being made available here in an English translation by Ruth Morris. The abridgements we have made to the original text mainly concern the detailed presentation of data and findings (charts, diagrams, appendix) of the experimental part of the study, in which the authors had three professionals interpret short scripted passages, sentences and isolated words. In this context, it may be interesting to note that the authors express their gratitude to "Miss Seleskovitch" for helpful information and for her interest in the study.

Pierre Oléron and Hubert Nanpon

RESEARCH INTO SIMULTANEOUS TRANSLATION

Translated by Ruth Morris

I

[. . .]

TO THE BEST of our knowledge, simultaneous translation[1] has so far not been the subject of any experimental studies. This is one of the reasons why in the present investigation we have limited ourselves to a relatively preliminary description of some of its aspects. We have considered a number of quantitative values, particularly those involving interpreters' output compared with that of speakers or a written translation. Other values are of more qualitative importance insofar as they enable the degree of correspondence, and hence the accuracy, of the translation to be assessed. However, we have focused on considering the phenomena in question in terms of how they occur over time, examining the speaker's activity relative to that of the interpreter. It is quite obvious that the term "simultaneous" is an approximation only, covering a fairly complex process whose variations must be presented by the analysis.

II

In principle, the technique we used is straightforward. It involves a two-track tape recorder. One of the tracks records the original text as output by the speaker, while the other records the translation provided by the interpreter. Next, the recordings must be transcribed in a visible form which will allow for analysis and measurements. This was achieved through the use of two galvanometric plotters connected to the tape-recorder outlets. [. . .] Finally, the resulting plottings have to be deciphered – the trickiest part of the exercise, and one which demands listening repeatedly to the recording. [. . .]

Data were collected in two conditions:

Condition A. Condition A involves recordings made "in the field." We took advantage of a UNESCO meeting to collect samples of speeches and their renderings in a number of different language combinations. In order to remain in the setting of translating oral texts, the recordings were restricted to off-the-cuff output produced during discussions and concerning non-technical matters. Of the resulting material, five passages were selected for special analysis. (See description below.)

The nature of the texts produced in this situation, while enabling a number of analyses to be carried out, is not without its drawbacks. In particular, improvisation leads to flawed presentations (hesitations, repetitions, incorrect language). As a result, the text is not organized "normally," and this impacts on the interpretation. Moreover, in practical terms, producing a transcript from the recordings in order to reconstitute the "texts" actually delivered by the speakers entails a great deal of work. As a result, we decided to make use of a more standardized situation.

Condition B. Condition B corresponds to an experiment carried out in the laboratory according to a predetermined design. We used texts which existed in a number of different language versions: extracts from the *UNESCO Courier*, and Saint-Exupéry's *Petit Prince*. There were three categories of texts:

1   "paragraphs" (4), ranging from 129 to 204 words (the word count being based on the French version);
2   sentences (14) ranging from 8 to 49 words;
3   individual words (46).

[. . .]

Prior to the experiment, the translations were reviewed and in certain cases, corrected when some passages had been rendered too freely. The amended texts were then recorded by mother-tongue speakers, and were then presented to the interpreters in tape-recorded form.

The translations were provided by three professional interpreters. [. . .] In the original research design, two different interpreters were supposed to work in each direction [. . .]. However, practical circumstances (interpreters not available, equipment malfunctions) made it impossible to implement this design. The quantitative characteristics of the samples appear in Table 1.[2]

Conditions A and B differ somewhat in terms of the speed at which the speakers spoke. The texts in A are presented more slowly than the paragraphs in B. This is obviously a result of the fact that the former involves improvised performances, including such features as hesitations and repetitions, which were cut out during the counting process. It should be noted that the relatively high speed at which material in Condition B was read, as well as the absence of a "situation-related" context (including the speaker's body language) which experts consider to be rather helpful, made the interpreters' task more difficult.

[. . .]

Table 1   Condition A: Description of samples.

Translation direction	Text	Number of words		Length (sec.)		Delivery rate (no. of words/min.)	
		Speaker	Int.	Speaker	Int.	Speaker	Int.
German–French	1	181	219	121	120	90	109
French–Spanish	2	202	168	84	84	144	120
English–French	3	117	114	68	70	103	98
French–English	4	192	186	98	97	118	115

III

(A) Quantitative characteristics of the translations

1 Translations compared with originals

From the data collected it is possible to determine the number of words produced, the length of speaking, and hence the rate of both speakers' and interpreters' outputs (Table 2).

2 Oral and written translation

Comparisons between the number of words produced in two different languages are clearly overshadowed by the fact that these languages do not have the same "density," or do not divide up linguistic units in the same way: negation requires one word in German (*nicht*), but two in French (*ne . . . pas*) and English (*do not*); French uses one word to indicate the future tense, while German and English need two; and so on. To interpret the results obtained in Condition A, it is necessary to define the standards for each of the languages. No such standards were available to us, and the few surveys which we carried out of works translated from one language into another could not be applied to the kind of limited sample with which we were dealing.

[. . .]

(B) Timing of original and translation

1 Temporal relations

The graphic "translation" of the original output relative to the translated one illustrates their respective timing; i.e. their temporal relations. While some of the

Table 2   Condition A: Indices for the central tendency and distribution of translation
delays (in seconds).

Translation direction	Text	Corresponding words	Average	Median	Interquartile range	Range
German–French	1	140	1.9	1.7	1.0	0.7–5.9
French–Spanish	2	110	2.7	2.6	1.6	0.9–7.1
English–French	3	79	2.6	2.4	0.7	0.5–4.7
French–English	4	93	5.4	5.3	1.7	0.9–11.1

findings resulting from scrutiny of the graphs will be discussed below, one deserves special study at this point: the structuring of the output texts, i.e. the distribution of continuous output and pauses. This structuring is indicative of how the output is divided up; clearly, the units are not words, but more comprehensive sequences, which should undoubtedly be considered systematically when a comparison is made between the original and translated utterances.

We did not do this here because of the complexities of the operation, particularly since the practical dividing up of the texts delivered does not always provide a faithful reflection of structuring in terms of words; for proper analysis, it would be necessary to have automatic counting resources. Pauses can have a range of meanings, and it is not easy to separate psychological factors (such as waiting for information) from linguistic ones (different organization of the respective languages) without a certain amount of analytical experimentation.

2 Determining the time delay between original and translation

To measure the time that elapses between original and translation the corresponding elements of the two outputs must be correlated. This can be done directly and without any loss when translating individual words. In the case of paragraphs and sentences, the situation is different, since certain terms are dropped in the translation, or are expressed by a number of words. Hence here we relate only to those words where a literal correspondence could be established. As a result, the number of elements used for these calculations is smaller than the number of words in the sample. (Other approaches could be imagined, of course, and there could be variations on how to calculate the correlation . . .)

From the technical point of view, the time delay (*décalage*) is determined on the basis of graphic recordings or plots, by measuring distances between points identified on the two tracks (original/translation). Obviously the accuracy of measurements is not absolute, particularly in light of the difficulties in identifying words in continuous texts; but it may be said that inaccuracies are minor relative to the order of magnitude of the values presented in the tables [. . .].

Statistical values. After determining the figures for the *décalage* between matched words, the indices for overall tendency (average and mean) were calculated, together with two indices for dispersion (the semi-interquartile range and the full range, i.e. between the lowest and highest values). The results are given in Table 2.

[. . .]

1. Overall, the distributions are asymmetrical in shape. This is the case wherever response times are concerned; it is impossible to drop below certain limits, while certain intervals may be extremely long.

2. There is considerable variation in median delay between samples (except in the case of words). The temptation is to attach responsibility to language factors and individual differences. The longest delays relate, for example, to the French–German texts. However, it is impossible to reach a conclusion on the basis of a single sample, particularly since the longest delays corresponded to a text where the interpreter found it increasingly difficult to follow. It is highly likely that individual differences exist between interpreters, perhaps relating to such factors as how much is grasped, work habits, familiarity with the language and the desire to be faithful to the original. Here again, more detailed studies are called for. Let us remember that many interpreters prefer to work in a direction in which they feel more comfortable. It was for this reason that we were unable to carry out our experiment in full, since two of our interpreters were unwilling to work in the direction less familiar to them. As a result, we were unable to evaluate whether this preference was reflected in different time delays.

Variations in length of delays over time. Delays do not lend themselves to straightforward statistical distribution: rather, they vary over time, becoming shorter or longer depending on variations both in the original speech and in the translation. [. . .] To illustrate this variation, graphs have been plotted, with time shown on the x-axis and delays on the y-axis, using the time which elapsed between matched words (original/translation). [. . .] For the data reflected by the graphs, a formal type of analysis may be conducted to study the interplay of the variables characteristic of oral output: speed of delivery, length and frequency of pauses. Clearly the interpreter falls further and further behind in the case of a rapid speaker who does not interject pauses; conversely, the interpreter will keep up better in the opposite situation. Again, an interpreter whose rate of delivery and use of pauses vary will fall behind (or not) to varying degrees. This analysis can be taken further, to include elements such as syllables or phonemes (a word may "dwell" on phonemes to varying extents, so that word length may be extended, with output rates being reduced as a result, without there being an increase in the quantity or length of pauses). This would result in a description which could take a precise quantitative form, even making it possible to try to come up with mathematical formulae somewhat similar to those used to describe such phenomena as traffic flow, or more complex ones (amount grasped, quantity placed in short-term memory, or storage abilities), setting a number of constants which must be complied with. To put it in more familiar terms which are closer to ordinary language, it is possible to describe the circumstances which correspond to various aspects of the plotted graphs: at this point the translator is hesitating, here he or she is correcting him- or herself, or speeding up or catching up by skipping certain parts of the text.

Such descriptions make it possible to understand a particular recording, but are short on general points. Examining the graphs may give rise to comments which are of more "clinical" significance, but nevertheless point to certain tendencies which an analysis of a larger number of more systematically structured samples might make it possible to state in greater detail. Some of these comments follow.

Some plots or parts of these plots can be considered as ascending systematically (rather than fluctuating). This is true of certain beginnings, and of the translation of short sentences. Here the interpreter begins to lag behind, and this lag will increase. Where short sentences are involved, it would appear that this can be explained by what has already been outlined: interpreters know that they are not under pressure, and consequently they take their time. Situations in which the delay becomes stabilized can be seen as resulting from the inherent progress of the text and the interpreter's concern not to fall too far behind, so that otherwise the amount which can be grasped and stored is not exceeded. This suggests that the concept of average lag actually covers a multitude of factors among which compromises are constantly being made.

Linguistic factors, particularly word order, must be given special consideration. When this order is different in the respective languages, the inevitable result is hesitations of varying degrees of obviousness. As an example, the fact that in German the verb or particle may come at the end of the sentence can generate major problems for the interpreter who is trying to maintain the natural order of the sentence in French or English. Alternatively, the interpreter may wait for the information contained in the verb (cf. the comment delivered as an aside by an interpreter at an international congress: "I'm waiting for the verb"), or will agree to violate some of the conventions of the language into which the rendering is being made.

More generally, the way in which each language divides up and structures information is undoubtedly a basic factor in determining how the translation is delivered relative to the original text. [. . .]

IV

Of the information generated in the course of this study, we have decided to highlight the aspect of time delay. We must start by emphasizing that when translating words, response time is around 1–1.2 seconds. During word-repetition experiments similar to the present one, but where the repetition is in the same language (Oléron and Nanpon 1964), the delay is around 0.6–0.8 seconds. Hence switching from one language to another produces a lengthening effect of around 0.4 seconds, or 50 percent. Since repetition within the same language is a mechanical phenomenon, it is noteworthy that switching from one linguistic system to another does not lead to a more substantial increase. Admittedly, translating individual words may be considered a mechanical process too, but not exactly of the same type; at the very least it is based on linguistic units (words), whereas straightforward repetition may involve more elementary ones (syllables), and the process is based on copying, which may (although this has not been proven) be simpler than associating elements which started out as heterogeneous ones.

It has been found that response times are distinctly longer in the case of texts. This is another fact worth bearing in mind. The interpreter works at some distance from the text heard – lapsed time can be considerable, sometimes as long as 10 seconds. In this process, it would appear that mechanisms are involved which tolerate considerable time delays in generating responses, though extreme delays are of limited significance only, since they often correspond to times when the translation is no longer following the text in a satisfactory fashion. The time delays which correspond to satisfactory performance are shorter, but can reach values which . . . are of the order of 2–3 seconds.

This discussion shows – as is obvious – that when it comes to interpreter performance, the time variable is not uniform. Once a delay reaches a certain length, it becomes problematic, interfering with the normal progress of the translation activity. More generally, the interpreter is part of a complex situation, and the variables considered account for only some of its aspects. In this connection, we can talk of strategies designed to try to control the situation and involving various compromises either in terms of accuracy, or in terms of correctness, when time constraints – particularly those arising out of over-rapid speaker speed – become excessive.

Separate research should be carried out into these strategies. However, in our view the importance of studying optimum situations should be stressed. Only in this way can one properly understand and analyze transcription [sic] processes. Excessive speed of delivery and lack of training or of familiarity with the subject matter are disruptive elements which conceal the actual structure of the phenomenon to be studied, at least during the initial stages of the study, which we have scarcely touched upon.

Another point which needs to be raised has to do with the relationship between the conditions of an analytical situation in a laboratory, and interpreters' hands-on activities. It goes without saying that we used professional interpreters to provide the transcription [sic] from one language to another in an oral setting, since this is an activity which relates very directly to what interpreters do at international conferences. However, it should be noted that specialists have made a point of emphasizing the differences between the two types of situation. In actual practice, the interpreter often receives the text (or at least a summary) of the paper to be translated, and this provides additional informational and in particular anticipatory elements (admittedly, this information must be digested, generating additional problems, but it undoubtedly makes things easier). On the other hand, in strictly oral translation situations, the interpreter may be assisted, as indicated above, by extra-linguistic aspects of the speaker's behaviour (such as body language and intonation). Furthermore, in the case of a genuinely oral style, whether an improvised presentation or the "oralized" presentation of a prepared text, information-diluting elements will be present. The result is increased redundancy, and the upshot is to slow down the presentation, thereby facilitating the translation task. It is obvious that the experimental situation chosen here eliminates these factors, displacing interpreters from their normal settings. Caution must therefore be exercised in generalizing from one situation to another.

Furthermore, it must be remembered that a psychological study of interpreters – particularly of those abilities other than knowledge of languages which can facilitate interpreter performance, such as the amount which can be grasped at one time, as well as the ability to concentrate on a number of different things and to perform several tasks simultaneously – might shed light on some aspects of how interpreting can be successfully performed, as well as providing insights into the mechanisms at work in the process.

Many other perspectives could be studied. In concluding, we would like to repeat that our own goal was strictly limited: this is simply a preliminary approach, restricted in terms of both design and implementation by the complex nature of the variables and the cumbersome nature of the analytical procedures applied. We trust that it will be followed by other investigations in which psychologists, linguists and professionals could, we believe, usefully cooperate.

Notes

1   Experts consider that the term "translation" should be used when referring to written texts, and reserve the term "interpretation" for situations which, like here, are purely oral (corresponding to the functions of the interpreter). We did not consider it necessary to adhere fully to this point of view because of the ambiguity, which is particularly awkward in a title, of the word "interpretation."

2   In all of the counts used in this study, hyphenated expressions were considered as single words. Also, the count did not include unintentional repetitions or false starts.

Reference

Oléron, P. and Nanpon, H. (1964) "Recherches sur la répétition orale de mots présentés auditivement," *L'Année Psychologique* 64: 397–410.

DAVID GERVER (1932–81) stands out among those who most decisively shaped the development of research on simultaneous interpreting. Gerver received a diploma in clinical psychology before proceeding to earn a doctorate in psychology from Oxford University for his thesis on "Simultaneous Interpretation and Human Information Processing" (1971), which reports experiments on the effects of factors likely to be encountered in authentic conference interpreting situations, such as rapid presentation rate, non-standard intonation and noise. Besides reviewing (and questioning) existing findings, Gerver also developed the first flow-chart model of the process, and posited the existence of a monitoring mechanism.

Gerver was the most prolific and varied of the early interpreting researchers, and co-edited what is clearly one of the most important books on interpreting: the proceedings of the 1977 Venice Symposium on *Language Interpretation and Communication* (Gerver and Sinaiko 1978), which attempted (none too successfully) to effect a dialogue between scientists and scholars in a variety of relevant disciplines. As a professor of psychology at the University of Stirling until his untimely death, he was also instrumental in establishing community psychological services, and prepared and presented a number of BBC radio and television programs on the relationship between the conductor and the orchestra.

The paper presented here is reprinted from *The Proceedings of the Second Louisville Conference on Rate and/or Frequency Controlled Speech* (1969).

Further reading: Gerver 1971, 1974a, 1974b, 1975, 1976, 1981.

David Gerver

THE EFFECTS OF SOURCE LANGUAGE PRESENTATION RATE ON THE PERFORMANCE OF SIMULTANEOUS CONFERENCE INTERPRETERS

Introduction

IN SIMULTANEOUS INTERPRETATION, as in most naturally occurring tracking tasks, the observer is often confronted with differential information load. For the interpreter, this may be due either to syntactic and/or semantic variability of the source language input, and/or to variability in source language presentation rate. In the present study, attention will be paid to the effects of presentation rate of the source language on the performance of simultaneous conference interpreters.

Goldman-Eisler (1968) and others have shown that most periods of speech consist not only of speech but also of silent intervals of varying temporal duration. Goldman-Eisler has suggested that the more of his output that the simultaneous interpreter can crowd into the source speaker's pauses, the more time he has to listen to the input without interference from his own output. Unfortunately for the interpreter, though, it is doubtful whether he can reliably predict input pauses and achieve the "ideal" distribution of his own speech time and pause times, i.e., to pause when there is input speech and to speak when there are input pauses. Even if he could do this, it is doubtful whether the simultaneous interpreter could cram much of his own output into input pauses, since the majority of pauses in speech are less than 0.5 second in duration, while only 20% to 40% lie between .5 and 1 second, 12% to 20% between 1 and 2 seconds, and very few above 2 seconds (Goldman-Eisler 1961).

While it is feasible that the interpreter could utilise input pauses, in view of the above mentioned limitations it seems more likely that he would attempt to cope with increase in input rate in other ways. He might, for instance, speak more and pause less, and increase his own output rate as input rate increased. Alternatively, he could pause more frequently and speak for shorter intervals at faster rates.

The purpose of this experiment, then, is to examine the effect of variation in input rate on the interpreter's performance by systematically varying the rate of presentation of a source passage. In order to ascertain the extent to which any variability in interpreters' performance may be due to difficulty in simply transmitting speech at faster rates, rather than to difficulty in carrying out the complex decoding and encoding processes involved in interpretation as input rate increases, all relevant measures of the interpreter's performance will be compared with those for Ss shadowing (repeating as they hear it) the same experimental message. Carey (1968) found that shadowers made more errors as input rate increased from 1 to 3 words per second (wps). Treisman (1965), using statistical approximations to French and English and presentation rates of 1.7 and 2.5 wps, found that information rate had a greater effect on the number of correct responses produced by simultaneous interpreters than by shadowers. Treisman also found that ear–voice span (the number of words S follows behind the speaker) was greater for interpreting than for shadowing. She attributed the differences in performance between interpreters and shadowers to the ". . . increased decision load between input and output required in translation: two selections need to be made, the first to identify the word or phrase heard, and the second to select an appropriate response. The shadowing task is simpler if it is assured, as is plausible, that a single central identification of the verbal unit serves for both reception and response, so that only one decision is required."

Treisman did not attempt to analyse her Ss' errors, but Carey employed four error categories: word omissions, word substitutions, additions of words, and distortions of words. Preliminary analysis of the protocols of Ss in the present study suggested that the term "discontinuity" rather than "error" was a more appropriate description of deviations from the input message found in the output of both interpreters and shadowers. Though omissions, repetitions, additions, and distortions can be regarded as errors, other phenomena found both in shadowing and interpretation, such as substitutions or corrections of words or phrases, are not necessarily errors but do involve some discontinuity in the message being transmitted. In the present study, the following categories will be employed: omissions of words, omissions of phrases, omissions of longer stretches of input of eight words or more, substitutions of words, substitutions of phrases, corrections of words and corrections of phrases.

Substitutions involve approximate or less precise responses which, though grammatical and meaningful, alter the meaning of a sentence in some way. Corrections are observed whenever S interrupts his output to correct previous words or phrases and are of particular interest in simultaneous interpretation for the light they shed on feedback mechanisms. Welford (1968) discusses the simultaneous interpreter's performance within the context of a "single channel" hypothesis and the role of feedback in human information processing during continuous tracking tasks. He states that simultaneous interpreters can, after long practice, acquire the ability to speak and listen concurrently because they learn to ignore the feedback from their own voices. The very fact of frequent corrections in the interpreter's output, however, shows that though interpreters may learn to ignore the *sound* of their own voices, they do not ignore the *meaning* of what they say.

Apart from these "discontinuities" in output, the dependent variables in this study will be: the number of words correctly shadowed or translated, ear–voice span, utterance times, and unfilled pause times. Fries (1952) defined an "utterance unit" as " . . . any stretch of speech by one person before which there is a silence on his part, and after which there is also silence on his part." For the purposes of this study, an utterance will be defined as any period of speech bounded by unfilled pauses, the criterion for an unfilled pause being a break in the speaker's utterance of not less than 250 milliseconds (msec.). Goldman-Eisler (1968) adopted this criterion, arguing that pauses up to 250 msec. might occur as part of ritardando effects or articulatory shifts between plosives.

Finally, the ratio of overall pause time to overall speech time will also be calculated since it has been hypothesized that the interpreter might try to redistribute his performance in time as input rate increases. Apart from redistributing speech time and pause time, the interpreter might become less variable in his output rates as information load increases. One noticeable characteristic of the delivery of conference interpreters is the frequency of ritardando and accelerando passages. That is to say that the interpreter will appear to dawdle over some words, rather like a person thinking of something else while he is speaking, and then speak very quickly as if under pressure to unload material in store. This, in turn, may be followed by a further ritardando passage, and so on. Another way of describing this type of output is in terms of the variability of the relationship between the number of words uttered and the time taken to utter them. In ritardando passages the interpreter may utter a few words in a given time, whilst in accelerando passages he would utter more words in the same time. At slower input rates, then, the interpreter may have time to vary his output rate, but not at the faster rates, and this would be reflected in the correlations between the number of words per utterance and the time per utterance at different input rates.

Method

A French text of 550 words (an extract from a speech at a United Nations Educational, Scientific, and Cultural Organization Conference on Human Rights) was recorded on tape at a rate of approximately 120 words per minute (wpm) by a male native French speaker. This master tape was systematically expanded and compressed in time by means of an Eltro Tempophon, the rate being changed at intervals of approximately 110 words. The output of the Tempophon was then rerecorded on a Revox G36 tape recorder, and the final experimental tape contained a continuous text with the following rates and passage lengths:

Rate wpm	95	112	120	142	164
Number of words	108	106	108	111	118

Subjects

The Ss were 10 professional simultaneous conference interpreters. Five of the Ss were allotted to the shadowing condition, five to the interpreting condition. The mother tongue of all Ss was English.

Procedure

All *Ss* heard the stimulus tape under language laboratory conditions. The experimental tape was relayed to *Ss'* individual booths from the main control booth and was recorded on the top track of each *S*'s tape. Subjects' responses were recorded on the bottom tracks of their tapes.

Interpreter *Ss* received the following prerecorded instructions: "You are going to hear a speech in French. You will probably notice that the speaker speaks more quickly as his speech continues. Please interpret the passage from French to English as you hear it."

Subjects in the shadowing group received the same instructions except that they were asked to repeat the words in French as soon as they heard them.

Treatment of Results

A 2 Groups x 5 Presentation Rate repeated measurements design (Winer 1962) was employed in analysis of variance of the results.

In order to measure *Ss'* utterances and pause times, both tracks of each *S*'s tape were transcribed on a paper record of a pen tracing of each channel. The pen recordings were obtained by replaying each *S*'s tape on a Revox G36 stereo tape recorder, and feeding the output from each channel to two speech trigger units attached to a modified Marconi Electro-encephalograph (EEG) pen recorder. In order to minimise pen onset and offset delays, which vary directly with signal level (Ramsay and Law 1966), the output from each channel of the trigger circuit was monitored on a multichannel display oscilloscope, whilst the tape recorder output was monitored on separate loudspeakers. The auditory signals could then be matched with visual traces of the operation of the trigger units to produce optimal onset sensitivity and minimal offset delay, by adjusting the sensitivity of the trigger circuits. [. . .]

After setting the appropriate level controls, the *E* followed the text from a typewritten copy and activated a marker pen on the EEG recorder at approximately every fifth word of the input text. . . . This practice provides a number of reference points against which to match the tape recording with the pen recording of each channel. The speed of the pen recorder transport was 3 centimeters per second. Both tape-recorded tracks were transcribed onto the pen recordings, and the measurements of ear–voice span, speech time, and pause time were then made.

Counting the number of words correctly shadowed was a straightforward task; but in assessing the correctness of interpretations, paraphrase was taken into account since a word-for-word translation was not expected and, indeed, would not have been a good translation from the interpreter's point of view.

Ear–voice span was calculated for shadowers at every fifth word of the input text in terms of the number of words not yet correctly repeated by the *S*. Words omitted entirely in shadowing were counted as part of the ear–voice span until the *S* had passed beyond the point at which they could have been repeated in the correct order. For interpreters, ear–voice span was calculated at every fifth word of the input text in terms of the number of words not yet translated by the *S*. Words omitted in translation were counted as part of ear–voice span until the interpreter had passed beyond the point where they could have been translated in context. Provided that some reasonable connection could be inferred between the interpreter's output and the original message, an error in translation was counted as a word translated and not as a part of ear–voice span. Here, too, paraphrase was taken into account, and there were specific rules relating to the number of words which could have been meaningfully translated into English. For instance, *ne . . . pas* was counted as one word from the *ne*, and articles in the original were not counted when they would not normally have been translated.

Results

Analyses of variance showed the following main and interaction effects:

1. Words correctly shadowed or translated. Significantly more words were correctly shadowed than translated ($F = 6.767$; $df = 1, 8$; $p < .05$), and the effect of presentation rate was also significant ($F = 24.752$; $df = 4, 32$; $p < .001$). As can be seen from Figure 1, the significant interaction ($F = 4.363$; $df = 4, 32$; $p < .05$) indicated that presentation rate had a greater effect on the performance of the interpreters than of the shadowers.

2. Ear–voice span. As can be seen from Figure 2, interpreters had significantly greater ear–voice spans than shadowers ($F = 56.304$ $df = 1, 8$; $p < .001$), and there was a significant effect of presentation rate ($F = 11.408$; $df = 4, 32$; $p < .001$). The

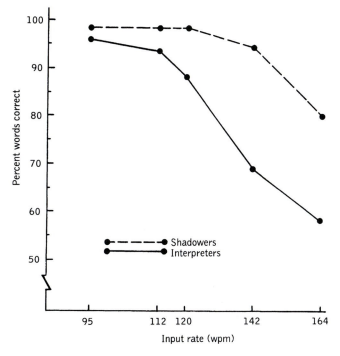

Figure 1   Mean % words correct.

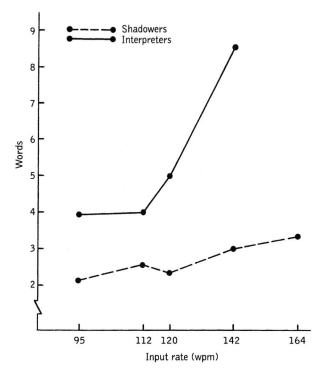

Figure 2   Mean ear–voice span.

significant interaction also indicated that presentation rate had a greater effect on interpreters (F = 5. 029; df = 4, 32; p < .001).

3. Number of utterances. Figure 3 shows that interpreters tended to produce more utterances (i.e., pause more often) than shadowers (F = 3. 742; df = 1, 8; p < .05), and that both groups produced significantly fewer utterances (paused less often) as presentation rate increased (F = 3. 377; df = 4, 32; p < .05). The interaction term (F = 0.064) did not approach significance.

4. Number of words per utterance. Figure 4 appears to show that shadowers produced more words per utterance than interpreters, and that there is a significant interaction between presentation rate and words per utterance, but these results do not approach significance on the analysis of variance.

5. Time per utterance. As can be seen from Figure 5, input rate had differential effects on the mean utterance times of shadowers and interpreters (F = 3. 09; df = 4, 32; p < .05). The effect of presentation rate was significant (F = 8. 57; df = 4, 32; p < .001), but there was no significant difference between groups.

6. Pause times. Though Figure 6 appears to show definite main and interaction effects, these results are not significant.

7. The ratio of total pause time to total speech time. On the average, interpreters maintained higher pause-speech ratios than shadowers (F = 8. 813; df = 1, 8; p < .001). Rate of presentation had a significant effect on pause-speech ratios for both groups (F = 3. 303; df 4, 32; p < .05), but the interaction term was not significant. These results are illustrated in Figure 7.

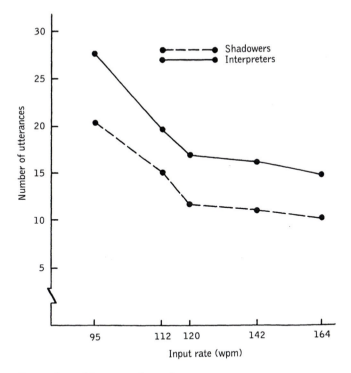

Figure 3   Mean number of utterances.

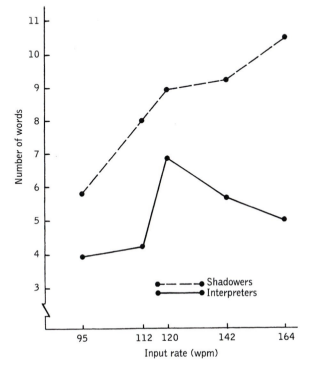

Figure 4   Mean number of words per utterance.

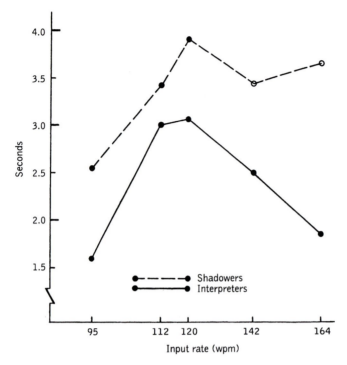

Figure 5   Mean utterance time (secs.).

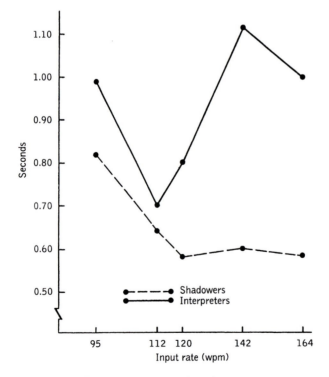

Figure 6   Mean pause times (secs.).

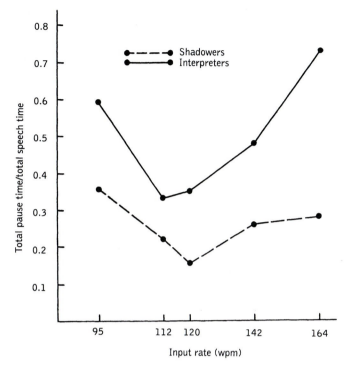

Figure 7   Ratio of pause time to speech time.

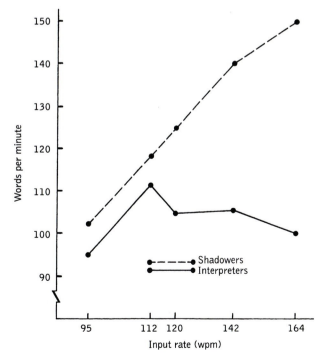

Figure 8   Mean output rates (wpm).

8. Output rate. As can be seen from Figure 8, shadowers maintained a consistently higher rate of output than interpreters ($F = 9.983$; df $= 1, 8$; p $< .05$). Presentation rate had a significant effect on the performance of both groups ($F = 4.697$; df $= 4, 32$; p $< .05$), and the interaction term was also significant ($F = 4.363$; df $= 4, 32$; p $< .01$).

9. Output variability. The correlations between words per utterance and time per utterance were calculated for Ss in each group at each presentation rate, and the weighted average correlations were then calculated (McNemar 1962). The plot of these relationships in Figure 9 shows that both groups became less variable in terms of their output rate per utterance as presentation rate increased.

Discontinuities in output

[. . .] The data are not suitable for an overall statistical analysis, but some tentative conclusions may still be drawn from the results.

1. From the totals for groups and rates, it can be seen that interpreters tended to produce more discontinuities than shadowers, and that these increased with increase in presentation rate.

2. Both groups omitted a similar number of single words, but interpreters omitted more phrases and longer passages. Here, too, there was an effect of presentation rate. The average number of words in phrases omitted by interpreters and

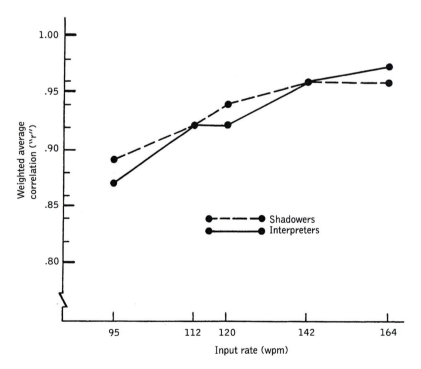

Figure 9   Weighted average correlations words per utterance/time per utterance.

shadowers was 3.7 and 4.3 respectively. The average length of longer omissions by interpreters was 15.2 words.

3. While shadowers substituted more single words than interpreters, the latter substituted more phrases. The average length of phrase substitutions was 4 and 3.3 words for interpreters and shadowers respectively.

4. Interpreters corrected more single words and markedly more phrases than shadowers. The average length of phrase corrections was 2.8 words for both groups. It was interesting to note that no words were omitted after corrections by shadowers, and that there were only four omissions after corrections (of phrases) by interpreters.

Discussion

The fact that significantly more words were correctly shadowed than were correctly interpreted suggests that any decrement in interpreters' performance was due to the effects of presentation rate on the processes involved in interpretation rather than to an inability to perceive and repeat the input message correctly. The results confirm Carey's (1968) finding that fewer words are correctly shadowed at the faster presentation rate. Carey's fastest rate was 180 wpm, while the fastest rate in the present study was 164 wpm. It is only at this last rate, however, that shadowers' performance deteriorates, whereas interpreters' performance falls off with each increase in rate. Both shadowers and interpreters had less time in which to perceive and speak at faster rates, but interpreters also had less time in which to decode from French and encode into English. Unlike the interpreter, the shadower only has to repeat, not to understand, what he hears. In a sense, shadowers' scores (words correct) are similar to intelligibility test scores, while interpreters' scores demonstrate both intelligibility and comprehension. As Foulke and Sticht (1967) have demonstrated, presentation rate has a greater effect on comprehension than on intelligibility, and it is to be expected, therefore, that interpreters should make more errors than shadowers at faster input rates.

As would be expected from Treisman's (1965) experiment, the ear–voice span was greater for interpreters than for shadowers. Though shadowers' ear–voice spans rose only slightly from slowest to fastest presentation rate, the interpreters' ear–voice spans almost doubled over the same range. When these results are considered together with Ss' output rates at each presentation rate, it can be seen that shadowers were able to increase their output rates as input rate increased at the cost of only a slight increase in ear–voice span. Interpreters, however, seemed only able to maintain fairly steady output at the expense of lagging further and further behind as input rate increased. There would seem then to be an optimal output rate for interpreters, and in order to maintain it in the face of faster input rates, they were forced to lag further and further behind.

Ear–voice span, whether for shadowing or interpreting, is attributable to the accumulation of items in some form of short-term buffer store, while previously received information is processed by a central mechanism. When shadowing, this process probably involves analysis of the auditory input at the level of the phoneme, syllable, or word, and direct recoding in terms of the articulatory movements required to produce the sounds just heard. In interpretation, however, more complex analysis of the input message must be carried out, and larger grammatical units must be involved in order to derive the deep structure of the source language message and translate to the surface structure and phonetic output of the target language. Since translation must involve larger "units" than shadowing, it seems reasonable to suppose that the major constituent or phrase might be the minimal unit of analysis in interpretation. One would, therefore, expect ear–voice span to be greater not only because processing takes longer, but because the constituent may also be the unit of storage.

It was hypothesized that interpreters would either reduce pause length and increase utterance length as input rate increased, or that they would pause more frequently and speak for shorter periods. A further prediction was that their output rate would become less variable as presentation rate increased. While only the last prediction has been supported by the results, it is worth noting that though shadowers were able to redistribute their performance in time in the manner predicted for interpreters, the latter were able to optimize their use of speech and pause times by speaking more and pausing less up to a presentation rate of 120 wpm, but then began to pause more and speak less. At input rates of 120 wpm and over, the interpreters were lagging further and further behind and making more and more errors. They spoke at a steady rate but only after longer pauses.

If, as was suggested above, shadowing involves a comparatively low level of processing, then it is not surprising that processing rate can keep track with input rate, at least within the range of input rates employed in this study. So long as the shadower can keep fairly close to the input he will need neither to utilise input pauses (where possible) nor to make extra pauses himself in order to process a backlog of material. The interpreter, having to cope with larger units before being able to translate, finds that as the intervals between items (words, phrases) become shorter than the time taken to process them, he must effectively slow down the rate at which he works. Finding that he cannot increase his own overall rates of processing and output, he appears to opt for a strategy of working in bursts and must lengthen pause times in order to do so. The extra time thus made available should enable him to cope with the increasing backlog of material in short-term store, but items in store accumulate and deteriorate faster than the interpreter can cope and, in fact, his performance falls off.

The principal effect of increasing presentation rate was to increase the number of discontinuities in all categories. Carey (1968), in order to account for his Ss' increases in errors in shadowing at faster presentation rates, concluded: ". . . when a speaking error is made, and monitoring indicates that what was spoken does not agree with the input, the mismatch may demand additional time that could have been devoted to perceiving the next section of input. Once speaking errors begin the result is a snowballing effect that results in a long stretch of omitted words." Contrary to this suggestion, however, the shadowers in the present study did not omit long stretches of words at faster input rates. Shadowers omitted mainly smaller units, whereas interpreters omitted more, and longer, passages at faster presentation rates.

At faster presentation rates the responses of both groups became less precise, as indicated by the larger numbers of word and "phrase" substitutions. It is worth noting that shadowers tended to substitute more single word units, whereas interpreters substituted more "phrases." These results, together with the fact that shadowers tended to correct words rather than "phrases," whereas interpreters omitted, substituted, and corrected "phrases" rather than words, suggests that interpreters do indeed work with larger units than shadowers. Though no attempt has been made here to analyze the structure of the "phrases" omitted, substituted, or corrected, that is to say whether they involve major or minor constituents, or whether discontinuities also occur between constituents, further research on these lines might help to answer the question as to the "unit" of storage, analysis, and monitoring in this complex information processing task.

The very fact that interpreters did correct their own output demonstrates that they do monitor what they say. These corrections are usually corrections of previous substitutions but may also be improvements or changes of already acceptable translations. In spite of the complexity of the operations involved, it appears to be possible for Ss to store input whilst both translating and monitoring their own output, without losing input either through interference or trace decay. Out of a total of 25 phrase corrections made by interpreters, only four were followed by omissions. It seems extremely unlikely that active rehearsal of Message 2 can take place while Message 1 is being translated, monitored, and corrected; and unless one postulated that attention can be switched rapidly between these operations, one is led to conclude that attention can be shared between input, translation, and monitoring. The difficulty with an attention switching model lies in the specification of the rate at which switching can occur and also of the duration of each switch. As Moray (1969) points out, the rate at which switching can occur depends upon the unit of analysis, and the larger the unit, the longer the duration. If, as seems likely, the unit of analysis in interpretation is the constituent, then the duration of the switch will be comparatively long. Even if this is between one-half and 1 second, one must still ask what will happen to input arriving while S is either interpreting or monitoring. The present evidence suggests that such information need not be lost, and an attention-sharing model seems most likely. At any rate, simultaneous interpretation appears to be a practical situation in which the processes associated with short-term storage need not involve covert repetition.

Conclusions

The aim of this study was not only to examine the effects of message presentation rate upon the simultaneous interpreter's performance over time, but also to study his output for cues as to the processes involved in so complex a skill.

If Ss have only to shadow a continuous message they are able to keep up with faster presentation rates by speaking more quickly, lengthening their utterances, and shortening pauses between utterances. When required to simultaneously interpret a message into a target language, faster input rates cause Ss to lag further and further behind and to make more errors than shadowers. In order to maintain a steady output rate, these Ss pause more and speak in shorter bursts. Though both shadowers and interpreters correct their errors, interpreters tend to work in units of 2–3 words or more. This, together with evidence from omissions and substitutions, suggests that the unit of analysis is the "phrase" for interpreters (where understanding is required) and the word for shadowers (where S is required to demonstrate perception rather than comprehension).

The picture emerges of an information-handling system which is subject to overload if required to carry out more complex processes at too fast a rate and copes with overload by reaching a steady state of throughput at the expense of an increase in errors and omissions. There is evidence that attention is shared within this system between the input message, processes involved in translating a previous message, and the monitoring of feedback from current output. Under normal conditions, attention can be shared between these processes, but when the total capacity of the system is exceeded, less attention can be paid to either input or output if interpretation is to proceed at all. Hence, less material is available for recall for translation, and more omissions and uncorrected errors in output will occur.

References

Carey, P. W. (1968) "Delayed Auditory Feedback and the Shadowing Response," unpublished PhD thesis, Harvard University.

Foulke, E. and Sticht, T. G. (1967) "A Review of Research on Time Compressed Speech," in *Proceedings of the Louisville Conference on Time Compressed Speech*, Louisville, Kentucky: University of Louisville.

Fries, C. C. (1952) *The Structure of English*, New York: Harcourt, Brace.

Goldman-Eisler, F. (1961) "The Distribution of Pauses in Speech," *Language and Speech* 4: 232–7.

—— (1968) *Psycholinguistics: Experiments in Spontaneous Speech*, London: Academic Press.

McNemar, Q. (1962) *Psychological Statistics*, New York: John Wiley.

Moray, N. (1969) *Attention: Selective Processes in Learning and Vision*, London: Hutchinson.

Ramsay, R. W. and Law, L. N. (1966) "The Measurement of Duration of Speech," *Language and Speech* 9: 96–102.

Treisman, A. M. (1965) "The Effects of Redundancy and Familiarity on Translating and Repeating Back a Foreign and a Native Language," *British Journal of Psychology* 56: 369–79.

Welford, A. T. (1968) *Fundamentals of Skill*, London: Methuen.

Winer, B. J. (1962) *Statistical Principles in Experimental Design*, New York: McGraw-Hill.

R ATHER EXCEPTIONALLY FOR a researcher in psycholinguistics, whose paradigms and findings could be seen as applying, at least indirectly, to interpreting, the contribution of Frieda Goldman-Eisler (1908–82) to the field of interpreting was a direct one, as she herself engaged in a series of experimental studies of simultaneous interpreting, and highlighted the advantages of using this "real task" to gain a better understanding of language processing.

Frieda Goldman-Eisler left Austria for Britain in 1934. After postgraduate studies at University College, London, she became a researcher at the Maudsley Hospital, where, among other things, she examined the association between breast-feeding and the development of personality traits, and the application of quantitative measures to the language of psychotherapeutic interviews. In 1955 she returned to University College, where, fifteen years later, she became the first scholar in the UK to hold the title of Professor of Psycholinguistics.

Goldman-Eisler's research came to focus on the study of pauses and pre-lexical hesitations as indicators of conceptual planning in spontaneous speech; her major findings are presented in her monograph, *Psycholinguistics: Experiments in Spontaneous Speech* (Goldman-Eisler 1968). Her observations of the interrelationship between temporal factors (speech rate, length of pauses) and the predictability of words in context were brought to bear on simultaneous interpreting, with important implications for the controversy between those who stress the language-pair-specific nature of the task and those who see it as transcending interlingual differences.

The paper presented here in somewhat shortened form was first published in 1972 in the second issue of the *Journal of Psycholinguistic Research*.

Further reading: Goldman-Eisler 1980; Goldman-Eisler and Cohen 1974.

Frieda Goldman-Eisler

SEGMENTATION OF INPUT IN SIMULTANEOUS TRANSLATION

Introduction

STUDIES OF PERCEPTUAL segmentation have shown that listeners impose subjective organization on speech input of an even delivery. Fodor and Bever (1965) were able to show by means of clicks that the continuous speech input is segmented according to the constituent structure of the sentence. Garrett, Bever, and Fodor (1966) considered that in the displacement of clicks in perception the effect of grammar might be only indirect. Perhaps, they asked, speakers tend to pause longer or give some noticeable cue at constituent boundaries which "attracts" the click to these positions rather than the grammatical division itself. By treating sentence recordings acoustically in such a way as to eliminate the possibility of such cues, they were able to show that the segments are not necessarily divided by any markers in the stimulus. They concluded that grammatical structure alone was enough to determine where interruptions were heard, and that this depended on a constructive process in the listener. Their task was a relatively simple one compared with that of the interpreter engaged in simultaneous translation, where segmentation of the speech perceived is based on comprehension rather than perception, to serve the processing of information in the translation act. One might say that, outside the laboratory, perception is always only a first phase in a chain of meaningful and vital activities, and that the situation of simultaneous translation is but one example of life situations in which perceptions are important initial phases. Its advantage for experimental study over other life situations lies in its clearly circumscribed directionality, its serial nature and structured complexity, the combination of which enables the experimenter to sort out and identify from objective records the various phases in the act of simultaneous translation. Even if speech was perceived as an even sequence of words, it is doubtful whether simultaneous interpreters could start translating as soon as the first word was perceived, and maintain a pace elicited by lexical units; whether, in other words, the unit of comprehension would be a lexical one. This seems to be the case in shadowing, where straightforward repetition is possible word by word (or even phoneme by phoneme). [. . .]

The situation of simultaneous translation is such that the conference interpreter must continuously monitor, store, retrieve, and decode the input of the source language while at the same time recoding and encoding the translation of the previous input.

One important aspect of both shadowing and simultaneous translation is the ear–voice span (EVS). This refers to the lag elapsing between the subject's or interpreter's monitoring of the input, and his actually repeating or encoding it, respectively. The EVS is, as one may expect, longer in simultaneous translation than in shadowing – about four to five words in translation and three words in shadowing, according to Treisman (1965). In this paper, we have concentrated on the EVS aspect of simultaneous translation. The conference interpreter proceeds in a series of fits and starts following behind the input. One would suppose that he starts as many steps behind as are necessary or sufficient to enable him to begin to translate, i.e., with an EVS of a certain length. As he continues, the EVS increases in length, and periodically accumulates until the amount of input to be stored seems to surpass the translator's storing capacity (see Figure 1). When this happens, the interpreter must catch up with the input, to bring the distance between target and source down to a manageable proportion.

The main questions are therefore: (1) What is the length and nature of the segments the interpreter needs to monitor before he can start encoding? (2) How does he segment the input? The paper is divided into two parts to examine these questions separately.

Technique

To sort out these events, a record of the temporal sequence of source input and target output is required. The events of simultaneous translation must, for inspection and study, be frozen into permanent form. This is done by transforming double-channel recordings of the source language and its simultaneous translation into parallel visual tracings showing vocal speech and hesitation pauses, as in Figure 2.

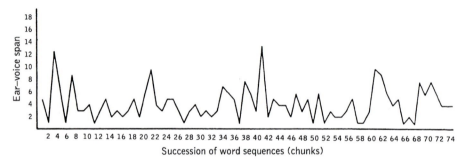

Figure 1   EVS between input and output chunks in simultaneous translation in order of succession in time.

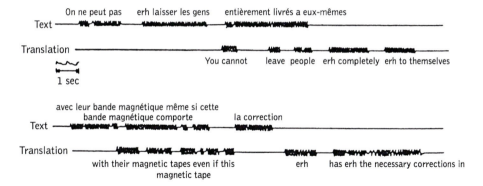

Figure 2   Record of text and simultaneous translation.

Material

It seemed essential to use competent interpreters, so that, having eliminated difficulties due to insufficient training, we could concentrate on those inherent in the linguistic and cognitive nature of the process. Six professional interpreters participated in the experiment: three English–French French–English, one English–French French–English as well as English–German German–English, and two English–German German–English. The material consisted of nine translations; three were translations from spontaneous English to French, three were from French to English (one spontaneous, two readings), and three were readings from German to English. The input texts were of varying input rate, and of very different types, within as well as between languages. (This is not as well planned as it should be, because it was not possible to synchronize the preparation of systematically arranged source texts with the availability of the professional conference interpreters.) The length of time taken up by each input of the source material was between 3 and 6 min., containing an average of about a thousand words per source input.

Part I

Ear–voice span, linguistic aspect

While we must assume that semantic comprehension precedes the onset of the translator's vocal production, the question remains: How much information does he require before he can begin to translate? More specifically, what constitutes the minimum sequence, the smallest unit below which translation cannot be started? This question must be supplemented by asking: (1) Is there a *preferred* EVS unit? (2) What is the *maximum* unit, i.e., how long an EVS can be tolerated without loss of text in the target?

Because the smallest possible step a translator can lag behind the source is one word, we can measure the EVS by the number of words, by lexical units. Another possible unit is the predicate phrase, i.e., the syntactical unit, NP + VP. Thus the EVS might be a lexical or a syntactical entity. The parallel traces of speech (see

Figure 2) enable us to examine the linguistic nature of the input preceding its corresponding translation.

Results

Minimum EVS

There were 2802 interpreters' responses (chunks of translation) based on 28 translations of 9 texts, and in 90–95% of cases the EVS consisted of at least a complete predicative expression. In only a mean proportion of 7.5% of cases was an EVS unit less than a complete NP + VP. This shows that on the whole, interpreters depend on information of a structural nature before they can start translation. The minimum EVS sequence is the NP + VP rather than just a word, and as will be seen later, the VP is a crucial part of the information required. Thus the unit of meaning upon which translators can act is not lexical but predicative, and the segmentation of the input flow follows from propositional principles. [. . .]

[. . .]

There is an indication that in translating from German, a larger chunk has often to be stored before starting translating than in English and particularly French.

It is clear from this that the crucial piece of information enabling interpreters to start translation is the predicate, and that any elements interpolated between NP and VP will extend to EVS. The greater frequency of long EVS units at the end of clauses, from which we have inferred a greater ease of storing, would tie in with this fact, comprehension having been facilitated after the verb has been decoded.

Part II

Ear–voice span, chunking aspect

[. . .] The process is such that the interpreter first monitors and stores, and then encodes in the target language (we shall be using the term "encode" as meaning encoding into the target language). During this period, the source may continue his utterance which again must be monitored and stored by the interpreter and subsequently encoded. This encoding proceeds after a certain sequence is monitored, and so on. Simultaneous translators sometimes cut into the source's continuous vocal input; at other times they may continue to monitor two or more vocal sequences of the input separated in the source by pauses, i.e., two or more input chunks, and encode them in one continuous sequence. Thus, while source and target language are uttered, as is all natural speech, in the form of alternate speech and silence periods (Goldman-Eisler 1958), there seems to be no systematic or predictable relationship between the two series of alternations. There are in fact three ways of segmenting this input: (1) encoding the chunks of speech as uttered in the source, (2) starting to encode before the chunk in the input has come to a halt (pause), or (3) storing two or more input chunks and then encoding. We shall refer to these three responses in terms of (1) identity, (2) fission, and (3) fusion, respectively, in the monitoring and decoding of input material.

In view of the fact that translators are highly motivated not to get too far behind, it seems reasonable to assume that the three types of segmentation of input are selected in accordance with the interpreter's need of and preference for a certain amount of information in the input to launch into translation. Factors to be considered in this context might be the capacity as well as the preference of the interpreter for storing or for anticipating, and the nature of the message.

Results

Our data were 208 identity, 1345 fusion, and 1149 fission responses; the mean frequency of occurrence for each of these responses was 11, 48, and 41 respectively. The proportions of each of the three operations varied from text to text. Equally all of them occurred side by side in different proportions in different interpreters.

Only 10.9% of the input was treated by the process of identity. When the input speech samples were divided into fast (Goldman-Eisler 1968) (pausing taking up less than 35% of input time) and slow (pausing taking up more than 35% of input utterance time), we found that for slow speech the mean proportion of identity responses was 13.8% or less while for fast speech the proportion was 7.7%. The difference is significant ($P < 0.05$).

It would seem then that the proportion of identical phrases in input and output is related to the rate of input: when input rate is slower, interpreters can make use of the pauses in the input to translate the chunks, as monitored. The fact that even then the identity response is relatively rare might be due to discrepancies between the temporal and semantic fitness, for the translators, of the chunks concerned: a comfortable input pace may be useless in terms of an EVS for starting translation if there is insufficient information in it. Individual differences seem to play a role (a) in the frequency of, and (b) in what is selected for the identity responses. [. . .]

An analysis of the identity chunks uttered by the interpreters shows them to be linguistically random and indicates no systematic occurrence.

The language factor

A much more powerful factor in the variation of identity responses emerged when these were divided according to the three languages. The mean proportions of identity responses were 6.6% when the source was English, 10.0% when it was French, and 17.1% when it was German, the differences being highly significant ($P < 0.01$). The fusion responses showed proportions of 49.3% for translations from English, 40.9% from French, and 49.8% from German. While these differences did not reach significance level, those between fission responses (47.3% English, 49.0% French, and 33.0% German) were significant ($F = 4.77$, dfs 2 and 25, $P < 0.05$). [. . .] In other words, whether translators begin to translate without awaiting the end of any input chunk, or whether they wait and store more than one such chunk before starting the translation, seems largely a matter of the nature of the particular language, and German clearly causes translators to store larger chunks of input before they begin to translate.

Discussion

This time the segmentation of the source text was analyzed using as criterion the occurrence of fission response as against fusion responses. Comparing chunks in the source with those in translations, we found that the interpreters tended to ignore the input chunkings and imposed their own segmentation on the text. In about 90% of cases they started translating before the input chunk had come to an end, or they delayed translation and stored more than one input chunk before starting, thus exhibiting a marked preference for constructive processes (fission or fusion) over purely receptive ones (identity). This behavior seems to be in line with the analysis-by-synthesis model of speech perception. The suggestion that the process of synthesis is partly under the control of the principles of grammatical organization has also been supported by George A. Miller (1962, 1969). The analysis of segmentation according to grammatical criteria in simultaneous translation shows that these principles prevail even when the linguistic task is highly complex and dynamic and entails a high degree of stress and pressure of time. In view of the likely disintegrating effects of such conditions it would not be too unreasonable to expect perceptual segmentation to recede from the active principles of grammatical organization toward a more passive, atomistic, and disorganized lexical segmentation. However, our data show that under such conditions simultaneous translation still follows mainly syntactical principles – it is as if, when really put to the test, processing cannot be bothered with *less* than predicative expressions.

This is also borne out by our data concerning the propositional nature of EVS segments, and in particular those showing that when translating from German, interpreters delay translation longer than when translating from French or English, most probably because the predicate in German comes at the end of the proposition, and objects or other modifiers precede it. It is only when the interpreter has decoded the predicate that he can start translating.

To test this proposition further we analyzed one of our texts to see whether the postponement of the verb in the clause had any bearing on the interpreter's choice of fusing input chunks as against intercepting them (fission). There were 115 EVS segments in the text and relating the number of words preceding the verb in each case and the number of fusion responses, we found a positive and significant relationship ($x^2 = 6.135$, $P < 0.02$). In other words, when the verb was uttered late in the clause the translator preferred to store more input and postpone the translation even if this entailed his not using for translation pause periods of the input.

This is in line with the result obtained by Healy and Miller (1970) showing the verb to be the main determinant of meaning. The verb in the authors' words "defines the plot; the subject merely indicates one of the actors."

Simultaneity of the processes of reception and translation

If the input were spaced in such a way that its pauses allowed time for the translation of each chunk of speech, so that the translation of sequence A could be sandwiched between sequences A and B, and the translation of sequence B between B and C, translation would in fact be sequential and not simultaneous. A personal enquiry among professional interpreters, incidentally, showed that a sequential arrangement would not be to their liking. Rather, they feel their own independent segmentation of the input to be an integral part of their performance, and deliberate segmentation at the source was not considered to be helpful. As the examination of the visual records shows, the real situation *imposes* simultaneity between the encoding of the translation of earlier source text, and the monitoring and decoding of the subsequent input. [. . .]

It is therefore clear that interpreters are capable of performing the complicated operations of monitoring, storing, and possibly decoding while engaged in the encoding into the target language of previously received sequences. The question is how these activities, and in particular decoding, were phased, i.e., in what order they are carried through, how decoding relates to storing, which of these is done automatically, and which receives attention.

If attention is focused upon the active part of translating and encoding, one would imagine that the input is stored in the "echoic memory" and is converted from sound image to meaning when its turn comes to be recoded into the target language. The term "echoic memory" refers to the kind of fleeting or transient memory which preserves auditory input long enough for the processes of speech perception to operate (Neisser 1967). If one accepts that the mechanism by which these processes operate is that of analysis-by-synthesis (Stevens 1960) – which is guided by such factors as context and expectation and must therefore be also under the control of the principles of grammatical organization – what would one visualize the sequence of operations to be? While the duration of echoic memory was found to vary inversely with the difficulty of the task used to measure it, Fraisse (1956, 1963), who estimated echoic duration on the basis of studies of rhythmic structure, arrived at the figure of 2 sec. This kind of duration would seem to be quite capable of accommodating the periods of EVS which were observed in our measurements. With most of the EVS segments containing not more than five elements, if we measure speech output at a rate of six syllables per second there would be twelve syllables in the echoic memory, which would amount to something like five elements. Can one therefore assume that in the speed of the total process of simultaneous translation, storage in active verbal memory is bypassed, and the stored but unprocessed input chunks are recoded and vocally encoded into the target language at the same time?

The alternative process would be if the recoding was done on reception of the input and stored, in its recoded form, while previously recoded sequences were encoded automatically. Attention would then be focused on the input, and the active verbal memory instead of the echoic memory would be involved. The fact that there is grammatical control, as shown by the criterion of "predicativeness" which determines the minimum EVS segment, indicates that it is by analysis-by-synthesis that the interpreter decides the earliest moment of launching into translation; the variety of lengths of EVS segments and the greater frequency of long EVS segments at the end of sentences would conform with the inverse relation of duration of echoic memory and difficulty of task. Such grammatical determination suggests that the first phase of processing at least, namely the segmentation, in accordance with grammatical principles, of the input stored in echoic memory, is not delayed but is part of the perception of the input, that in fact the segmented input is decoded on reception. If at this stage previously decoded material needs to be encoded in translation, the most economical procedure seems to be to store the now decoded sequence in the active verbal memory as segmented, and recode into the target language only when encoding. Recoding a sequence and storing it for later encoding, i.e., making higher level decisions prematurely would, it seems, strain the system unnecessarily. If we accept this, the acts which would be performed simultaneously would be monitoring and segmenting, which implies decoding, on the one hand, and recoding and encoding on the other. It is the writer's supposition that the latter sequence of processes is the more automatic one, and that decoding the input, involving comprehension, is the one requiring most attention. This will have to be demonstrated.

References

Fodor, J. A. and Bever, T. G. (1965) "The Psychological Reality of Linguistic Segments," *J. Verb. Learn. Verb. Behav.* 4: 414–20.

Fraisse, P. (1956). *Les structures rhythmiques*, Louvain, Belgium: Publications Universitaires de Louvain.

Fraisse, P. (1963) *The Psychology of Time*. New York: Harper & Row.

Garrett, M., Bever, T. and Fodor, J. (1966) "The Active Use of Grammar in Speech Perception," *Percep. Psychophys.* 1: 30–32

Goldman-Eisler, F. (1958) "Speech Production and the Predictability of Words in Context," *Quart. J. Exper. Psych.* 10: 96–106.

—— (1968). *Psycholinguistics: Experiments in Spontaneous Speech*, London and New York: Academic Press.

Healy, A. F. and Miller, G. A. (1970) "The Verb as the Main Determinant of Meaning," *Psychonomic Sci.* 20: 6.

Miller, G. A. (1962) "Decision Units in the Perception of Speech," *IRE Transactions in Information Theory*, IT-8: 81–3.

—— (1969) "The Organization of Lexical Memory: Are Word Associations Sufficient?," in *The Pathology of Memory*, New York: Academic Press.

Neisser, U. (1967) *Cognitive Psychology*, New York: Appleton-Century-Crofts.

Stevens, K. N. (1960) "Toward a Model for Speech Recognition," *J. Acoust. Soc. Amer.* 32: 47–55.

Treisman, A. M. (1965) "The Effects of Redundancy and Familiarity on Translating and Repeating Back a Foreign and a Native Language," Medical Research Council, unpublished report, PLU/65/12.

FOLLOWING UPON THE groundbreaking study by Oléron and Nanpon (1965), Henri Barik, a French-born Canadian, sought to examine interpreters' output in both quantitative-temporal and qualitative-linguistic terms. In his "Study of Simultaneous Interpretation," the first doctoral dissertation on interpreting by a non-interpreter, Barik (1969) reported pioneering experimental research, for which he received honorable mention in the Creative Talent Awards Program of the American Institutes for Research in the Behavioral Sciences. Interestingly, as Barik was conducting his research in the Department of Psychology at the University of North Carolina, David Gerver was doing very similar work in relation to his 1971 dissertation – though neither was aware of the research activities of the other. As Barik himself puts it (personal communication), this was "a good example of Zeitgeist in action."

Though his professional focus in recent years has shifted to other areas – notably test development, French immersion and bilingual education assessment in Canada – Barik retains an abiding interest in simultaneous interpreting research.

The paper reprinted here is the second of two articles by Barik (1973, 1975) which appeared in the journal *Language and Speech*. Complementary to the prior publication (Barik 1973), which contains a full description of the experimental design, the 1975 paper addresses various types of "content departures" (errors) and other linguistic findings, some of which had to be omitted here for lack of space. (Among other things, the complete version also discusses the relevance of the locus of pauses in the speaker's delivery, various lexical and syntactic difficulties, and interpreters' "flaws" of delivery.)

Further reading: Barik 1969, 1971, 1972, 1973, 1994.

Henri C. Barik

SIMULTANEOUS INTERPRETATION
Qualitative and linguistic data

IN SIMULTANEOUS INTERPRETATION, the interpreter's or translator's (T's) version may depart from the original or speaker's (S's) version in three general ways: the T may omit some material from the original version, add some material, or substitute material which, if it is at considerable variance with the original version, may constitute an "error" of translation. We present here data relating to the incidence of these events and their relationship to various characteristics of the input materials, i.e., the texts being translated.

Method and input data

The design of the study is described elsewhere (Barik 1969, 1973). Briefly, two experienced or professional conference Ts, two "student" Ts (recent graduates of a program in interpretation) and two "amateur" Ts (thoroughly fluent bilinguals active in the area of language but with no experience in interpretation) were required to do the simultaneous interpretation of several texts from either their weaker (second or acquired) language into their dominant (native) language (W to D translation) or vice versa, from their dominant into their weaker language (D to W translation). In each category of T, one was English-dominant, with French as his/her weaker language, and the other French-dominant, with English as his/her weaker language.

The texts translated represented four types of material: spontaneous speech, semi-prepared material (a non-technical lecture), prepared material intended for oral delivery (a non-technical formal speech), and prepared material intended for the written medium (the reading of a non-technical article). There were two instances of spontaneous speech; in one the speaker elaborated a story around a picture presented to him, in the other he discussed a film. The prepared speech and written text were identical in content in French and in English, but the spontaneous (story and film discussion) and semi-prepared (lecture) texts differed in the two languages, though the two language versions were roughly comparable in nature.

The Ts listened to the texts on tape, and translated them as they went along. Their translations were recorded on a second track of the tape, permitting subsequent simultaneous monitoring of both original and translated versions. Of eight passages, the T translated five (each of the 5 texts described above) from his weaker into his dominant language, and three from his dominant into his weaker language (the dominant-language versions of the story, lecture, and second half of the written text, the first half of which was used for W to D translation).

[. . .]

Types of translation departure

Within the three categories of translation departures noted earlier – omissions, additions and substitutions or errors of translation – several types may be defined, as outlined below. A more detailed description of these events and of the procedure followed to arrive at this categorization is to be found elsewhere (Barik 1971).

(1) *Omissions*, referring to items present in the original version, which are left out of the translation by the T (exclusive of contextually irrelevant repetitions, false starts, fillers such as "you know," etc., and excluding also material not to be found in the translation due to its involvement in a substitution or error of translation, which necessarily consists of the "omission" of one item and the "addition" of another in its place).

Four main types of events fall under the heading of omissions:

(a)   *O1*, skipping omission: the omission of a single lexical item such as a qualifier or a short phrase which appears to be skipped over by the T and which is of minor consequence.

> E.g. S version: . . . un instrument *assez* difficile . . .
> (. . . a *rather* difficult instrument . . .)
> T version: . . . . a difficult instrument . . .

(b)   *O2*, comprehension omission: the omission of a larger unit of text due to the T's inability to comprehend or translate it, resulting in a definite loss in meaning and sometimes in disjointed speech.

> E.g. S version: . . . depuis l'époque ou *il avait coutume de venir nous voir* il y a des années à la Jamaïque. Je n'ai jamais *admiré ou aimé personne plus que lui* . . .
> (. . . since the time when *he used to come to see us* years ago in Jamaica. I have never *admired or loved anyone more than him* . . .)
> T version: . . . since the time when years ago . . . I have never . . .

(c)   *O3*, delay omission: the omission of a larger unit of text, similar to *O2*, but seeming to be due primarily to the delay of the T in relation to S (as judged from monitoring the two versions) at a particular point in the text, which causes him to fail to register or to have to bypass part of the text in order to catch up. The assumption here is that T may have been able to translate the omitted segment had he not lagged too far behind at that point. There is a certain subjective element in determining whether a particular instance of omitted material represents an omission of type *O2* or *O3*; functionally, the two types are equally disruptive.

(d)   *O4*, compounding omission: omission associated with the T's regrouping or compounding of elements from different clause units, resulting in a sentence with a meaning slightly different from the original, though the gist of the latter is retained.

> E.g. S version: *J'étais à Londres* mercredi soir *lorsque* la nouvelle s'est répandue . . . que . . .
> (*I was in London* Wednesday evening *when* the news spread . . . that . . .)
> T version: Wednesday evening the news spread that . . .

This instance is not a case of disjointed translation (. . . Wednesday evening . . . the news spread that . . .) as in *O2*, since the T's delivery is quite smooth, and it appears that he selectively omitted certain items and regrouped material from different clause units, forming a new entity. This type of omission, though not too common, is rather interesting.

(2) *Additions*, referring to items not to be found in the original, which are added to the text by the T (exclusive of repetitions, false starts, etc., on T's part, and of new material introduced in conjunction with a substitution or error of translation).

Here also, four types of events may be specified:

(a)   *A1*, qualifier addition: the addition by the T of a qualifier or short qualifying phrase not in the original version.

> E.g. S version: . . . ils gardaient tous deux enraciné en eux . . .
> (. . . they both kept rooted within themselves . . .)
> T version: . . . they both had *deeply* rooted within themselves . . .

(b)   *A2*, elaboration addition: similar to *A1*, but more elaborate and more extraneous to the text.

> E.g. S version: . . . Je dois rester conscient de ce qui est juste . . .
> (. . . I must remain aware of what is just . . .)
> T version: . . . I must be aware *and conscious* of what is just *and fair* . . .

Addition types *A1* and *A2* could in fact be combined into a single category.

(c)   *A3*, relationship addition: the addition of a connective or of other material which introduces a relationship among sentence units not specified in the original.

> E.g. S version: . . . J'ai beaucoup apprécié aussi l'interprétation du film. Les deux grandes vedettes étaient
> (. . . I also very much enjoyed the performance of the actors. The two main stars were . . .)
> T version: . . . I also enjoyed very much the performance of the actors . . . *because* the two stars were . . .

(d)   *A4*, closure addition: addition which accompanies rephrasing, omission or misinterpretation on the part of the T and which serves to give "closure" to a sentence unit, but does not add anything substantial to the sentence.

> E.g. S version: . . . des messieurs qui décident . . . du choix des livres qu'ils vont publier et de la façon dont ils vont le faire . . .
> (. . . persons who decide . . . which books they are going to publish and the way in which they are going to do it . . .)
> T version: . . . men who decide . . . the selection of the books which are going to be published and how they're going to be offered *to the public*.

It is surmised in this example that the T has misinterpreted some of the text, possibly misunderstanding something relating to "offert" ("offered") instead of "le faire" ("to do it"). To give closure to the sentence, the phrase "to the public," which is extraneous to the text, is added, though it too may be due to a misunderstanding of the word "publier."

A few other instances of minor "additions" were noted, which, however, were disregarded, such as the frequent addition of the connective "and" between separate units, the specification of an item expressed pronominally in the original, etc.

(3) *Substitutions and errors*, referring to material substituted by the T for something said by the S and involving a speech segment ranging from a single lexical item to a complete sentence unit. Five types of substitutions (errors) were recorded:

(a)   *E1*, mild semantic error: an error or inaccuracy of translation of some lexical item, which only slightly distorts the intended meaning. Such errors may be associated with an awkward translation. The inaccuracy is restricted to the lexical item or expression, and does not affect the rest of the unit of which it is part.

> E.g. S version: . . . il n'a jamais montré de *malveillance* ni de méchanceté . . .
> (. . . he never showed *ill-will* or *maliciousness* . . .)
> T version: . . . he never showed an *evil mind* or an *evil reaction* . . .

The T's version is slightly awkward and inaccurate, but the gist of what is said is fairly well retained.

(b)   *E2*, gross semantic error: error of translation of some lexical item which substantially changes the meaning of what is said. Here again, the error is primarily in terms of a specific item and does not affect the rest of the unit. Three types of events fall in this category:

(i)   error due to confusion with homonym or near-homonym.

> E.g. S version: . . . l'autocritique est *l'arme* secrète de la démocratie
>> (. . . self-criticism is the secret *weapon* of democracy . . .)
>> T   version: . . .   (self-criticism   is)   the   secret   *soul*   of democracy . . .

In this example the T apparently misunderstood "l'âme" (soul) for "l'arme" (weapon).

(ii)   error due to confusion of reference, having its basis in the text.

> E.g. S version: . . . ce qui n'empêche pas les enfants de la nouvelle génération d'être plus grands que leurs *parents* . . .
>> (. . . which does not prevent the children of the new generation from being taller than their *parents* . . .)
>> T version: . . . which doesn't prevent children . . . from being taller than their *children* . . .

This type of error is possibly less damaging than that in (i) above, since the listener can probably figure out the T's mistake, which might not be the case in (i).

(iii)   "straightforward" error of translation, not due to confusion.

> E.g. S version: . . . et (il) *se demande*, avec quelque angoisse . . .
>> (. . . and he *is wondering*, with some anxiety . . .)
>> T version: . . . and he *looks*, with some anxiety . . .

The translation of "se demande" (to wonder) as "to look" constitutes a substantial semantic error, apparently not due to confusion with another item in the text.

There are thus two categories of semantic errors, one referring to mild errors or substitutions which more or less retain the meaning intended by the S, the other referring to more "serious" errors involving a substantial change of meaning. The other three categories of errors refer to translation departures which involve larger segments of text and represent differing degrees of departure rather than distinct types of errors:

(c)   *E3*, mild phrasing change: the T does not say quite the same thing as the S, but the gist of what is said is not affected.

> E.g. S version: . . . dans ce Conseil *qu'il a si fortement marqué de* sa personnalité . . .

(. . . in this Council *which he so strongly marked with* his personality . . .)

T version: . . . in this Council *to which he gave so much of his* personality . . .

Such phrasing changes are very mild and are generally acceptable within the context of simultaneous interpretation, where T is allowed a certain latitude in his wording.

(d)   *E4*, substantial phrasing change: here, the change in phrasing is more marked and leads to a difference in meaning, but the overall gist of what is said by the S is not too distorted.

E.g. S version: . . . je trouve que ce film est une réussite, une manière de réussite . . .

(. . . I think that this film is a success, a kind of success . . .)

T version: . . . I would like to say that this is an excellent film, that it was a great success . . .

The T here has substantially rephrased what the S was saying, making the statement much more positive than the original, but his translation retains the gist of the message.

(e)   *E5*, gross phrasing change: a translation departure which represents a considerable difference in meaning and is thus quite erroneous. Such errors may be attributable to different events:

(i)   "straightforward" error of translation.

E.g. S version: . . . qui occupent dans cette maison un emploi salarié . . .

(. . . who hold in this [publishing] house a salaried position . . .)

T version: . . . who are even paid by this publisher . . .

(ii)   the T seems to "make up" something on the basis of some part of the text. This may be due to his lack of comprehension of what is said, or because of his lagging too far behind the S, which prevents him from fully understanding what S has said, and he consequently tries to "fib" his way through the text on the basis of some word in it.

E.g. S version . . . je dois garder enracinés en moi certains principes . . .

(. . . I must keep rooted within myself certain principles . . .)

T version: . . . (substantial delay) . . . and there are certain roots to this . . .

(iii)   error due to misunderstanding of some item:

> E.g. S version: . . . (des écrivains qui) . . . n'y occupent *aucun* autre emploi sinon celui de lecteur . . .
>
>> (. . . [writers who] . . . hold there *no other* position except that of a reader . . .)
>>
>> T version: . . . they have *another* job which is that of a reader . . .

The T here appears to have misunderstood "un autre" (another) for "aucun autre" (no other), resulting in a meaning almost opposite to what the S said. This type of error is similar to type *E2i*, but it affects the meaning of a whole unit rather than just one word.

Other events were also classified in category E5: meaningless or confused translations, reversals of meanings, transforming a question into a statement, etc.

The above description summarizes the main types of departure noted between original and translated versions. The coding scheme developed was intended to provide only a general categorization of events. Within each class of events, further refinements could be made. Other categorization schemes may also be advanced. Gerver (1969), for example, refers to departures between original text and translation as discontinuities and specifies eight categories of such events: omissions of words, omissions of phrases, omissions of longer stretches of input of eight words or more, substitutions of words, substitutions of phrases, corrections of words, and corrections of phrases. As can be seen, there is considerable overlap between Gerver's coding scheme and the one described here.

Results

Each category of translation departure will now be considered in terms of frequency of occurrence of events and their relationship to certain characteristics of the input materials. Additional linguistic observations made in the course of the investigation are also noted.

(1) Omissions

In looking at omissions, two basic measures may be considered: number of instances of omissions, and amount of material omitted.[1] Since the texts differed in length, the number of omissions was standardized to a common text length of 100 words of original text (excluding words associated with repetitions, false starts, etc.) to permit cross-text comparisons.

(In the following paragraphs, reference is made to the performance of individual Ts. To facilitate discussion, the Ts will be identified as PE, SE and AE for professional, student and amateur English-dominant Ts, and PF, SF and AF for professional, student and amateur French-dominant Ts.)

On overall omission measures, as expected, among English-dominant Ts, the professional PE makes the least number of omissions (2.4 per 100 words for W to D translation, 2.2 for D to W translation) and omits the least amount of material (approximately 6% for translation in either direction). The student SE makes 5.6 omissions per 100 words and omits 22% of the material in W to D translation, with corresponding figures of 3.8 omissions and 9% omitted material in D to W translation. For the amateur AE, the figures are 6.3 omissions and 23% omitted material in W to D translation, and 6.0 omissions and 19% omitted material in D to W translation. Thus for both PE and AE, the overall omission measures are similar in W to D and D to W translation, while SE tends to make fewer omissions and omit less material in D to W translation.

Of PE's omissions, 83% are of the minor "skipping" type (01) in W to D translation and 65% in D to W translation, with most of the remaining omissions being of the 03 delay type (11% for W to D and 25% for D to W translation). PE thus makes very few type 02 (comprehension) and 04 (compounding) omissions. For SE and AE, only approximately half (49% for SE, 45% for AE) of their omissions in W to D translation are of the minor type 01, while the other half is composed mostly of the more disruptive type 02 and 03 omissions (20% and 27%, respectively, for SE; and 17% and 34% for AE). In D to W translation, SE and AE fare somewhat better, a greater proportion of their omissions being of the minor skipping type (75% for SE, 65% for AE), with the rest being primarily 02 and 03 types. Omissions of type 04 (compounding) are rather uncommon and do not represent more than 5% of omissions for any one T across either set of texts (W to D or D to W).

[. . .]

Among French-dominant Ts, the data reveal that it is the student SF rather than the professional PF who makes the least number of omissions (2.1 and 2.7 omissions per 100 words for W to D and D to W translation, respectively, for SF, vs 3.5 and 3.8 omissions for PF) and omits the least amount of material (5% for W to D and 7% for D to W translation, vs 10% for PF for either direction of translation). These findings are not as disconcerting as they may appear, for this particular student T (SF), who had completed the approved program in interpretation when tested, was judged to be of outstanding ability by her professors, and may in fact be considered of professional calibre (in contrast to the English-dominant student SE who, although having completed the same program, was clearly less competent than SF). In addition, it is not unlikely that "seasoned" professional Ts are more apt to consciously choose to skip over or omit some items judged superfluous, which would affect the omission measures associated with their performance. As for the amateur AF, she makes 5.0 omissions per 100 words and omits 19% of the material in W to D translation, with corresponding figures of 4.0 omissions and 10% omitted material in D to W translation.

[. . .]

When looking at the omission data in relation to the segmentation characteristics of the input texts, negative correlations are obtained in the case of all 6 Ts (across the 5 W to D texts) between either omission measure and number of grammatical pauses (per 100 sec. of texts) in the original; thus, the more often the S pauses at grammatical juncture points in his delivery – which pauses the T can presumably make use of to deliver part of his translation – the fewer omissions the T makes ($r <$ -0.65 in 3 of 6 cases) and the less material he omits ($r <$ -0.65 in the case of 5 of the Ts). [. . .]

(2) Additions

The two measures of additions to consider are number of instances of additions and amount of material added by the T (the proportion which the number of words associated with added material represents of the total number of words in the T's translation, excluding words relating to repetitions, false starts, etc.). The number of additions is calculated on the basis of the amount of original material effectively translated. Thus, if in the translation of a 100-word text the T failed to translate 20% of the material (20 words) and one instance of added material was recorded, the addition index would be 1 addition per 80 (translated) words, or 1.25 additions per 100 words. The number of additions is thus based on the number of words in the original version which are translated (obviously not in terms of literal word-for-word translation but in terms of meaning equivalence) rather than on the number of words in the translation. To permit cross-text comparisons, the number of additions index was standardized to a common base of 100 (translated) words of original text.

   The data reveal that very little material is added to the texts by the Ts, the mean number of additions over the 5 W to D texts ranging from 0.3 to 2.3 per 100 translated words of text, and the mean amount of material added from 0.5% to 5.4%. The vast majority of additions are of the minor *A1* and *A2* types, representing slight qualifications or elaborations. Very few additions of types *A3* and *A4* (relationship and closure additions, respectively) are recorded.

[. . .]

(3) Substitutions and errors

As in the case of additions, the number of mistranslations or errors committed by the T is calculated on the basis of the amount of original material (number of words) effectively translated, i.e., excluding from the word total those words associated with omitted material, since for such material the possibility of concomitant errors is effectively removed. To permit cross-text comparisons, that measure was again based on a set length of 100 (translated) words of original text. In the case of errors, a measure relating to the amount of material involved in such events is not as readily calculable as in the case of omissions and additions, since whereas for the latter the amount of material affected is reasonably clearly delineated, this is not quite the case for substitutions and errors, particularly where lengthy phrasing changes are involved, some parts of which may represent accurate translation while others do not. The amount of material associated with an error may also be largely fortuitous and inaccurately reflect upon the "seriousness" of the event; whereas in the case of omissions it may be assumed that the longer a particular omission, the more disruptive its effect on the worth of the translation, the same does not apply in the case of errors: a short but gross phrasing or semantic error may be more disruptive than a lengthy but mild phrasing change. For these reasons, the number of errors committed is judged the more appropriate measure.

Among English-dominant Ts, as expected, the professional PE makes fewer errors than the student SE, who in turn makes fewer errors than the amateur AE (an average of 2.8 and 2.4 errors per 100 translated words for PE for W to D and D to W translation, respectively, vs comparable figures of 3.4 and 3.7 for SE and 4.0 and 5.0 for AE). Some reversals occur, notably in relation to the W to D lecture, on which PE makes more errors than the other two Ts, that text in fact showing the greatest number of errors for PE (3.6 per 100 translated words) but the least or next to least number of errors for the other two Ts (2.6 in each case). The reason for this discrepancy is to be found in the omission measures associated with this text, which show PE omitting 9% of the material but SE and AE almost fully a third (32% in both cases). Thus for this passage the less qualified Ts choose to omit material outright when faced with difficult sections, whereas the professional T attempts a translation and is thus more open to the possibility of errors. It must thus be borne in mind that number of errors cannot be considered independently of other events, such as amount of material omitted. [. . .]

[. . .] As in the case of omissions, the coding system for errors probably favours the less-qualified T while penalizing the more-qualified T to some extent because of his very expertness. In coding errors, the main concern is with the "transfer" of the information from the original version to the translation, and not with how "elegantly" that information is conveyed. A distinguishing characteristic between more-qualified and less-qualified Ts is the degree of literalness of their interpretations: those by amateur Ts are typically very literal, being in many instances almost word-for-word "verbal transpositions" rather than translations, whereas those by professional Ts are substantially more in agreement with the idiom of the target language. Translations by amateurs are thus considerably more "awkward" and less intelligible than those of more-qualified Ts, but this is not reflected accurately in the coding system. [. . .]

In the main, the error data . . . do not appear to show any particularly notable relationships, and a possibly more useful function may be served by giving some specific examples of errors committed in translation and trying to see how or why they arise. [. . .]

(4) Translation disruptions

Part of the reason for the relative lack of "meaningful" results and for the discrepancies associated with the error data stems from the fact that, as pointed out, the incidence of errors is not a fully independent event, since it relates to some extent to the degree to which material is omitted in translation. Even though the error index is based on the amount of material effectively translated, functionally it is still not independent of the amount or nature of the material omitted. Supposing, for example, that the T has recourse to a strategy of generally omitting sections which he is unable to translate accurately and attempts to translate only those parts which are more straightforward, there are likely to be proportionally fewer errors in relation to the material translated than if the T attempts to translate all sections of the text, at the risk of making errors.

Since both omissions and errors are disruptive of translation, the two event categories may be combined and a general measure of translation "disruptions" considered. In doing this, the basis for calculation once again becomes the total original text rather than the translated sections only.

When omissions and errors are so combined, the emerging pattern is rather more consistent with what may be expected. In the case of English-dominant Ts, PE shows substantially fewer disruptions than SE on all texts, while the latter in turn shows fewer disruptions than AE on all texts but one. Averaging across texts, PE makes 5.0 translation disruptions per 100 words in W to D translation, vs 4.5 in D to W translation. The corresponding figures for SE are 8.3 and 7.2, and for AE 9.4 and 10.0. [. . .]

One further finding relating to disruptions of translation may be mentioned, which may be of some "practical" significance. With respect to omissions, it may be expected that the more material the T omits in translation, the smaller will be his verbal output in relation to that of the speaker. This is in fact the case; for all six Ts, when considering the 5 W to D texts, there is in most instances a high negative correlation between the amount of material omitted by the T and the ratio of the number of words (or syllables) in the T's version to that in S's. In other words, the greater the omission index for T, the smaller, proportionally, the verbal output of the T relative to that of the S. This relationship holds whether or not words associated with repetitions, false starts, etc. in either version are considered. The easiest measure to calculate, evidently, is the total number of words in each version, inclusive of repetitions, etc., and the negative correlation between amount of material omitted by T and T-to-S word total ratio is significant at $p < 0.10$ in the case of all six Ts. Moreover, when errors of translation are also taken into consideration and translation disruptions as a whole considered, the finding remains the same: the greater the proportion of original text associated with translation disruptions (omissions plus errors), the smaller the ratio of number of words in T's version to that in S's ($r < -0.65$ in all 6 cases across the 5 W to D texts). The findings hold also if only "serious" disruptions are considered.

[. . .]

If omissions and errors are interpreted as rough indices of quality of performance, what these findings imply is that the ratio of number of words in T's version to that in S's may serve as a gross measure of evaluation. Of two translations of the same text (involving the same language combination) by interpreters of similar calibre or experience, the one revealing the higher T-to-S word total ratio (allowing evidently for some leeway), presumably, might be expected to be the "better" of the two. This issue may be worth investigating in greater detail, with independent judgments on the quality of interpretations from experts in the field. [. . .]

[. . .]

Without in any way prejudicing the performance of interpreters, it may be said that the T's speech is generally less smooth than "natural" speech and contains a substantial number of false starts, retraces, and other minor "flaws" of pronunciation and delivery. This is apparent from a consideration of the transcripts. Many of the false starts are of an anticipatory nature, the T starting to say a word which comes only later. Some are also traceable to interferences from the source language.

The occurrence of retraces and corrections in the T's utterance, as Gerver (1969) points out, indicates that Ts do in fact monitor their own output.

[. . .]

Also to be taken into account, as already discussed, are the shortcomings of the coding scheme, which is insensitive to the "elegance" of the translation but considers only the degree of correspondence between original and translated versions, and thereby favours novices, whose translations tend to be quite literal, relative to more qualified Ts, whose translations are more idiomatic and thus more open to slight phrasing changes and other minor "disruptions." The coding scheme does not directly reflect on the overall intelligibility of the translation, nor on such other vital aspects of delivery as intonation, cadence, etc. The data for the amateurs are thus not directly comparable with those of trained Ts as indices of adequacy of performance.

[. . .]

One vital factor which clearly affects quality of performance in interpretation, as was seen, is the T's ability to segment the incoming message at appropriate linguistic boundaries, an issue which is closely linked to the time lag which the T observes in relation to the S and which relates to the question of what constitutes the "unit" of translation. These related items have been considered by several other investigators (Gerver, 1969; Goldman-Eisler, 1972; Kade and Cartellieri, 1971; Oléron and Nanpon, 1965; Treisman, 1965). The issue of the translation unit is not easily resolved. It is apparent that the T considers meaning units rather than single words, but the size of the unit may itself be influenced by a number of factors pertaining to delivery characteristics such as S speech rate, extent and locus of pausing, etc. There is a need for further systematic research on these issues and others raised in the present investigation.

Note

1   The number of instances of omissions *per se* is not a complete index of performance since, quite obviously, different instances may involve different amounts of material. There is, however, a high positive correlation between the two measures ($p < 0.05$ in the case of 5 of the 6 Ts).

References

Barik, H. C. (1969) "A Study of Simultaneous Interpretation," unpublished PhD dissertation, University of North Carolina, Chapel Hill.

Barik, H. C. (1971) "A Description of Various Types of Omissions, Additions and Errors of Translation Encountered in Simultaneous Interpretation," *Meta*, 16: 199.

—— (1973) "Simultaneous Interpretation: Temporal and Quantitative Data," *Language and Speech*, 16: 237.

Gerver, D. (1969) "The Effects of Source Language Presentation Rate on the Performance of Simultaneous Conference Interpreters," in *Proc. 2nd Louisville Conf. on Rate and / or Frequency Controlled Speech*, University of Louisville, p. 162.

Goldman-Eisler, F. (1972) "Segmentation of Input in Simultaneous Translation," *J. Psycholing. Res.* 1: 127.

Kade, G. and Cartellieri, C. (1971) "Some Methodological Aspects of Simultaneous Interpreting," *Babel*, 17: 12.

Oléron, P. and Nanpon, H. (1965) "Recherches sur la traduction simultanée," *J. Psychol. Norm. Pathol.* 62: 73.

Treisman, A. M. (1965) "The Effects of Redundancy and Familiarity on Translating and Repeating Back a Foreign and a Native Language," *Brit. J. Psychol.* 56: 369.

Part 2

Laying Foundations

INTRODUCTION

THE POTENTIAL OF the psychological and psycholinguistic approaches to interpreting, which show a high degree of interdependence, did not escape scholars within the field of interpreting itself. While not all of them drew directly on the groundbreaking research presented in the previous section, their emphasis on ecologically valid research design, and the insights gleaned from their own experience as practitioners, added a vital new dimension to the experimental direction of the earlier work.

Ghelly V. Chernov investigated simultaneous interpreting in a paradigm which rested upon Soviet scholars' theories of human activity. His model of "the underlying psycholinguistic machinery" (1992: 151) posits the redundancy of natural languages as the essential factor enabling human communication. This redundancy in turn allows for the probabilistic prediction of the incoming message, which Chernov (1979, and in this volume) regards as the crucial mechanism in the process of simultaneous interpreting. His account of the subconscious semantic analysis of the message draws on the linguistic notions of theme and rheme as well as the cognitive structural concepts related to the organization of semantic information in memory. Thanks to his close collaboration with psychologist Irina Zimnyaya (Zimnyaya and Chernov 1973), Chernov was able to develop and test his probability prediction hypothesis, and demonstrate, *inter alia*, that interpreters' top-down semantic processing can override the information present in the actual input; that message comprehension – and reproduction – by the interpreters is in direct relation to the theme–rheme structure of the message; and that the redundancy of the source-language message permits interpreters to introduce varying degrees of compression. The latter finding was further explored particularly by scholars in the "East" such as Alexieva (1983) and Kutz (1990). In a replication study some twenty years later, Carlet (1998) tested Chernov's main hypothesis and found that deviations in the expected semantic content of a message tended to impede processing inasmuch as the interpreter was unable to incorporate the utterance into the message as anticipated. More generally, the ideas developed by Chernov are also reflected in the discourse-oriented perspective on interpreting which gained ground in the 1990s (see Part 5).

A contemporary of Chernov's in the "West," **Hella Kirchhoff**, of the University of Heidelberg, also dealt with processing operations such as anticipation and compression. Though most of her writing had a pedagogical focus and remained unpublished, the few papers that do appear in the literature deal mainly with conceptual aspects of interpreting within the broad theoretical framework advanced by translation scholars of the so-called Leipzig School. Building upon the work of Otto Kade (1963, 1967, 1968; Kade and Cartellieri 1971), Kirchhoff tapped the psycholinguistic literature of the day to formulate a model of the simultaneous interpreting process couched in the terminology of information/communication theory (1976a, and in this volume).

Aiming at a comprehensive account of processing issues, she drew attention to the role of strategies (developed in the literature on foreign-language acquisition in the 1970s) in simultaneous interpreting, as manifested in interpreters' use of anticipation, syntactic reformulation, and various forms of compensation for cognitive overload. Kirchhoff explored the complex interrelationship between time lag, memory constraints and predictability, and paid particular attention to language-pair-specific factors. The latter concern was shared by Salevsky, who, as a student of Kade's, devoted a large empirical study to the quest for strategies in Russian–German simultaneous interpreting (Salevsky 1987; cf. also Gile [et al.] 1997: 115–16). Aside from the reflection of her work in Kurz (1983) and Stenzl (1983), Kirchhoff's influence is even more directly evident in the work of Kalina (1998), whose research at the University of Heidelberg elaborated on both the conceptual framework of strategies (Kohn and Kalina 1996) and the didactics of interpreter training. An issue which was first raised by Kirchhoff (1976a, and in this volume) was the need for – and difficulty of – adapting source-culture-bound messages to the communicative needs of receivers with a different sociocultural background. This observation was explored further by Kondo (1990) from a Japanese perspective, and by Dam (Kondo and Tebble 1997: 158), who suggested that "the ideal role of the interpreter is to serve not only as a linguistic but also as a cultural mediator" (see Part 7). The claim that the interpreter's (and translator's) output should be fully functional within the target culture is at the heart of the *skopos* theory, which was developed by Kirchhoff's Heidelberg colleague Hans Vermeer (Vermeer 1989, 1996) and applied to simultaneous conference interpreting by Pöchhacker (1994a, 1994b, 1995a).

The assumption that language-pair-specific strategies play a central role in the interpreting process, as upheld by Kirchhoff in the tradition of the Leipzig School (cf. also Römer 1968; Dalitz 1973), was diametrically opposed to the credo of the so-called Paris School as represented by **Danica Seleskovitch**. Convinced that neither the linguistic theories prevailing through the late 1960s nor psychological experimentation in the language laboratory was suitable to explain the interpreting process, Seleskovitch (1976: 95) insisted on the observational study of authentic data from professional practice, and maintained that "the theory of interpretation is not concerned with descriptive or comparative linguistics but with speech performance; it studies and compares the original message with that conveyed by the interpreter and endeavors to discern the interplay of thought and language through the evidences supplied by the processes of understanding and expressing." On the basis of an experimental investigation into note-taking in consecutive interpreting (Seleskovitch 1975, and in this volume), Seleskovitch came to assert that the linguistic units in the original message are first converted into "deverbalized" structures, or units of sense, and only then reformulated in the target language (Seleskovitch 1978). This *théorie interprétative de la traduction*, also known as the *théorie du sens* (García-Landa 1981), formed the underpinning of a series of dissertations completed in the doctoral program at the *École Supérieure d'Interprètes et de Traducteurs* (ESIT) of the University of Paris III/Sorbonne Nouvelle (e.g. Déjean le Féal 1978; García-Landa 1978; Lederer 1978a; Driesen 1985; Donovan 1990; Laplace 1994). Whatever the theoretical and empirical innovation with which one may credit this school of thought (cf. Gile 1990a; García-Landa 1995), the Paris School's paradigm of *traductologie* (translation and interpreting studies) was an important stepping-stone in the institutionalization of research on interpreting, and laid the foundations for the subsequent establishment of IS as a discipline.

The work begun by Seleskovitch with a focus on consecutive interpreting was developed further by **Marianne Lederer**, who carried out a comprehensive empirical study of simultaneous interpreting and formulated a model of the mental operations comprising the task. Central to her conceptualization of the process is the notion of cognitive complements – the interpreter's knowledge of the world, of the setting and circumstances, and of the broader context, which is brought to bear on the linguistic meaning of the incoming message so as to form "sense" (Lederer 1978b, and in this volume): "Only cognitive complements can explain fully the nature of interpreting and vindicate interpreters' assertion that understanding speech goes further than understanding language" (1990: 59). Lederer collaborated with Seleskovitch in formulating a *Pédagogie Raisonnée de l'Interprétation* (Seleskovitch and Lederer 1989; English translation 1995: *A Systematic Approach to Teaching Interpretation*) and has been active in extending the *théorie du sens* to written translation as well (Lederer 1994).

Coming from very different geo-academic traditions, but essentially sharing a common background in interpreting and interpreter training, the four writers whose work is represented in this Part draw attention to the role of inferencing based on linguistic and extra-linguistic background knowledge, and to the ways in which the underlying meaning, rather than the surface form of the message is at the heart of interpreting, in terms of both the process (see Part 3) and the product (see Part 5).

THE LEADING REPRESENTATIVE of the "Soviet School" of Interpreting Studies, Ghelly Chernov (1929–2000) had a distinguished career both as a professional conference interpreter and as a researcher and academic. His name is closely linked with the Maurice Thorez Institute of Foreign Languages (now Moscow Linguistic University), where he studied for his diploma in translation in the late 1940s and early 1950s, defended his Candidate of Sciences dissertation in philology, and started teaching in 1955. In the early 1960s he joined the Interpretation Service at the United Nations in New York, where he was to become Chief Interpreter of the Russian Section from 1976 to 1982. In between his two six-year stints at the UN, he returned to the Maurice Thorez Institute and, as an associate professor, organized a research seminar for instructors and postgraduate students. In that framework, psychologist Irina Zimnyaya and Chernov conducted a crucial experiment to test the hypothesis, first advanced in writing by Zimnyaya and Chernov in 1970, that "probability prediction" was the major psycholinguistic mechanism underlying simultaneous interpreting. Chernov developed this line of research in his post-doctoral thesis (Chernov 1978), which, aside from Shiryayev's (1979) monograph, remains the most significant work in the Russian literature on (simultaneous) interpreting. In 1987, during his eight-year term as Director of the conference interpreting department, he published another monograph (Chernov 1987) to serve as a textbook on simultaneous interpreting studies.

The article reprinted here in abridged form was originally published in *Language and Speech* in 1979. The passages omitted for reasons of space mainly concern example-based explanations of the linguistic concepts of theme vs. rheme, and lexical meaning vs. propositional content (sense).

Further reading: Chernov 1977, 1978, 1985, 1987, 1992, 1994, 1999.

Ghelly V. Chernov

SEMANTIC ASPECTS OF PSYCHOLINGUISTIC RESEARCH IN SIMULTANEOUS INTERPRETATION

Probability prediction as a basic mechanism of simultaneous interpretation

[. . .]

THAT NATURAL LANGUAGES are redundant is a well-known fact. It is also known that redundancy in speech tends to increase when the speech becomes standardized (reaching about 96% for airport control tower to pilot communication (Frick and Sumby 1952)). I assume that redundancy constitutes a basic quality of human language communication, making for the predictability of the incoming message.

There are two sources of redundancy in human discourse: (1) the plain fact of iteration of certain linguistic features; and (2) the interdependency of the linguistic components of the message, the fact that message units (certain sequences of sounds, words, word combinations or phrases, sentences, etc.) are formed according to rules, which makes them interdependent, and which also boils down to a situation in which the speaker "tends to repeat himself" (Miller 1963, p. 103).

Let me make it clear that I do not propose the application of a pure Markovian model to the process of speech perception. Such an approach should be rejected not only for the reasons advanced by Miller and Chomsky (Miller and Chomsky 1963), but also because we do not know the sequences of which units (phonemes, letters, or words) we are to consider. I would rather suggest a mechanism in the general spirit of Osgood's proposal (Osgood 1963), in which transitional probabilities interconnect not the units of one level, but the whole hierarchy of structures in language, simultaneously at a number of levels,[1] with an important proviso that the structural relations in speech develop in multidimensional dynamics. Thus, I propose a model framework providing for (i) a concurrent dynamics of probability prediction at a hierarchy of levels[2] and (ii) an interdependence of levels.

I suggest that the levels at which transitional probabilities are defined should be sought above all in the semantics of the message – its formal grammatical structure – although the important factor of predictability is of secondary significance. Henceforth, I will be interested primarily in semantic redundancy (versus information density) in a message, which permits the full involvement of the probability prediction mechanism in simultaneous interpretation.

Semantic redundancy: a source of prediction of message development

Leaving aside the lowest phonematico-syllabic level and the level of syllabic ensembles encoding morphemic structures of words . . . , I would like to begin with semantic levels that work towards the formation of a dynamic internal programme (Leont'ev 1968) of the TL communication, or its *plan* (Miller, Galanter and Pribram 1960): a verbal level of words combining into phrases and their underlying semantic structure; the level of an utterance and the thematico-rhematic communicational relations underlying an utterance. I will then pass on to semantic relations in a discourse, while the situational factors of the communication, tending as they do to increase the overall redundancy of the message (Chernov 1975), will necessarily remain beyond the scope of the present paper.

In our experiment of 1970 (Zimnyaya and Chernov 1970, 1973; Chernov 1973, 1978), utterances of two types were embedded in the texts offered for simultaneous interpretation.[3]

Type A utterances were such as to make their endings appear highly predictable to the interpreter, while the actual endings were unexpected:

> . . . We are trying to transform subsistence economies into modern societies with modern industry and modern agriculture. Very often we are told that
>
> (1) *Rome was not built in a day*. Of course, we realize that
> (2) *Rome was not built in a dale*, that it was built on seven hills . . .

The subjects were expected to continue towards the wrong completion of the utterance (2), in accordance with their hypothesis of its most probable conclusion, prompted by its beginning and by the previous utterance (1); or to halt their interpretation and omit the utterance (2) altogether, due to a belated awareness of the wrong *plan* and their inability to alter it because of lack of time. The results obtained from a total of 10 type A utterances, and a total of 80 analysable cases, were as follows:

23.75%   correct translations,
37.5%   translations according to the "prompted prediction";
38.75%   no translation of the given utterance;

in other words, a total of 76.25%, as predicted.

Type B utterances, although perfect sentences in form, were semantically non-sensical in that each succeeding word did not combine with the preceding one. The test sentences were again embedded in a plausible context, e.g.:

... we must [now] slightly digress to deal briefly with an extreme case of translation difficulty. A sentence

(3) *The ugly beauty rattled up to the top of the sour valley*

could provide an appropriate example. This is a . . .

It was assumed that due to the practical impossibility of building a "hypothesis" of the semantic development of the utterance, the mechanisms of SI would partially or completely break down, with hesitation pauses and errors resulting in the TL speech.

The results obtained from 14 utterances and 112 analysable cases were as follows:

10.71%   correct translations;
35.71%   no translation;
53.58%   errors or partial losses in translation;

i.e., a total of 89.29%, as predicted.

Type A utterances do not require much discussion except that they provide a clear-cut demonstration of the importance of the verbal predictability of a message.

Type B utterances illustrate several subtler points of the semantic level of the probability prediction mechanism in SI.

Indeed, syntactically they make up perfect sentences where the phrase structure . . . is perfect. Besides, they all consist of normal, meaningful words, each of which would have a detailed definition and description in the dictionaries. The difficulties apparently arise out of the semantic incompatibility of the words; moreover, although perfectly structured, words when thus combined are said not to make sense.

It would now be appropriate to give a brief explanation of the difference between *meaning* and *sense*, as the two terms will be used hereafter in this paper. If we take utterance (3), every word in it has a meaning, although we say that the utterance as a whole is senseless. According to Zhinkin (1970), information in human speech, besides being encoded verbally, is also encoded in sense-producing word combinations. A minimal unit of sense is defined as "a measure of information change in two combining words" (Zhinkin 1970, p. 77); and sense, as "such information-containing sequence which may be transformed into a sequence of synonymously interchangeable words, yet is not itself a sequence of words, and such which sets certain limits to information content within which the sequence may be continued" (Zhinkin 1970, p. 83).

If *meaning* is a notion pertaining to a word (or its phraseological equivalent), *sense* can only appear through predication, explicit or implicit (underlying).

[. . .]

The results of the experiment show that surface syntactic relations are rendered much more readily than deeper semantic relations. In fact, the sentential form was rendered correctly in over 70% of the cases analysed while only 10.7% of the total were semantically correct translations.

Thus at the level of an utterance we see that even if the sentential form of the utterance can be rendered correctly, an utterance cannot be simultaneously interpreted (an apparent overloading of the information-processing mechanism can be observed) if the utterance itself does not make sense. That, in turn, happens when the semantic structures of the words of the utterance do not combine, due to the lack of common semantic primitives in their semantic structures.

There are several considerably developed attempts at formalizing the underlying semantic structure of sentences in contemporary linguistic semantics (Fillmore, Chafe, Apresian, Zholkovsky, etc.); some of these models have been computer tested (Schank and Colby 1973; Norman and Rumelhart 1975). Yet none of them may as yet claim to represent more than a fragment of the total structure of semantic components and semantic relations of a natural language as a whole. That explains why I had to resort to an *ad hoc* procedure of semantic decomposition of utterances in the experimental discourse.

Let us consider a sentence from the experimental series of brief United Nations General Assembly speeches.

(4) "I now give the floor to the distinguished delegate of India."

"I now give" = "I give" ("now" is redundant since the verb already contains a semantic component indicating the present). "I give the floor to" = "I call on" = "I recognize"; all have one Russian equivalent used in official cases. In "the distinguished delegate of" the word "distinguished" has a purely pragmatic meaning in the utterance and for all practical purposes is a neutral form, a customary manner in which a chairman addresses a delegate. Nevertheless its absence may acquire a certain pragmatic significance if conspicuously dropped by the chairman, but not necessarily by the interpreter.

Indeed, situationally, practically the whole utterance is redundant, the only informative element being the name of the country the speaker represents – in our case, "India."

[. . .]

Cumulative dynamic analysis and probability prediction field

Some important points concerning the semantic level of the probability prediction and anticipatory synthesis mechanism in SI, both in an utterance and in discourse, may be observed in Figure 1.

SL and TL messages were transcribed from a two-track magnetic tape on which both recordings were made simultaneously in the process of interpretation and later analysed for real time to the nearest 10 msec. of duration for each chunk of speech and each pause between the two chunks. Thus, the line for "I would like to touch"

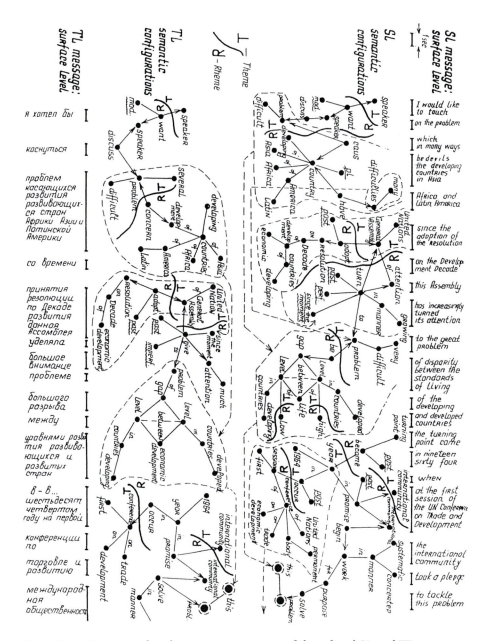

Figure 1   Compound real time representation of the related SL and TL messages
obtained in an experimental study of the SI mechanism.

(upper right corner) represents about 1,250 msec.; the blank spaces between speech
chunks represent pauses; while the whole diagram stands for about 35 seconds of
discourse. A horizontal section at any point of the diagram would represent a precise
moment in time.

Its central part is a semantic representation of the corresponding SL and TL
messages on the deepest traceable level of "natural" semantic decomposition as

extracted for each utterance from the 10 available translations obtained from the transcripts of recorded TL messages produced by subjects in the experiment. Hence, the dots do not represent semantic primitives but rather semantic components and configurations, as the case may be. The verb-components are shown as governing certain referential nouns (see the direction of arrows), while curves separating *theme* and *rheme* indicate the direction that the evolving message takes at each juncture (from *theme* to *rheme*). The dotted lines encircle complex configurations, while the dotted arrows point to the anaphoric components further in the message. The thick dots surrounded by dotted circles in the lower part of the diagram represent "this problem" as a cumulative complex semantic configuration.

Semantic components form configurations that go beyond the limit of one utterance. In fact, even during the course of a few utterances they form a highly developed *sense and semantic structure*. Certain components cluster around others, while these others tend to form "centers of gravity," attracting new elements of sense as the message develops. They, in turn, form main themes, or topical structures, that establish links among themselves in discourse, to form a constellation of semantic configurations.

In the resulting TL message "constellations" tend to be slightly thinner than in the SL diagram due to the thinning out of semantic configurations, some of whose elements are lost in the process, (while others are added from the situational context and the interpreter's long-term memory, triggered by association). The important thing for the interpreter is to keep mental track of, and transfer as accurately as possible, the relations of semantic components, since it is they that make for the appearance of sense out of the stock of semantic components provided by natural language and activated in discourse.

We shall now pass on to the probability prediction field that tends to be built up as the message develops. The hypothesized method of building a growing semantic field in the interpreter's memory will be called *cumulative dynamic analysis* (subconsciously performed by the interpreter) (Chernov 1977).

I assume that the process of understanding presupposes frequent resort to semantic decomposition of word meanings that form part of semantic configurations underlying the utterances in discourse. This hypothesis provides a plausible explanation of certain facts observed both in experimental translations and in live simultaneous interpretation of the type described in connection with (4).

[. . .]

"Understanding" of the semantic and sense structure of the incoming message consisting of a series of interconnected utterances is a dynamic process which covers:

— the gradual, yet discrete, addition of new semantic (rhematic) components to those already foregrounded, effected through acts of predication and completed with the appearance of a higher order (synthetic) semantic configuration;

— bridging sense gaps through decomposition of surface-level sense structures of incoming utterances, their rearrangement and subsequent recomposition into higher-level semantic units;

— establishing new links and relations between the incoming (rhematic) and previously foregrounded (thematic) semantic components and combining them into a new sense structure with fewer, more complex semantic configurations;

— finally, fitting this semantic structure into the larger picture of the situational context and the hearer's knowledge.

This process must logically result in the growing semantic redundancy of the message for the simultaneous interpreter, as long as the message continues to develop, and in facilitating the probability prediction process at all levels of generation of the *internal programme* or *plan* of TL utterances.

The suggested overall picture seems to agree well with:

— the prevailing psychological conceptions of increasing the amount of information a human brain is capable of processing in its short-term, or "operative," memory by re-encoding it into fewer "chunks" with a higher information density per "chunk" (Miller 1956);

— computer models of language understanding and information processing (Schank and Colby 1973; Norman and Rumelhart 1975);

— our own experimental data showing that the semantic components of a text, first introduced as *rhemes* at the surface level of utterances, are significantly more often rendered correctly in SI than those whose original rhematic nature is concealed at the deep semantic level and which require an explication, or a bridging of the sense gap in discourse. An analysis of 11 semantic configurations representing main thematic components of a text, with 10 subjects performing SI, showed that if the component is first introduced in the text as a surface-level rheme, we obtain from 80 to 100% correct translations – as against 30 to 40% correct when it is introduced as a dependent member (an attribute or a modifier) of a surface theme. In other words, we observe here a deterioration in the mechanism of probability prediction in cases of sense gaps, which signify a reduced level of redundancy;

— certain linguistic facts, such as nominalizations, the category of definiteness (regarded by Chafe as a contextual semantic feature), or the introduction of subject clauses with a possibility of their subsequent transformation into noun-phrases with a deictic determiner, of the type:

> The United Nations adopted a resolution ⟹ the adoption of a resolution by the United Nations . . .; or ⟹ that the United Nations adopted a resolution . . . ⟹ the fact that the United Nations adopted a resolution . . . ⟹ this fact . . .

Some other typical examples:

> the situation where . . . ⟹ this situation
> the idea that . . . ⟹ this idea
> the assumption that . . . ⟹ this assumption, etc.

The paraphrastic power of natural languages, including the stores of lexical units allowing for generalizations and generic terms that can be used for specific ones, should also be considered under this heading.

It is interesting to note that the cumulative dynamic analysis of the type I am proposing results . . . early in the text . . . in a semantic configuration that provides a full framework for probability prediction of further utterances in the text [. . .].

Yet the factor of time pressure typical for SI seems to hamper this process and sometimes to result in translation lapses and errors (Barik 1975), leaving even wider sense gaps for the hearer of the message in TL to bridge. This brings us to the question, "Can non-sense also be rendered in SI?" One aspect of this question has been dealt with rather in detail in the discussion of (3). But there is yet another aspect, namely, the following: what makes plenty of sense to one, may make no sense at all to another. In other words, the success or failure of interpretation also, and to a very great extent, depends on the interpreter's and hearer's thesaurus of concepts, or the knowledge contained in their long-term memory. The latter brings me to the question of training conference interpreters. Unfortunately, this subject cannot be considered here for lack of space. However I cannot bypass it completely, for training tends to inculcate additional in-built potential factors of redundancy in the interpreter's long-term memory.

Redundancy in the thematic structure of discourse makes it possible for the interpreter to introduce a varying degree of lexico-semantic compression in the TL message, normally resulting in greater information density in the TL message.

[. . .]

We may assume that the *semantic configuration in the TL message tends to be less complex than a corresponding configuration in the SL message*, although the latter would not necessarily result in a poor translation. However, it must result in greater information density in the TL message, which explains why simultaneous interpretation through relay is often discouraged.

Conclusions

A simultaneous interpretation model framework, such as the one that I have suggested, is based on the assumption that probability prediction concerns the successive units of sense (semantic components and their relationships) in an SL message, while the interpreter is engaged in the anticipatory synthesis of verbal components of the TL message he is in the process of regenerating.

Of necessity, I have dealt here only with the semantic component of the suggested model, for the reason that semantic studies nowadays seem to provide the greatest possibilities of building a complete model of the SI mechanism as a language performance model. The semantic component of the suggested model interacts most closely with the individual's store of knowledge in general (Chafe 1972), and with the situational context of a communication, in particular (Chernov 1975, 1978). This does not mean that I am disregarding the syntactic component of the model. Studies in syntactic transposition of a text indeed have an important role to play in SI models, both for pairs of languages with similar syntactic structures and, even more, for language combinations with dissimilar syntactic structures.

In general, it is possible to predict that the higher the degree of divergence of thematico-rhematic semantic structure ("deep" structure) and surface syntactic structure in SL, the greater the constraints on simultaneous interpretation. It is likely that this field would prove a fascinating area for research.

Limitations of space do not allow me to include in my consideration various factors of the situational extralinguistic context of the communication that may add very significantly to the redundancy of a message, both for the simultaneous interpreter and for the hearer of the recoded message in TL (Chernov 1975, 1978).

I have tried to show that redundancy at a series of levels (whose exact structure and number we have yet to establish) in discourse, is a unique and very powerful basis for a probability prediction mechanism in SI; that it is worthwhile to focus the attention of researchers interested in SI on the achievements of linguistic semantics so that they may borrow ideas for their necessarily communicational "bilingual" performance models; and that in so doing it would be wise to bear in mind the situational context and the need to improve the very instrument of prediction mechanism through in-built redundancy potential in the mechanism as such.

We believe that, on the basis of the criteria suggested above, further psycholinguistic research into the theory of simultaneous interpretation should take into account the following considerations.

(1) No future SI model should contradict (or ignore, for that matter) psychological data (human information processing, attention, memory and speech psychology) or lack a thorough experimental basis.

(2) Since simultaneous interpretation normally involves *simultaneity of listening and speaking*, all experiments in the field should be carried out on "normal" (average) speech rates and "normal" (average) pause-to-speech ratios ("normal" speech density, or values of hesitational factors), unless the study of deviations proper constitutes the aim of an experiment.

(3) Experiments in SI should always involve texts (complete communications) as opposed to separate words and unrelated sentences. Experiments of the latter type cannot be conclusive as to the mechanism of simultaneous interpretation as such.

(4) The degree of verbal and semantic redundancy in a message depends on the involvement of as many verbal, semantic, syntactic and situational factors as possible. Among the complex semantic relations in discourse, it is the sense of the message that forms the invariant in SI. Hence, a basis for research should be sought in linguistic semantics, semantic syntax, linguistics of the text and communicational studies.

As Lewis Carroll's Duchess once said, "Take care of the sense, and the sounds will take care of themselves."

Notes

1   For objections to Osgood's proposal, cf. Fodor, Bever and Garrett (1974).
2   This would agree with the psychological model of multichannel information processing in simultaneous interpretation (Gerver 1975).
3   A series of short United Nations General Assembly speeches (English–Russian combination), a popular lecture on translation (English–Russian combination), and a popular lecture on problems of linguistics (Russian–English combination), 20 minutes each. Eleven experienced simultaneous interpreters used as subjects performed interpretations recorded on one track of a two-track tape, the record of the original being on the other.

References

Barik. H. C. (1975) "Simultaneous Interpretation: Qualitative and Linguistic Data," *Language and Speech* 18: 272–94.

Chafe, W. L. (1972) "Discourse Structure and Human Knowledge," in R. O. Freedle and J. B. Carroll (eds), *Language Comprehension and the Acquisition of Knowledge*, Washington, DC, pp. 41–69.

Chernov, G. V. (1973) "Towards a Psycholinguistic Model of Simultaneous Interpretation" (in Russian), *Linguistische Arbeitsberichte* (Leipzig) 7: 225–60.

—— (1975) "Communicational Situation of Simultaneous Interpretation and Redundancy in a Message" (in Russian), *Tetradi Perevodchika* 12: 83–101.

—— (Černov) (1977) "Kumulative dynamische semantische Analyse des Eingangstextes beim Simultandolmetschen," in O. Kade (ed.) *Vermittelte Kommunikation, Sprachmittlung, Translation*, Leipzig, pp. 93–104.

—— (1978) *Theory and Practice of Simultaneous Interpretation* (in Russian), Moscow.

Fodor, J. A., Bever T. G. and Garrett, M. F. (1974) *The Psychology of Language*, New York.

Frick, F. C. and Sumby, W. H. (1952) "Control Tower Language," *J. Acoust. Soc. Amer.* 24: 595–6.

Gerver, D. (1975) "A Psychological Approach to Simultaneous Interpretation," *Meta* 20: 119–28.

Leont'ev, A. A. (1968) *Psycholinguistic Units and Generation of Speech Utterances* (in Russian), Moscow.

Miller, G. A. (1956) "The Magical Number Seven, Plus or Minus Two: Some Limits on our Capacity for Processing Information," *Psych. Review* 63: 81–96.

—— (1963) *Language and Communication*, New York.

—— and Chomsky, N. (1963) "Finitary Models of Language Users," in R. D. Luce, R. R. Bush and E. Galanter (eds), *Handbook of Mathematical Psychology*, 2nd edn New York.

——, Galanter, E. and Pribram, K. H. (1960) *Plans and the Structure of Behavior*, New York.

Norman, D. A. and Rumelhart, D. E. (1975) *Explorations in Cognition*, San Francisco.

Osgood, C. E. (1963) "On Understanding and Creating Sentences," *American Psychologist* 18: 735–51.

Schank, R. C. and Colby, K. M. (1973) *Computer Models of Thought and Language*, San Francisco.

Zhinkin, N. I. (1970) "Grammar and Sense" (in Russian), in V. A. Zvegintsev (ed.) *Language and Man* (in Russian), Moscow, pp. 63–85.

Zimnyaya, I. A. and Chernov, G. V. (1970) "On the Role of Probability Prediction in the Process of Simultaneous Interpretation" (in Russian), in *Problems of the Theory and Methods of Teaching of Translation* (in Russian), abstracts of conference papers, mimeo, Moscow.

—— (1973) "Probability Prediction in Simultaneous Interpretation" (in Russian), in *Advanced Publications on Experimental Research in Psycholinguistics* (in Russian), mimeo, Moscow.

FOR FORTY YEARS, until her retirement in 1983, Hella Kirchhoff headed the Italian section of the School for Translators and Interpreters at the University of Heidelberg. She had enrolled there as a student in 1938 after completing her secondary education in Trieste, where her German-speaking parents had made sure that she also became fluent in French and English. After only three semesters she was given teaching responsibilities and, three years later, was put in charge of all translation and interpreting training in Italian. The (open) secret of her success was her perfect German–Italian bilingualism, which, in her account, made her a "natural" for (simultaneous) interpreting. Nevertheless, with clearly a full job on her hands, she never pursued a professional career in interpreting but instead devoted her academic life to teaching translators and interpreters.

Having obtained a doctorate in Romance languages in the early 1950s, she did not start writing on interpreting until twenty years later, after a chance encounter with research on bilingual performance had sparked her interest in the study of interpreting. In her (few) publications on the subject, she blended psycholinguistic insights with the translation-theoretical foundations of the Leipzig School. Her didactic approach, while stressing the crucial role of bilingualism, foregrounded language-pair-specific problems and strategies for resolving them. Her 1974 manuscript on teaching interpreting (*Eine Didaktik des Dolmetschens*) remained unpublished.

The paper reprinted here was originally presented at a conference in Germersheim in 1975 and published in the proceedings (Kirchhoff 1976a). It was translated into English – without the Italian–German examples drawn from empirical diploma theses under Kirchhoff's supervision (e.g. Amoser 1969) – by David Sawyer in cooperation with the editors.

Further reading: Kirchhoff 1976b.

Hella Kirchhoff

SIMULTANEOUS INTERPRETING
Interdependence of variables in the interpreting process, interpreting models and interpreting strategies

Translated by David Sawyer

THE FOLLOWING IS an attempt to describe the process of interpreting using concepts from information theory.

1 Description of the interpreting process

In simultaneous interpreting (SI), the interpreter, using technical equipment, perceives a sender's source language (SL) message in segments, processes it and renders it immediately and continuously in the target language (TL) for a receiver. The use of the term "simultaneous" is justified only from the perspective of an observer, who (with the exception of non-overlapping intervals) experiences the sender's production of information, the interpreter's reception and reproduction of the information, and TL reception as concurrent processes. The continuous production of equivalent TL segments can never take place at the same time as the production of SL segments, even if the interpreter has outstanding anticipation skills. Therefore, we can refer to this process as being quasi-simultaneous at most or, more aptly, as requiring a phase shift from SL input to TL output.

1.1 Simultaneous interpreting can be described as a multi-phase process that takes place sequentially while sender output, except in the case of pauses, is being produced, and must be processed continuously. The basic process involves four phases:

– Decoding of a SL segment
– Recoding
– TL production
– Output monitoring (self-correction if necessary)

⎤ Attention to
⎦ ongoing input

There are variants of this basic process, which are due mainly to text structure and the relationship between the two languages and in which storage operations or information reduction operations (see 3.1.3.5) come into play. An example of a variant involving storage operations is the rendering of the following German passage into a Romance language:

                    Aa   B
/ / *Der Minister und sein Gefolge haben*   / / *nach erfolgreichen Verhand-*
[/ / The Minister and his delegation have // after successful negotiations

                         Ab
lungen mit dem Gastgeber / / *die Stadt verlassen* / / *und sind*
with the host   // left the city   // and have

        C
nach Bonn zurückgekehrt. / /
returned to Bonn. / /]

Decoding of partial segment Aa
Storage of Aa
Decoding, recoding / production of B
Decoding of partial segment Ab
Retrieval of segment Aa and recoding of Aa plus Ab
Production of complete segment A

⎤ Attention to
⎦ ongoing input

1.2 The parallelism of SL input and TL output can be visualized by a two-tier model with multiple-phase structure. The model depicts the segmentation of input and the phase shift in output.
Basic process:

SL	Segment A	Segment B	Segment C
TL	Segment A	Segment B	Segment C

The variant involving a storage operation (see above) shows the anticipatory production of segment B in the output.

SL	Segment Aa	Segment B	Segment Ab	Segment C
TL		Segment B	Segment Aa + Ab	Segment C

2 Interdependence of variables

2.1 Relation of SL to TL: The degree of correspondence in a language pair is a decisive variable. If the syntactic structures of the two languages are similar, the interpreter is usually not required to replan syntax in the TL and can work without a high probability risk. The cognitive load in simultaneous interpreting between structurally similar languages is lower than that of a monolingual paraphrasing task, despite the need for recoding. In simultaneous interpreting between structurally divergent languages, the interpreter will need to process larger segments. Proceeding with TL production before syntactic disambiguation involves a high probability risk. If divergent structures coincide with segments carrying a high subjective information value per unit of time, the interpreter's processing capacity may be overloaded, and information loss may occur.

2.2 SL text: The syntactic complexity of the SL text is barely relevant when languages are structurally similar, unless it makes text comprehension more difficult. In the case of structurally divergent languages, syntax is of decisive importance for the choice of processing strategy. The subjective information value of the text has an impact on the segmentation strategy. If the information value is low, the interpreter can reduce the probability risk by maintaining a greater distance from the original without straining processing capacity. Texts that are addressed to TL receivers, taking into account their communicative possibilities and needs, are easier to interpret simultaneously than texts with a distinct SL orientation. The adaptation of such texts to the communicative needs of receivers with a different sociocultural background is possible only to a very limited extent. [. . .] For instance, clarifying an expression by giving an explanatory paraphrase is not feasible during SI for reasons of time, whereas it is very well possible in consecutive interpreting. What is however feasible are adaptations to the stylistic conventions of the TL as well as emotional attenuation or emphasis.

[. . .]

2.3 Sender performance: The communicativity of the sender's delivery facilitates appropriate segmentation of the message, particularly with regard to the speaker's pauses. The presentation rate, which the interpreter cannot influence, has an impact on all operations of the process: all phases are under time pressure. When language structures diverge, a high presentation rate is particularly stressful. An extremely low presentation rate, on the other hand, also has a negative impact if it forces the interpreter to carry out complex storage operations that make problem-solving more difficult than at an average rate of presentation.

2.4 Technical equipment: The entire process depends on fully functional simultaneous interpreting equipment and is thus particularly susceptible to disruptions (incorrect switching by the technician or individual listeners, speakers turning away from the microphone, etc.).

3 Processing operations and strategies

Simultaneous interpreting is a complex cognitive process. The individual steps in problem-solving (processing of segments) can be divided into component operations which must occur in a certain sequence (see model in section 1.1) and in a pre-determined time frame. Each component operation has an impact on the overall solution, because the output of one data-processing stage serves as the input condition for the next one. The results of problem-solving operations are determined by the efficiency of the strategies employed. Strategies indicate which decisions must be taken in a given situation or in view of certain probabilities so as to reach a goal within a behavioral plan. SI strategies determine, among other things, decisions on the timing of the start of processing operations (segmentation), decisions to delay operations or keep data (parts of segments) available, decisions concerning the types of necessary operations (information selection and reduction), and decisions concerning processing speed and the overall load sustainable at a given time. Interpreting strategies are subject to continuous improvement until they become optimized and, if possible, automatic.

3.1 Decoding: In the basic form of the process, decoding is linked to recoding.

3.1.1 Segmentation strategy (basic process): Appropriate segmentation into function units is a prerequisite for text processing. In contrast to a normal monolingual listening situation, a function unit is determined not only by the structure of the SL (in which case it would correspond to a complete meaning unit or presuppose strong expectations for the continuation of the meaning unit, and can be defined primarily by linguistic criteria). Rather, the function unit is determined by both decoding and recoding conditions. A function unit in simultaneous interpreting can be defined as the smallest possible decoding unit in the SL for which a 1:1 relationship can be established with a TL segment.[2] It depends not only upon the structure of the SL but also upon the equivalence relation between the SL and TL. A function unit is a variable that can be defined by translation-linguistic criteria.

While in a monolingual listening situation the SL decoding unit can be viewed as fixed (within the range of possible decoding strategies, of course), the SL function unit in simultaneous interpreting is of a dynamic nature, because it varies, depending on the equivalence relation linking the SL with a TL.

The size of a function unit is however limited. While the lower limit for the size of a processing segment is determined unequivocally by the above-mentioned criteria, the upper limit is determined by the processing capacity of the individual. The subjective information value of a segment must not exceed the individual's processing capacity in relation to the time available. The upper limit of the segment is thus determined by psychological and information-theoretical criteria which must be taken into account. The latitude for the interpreter's choice of timing therefore lies between the following two limits:

—   The lower limit (minimum size of the segment, minimum time lag) requires grasping the minimum SL unit for which there is a 1:1 equivalent in the TL, or presupposes strong expectations for continuation.

– The upper limit (maximum size of the segment, maximum lag) is determined not by the volume of text but by the total amount of information that must be processed within a maximum time frame of 10 seconds.

If the interpreter cannot grasp a function unit as a complete whole before reaching his capacity limit, he must begin transferring the segment (before complete syntactic and semantic disambiguation) solely on the basis of his expectations. In doing so, the interpreter assumes a risk that is inversely proportional to the correct anticipation of how the segment will develop. (Deviations from the lower limit may occur in language combinations with parallel syntactic structures. Choosing a start-ing point below the lower limit involves almost no risk if lexical disambiguation is assured through context and situation.) Based on the above description, the inter-preter's optimum starting point would have to lie where a maximum amount of certainty and a minimum load on capacity are ensured. The optimum starting point would have to correspond to the respective limits of the smallest recoding unit. In practice, however, this is not usually the case. Although the starting point mostly lies within the limits below which incorrect planning and production may result and above which information may be lost, it does not correspond to the theoretically defined optimum.

Comparisons between SL input and TL output show that experienced inter-preters strive to adapt their segmentation strategies primarily to the sender's rhythm of speech. While the performance of beginner interpreters is characterized by high variations in speed and disruptions in the speech/pause ratio, the experi-enced interpreter accepts both the risk of anticipation and a greater load on capacity arising from the storage of grammatical and semantic information for the sake of maintaining a steady output rate.

In addition to this consistent rhythm of speech, a moderate time lag allows the interpreter to free himself from the surface structure of the SL text and optimize the communicative effect of the TL text. In the interest of the effectiveness of his message, the interpreter is thus willing to sacrifice certainty and economy to a great extent. Such behavior presupposes the building up of strong expectations and the mastery of additional strategies.

3.1.2 The interpreter's ability to anticipate: The construction of expectations depends on linguistic and extra-linguistic determinants.[3] The interpreter's ability to anticipate is defined on the one hand by his linguistic competence, i.e. his knowledge of syntactic and semantic regularities in the SL and the use of information from previously processed text, and on the other hand by his knowledge of the situation, especially the role of the sender and his typical behavior in that role and situation, and the interpreter's prior knowledge of the subject. As a rule, the certainty with which the interpreter can anticipate will increase (in other words, the subjective information value of the text will decrease) as the interpretation progresses, because it becomes easier for the interpreter to recognize and predict the performance characteristics of the sender and the subject matter. The experienced interpreter is rarely mistaken in his expectations. If he is wrong and notices this in time, he will modify his plan, or make corrections. If this is not possible due to time constraints, there will be distortions and losses of information.

3.1.3 Additional processing strategies: The interpreter's processing capacity limitations, time constraints, structure-related processing difficulties, and the necessity of producing a TL text that does not differ from a spontaneously spoken text, lead to the formation and use of strategies which can be described as follows:

3.1.3.1 Extraction and separate processing of free-position parts of larger semantic structures, together with storage of text elements to be processed [. . .][+]

3.1.3.2 Flexible sentence planning when the continuation of the utterance is uncertain, so as to permit modifications of the interpreter's output plan [. . .]

3.1.3.3 Use of neutral padding expressions [. . .]

3.1.3.4 Additions to fill hesitation pauses: Long pauses make a negative impression on the receiver, who may suspect information loss, and must be filled as far as possible (repetition as paraphrase or addition).

3.1.3.5 Information reduction: Waiting for the disambiguation of long passages up to the limit of processing capacity is recommended only in extreme cases of unclear continuation of the text. In that event, excessive lag and overload can be reduced through selection (omission of irrelevant information), which quickly restores normal processing operations. [. . .]

3.2 Recoding: If adequate segmentation of the text is assured, recoding is determined by the way the interpreter relates SL segments to TL segments. Conventional patterns, stereotypical phrases, and sequences familiar to the interpreter are matched without problem, i.e. almost automatically. Complex structures and rare sequences require sophisticated, cognitively controlled assignment procedures. Recoding usually occurs in the direct presence of the SL segment, which is documented by output corrections for deviations from the original segment. Only at an extended lag will the latter become cognitively unavailable.

Research on bilingualism explains the interpreter's recoding procedures during simultaneous interpreting on the basis of the hypothesis that both linguistic systems (SL and TL) are in operation at the same time, with the input switch set to the SL and the output switch to the TL.[5] In the interpreting literature, recoding is presented as an almost automatic activity. In the SI model of Seleskovitch,[6] the recoding phase is entirely absent, which suggests that skilled interpreters control the recoding process without becoming aware of it.

In this context, the question arises as to whether the interpreter rapidly considers a range of possible TL variants and is able to make a definite selection among alternatives, or whether he restricts possible alternatives as part of preliminary decision-making and only considers standard variants.

3.3 Reproduction: TL output must be continuous and achieve optimum communicative effect. Normally, the interpreted text has the appearance of a spontaneous speech. Individual features of sender performance remain largely intact, and undesired deviations from SL norms are corrected. Plan changes and anacolutha in the SL text can usually be offset only with difficulty or not at all; the interpreter can however improve on the delivery of the message. Under difficult conditions, the degree of spontaneity in reproduction may decrease, and there may be fluctuations in rhythm due to hesitation and deviations from standard syntactic and lexical usage. If the interpreter is unable to cope, there will be plan changes, anacolutha, violations of standard usage, frequent corrections, and ultimately distortions and losses of information.

3.4 Output monitoring and self-correction: Like any act of speech, simultaneous interpreting involves the monitoring of output and, if necessary and possible, the correction of performance errors on the phonological, syntactic and lexical levels. A characteristic of the SI process is the ongoing monitoring of output segments for functional equivalence. Errors occur mostly due to interference and pre-mature translation before the lexical or syntactic disambiguation of a segment. Naturally, the interpreter will not become aware of errors of competence. Nor will every performance error that is registered also be corrected, as error toler-ance varies from one interpreter to another and time pressure may lead the interpreter to forgo correction so as not to jeopardize the simultaneity of the interpretation. Among beginners, the number of corrections (under time pres-sure) will remain constant despite a rising error rate when little processing capacity remains available for this final operation in the problem-solving process. If the interpreter's processing capacity is exhausted, corrections are no longer possible.

4 Multiple task performance

In simultaneous interpreting, multiple task performance is required in all phases for much of the time, i.e. the interpreter must divide his attention between two com-plex tasks of equal importance. The phenomenon of multiple-task performance has been studied at length in psychology, and two basic hypotheses have been developed:

1   Data are processed sequentially; concurrent linking of different data is not possible, because there is room for only one content item in the processing center.
2   The individual's total capacity allows for parallel processing of different data.

The question as to whether in SI SL input and TL output are processed in parallel or sequentially has not yet been answered. Following Peterson,[7] we assume that the interpreter can make use of both strategies. Multiple-task performance does not appear to place a great burden on the interpreter, as is stated unanimously in the interpreting literature. Barik's measurements of SL input and TL output synchron-ization[8] clearly show that multiple-task performance encompasses almost half the total activity. This could be reduced if the interpreter felt it were necessary, as shown by the comparative findings:

Sender speaking	Interpreter speaking	42%
Sender speaking	Interpreter silent	18%
Sender silent	Interpreter silent	12%
Sender silent	Interpreter speaking	28%

Multiple-task performance becomes a problem if task completion requires cognitive decisions which, in sum, reach or even exceed the individual's processing capacity limit. In this case, multiple-task performance can be accomplished only with the help of particularly efficient processing techniques (selection and concentration of information).

5 Memory in simultaneous interpreting

In our view, simultaneous interpreting cannot be seen as a learning process in the sense of a "lasting change of behavior" nor as a learning process comparable to consecutive interpreting, with medium-term retention and reproduction of the total information content of the text. In consecutive interpreting, data are stored fundamentally in long-term memory (LTM), whereas in simultaneous interpreting they are stored in short-term memory. The interpreting literature reflects conflicting opinions on this topic among professional interpreters. Our view is as follows: simultaneous interpreting generally involves latent learning, i.e. text passages or individual elements remain cognitively present after simultaneous processing even without the intention to learn. Similarly, ongoing adaptation to the speaker (speaking style, rhythm of speech, use of individual linguistic patterns, etc.) occurs unconsciously, and interpreting strategies are acquired during the process. Memorization of the entire text content in long-term memory is possible in SI only by intentional learning. However, the interpreter will want to do so only if he requires a full contextual understanding for processing the text. He will not store information in long-term memory if he is doing routine work or if he can do without contextual knowledge, so as not to tax his capacity unnecessarily and keep "channel capacity" available for the simultaneous interpreting process. The interpreter will not be able to store information in long-term memory at all if the complexity of the task does not leave any processing capacity available. Pinpointed learning is also based upon the intention to learn: individual statements or linguistic elements are retained so that they can be used again later.

6 Summary

If we want to distinguish specific interpreting behavior from general encoding and decoding behavior in monolingual communication, the text-processing conditions described above result in the following requirements specific to the simultaneous interpreter:

6.1 Continuous input places all phases of the process under time pressure: The interpreter must work at a high processing speed and must be highly resistant to stress.

6.2 Appropriate SL segmentation is a decisive operation in the SI process: The interpreter must have excellent competence in the SL and TL.

6.3 The TL text should exhibit a balanced speech/pause ratio: Maintaining a steady rhythm requires the ability to develop strong expectations (implying rapid adaptation to sender performance and knowledge of the topic) and to concentrate information (for recovering from excessive lag).

6.4 The TL text must guarantee functional equivalence: The interpreter is expected to be able to relate equivalent TL segments to the SL segments rapidly and with certainty and to process frequently occurring sequences automatically.

6.5 The need for multiple task performance presupposes the ability to cope with multiple loads: The process as a whole can be accomplished only on the basis of the full mastery, continuous improvement and automatization of the necessary interpretation strategies.

Notes

1   F. Goldman-Eisler and M. Cohen, "An Experimental Study of Interference between Receptive and Productive Processes Relating to Simultaneous Translation," *Language and Speech* 17 (1974).

2   Cf. O. Kade, *Zufall und Gesetzmäßigkeit in der Übersetzung*, Beiheft 1, *Fremdsprachen* (Leipzig, 1968), p. 90.

3   L. Römer, "Einige syntaktische Gesetzmäßigkeiten beim Simultandolmetschen," Beiheft 2, *Fremdsprachen* (Leipzig, 1968).
    G. Dalitz, "Zur Beschreibung typischer Vorgriffsfälle beim Simultandolmetschen," Beiheft zu *Fremdsprachen* 5/6 (Leipzig, 1973).

4   G. Ilg, "Psittacisme decalé où la Plume de ma Cabine," *L'Interprète* 2 (1972).

5   J. Macnamara, "The Bilingual's Linguistic Performance – A Psychological Review," *Journal of Social Issues* 23 (1967); J. Macnamara, M. Krauthammer and M. Bolgar, "Language Switching in Bilinguals as a Function of Stimulus and Response Uncertainty," *Journal of Experimental Psychology* 78:2 (1968).

6   D. Seleskovitch, *L'interprète dans les conférences internationales*, Minard–Lettres Modernes (Paris, 1968).

7   L. R. Peterson, "Concurrent Verbal Activity," *Psychological Review* 76 (1969): 376–86.

8   H. C. Barik, *A Study of Simultaneous Interpretation*, Diss. University of North Carolina, (Chapel Hill, 1969).

WHENEVER THE STUDY of interpreting is discussed in a broader, historical perspective, it is bound to include reference to the concept of deverbalization and to the *théorie du sens*, as conceived and formulated by Danica Seleskovitch (1921–2001). Her 1968 monograph, which captured the essence of the profession, took IS well beyond the language-pair-specific comparative study of lexical and grammatical systems, and laid the foundations for her own doctoral work, and that of her many disciples. Seleskovitch, a practitioner whose distinguished career included the position of Secretary General of AIIC, was among the first to stress that oral translation is never carried out on a word-for-word basis, and that the processing of utterances is never tantamount to the processing of words or sentences in isolation (Seleskovitch 1962). Seleskovitch made the "sense"-based conception of the interpreter's performance the cornerstone of her 1973 doctoral dissertation on consecutive interpreting (Seleskovitch 1975), from which the pages reprinted here (pp. 56–67, 179–181) are taken.

Apart from her research, the dominant position held by Seleskovitch and the "Paris School" in the field of IS in the 1970s and 1980s was primarily due to the launching, in 1974, of a doctoral research program at the Sorbonne Nouvelle School of Interpreters (ESIT) in Paris, where Seleskovitch taught interpreting for more than thirty years until her retirement, in the position of Director, in 1990. Not surprisingly, her work exhibits a close link between theory and training, as reflected in the *Pédagogie raisonnée de l'interprétation* (Seleskovitch and Lederer 1989). The latter was published in 1995 in an English translation by Jacolyn Harmer, who also produced the English version of the excerpt presented here.

Further reading: García-Landa 1981; Seleskovitch 1968, 1976, 1978, 1982, 1999; Seleskovitch and Lederer 1984, 1989.

Danica Seleskovitch

LANGUAGE AND MEMORY
A study of note-taking in consecutive interpreting

Translated by Jacolyn Harmer

Word association, and eliciting words

WHY IS LITERAL translation so much easier than translation involving deeper reflection? The answer is simple: the first requires much less mental effort. Our tendency to want to expend the least possible effort explains why we often resort to stereotypical, or formulaic, language rather than mentally searching for the precise translation of words whose conceptual boundaries are unaffected by context, or endeavoring to interpret the message. In other words, we somewhat automatically string words together by word association. At the end of the eighteenth century two physicians, Baillarger and Jackson, looked at this word-association process and drew a distinction between voluntary language production and reflex language production. According to Alajouanine,[1] this is how Baillarger defined these terms:

> [. . .] some patients manifest an unusual phenomenon: they are unable to produce certain words when they want to, no matter how hard they try. Then, a few minutes later, they utter those very same words involuntarily. It seems they have lost the ability to perform the voluntary, motor act of word production, while their spontaneous word production motor ability remains unimpaired.

This dual voluntary/reflex nature of language is also apparent in the transition from one language to another in what I would call a "literal" translation versus a more reflective one. In the case of a literal rendition from English into French, the French word appears because it resembles the English one; or it comes to mind by word association because it is frequently used as a translation for the English word. A reflective translation results from a search for meaning and intentional eliciting of the appropriate corresponding term. Literal translation can be likened to stereo-typical, or formulaic language, in which one word leads to the next, and reflective translation corresponds to deliberate, or voluntary, word production where the "concept" evoked by the first word elicits another word by intentional effort. The first process is easier and faster than the second but frequently quite imperfect.

I will take an example of voluntary word production from my own experience. The participants at a weather-stripping products conference were discussing the format of an advertising brochure. The Germans proposed a "Ringbuch." I saw what they meant but could not produce the French term for the concept in my mind. For quite some time, while continuing to interpret simultaneously, I said "feuillets détachables" (loose leaf/detachable pages), while subconsciously still searching for the term for what I had in mind. As I imagined the bookstore where I usually buy my stationery, and saw myself talking with the sales assistant, the word "classeur" (ring-binder) finally occurred to me in *verbal* form and I was able to slot it into my interpretation. To borrow from computer terminology, thought functions in ana-logue mode. Imagining a situation activates a sufficient number of inextricably linked data saved in our mental storage for the missing link to appear in its verbal form. The process of eliciting the right word starts with an awareness that a precise term exists and ends with its verbal appearance. And yet this same analogue way of functioning also explains the infelicitous appearance of literal translations.

Literal translation (i.e. reflex, unthinking translation) and reflective translation are not two different methods used in different cases, depending on the circum-stances or the words to be translated. Nor is it true to say that one is always correct and the other always wrong. The correctness of a translation must be judged accord-ing to the result and not the process by which the result is obtained. If the word in the translation refers to exactly the same thing as the word in the original, the translation is correct, regardless of the reflective effort expended. During the first day of interpreting at a conference, "Mantel" might be repeatedly translated as "virole" (shell), a term which becomes reflex and just as unthinking as translating the term by the cognate "manteau" (coat, jacket) – which it could well be in other contexts. This does not mean it is incorrect.

Automatic word association can in fact rescue the interpreter who has identi-fied something but is having trouble coming up with the exact corresponding term in the other language. Our students all know that when they cannot find the word they want in their mother tongue, all they have to do is quickly say something aloud in the semantic field of the word they are looking for, and it will then surface spontaneously – in other words, instead of trying to find the word, try to jog it loose with stereotypical utterances. Take the example of a student who could not think of the French equivalent for *Giftgas* (toxic gas) during a German>French consecutive exercise. Although he knew it was wrong, he tried working round the French word *poison* (*poison* = *Gift* in German), all the while looking for the right word: "des gaz . . . des gaz . . ." (". . . gases . . . gases"). I prompted: "les gas d'échappement des voitures sont extrêmement . . ." (vehicle exhaust gases are extremely . . .), and before I was able to finish the sentence, he came up with "toxique" (toxic).

Reflective translation does not demand a constant effort to elicit the right terms (interpreters are not walking dictionaries). Nevertheless, such an effort must be made a certain number of times for the association of two words to become a reflex, one eliciting the other spontaneously for the remainder of the conference.

"Reflex" translation is so often wrong because no initial mental effort has been made to associate a word in one language with the corresponding word in another. Many literal translations are so purely stereotypical in form that I sometimes say: just as there is thought without speech, there is also speech without thought . . .

Technical terms are among the words always noted and translated in consecutive interpreting. During a conference, the interpreter often initially notes them in the original language. As the speech progresses, and once the interpreter has started to interpret, a subconscious effort elicits the corresponding word in the other language. It is very rare for the right word not to come to mind when needed. As the conference proceeds and the specialized terms come up again and again, their correct translation becomes a reflex – and the interpreter will begin noting down the technical term directly in the target language.

Some examples taken from the corpus

Some examples of translations of polysemic words can be found in two passages from Speech 2 (Part 2, paragraphs 1 and 4). All subjects in the experiment noted these words (whether in English or French) and included them in their interpretation.

The first paragraph says:

> Let's look at PRIMARY PRODUCTS. And I think we should here distinguish between two categories: on the one hand, we'll set TEMPERATE FOODSTUFFS and on the other RAW MATERIALS of various sorts and TROPICAL FOODSTUFFS.

(The emphasized words correspond to the words noted down from this paragraph.)

Let us first look at the term which has been translated most consistently by all subjects: *raw materials*. We find:

> Matières premières (**A, E, F, D, M, K, I**)[2]
> Matières premières proprement dites (**G**)
> Matières premières industrielles (**L**).

H, N, B and **C** did not interpret Speech 2, which is why we have only nine subjects. All interpreters say "matières premières" (raw materials), except for two (**G** and **L**) who had already used "matières premières" for *primary products* and who clearly want to distinguish between the two terms *primary products* and *raw materials*.

Raw materials typifies the kind of expression which is constructed differently in English and French. The English term marks the state "raw"; the French term marks the stage in the processing process "premières" (first). This expression cannot be translated by simply converting each of its composite terms into the other language. *Raw materials* "elicits" *matières premières*: "translating" first *raw* and then *materials* does not work. Someone familiar with both the English expression and its French equivalent might find this example rather obvious because when you hear the term *raw materials*, *matières premières* comes just as easily to mind as *cinquante* when you hear *fifty*. However, someone who recognizes the two expressions and the object itself, but who is unfamiliar with certain underlying concepts (an all too frequent occurrence when it comes to translating technical terms), might easily be misled into translating each component separately.

In the above example, most subjects gave a "semi-automatic" translation of *matières premières* for *raw materials*. This solution disregards the distinction made by the speaker between "primary products" and "raw materials." Only **L**, who always seems to prefer exegesis over transcoding, goes further, specifying that the speaker means "matières premières industrielles."

The English original text says:

> Let's look at primary products. And I think we should here distinguish between two categories: on the one hand, we'll set temperate food-stuffs and on the other, raw materials of various sorts and tropical foodstuffs.

Since the term "primary products" includes both foodstuffs and "matières premières" (raw materials of various sorts), clearly the latter refers to products that require processing.

For *primary products* the subjects note:

> matières premières (**G** and **L**)
> produits primaires (**A, D, M, I**)
> produits de base (**K**)
> produits (**E** and **F**).

The subjects carefully distinguish in French between the two English terms "primary products" and "raw materials." However, all except for **L** make that distinction by word choice alone: produits primaires – matières premières; produits de base – matières premières.

Now let's look at *temperate foodstuffs* and *tropical foodstuffs*. For *tropical foodstuffs* the subjects noted:

> produits alimentaires tropicaux (**G, L, F, D, M, K, I**)
> produits tropicaux (**E**)
> produits alimentaires de culture tropicale (**A**).

For *temperate foodstuffs*:

> produits alimentaires tempérés (**G** and **M**)
> produits alimentaires de régions tempérées (**L, F, K, I**)
> produits alimentaires de culture tempérée (**A**)
> produits alimentaires naturels aux pays tempérés (**E**)
> produits alimentaires des zones tempérées (**D**).

The term *produits tropicaux* exists in French: it is a normal French expression. All subjects, except for one (**A**), therefore do not hesitate to use it for *tropical foodstuffs*. However, for the analogous term *temperate foodstuffs*, we see that the translation is not quite as automatic. Since the subjects are not aware of a direct correspondence in the target language, some (**M** and **G**) translate the term literally ("produits alimentaires tempérés") while others prefer to explain the concept.

What we are seeing here is the interpreting process at work. We already saw the same phenomenon with listed items. However *translatable* a word or expression may be, that does not obviate the need to *interpret* it in context. The more we move away from analyzing the meaning of the words at the level of the language system to focus instead on the speech act in its particular circumstances and much broader context, the more we will be able to interpret instead of transcode.

We see the same kind of alternatives (literal translation or explanation) when we look at *tariff on wheat* (Speech 2, part 2, paragraph 4):

> And the kind of thing we have in mind when we mention temperate foodstuffs is, for example, the chicken war between the U.S. and the Six, and the tariff on wheat, and so on and so forth.

For *tariff on wheat* we find:

> négociations portant sur le blé américain (**G**)
> problèmes tarifaires du blé (**L**)
> droits de douane sur le blé (**A**)
> problèmes tarifaires concernant le blé (**E**)
> droits de douane pour le blé (**F**)
> accords sur le prix des céréales (**D**)
> tarifs sur les blés (**M**)
> tarifs ou droits de douane frappant les céréales (**K**)
> tarif du blé (**I**).

Most subjects "translate" the expression, while **D** ("accords sur le prix des céréales") and **G** ("négociations portant sur le blé américain") truly interpret it.

The relevant passage is in Speech 2 (part 2, paragraphs 16 and 17):

> In fact, I think I should remind you that the whole business of the international trade in temperate foods, is a problem for developed countries; that is to say, it's become a problem between North America and the Six, between the Six and the Commonwealth, between the Commonwealth and North America, and so on and so forth.
>
> And the kind of thing we have in mind when we mention temperate foodstuffs is, for example, the chicken war between the U.S. and the Six, and the tariff on wheat, and so on and so forth. Now this is not of much importance to the great majority of the less developed countries.

D's notes for this passage look like this:

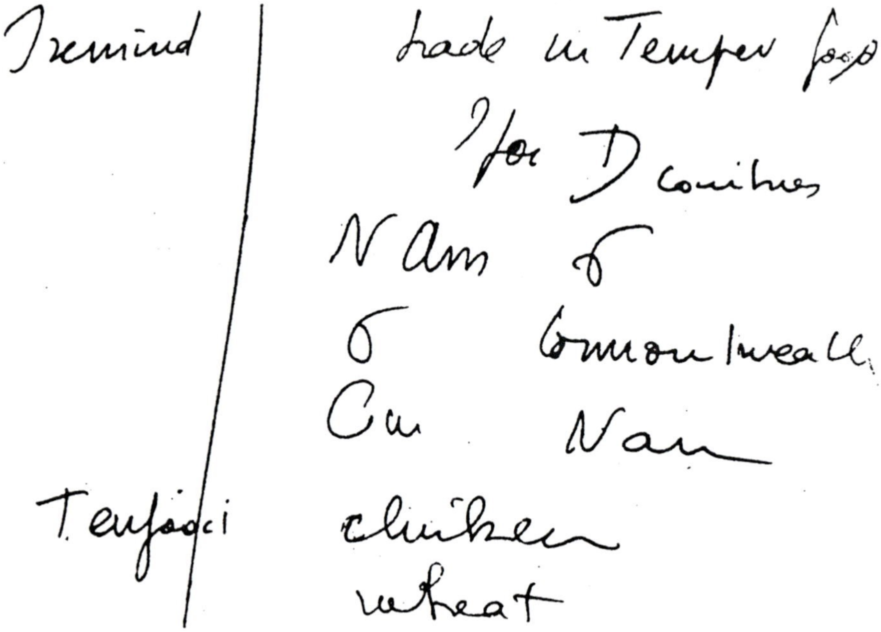

I remind

T enfood

trade in Temper   food

? for D   countries

N Am   6

6   Commonwealth

CM   N am

chicken

wheat

D says:

Je dois en effet vous rappeler que le problème des échanges commerciaux portant sur les produits alimentaires tempérés se pose surtout aux pays industrialisés: ce sont les problèmes qui se posent à propos des échanges entre les six pays du Marché Commun et les États d'Amérique du Nord, ou bien entre le Marché Commun et le Commonwealth, ou bien encore entre le Commonwealth et l'Amérique du Nord. Et ici il faut se souvenir de la guerre du poulet, des ACCORDS SUR LE PRIX DES CÉRÉALES, etc. mais ces problèmes d'exportation de produits alimentaires de zone tempérée ne sont pas très importants pour les pays en voie de développement.

[Back translation:

> Indeed, I must remind you that the problem relating to trade in temperate foodstuffs arises particularly for industrialized countries; these are the problems that arise in connection with trade between the six countries of the Common Market and the states of North America, or between the Common Market and the Commonwealth, or even between the Commonwealth and North America. And here we must recall the chicken war, the AGREEMENTS ON THE PRICE OF CEREALS, etc., but these problems concerning the export of foodstuffs from temperate zones are not very important for the developing countries.]

A closer look at **D**'s notes reveals something rather amusing: between "T enfood" and "chicken," the color of the ink changes. **D** had to switch pens just at that point and stopped taking notes for an instant. My guess is that this explains why **D** has no note for "tariff." Distracted for just a second, the interpreter missed the term; this is confirmed when the term is omitted in the interpretation. The word "war" was not noted either, although it is in the interpretation, indicating that the interpreter had caught it.

D has only "wheat" in his notes. A distraction lasting a fraction of a second prevented him from analyzing the message while taking notes. As a result, his sole prompt is a single scribbled note, a word that went straight from ear to hand, with no analysis in between. When the time comes to interpret, **D** has just his notes to help him understand this word. What is striking here is not really the pen change, nor the omission of one word in the notes; it is the way **D** copes with a gap in meaning. The word *wheat* by itself could of course be translated literally, yet clearly **D** cannot say: "il faut se souvenir ici de la guerre du poulet, des céréales . . ." (here we must remember the chicken and cereals war . . . .). Since he missed the word *tariff*, **D** did not grasp the context: "échanges entre la Communauté et le reste du monde" (trade between the Community and the rest of the world). However, in a flash, a line of logic runs through his mind: he must attach meaning to this isolated word in his notes. Setting "wheat" in the general context of trade between industrialized countries, and (though I am only guessing) probably thinking of the International Wheat Council negotiations on the "Wheat Agreement", the wheat-importing and -exporting countries' charter, **D** interprets the word *wheat* so that it takes on meaning. He says:

> *accord sur le* PRIX *des céréales* (agreement on cereal PRICES).

G also has only "*blé*" (wheat) in his notes and says: "*négociations portant sur le blé américain*" (American wheat negotiations). In this case, the interpreter probably chose not to note *tariff*. Familiar with the context, he knows that customs duties imposed on wheat imports into the Community are being negotiated with the United States and that the Kennedy Round is about to start and so did not need to note *tariff*. The word *blé* (wheat) alone is enough to enable him to recall what was said and to interpret.

Appendix: the experiment

Description

Our priority was to ensure that this experiment was conducted under the same conditions that would be found in practice. We also wanted to avoid the glaring mistakes sometimes made by observers who have a poor understanding of what they are going to observe.[3]

Consequently, all Paris-based members of AIIC (International Association of Conference Interpreters) currently with the following language combinations were invited to volunteer as subjects: French as mother tongue (A language), English as a professionally active language (B language).[4]

Of the 51 AIIC members who were potential subjects, 13 participated in the experiment. All subjects' identities were protected.

For obvious reasons, French and English were selected as appropriate languages for the experiment.

There are two modes of interpreting: simultaneous and consecutive. As we were starting practically from scratch, I thought it best to focus on the mode first used in practice, i.e. consecutive. This mode must be taught before simultaneous interpreting can be taught;[5] our experience indicates that someone who excels at consecutive interpreting is able to do simultaneous interpreting.

My greatest concern was to ensure that the experiment faithfully reflected reality wherever possible. The experiment was therefore designed around certain fundamental parameters: oral extemporaneous style, length of discourse, natural rhythm of delivery, current topic, single delivery of each speech.

Some conditions could not be met:

- in meetings, the context always frames the discussion – this factor will inevitably be missing in the case of an interpretation performed in the laboratory;
- it was not possible to obtain interpretations with both *the live speaker* and *the intended target audience* present. Recorded speeches were used instead of live speakers;
- it was not possible to arrange for the original speech to be *delivered and interpreted at the same time*;
- lastly, some subjects did something that interpreters do not normally do: in this case it was because *they knew their interpretation would be recorded.* They tried to stick close to the text to keep the words of the original and the interpretation parallel.

Now I will describe the procedure. Each interpreter listened to the first part of the speech while taking notes; he was told when the section to be interpreted began; he continued to take notes and then interpreted as soon as the speech was over. His interpretation was recorded. *He did not hear his own interpretation again, nor the original speech.* The subject was thus interpreting under conditions that reflected common practice.

Next, the interpreter was asked about his notes and was free, of course, to make some personal comments. The interview was also recorded and then transcribed.

In order to guarantee objectivity, the experiment was conducted by Ms. C. Gravier who is not an interpreter. I would like to thank her for her insightful work during the interviews and for her meticulous records.

[. . .]

Notes

1   *L'Aphasie et le langage pathologique*, pp. 243–51.
2   The interpreters who participated in the experiment are identified by letters only.
3   Oléron and Nanpon (Laboratoire de Psychologie Génétique, Faculté des Lettres et Sciences Humaines, Paris) [Genetic Psychology Laboratory, Faculty of Humanities and Human Sciences, Paris] in "Recherches sur la Traduction Simultanée" (1963 and 1965) had a series of errors in their experimental conditions: use of written texts, translations of translations, speakers not speaking extemporaneously, reading speed instead of discourse speed, isolated utterances and words, etc.
4   AIIC classifies Members' working languages [A] and [B] as follows;

- "Active languages: those into which the interpreter works"
- "[A] language: the interpreter's native language (or another language strictly equivalent to a native language), the member's main active languages . . ."
- "[B] language: active languages other than the interpreter's native language, of which she or he has a perfect command" (NB: "in interpretation").

5   Cf. "Colloque sur l'enseignement de l'Interprétation" [Symposium on the Teaching of Interpreting], International Association of Conference Interpreters (AIIC), 1965.

Chapter 2.4

THE IDEAS SET forth by Seleskovitch were further studied and extended, both independently and in collaboration with her, by Marianne Lederer, herself a practicing interpreter and an interpreter trainer. As one of the first doctoral students in the research program on *Science et technique de l'interprétation et de la traduction* (*Traductologie*) at the Sorbonne Nouvelle School of Interpreters (ESIT), Lederer defended her doctoral thesis, *La traduction simultanée – fondements théoriques*, in the late 1970s. She was subsequently appointed full professor at Université Paris XII and, in 1985, at Université Paris III – Sorbonne Nouvelle, where she went on to become Director of ESIT (1990–9) and Head of the University Research Center for Translation Studies.

The paper reprinted here, first published in the Proceedings of the 1977 Venice Symposium (Lederer 1978b), presents Lederer's early investigations of simultaneous interpreting, preceding the more extensive empirical and theoretical analyses presented in the published version of her doctoral dissertation (Lederer 1981).

Lederer's later work focused on written translation, where similar aspects were found to be universally valid, whatever the situation and whatever the language pair. Among her many publications are *Études traductologiques – travaux réunis par M. Lederer* (1990) and *La traduction aujourd'hui – le modèle interprétatif* (1994), as well as several volumes on interpreting in collaboration with Seleskovitch.

Further reading: Lederer 1981, 1982, 1990, 1994; Seleskovitch and Lederer 1984, 1989.

Marianne Lederer

SIMULTANEOUS INTERPRETATION
Units of meaning and other features

IT IS CERTAINLY fit and no coincidence that this symposium devoted to interpretation should bring together psychologists, linguists and interpreters. Interpreting is a human performance in which cognitive activity is first and foremost; it therefore leads us into the field of psychology with no need to resort to special experiments; in this field the connection between thinking and speaking can be observed as it materializes with each segment of speech so that investigations into interpretation also pertain to psycholinguistics. Since it implies a comparison of speech acts in different languages it also obliges us to tread on linguistic ground. Thus interpreters can rejoice in having the opportunity of comparing their results with those obtained by psychologists, linguists and psycholinguists.

For a number of years, our research team at Paris University (Sorbonne Nouvelle) has been recording speeches and discussions at multilingual international conferences and comparing not only speeches and their interpretations but also speeches in different languages. We have collected a wealth of evidence which is as yet far from being entirely exploited; yet a number of conclusions seem now sufficiently ascertained for me to try and present a short extract of a speech and its simultaneous interpretation and to discuss some of the evidence obtained.

As a preface however, I should like to stress how important it is to consider what interpretation is supposed to achieve before embarking on a detailed study of the processes involved. Everything that is spoken in a booth in response to speakers' utterances is interpreting and representative of the state of the art; in a study that would propose to survey the present state of the profession, all types of interpretation would have to be taken into consideration. This, however, is not the purpose of our research team: we concentrate on the process of interpretation that establishes communication. We believe that in doing so, we determine not only what such interpretation is, but also what speech behaviour consists of. Seen from this angle it becomes a truism to state that interpretation, to be taken as an object for investigation, has to establish communication.

A fundamental precept has therefore guided our selection of recordings at international conferences: we have always checked that discussions in the meeting room have developed unhampered by the variety of languages used. Delegates speaking different languages and listening to the interpretation of languages they do not know must be able to understand each other as if they were communicating directly through one and the same language: that is a basic prerequisite for interpretation to be considered worth studying as a process. The best way of judging the quality of interpretation is to listen to a discussion period where people put questions to each other. If all this is carried out in two or three languages, and people prove satisfied with the replies, it can be said that communication was established, that the interpretation was successful and that the process involved was representative.

We also have to bear in mind that the findings on any process under investigation can be distorted if extraneous factors confuse the basic issue. Interpreting is free speech and it should be investigated in connection with spontaneous speech, i.e. extemporaneous interventions and not prepared statements or papers being read out. When we speak, our thoughts are paramount in our minds and words follow suit without our paying attention to them. We think as we speak and so does the interpreter listening to us. When we read out a text however our thinking has already taken place and our thoughts, instead of controlling our words, are merely aroused by them, sometimes we even bypass thinking altogether. The interpreter's performance is not the same in both cases; when translating from texts being read out he has to overcome problems that are quite different from the process of understanding and stating that which was understood which he carries out normally.

A further fact is worth mentioning before embarking on a more detailed account of some of my findings: it is a recurrent fact that at the beginning of any meeting there is much more language transposition or transcoding than later on. This constantly recurring phenomenon can be explained: as long as too much of what is meant remains unknown to the interpreters (although perfectly known to all participants, and therefore unsaid by the speaker) their only recourse is to lag as little as possible behind the speaker's words so as to translate his language. By and by, as the meeting goes on, interpreters analyse the tiniest bits of information, probe more and more deeply into the intended meaning of speakers and, as this stored knowledge builds up, their interpretation departs from the linguistic meaning of the source language and consequently their rendering becomes more natural and their language more native.

The very short passage upon which I am going to comment – it took the speaker 36 seconds to utter it – has been extracted from a panel discussion which was part of a three-day meeting organized last March by the Sugar Industry on the general theme: "Sugar, Diet and Health". This panel discussion took place on the afternoon of the second day; interpreters had already heard and translated papers on sugar and obesity, sugar and diabetes, sucrose and brain chemistry and sucrose and sports. They were therefore quite familiar with the various topics speakers might touch on.

This passage in English and its interpretation into French was chosen from a number of transcripts of recordings I made at that conference. It is intended to be an example of a few of the features that appear when studying simultaneous interpretation. It is of course not the sole basis for the conclusions I shall be presenting here, and not exhaustive as a substratum either. Much more can be said about simultaneous interpretation and its implications for language and memory than I could possibly say within this short time. [. . .] This paper is meant as a typifying example of results obtained so far. The passage is taken from a panel discussion on the role of sugar in the soft drink and food industry; Mr Brooks from Canada is speaking; here are the first sentences of his statement:

> I don't really want to get into the paper that I am presenting this afternoon, but it bears upon the matter that at present is being discussed. I think this is an extremely important point. Apart from certain necessary defensive work from sucrose manufacturers and sucrose users, there is a real need to identify where, within the normal society, sucrose and similar sugars are playing important positive roles. Dr Kingsbury's comments with regard to the sportsmen are pertinent. He is right also to identify the possibility of other needs at other times.

And here is the transcription of the recording showing the parallel development of original and translation:

APART   FROM   CERTAIN   NECESSARY   DEFENSIVE
Je crois   que   le   problème   est   extrêmement

WORK   FROM   SUCROSE   MANUF-
important.   A   part certains   travaux

ACTURERS   AND   SUCROSE   USERS
nécessairement   défensifs

THERE   IS A REAL   NEED   TO   IDENTIFY
de la   part des fabricants   et des   industries utilisatrices de saccha-

WHERE   WITHIN   THE   NORMAL   SOCIETY
rose,   il   faut   préciser

SUCROSE AND SIMILAR SUGARS ARE
                le

PLAYING IMPORTANT POSITIVE ROLES.
                rôle positif et important du saccharose et autres sucres

DR. KINGSBURY'S COMMENTS
chez les bien-portants.

WITH REGARD TO THE SPORTSMEN
Ce que Monsieur Kings –

```
ARE      PERTINENT.     HE   IS  RIGHT   ALSO
bury vient   de nous        dire  à propos  des sportifs est

TO      IDENTIFY     THE   POSSIBILITY
extrêmement          pertinent.    Il a aussi

OF  OTHER   NEEDS   AT   OTHER   TIMES
raison                de              dire qu'il y a

I   DON'T  THINK   THE   TOPIC  IS   A   SIMPLE   ONE
d'autres   besoins   à certains   moments au  plutôt  chez d'autres

WHEN IT GETS DOWN TO IT I .................
personnes.
```

The reader will notice that at the beginning of the transcription, the interpreter is still rendering the previous sentence and that, whilst he is still translating the end of the passage, the speaker is pronouncing a new sentence. This is a reminder that the interpreter receives a continuous stream of information and that interpretation, although shown here on paper, should not be analysed as if it was written translation.

I have arbitrarily subdivided the 36 seconds extract into segments of three seconds each in my presentation in order to present the way the speaker's and interpreter's parallel speeches develop. I have very roughly superimposed the words simultaneously pronounced by them in an effort to reproduce (although very sketchily) what can be heard when listening simultaneously to tape recordings of the two languages.

The time lag between speaker and interpreter

When looking at the transcript it can be observed that there are times when interpretation follows fluently upon the speaker's output with a delay of between 3 to 6 seconds. There are other times however when the interpreter pauses and lets the speaker get very much ahead of him. And there are still other times, usually following a pause in the interpreter's rendering, when the flow of words coming out of his mouth increases to a very quick delivery. Why does this happen and how can it be explained? Let us look at the sentence: *"He is right also to identify the possibility of other needs at other times."* Up to: "He is right also . . .", the interpretation is very fluid, developing smoothly and quickly.

"Ce que Monsieur Kingsbury vient de nous dire à propos des sportifs est extrêmement pertinent. Il a aussi raison de . . ." follows with no hesitation upon the previous sentence but then, upon hearing " . . . to identify the possibility . . . ", there is a pause of over one second, quite a remarkable interruption in such a quick delivery.

I suggest that this pause was necessary for the interpreter to get the amount of information required for his understanding of the speaker's meaning. *To identify the possibility* does not mean anything; more is needed to give this set of words some sense: the interpreter needed to hear "*of other needs at other times*". With lightning speed he was then able to connect these words with the information stored in his cognitive memory. He had translated Dr. Kingsbury's statement approximately ten minutes before translating the Canadian delegate. We have a proof of his remembering, for upon hearing "*Dr. Kingsbury's comments . . .*" he said: "Ce que Monsieur Kingsbury *vient de nous dire . . .*" His words there stem quite normally from sense, a combination of previous knowledge and immediate language understanding. But understanding "*to identify the possibility of other needs at other times*" requires more than the mere recollection of having heard the speech a short while ago.

If interpreting was mere language transposition, nothing could have prevented the interpreter from saying: ". . . *d'identifier la possibilité d'autres besoins à d'autres moments*". The English sentence: "He is right also to identify the possibility of other needs at other times" contains nothing but familiar words, arranged in a syntactic order which can easily be transposed into French. The fact that in his rendering the interpreter chose to say something else ("Il a aussi raison de dire qu'il y a d'autres besoins à certains *moments ou plutôt chez d'autres personnes*") points to a more complex process than a mere understanding of language. To start with, the interpreter does translate literally " . . . *of other needs at other times*" with "*d'autres besoins à d'autres moments*"; he apparently wants to catch up with the speaker but having understood what was meant, he immediately corrects himself by adding: ". . . *ou plutôt chez d'autres personnes*".

Understanding sense is adding a cognitive element to language meaning. What happened here is that the words "*other needs at other times*" merged with previously stored relevant knowledge, as evidenced by the addendum: ". . . *ou plutôt chez d'autres personnes*", that refers to information that has been in store for about ten minutes. In going through Dr. Kingsbury's statement, I found the following sentence:

> There are definitely times when there is a physiological need for sugar in the drinks, not only I think for athletes and sportsmen, but also in children, convalescents, people that aren't physically very active . . .

Of course the interpreter could not have remembered this sentence word for word, but his recollection of the substance was aroused by the mention of "*other needs at other times*", and the conjunction of the two made sense.

The choice of words

Understanding is not the only process of the human mind that can be studied in interpretation. The interpreter is not only a listener, he is also a speaker and while his words are determined by his understanding of the speaker's intended meaning, to some extent they are also based on the speaker's language.

In our example, the words "*sucrose and similar sugars*" are translated into French: "*du saccharose et autres sucres*". Here a word in French (*saccharose*) appears to have been called up to match the English sucrose; the same can be said of *sugar* = sucre, or *important positive* = *positif et important*,etc.

Words that match in translation do so for a number of reasons that do not reflect identical psychological processes. In a previous publication (Lederer 1973), I identified three ways which seem to underlie word matching in translation. The first one I called "glissement phonétique" (phonetic shift): in the present case (E) *positive* = (F) *positif* or (E) *important* equating (F) *important*. A change in pronunciation brings a word from one phonological system over to another and the English word is turned into a French word. The "glissement phonétique" is in some cases fully justified, when controlled by sense as in the present case. At other times it is an important source of language contamination; thus (E) *material* becomes all too often (F) *matériel*, or (E) *to ignore, ignorer*, etc. In simultaneous interpreting, where both languages are constantly present at the same time in short-term memory, it is a great temptation to take a shortcut and be contented with the change in phonetics under the misguided impression that words phonetically similar are semantically identical; fighting this natural trend is one of the main problems in the translation of languages that resemble each other, such as English–French or Italian–French.

The second way words can be matched in translation is through a translation of primary meanings: the word that comes first to mind as an equivalent to the English word is the word that fits the translation; here we find *sugar* = *sucre, needs* = *besoins, manufacturers* = *fabricants, sportsmen* = *sportifs*, etc. The process involved here is very much what most people think interpreting amounts to; the only mental processes appear to be the recognition and transposition of language meaning. Figures are the typical instance of that process in interpretation and yet they are the arch foes of many of the best interpreters who fail to hear and translate correctly even two-digit figures, while having no problem in grasping the most intricate arguments. One finding of immediate interest in connection with figures is related to the interpreter's lagging behind the speaker: whenever figures are rendered correctly although they are embedded in a complex argument, the interpreter abruptly catches up with the speaker and pronounces the figure almost immediately after hearing it. It seems that figures have to be repeated while still within the span of short-term memory.

Primary meaning translation is a process that often proves successful but that just as often can fail. In the present case, *sucre*, for *sugar* is appropriate but in numerous cases primary meanings translated with no regard to sense are not immediately intelligible; so for instance (E) *challenge* is always rendered in French by *défi* or (E) *account for* by *rendre compte*, although *expliquer* is available and much more to the point in French.

Finally a third way of matching words is the deliberate calling up of a specific term to match a given word. Thus (F) *saccharose* for (E) *sucrose*. There the interpreter not only has to find the specific term that does not automatically associate itself with the English, as *sucre* did with *sugar*; he also has to consciously refrain from "glissement phonétique" (*sucrose* would sound so natural in French!). In other cases he would have to repel the primary meaning translation; for instance in the case of "*a fleet of engines*", "*parc de locomotives*" has to replace the automatic urge to say "*flotte*" or "*flotille*" before becoming automatically associated with "*fleet*" after having been said a few times. In the case of *saccharose*, it can be assumed that since this interpretation took place on the second day of the meeting, the calling up of the word did not require a conscious effort on the part of the interpreter, for whom the equivalent had probably by then become automatic reflex. But the phenomenon of having from time to time to summon consciously a word or an expression is too common in interpretation not to be mentioned here.

The verbal manifestations of sense in interpretation

In our English–French extract it is striking to note a constant intertwining of what might appear to be a word for word translation and of phrases that, although initiated by the words of the speaker, do not resemble them literally. A number of the words and phrases heard in English by the interpreter are transposed into French: "*A part certains travaux nécessairement défensifs de la part des fabricants*" is a literal translation of "*Apart from certain necessary defensive work from sucrose manufacturers*". This does not mean that the interpreter, when doing that literal translation, puts his intellect at rest. That he understood and not only repeated "*defensive work*" comes out clearly in the way he later translates "*within the normal society*" with "*bien-portants*".

Here a few words of explanation may be necessary: sugar manufacturers are not only doing promotion and marketing work in order to boost their sales, they also subsidize a number of laboratories doing research on the role of sugar in diabetes, coronary diseases, dental caries, etc. in the hope that results will ultimately show that sugar is not as bad for health as currently held by public opinion. The meeting brings together a number of scientists who have submitted papers on their findings in those various fields. The interpreter knows all this; he therefore cannot but understand what "*necessary defensive work*" means. The verbal manifestation of his understanding is found in the French rendering:

> *il faut préciser le rôle positif et important du saccharose et autres sucres chez les bien-portants.*

There is nothing in this French sentence that resembles phonetically or semantically the phrase "*within the normal society*". No better example could be found of the way in which something that is understood not only can be rendered in a form that is entirely alien to the original form but also kept in store for a period exceeding the short-term memory span, and rendered at a place that is adequate in French.

"*Defensive work*" meant research work on various diseases. "*Normal society*" where sugar is playing a positive role, means "*bien-portants*". The choice in French of words differing from the English words shows that the interpreter understood both this part of the sentence and the first part on defensive work. We find a similar example of language disparity in the same sentence, where "*sucrose users*" is rendered by "*industries utilisatrices de saccharose*". The speaker could not have meant the end users, the panel discussion is on the role of sugar in the soft drinks and food industry. This is obviously what the speaker meant by "*sucrose users*". The interpreter makes this even more obvious by stating it explicitly.

The difference between sense and linguistic meaning is clearly revealed in the two equivalents I have just shown : *users* = *industries utilisatrices*, *normal society* = *bien-portants*, or earlier, *comments* = *vient de dire*. This variance in the interpreter's expression as compared to the basic meanings of words is the tangible evidence that can be seized upon to probe into nonverbal thinking. The point here is not how interpreters arrange their phrases syntactically so as to fit the requirements of their own mother tongue, but the fact that their wording reflects more than the knowledge of two languages and the ability to establish equivalents between the two. It reflects the thinking process that goes on during interpreting, something which obviously is not unique to interpreters or interpretation but applies to the understanding process in general.

Units of meaning

My investigations of recordings of interpretations led me to put forth the general concept of units of meaning. I suggest that such units are segments of sense appearing at irregular intervals in the mind of those who listen to speech with a deliberate desire to understand it. As long as there is nothing but words available, such as in our case: ". . . to *identify the possibility* . . ." recognition of language sounds is possible (at least in most cases, even though recognition of sounds often requires the assistance of sense), but no additional mental operations can be carried out. With the appearance of *"other needs"*, the words present in short-term memory seem to pull together and merge with the recollection of knowledge acquired since the beginning of the meeting, all of a sudden making sense.

A colleague of mine who is preparing her Doctor's degree at our University, Miss Bertone, has drawn a parallel between the emergence of sense and Jacques Lacan's *point de capiton*. For Lacan, understanding is achieved with the last word of sentences, when words seem to pull together to give birth to an idea. He compares the process of understanding with the mattress maker's pulling up his thread every few stitches, making the *point de capiton* that divides up his fabric at regular intervals (Lacan 1966).

Chunks of sense appear in interpretation whenever the interpreter has a clear understanding of a speaker's intended meaning. They can be preceded by a slight pause or come after a few probing words that are literally translated. At other times they are rendered immediately, as *"ce que Monsieur Kingsbury vient de nous dire"* for *"Dr Kingsbury's comments"*. Units of meaning are the synthesis of a number of words present in short-term memory associating with previous cognitive experiences or recollections; this merging into sense leaves a cognitive trace in the memory while the short-term memory is taking up and storing the ensuing words until a new synthesis occurs and a new cognitive unit adds up to those previously stored in the cognitive memory.

Word prediction and sense expectation

Units of meaning are not a grammatical segmentation of language into syntactic units. It often happens in ordinary life that we grasp the intended meaning of a speaker before he finishes his sentence. This also happens to interpreters. Anticipation can take different forms: either the interpreter actually says a word (the verb for

instance) before the speaker has uttered the corresponding word or, more commonly, he puts in a word at the correct place in his French sentence which, if
compared in time, is uttered after the original, but so soon afterwards and at so
correct a place in his own language that there is no doubt the interpreter summoned
it before hearing the original.

When studying these anticipations a clear distinction should be drawn between
anticipations based on sense expectation and anticipations based on language prediction. In the first case the interpreter who is piling up one unit of meaning after the
other in his cognitive memory (they do not keep separate there, but they all contribute to his understanding of the speech as it unfolds) knows, rightly or wrongly, what
the speaker is aiming at. In the other case he predicts the appearance of words that
frequently occur together in speech. We have an example of this stochastic process
in our passage here. The speaker, to wind up his sentence, says ". . . *where, within
normal society, sucrose and similar sugars are playing important positive roles*".

The interpreter who had been speaking rather quickly while the speaker was
uttering the beginning of that sentence remains silent while hearing: ". . . *society,
sucrose and similar sugars are playing important . . .*"; the only word he pronounces is
"*le*"! Then he gets the hint and resumes speaking: ". . . *rôle positif et important du
saccharose et autres sucres chez les bien-portants*".

(F) "*rôle*" is pronounced practically at the same time as the English word "*important*". It is a fact that anyone would expect the word "roles" (or any other word with a
similar semantic content) after hearing: "*There is a real need to identify where, within the
normal society, sucrose and similar sugars are playing important . . .*"

Sense expectation is different.

I shall have to resort to interpretation from German into French where evidence of sense expectation is easier to collect, since the syntactic structures of
German and French are wide apart and literal translation less frequent. The following example is an extract from an extensive study of simultaneous interpretation
which is now nearly completed.

At a railways meeting the representative of an international financial body with
headquarters in Switzerland said the following sentence

> *Die Schweizerischen Bundesbahnen haben uns angeboten diese Presseveran-
> staltung, die vom Vertreter des kommerziellen Dienstes . . .*

I stop here to show what the interpreter said in French in the meanwhile:

> "*Les CFF nous ont offert de nous aider à organiser . . .*"

The French word *organiser* coincides in time with the last German word quoted so
far, *Dienstes*; so there is clear evidence that ". . *nous aider à organiser . . .*" is an
anticipation. *Organiser* is language prediction : "*Die Schweizerischen Bundesbahnen haben
uns angeboten diese Presseveranstaltung . . .*" calls for something semantically equivalent
to *organiser*. We shall see that the German word was *durchzuführen*. But where does
nous aider come from? "*Les CFF nous ont offert . . .*" is closely matching "*Die
Schweizerischen Bundesbahnen haben uns angeboten . . .*" but why ". . . *de nous aider à
organiser*", where only the word *organiser* could be expected in association with

Veranstaltung? The sense expectation *aider à* is vindicated by the end of the German sentence:

> *Die Schweizerischen Bundesbahnen haben uns angeboten diese Presseveran-staltung, die vom Vertreter des kommerziellen Dienstes in der Gruppe Guignard vorgeschlagen worden war, gemeinsam mit uns durchzuführen.*

So *aider à organiser* was anticipating ". . . *gemeinsam mit uns durchzuführen*".

Sense anticipation is easy to explain. In our case, the speaker has been giving details for several minutes about the way his company intended to organise a presentation to the press of various new types of passenger cars. So obviously when he starts saying: "*Die Schweizerischen Bundesbahnen haben uns angeboten diese Pres-severanstaltung . . .*", this could not merely call for "*durchzuführen*", since his company was also involved. Once again we have here an example of the way cognitive memory constantly intervenes in communication.

In this short paper and with the few examples that could be drawn from 36 seconds of speech, I have tried to show some of the extraordinary complexity involved in speech understanding and oral translation. If interpreting was mere shadowing in another language, consisting of translating the individual meaning of each successive word in the speaker's output, or if it was just translation of language with only problems of syntactic restructuring and occasionally technical terms, it would be an interesting but limited field of investigation.

As it involves a complex series of cognitive activities, it offers I believe an avenue for an investigation of the thinking processes involved in understanding and speaking. This avenue might not have been opened up, and the thinking processes might have remained in their black boxes, had the comparison of interpretation and original speech yielded no different results from the comparison of languages as such.

Much that is revealed by interpretation is nothing other than normal speech mechanisms. I hope these few glimpses of how interpretation operates will contribute to their better understanding.

References

Lacan, J. (1966) *Ecrits*, Paris: Seuil.
Lederer, M. (1973) "La traduction: transcoder ou réexprimer?", *Etudes de Linguistique Appliquée* 12, Paris: Didier.

Part 3

Modeling the Process

INTRODUCTION

A S IS EVIDENT from the studies presented in Parts 1 and 2, early research on interpreting, which was largely confined to the simultaneous mode, was essentially concerned with the psycholinguistic processes involved in the activity. This focus on the cognitive process(es) remains an enduring feature in contemporary Interpreting Studies. In the words of Gile (1994: 152), "Most researchers would probably agree that the medium and long term objective of present day interpretation research is to gain a better understanding of interpretation processes." Similarly, Moser-Mercer (1994a: 15), in describing what she views as the two main paradigms in the IS research community, states: "Both concentrate on the process of interpreting and not on the product." So does this part, in which the notion of "process" will be used in a broad sense, mainly to distinguish it from the "product" of interpreting, which forms the theme of Part 5. While the three papers in the present part tend to focus on the micro-level cognitive processes "inside" the interpreter, they can also be situated within a broader perspective on the interpreting process, thus covering the role and impact of "external" variables as well.

Efforts by IS researchers to construct models of the interpreting process have exhibited considerable variety, not least in terms of the level of abstraction chosen by the analyst, and of the theoretical line of approach to the "reality" to be modeled: the first detailed process model of simultaneous interpreting, put forward by Gerver (1971, 1976), rested on findings from experimental research in an information-processing paradigm (cf. Part 1); B. Moser (1976, 1978) adapted Massaro's (1975) speech comprehension model to the simultaneous interpreting process; Kirchhoff (1976a, and in this volume) built upon translation-linguistic and information-theoretical foundations for her (psycholinguistic) communication model, later taken up by Kondo (1990); Chernov (1978, 1979, and in this volume) used psycholinguistic research to develop a redundancy-based probability prediction model; Lederer

(1978a), on the other hand, based her model of eight constituent operations on an observation of output data; whereas Roothaer (1978) adapted an early psycholinguistic speech production model, and Mackintosh (1985) suggested applying the Kintsch and van Dijk (1978) model of discourse comprehension and production to both simultaneous and consecutive interpreting; drawing on some of these processing models developed for spoken-language interpreting, Cokely (1985, 1992) developed "a sociolinguistic model" of the (sign-language) interpreting process – and the list could obviously be continued beyond the first one and a half decades of modeling efforts.

The two best-known full-process models as well as several partial models of the interpreting process are reviewed in the first paper of this part by **Barbara Moser-Mercer**, herself the author of an early information-processing model of (spoken-language) simultaneous interpreting. Her emphasis is on models which are fine-grained enough to allow for their experimental testing and verification. Apart from the cognitive psychological and neurolinguistic methodologies envisaged for this task, the approach to modeling described by Moser-Mercer (1997a, and in this volume) is also closely linked to efforts at computer-based implementations of translational natural-language processing, such as those by Lonsdale (1996, 1997) for simultaneous interpreting, and by Kitano (1993), LuperFoy (1996, 1997) and researchers in the Verbmobil project (Jekat and Klein 1996; Jekat 1997) for automatic dialogue interpreting.

Elsewhere, in a more extensive review, Moser-Mercer (1997b) also gives a critical assessment of the neurolinguistic model by Paradis (1994) and takes up some of the broader issues involved in modeling simultaneous interpreting as a complex, time-constrained, multiple cognitive-processing task. While she reaffirms the methodological rationale for decomposing the interpreting process into separate stages or skill components, she also stresses the need to move beyond discrete processing stages and the respective subskills to account for interpreters' dynamic strategies. One such (simultaneous) interpreting strategy, which can be related to the "prediction features" in the models by B. Moser (1976, 1978), Chernov (1978) and Lederer (1978a, 1981), is "anticipation," which has been the subject both of numerous investigations (e.g. Dalitz 1973; Mattern 1974; Lederer 1978a, 1981; Salevsky 1987; Adamowicz 1989; Gile 1992; Jörg 1995, 1997; Kalina 1998; Riccardi 1998; Van Besien 1999a, 1999b) and of didactic proposals (e.g. Kurz 1983; Van Dam 1989; Viaggio 1992; Kalina 1998). Similarly, "compression" (chunking, condensing) has been addressed as a processing strategy in both simultaneous and consecutive interpreting (e.g. Alexieva 1983; Mackintosh 1985; Hu 1990; Kutz 1990; Dam 1993; Sunnari 1995). A theoretical and didactic approach to (conference) interpreting that is wholly centered on the notion of strategy was put forward by Kalina (Kohn and Kalina 1996; Kalina 1998), whose broad usage of the term subsumes (reception and production-related) text-processing operations like segmentation, inferencing, syntactic transformation, coherence-building or delivery under the heading of "strategic processes." Kalina (1998) in particular emphasizes the link between strategies and process models, on the one hand, and processing strategies and (teachable) skills, on the other.

The application of theoretical modeling to interpreter training, more specifically aptitude testing, has been described for both of the early full-process models of simultaneous interpreting (cf. Gerver *et al.* 1984; Moser-Mercer 1984, 1985, 1994b), and Moser-Mercer (1997a: 8, and in this volume) affirms that her cognitive-science-based model "has been used fairly extensively for pedagogical purposes." In contrast, the more holistic processing model by **Daniel Gile** originated as an intuition-based didactic model (1985a) and was subsequently applied in empirical research, both by Gile himself (e.g. 1999b) and by others (e.g. Dawrant 1996; Schjoldager 1996; Lamberger-Felber 1998). Gile's Effort Model (*modèle d'efforts*) was first formulated for simultaneous interpretation (Gile 1985a) and was later extended to consecutive interpreting and sight translation (Gile 1995a, 1995c, 1997, and in this volume). Gile's model is not so much a fine-grained analysis of the sequential cognitive processing operations in interpreting as a conceptual tool for explaining interpreters' performance limitations as a result of cognitive constraints. The notion of limited attentional resources or "processing capacity," which can be traced back to early work on simultaneous interpreting (e.g. Gerver 1971; Kirchhoff 1976a), is at the heart of Gile's account of the interpreting process and crucial to his discussion of interpreting strategies and tactics. In contrast to the idealistic conception of the Paris School, as represented by Seleskovitch and Lederer (cf. Part 2), Gile focuses on professional interpreters' processing failures, and accounts for them in terms of attention management difficulties intrinsic to the process. Equally antithetical is Gile's foregrounding of processing issues specific to particular language pairs – a topic which is addressed prominently also in the third paper in this part.

The "cognitive-pragmatic analysis" of the interpreting process developed by **Robin Setton** in his PhD research (1999a) goes beyond – and, in some sense, reconciles – existing theoretical approaches: while accepting a cognitive-science orientation for (simultaneous) interpreting research, Setton faults information-processing models, both of the sequential architectural and of the holistic type, for lacking an operational account of contextualization. At the same time, he is basically sympathetic also to the "interpretive theory" (*théorie du sens*) of the Paris School and its foregrounding of extra-linguistic knowledge and context (cf. Part 2), but disqualifies the key notion of "sense" as essentialistic and underspecified. Setton also acknowledges the merits of the *skopos* theoretical model of interpreting as a complex course of action (Pöchhacker 1994a, 1994b, 1995a), with all its social, psychological and textual variables and relationships, but rightly points to its limitations in making its rich and open-ended account of the situational context operational for an online analysis of the process. (The same would have to be said about Cokely's (1992) "sociolinguistically sensitive model," which posits a broad bicultural knowledge base ranging from syntactic, semantic and contextual knowledge to associated relations and cultural awareness, without specifying its step-by-step operation in the interpreting process.) Endeavoring to move beyond what he acknowledges as the three most influential contemporary approaches, Setton (1999a) draws on cognitive linguistics (mental models, relevance theory) to fashion an analytical tool for "intermediate representations" with which to overcome what he graphically describes as the "towering challenges: Knowledge, and its still fuzzy relationship with Context, which in previous usage seems ambivalently to straddle the objective and the subjective, smeared across the text and the rest of the environment" (1999a: 60).

The account offered by Setton (1998, and in this volume) is arguably the most comprehensive and sophisticated model of the interpreting process in IS today. Re-affirming both the role of linguistics in the framework of cognitive science and the need for detailed step-by-step corpus analysis, Setton professes interdisciplinarity while at the same time demanding an immediate link with authentic interpreting practice. What is more, Setton's approach also seems germane to the discourse analytical paradigms used for the study of interpreting in dialogic community settings (cf. Wadensjö 1992, 1998; Meyer 1998; Mason 1999), establishing as it does an integrated account of the complex dynamics of the cognitive processes, the (con)textual variables in the act of communication (see Parts 4 and 5), and the constraints and relationships of the interactional setting (see Part 7).

F**OLLOWING HER TRAINING** as a conference interpreter (at the University of Innsbruck) in the early 1970s, Barbara Moser was among the first practitioners to follow up their professional education with a doctoral dissertation on interpreting. Unlike her contemporaries at ESIT in Paris, she sought to apply advances in other disciplines, especially psycholinguistics and cognitive psychology, to her groundbreaking work on modeling the process of simultaneous interpreting. Indeed, she has championed this interdisciplinary approach ever since and has cooperated closely with researchers in the cognitive sciences, not only in carrying out empirical studies on topics like aptitude testing, expertise and stress in simultaneous interpreting (e.g. Moser-Mercer *et al.* 1998, 2000), but also in the launch, in 1996, of *Interpreting*, the first international refereed journal devoted solely to the study of interpreting.

Remaining active as a conference interpreter and AIIC member throughout, Barbara Moser-Mercer has had a distinguished career as an educator in the field of conference interpreting. She has held top leadership positions both at the Monterey Institute of International Studies, where she also set up a degree course in terminology and machine translation in the 1980s, and at the École de traduction et d'interprétation of the University of Geneva, where, as Professor of Conference Interpreting and Vice-President, she launched international "training the trainers" courses as well as a doctoral research program.

The paper reprinted here was originally published in a volume of papers from an international workshop on *Machine Translation and Translation Theory* (Hildesheim, 1994), which included several contributions on automatic dialogue interpreting.

Further reading: Moser 1978; Moser-Mercer 1997b.

Barbara Moser-Mercer

PROCESS MODELS IN SIMULTANEOUS INTERPRETATION

[. . .]

The complexity of the interpreting process –
full process models

THE COMPLEXITY OF the interpreting process has without doubt daunted many researchers who might have been interested in developing research models. The two full process models developed in the 1970s (Gerver 1976; Moser 1976, 1978) built upon the then fairly novel approach to psychological inquiry: the information processing approach.

Both researchers proceeded on the conviction that advances in understanding the interpreting process would not come from applying the introspective method, which does not, by itself, lead to precise and quantitative knowledge. Psychologists have been able to point to the limitations of this method by showing that the causes of human behavior are by and large not understood (Massaro 1989). While documenting phenomenal experience in interpreting was considered an important activity, it was judged to be totally insufficient in terms of providing researchers with the type of consistent theoretical framework necessary to study methodological, logical, and theoretical issues in a consistent and coherent manner.

While neither researcher pretended to offer a model that corresponded to the real-life phenomena, their motivation was to offer formal representations of the state-of-the-art knowledge of the interpretation process and to encourage consistency in researching it, to permit specific predictions about certain stages during processing, as well as to develop empirical tests of such predictions. It was understood that as new empirical evidence was obtained the authors would be obliged to modify their models (Flores d'Arcais 1978).

Gerver's model

In Gerver's model of the simultaneous interpretation process (see Figure 1) two main aspects of the process can be described:

- Permanent structural features (various types of memory systems)
- Control processes to be selected at the option of the interpreter (and that potentially co-determine the distribution of attention to the different components of the task).

Gerver postulates the existence of some kind of buffer storage (temporary storage) in which information can be acquired while the interpreter operates on the translation of a previous message segment. This buffer storage is necessary to maintain the results of intermediate steps of analysis. Gerver then goes on to outline the operations in short-term operational memory (Gerver 1976: 194) which would cover all the operations after retrieval of information from the buffer.

"Decode and store" refers to the decoding of phonetic representations of each segment of the source language message and to understanding the underlying structure. At some point understanding of the message by the interpreter occurs, although this is not explicated in the flow-chart. Thus, the transfer problem is not touched upon at all.

The interpreter then may choose between checking (testing) his translation for goodness of fit to the original before beginning output or deciding to begin production at once. Even if he chooses the second path he will still match the output with the original message or with whatever memory trace of this message is still available. If no match or a mismatch occurs, the interpreter will stop output and retry or stop and continue if time for retry is insufficient. There is good support in the literature for the hypothesis that a message remains in temporary storage sufficiently long to be compared to the target language version (see Treisman 1964 for experimental evidence, accounts of restarts, and corrections in many other experiments).

Gerver concludes that his model is but a first approximation to a model of the processes involved in simultaneous interpretation and that various aspects of the model "can either be made more explicit or discarded in favor of more likely hypotheses" (Gerver 1976: 202).

Moser's model of the simultaneous interpretation process

This model is based on the information-processing model of understanding speech by Massaro (1975) and represents a flow diagram of the temporal course of simultaneous interpretation (see Figure 2). Boxes represent structural components that describe the nature of the information stored at a given stage of processing, whereas the intermediate headings represent functional components, describing the individual operations performed at a particular stage of processing. Each diamond represents a decision point in the process, provision is made for rehearsal loops even if a decision furnishes a YES-answer. This is due to the simultaneity of certain

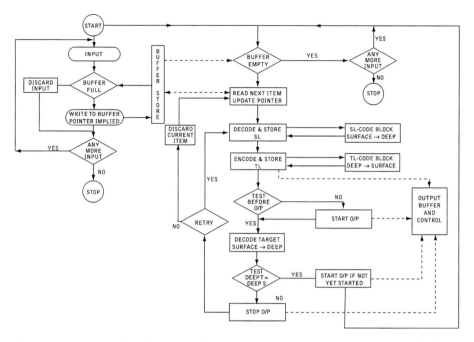

Figure 1   A model of the simultaneous interpretation process (adapted from
Gerver 1976).

processing stages when attention is devoted both to the incoming message and to the
operations involved in the target language output.

The processes described in the central column are presumed to occur in
working memory with constant access and feedback to long-term memory (LTM).
Contrary to certain interpretations of this model (Sánchez Martínez 1988) the
double-headed arrows to LTM do not represent exclusive lines of access to a
particular type of information in LTM. Bottom-up processes (immediate input
processing) and top-down processes (knowledge of the world interacting with new
information) occur at every stage of the process.

This model features a decision point PREDICTION POSSIBLE not mentioned
at all in the Gerver model. It appears relatively late in the flow-chart. Several
colleagues have tried to argue it should appear earlier in the process, but without
having already processed a certain amount of prior information prediction on future
input is simply not possible.

The question now arises as to how useful these two full-scale models have been
in further analysing the interpretation process. There is no literature on the use of
Gerver's model in an experimental setting and, due to the author's untimely and
early death, he himself was not able to interpret new research findings in light of his
model. As to my own model, it has been used fairly extensively for pedagogical
purposes (design of introductory courses in simultaneous interpretation) and provided the basis for a long-term study on aptitude testing (Moser-Mercer 1984).
Although Sánchez Martínez (1988) indicated using the model to interpret empirical
data from simultaneous interpretation, he did in fact not make use of it but reverted
to purely intuitive interpretations of the evidence.

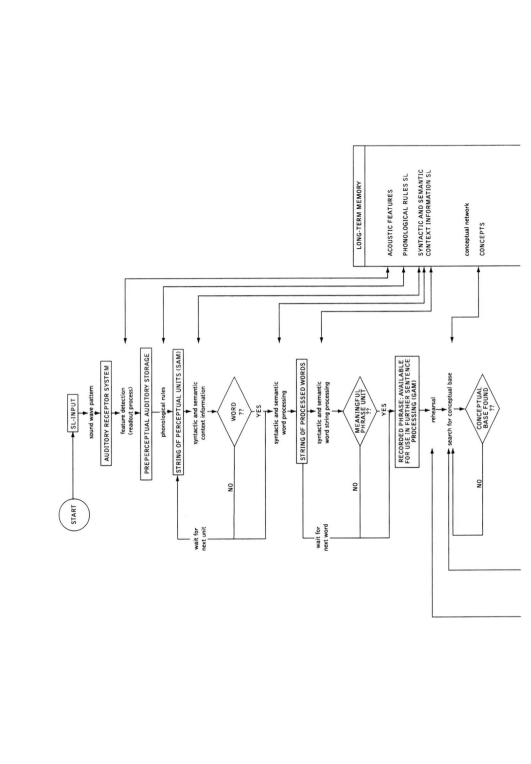

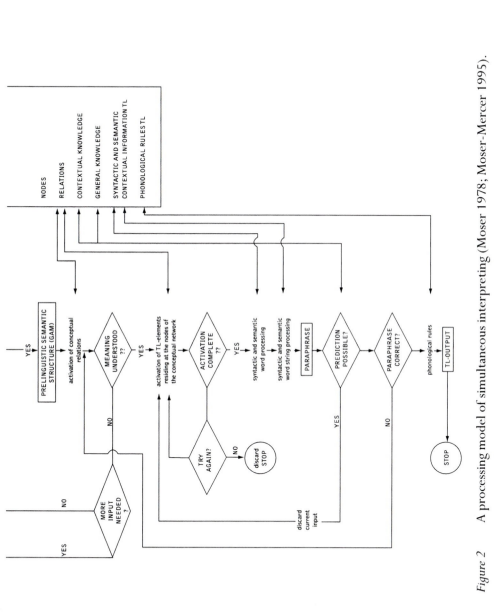

Figure 2   A processing model of simultaneous interpreting (Moser 1978; Moser-Mercer 1995).

Partial process models

This category includes experimental approaches to interpreting that led to partial adaptations of models developed for language processing: Lambert (1983), Dillinger (1989), Darò and Fabbro (1994).

Lambert's (1983) depth-of-processing model

In 1972, Craik and Lockhart challenged the information-processing approach and offered levels-of-processing as an alternative to the standard information-processing stage model. In this approach it is assumed that our memory is dependent upon the depth (level) of processing of incoming information. The deeper one processes this information the more one should retain.

Lambert proposed four possible levels of depth of analysis: consecutive interpretation, listening, shadowing and simultaneous interpretation. Higher retention scores were obtained following listening and consecutive interpretation and lower scores followed shadowing and simultaneous interpretation. During the two tasks that required no concurrent vocalization retention was higher: vocalization may have possibly masked the auditory stimulus, less information may have been available for processing, thus less information was retained. Lambert, however, ran into the same problem as other researchers working in this paradigm, i.e. the testability of this theory. The measurement of depth of processing appears extremely difficult and the only assessment is by memory performance (Baddeley 1978, in Massaro 1989) which renders the notion of depth of processing circular.

The study of component processes of simultaneous interpreting (Dillinger 1989)

Dillinger focused on possible differences in comprehension processing between bilinguals with no prior interpreting experience and experienced conference interpreters. Contemporary cognitive science conceives of text comprehension "as a set of quasi-independent component processes which are said to construct and transform in different ways multiple mental representations of the input text, based both on text properties and on different types of prior knowledge" (Dillinger 1989: 12). Working on the basis of a model of text comprehension by Frederiksen (1975), Dillinger isolates the processes of the language processor (lexical processing, syntactic processing, and proposition generation or semantic interpretation) and those of the general cognitive system; the latter are assumed to function inferentially to enhance the coherence of the output of the language processor, for example by filling in missing elements, by organizing it in terms of macrostructures, schemas, frames, and by integrating it with existing knowledge. He also assumes that "input will always be represented at the maximal level of representation to which its analysis can be taken by the processor" (Marslen-Wilson and Tyler 1980: 66 in Dillinger 1989: 13).

Some of Dillinger's findings came as a surprise at least to this author, in particular his experimental proof that experience had a weak quantitative effect on interpreting overall (experienced interpreters performed 16.6 % more accurately than the inexperienced bilinguals). He found some support for the notion that experienced interpreters may have learned to be more selective in the surface information they will process semantically. That is, for the experienced interpreter the subprocess of proposition generation may be more closely tailored to the needs of subsequent frame processing. He came to the conclusion, on the basis of his data, that experienced interpreters have not acquired any special set of abilities, rather that normal comprehension processes are more flexible than previously believed.

Thus, comprehension in interpreting is not a specialized ability, but the application of an existing skill under more unusual circumstances (Dillinger 1994) and comprehension in interpreting is characterized by all of the same component processes as listening, with an emphasis on semantic processing, in particular proposition generation. He concludes from this that the interpreter's performance is limited by the same broad parameters that limit text comprehension in general, i.e. the nature of the text itself and the prior knowledge that they can bring to bear on understanding it. He left open the question whether the findings would be the same with more complex text materials or at higher presentation rates and limited his research to the comprehension part of the interpreting process, deliberately leaving out memory and production.

Memory systems in simultaneous interpretation (Darò and Fabbro 1994)

Darò and Fabbro propose a general model of memory during simultaneous interpretation which is based on the principles of memory put forward by Baddeley (1990) and Tulving (1987). Recent research in memory has led to a revision of concepts underlying short-term and long-term memory.

For short-term memory Baddeley (1986, 1990) substitutes a system called working memory. Working memory is responsible for both retaining and processing information while at the same time contributing to essential cognitive activities such as reasoning and comprehension. Working memory has three components; the most important is the central executive which regulates information flow within working memory, retrieves information from other memory systems such as LTM and processes and stores information.

There are two additional slave systems: the phonological loop maintains verbally coded information, while the visuo-spatial sketchpad is involved in the short-term processing and maintenance of material which has a strong visual or spatial component. The central executive allocates inputs to the phonological loop and the sketchpad system; these activities are driven by processing resources within the central executive, but which have finite capacities. Among the cognitive tasks that involve the central executive are: mental arithmetic, recall of lengthy lists of digits, logical reasoning, random letter generation, semantic verification, recollection of events from LTM, etc.

Theoretical progress on the central executive has been relatively slow, and experimental methodologies for studying the nature and extent of executive involvement in particular tasks are still under development.

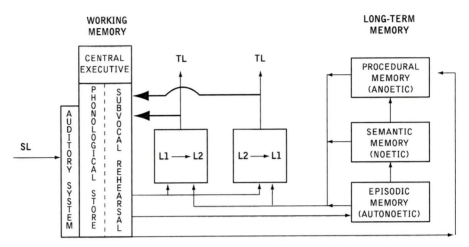

Figure 3   A general model of memory during simultaneous interpretation (Darò and Fabbro 1994).

Much of the current work on the regulatory functions of the central executive is guided by a model of attentional control of action developed by Shallice (1982, 1988; Norman and Shallice 1980). Action is controlled in two ways. Well-learned or "automatic" activities are guided by schemas that are triggered by environmental cues. Schemas can be hierarchically organized. Skilled drivers, for example, will have a driving schema that activates subroutines such as steering, gear-changing and braking schemas. When driving, the driving schema will be activated and all its subroutines primed, so that the sight of red lights at the rear of the car ahead should suffice to provide the environmental cue to trigger the braking schema.

Potential conflicts between ongoing schema-controlled activities can be resolved routinely by a contention scheduling system. But when novel activities are involved, there is a higher-level central executive (or supervisory attentional system, SAS) that intervenes to control action. SAS inhibits and activates schemas directly and so can override the routine process of contention scheduling. By combining the powerful but resource-demanding SAS and the autonomous process of contention scheduling, human action is controlled by an efficient and responsive system.

Darò and Fabbro (1994) conclude on the basis of data from experiments on verbal memory and phonological interference during simultaneous interpretation that working memory starts processing the source-language input prior to its translation into the target language. Verbal chunks are held for about 10 seconds and then either fade away or are further processed. At this stage, the verbal chunks can be transferred to the translation systems or to the long-term memory systems of explicit (episodic and semantic) and implicit (procedural) memory, where they may be stored. Sometimes, however, a series of chunks is not immediately translated, but processed and coalesced with the contribution of long-term memory systems into a sentence comprised of these chunks. Long-term memory assists the neurofunctional systems that account for the translation process. Reduced recall found by Darò and Fabbro (1994) as well as Lambert (1989) and Isham (1994) is partially due to phonological interference from the TL message with subvocal rehearsal procedures in working memory.

Ongoing research

Investigations such as these into the human memory systems in conjunction with findings from neuropsychology and neurophysiology may well bring us a step closer to understanding the interpreting process and any strategies the interpreter might employ. The performance of a simultaneous interpreter depends on the possibility of monitoring, shifting and distributing selective attention on different parallel tasks, a capability which is partly unconscious and partly voluntary. Neurophysiological research indicates the high degree of automaticity of a large number of unconscious processes.

Daneman and Carpenter (1980, in Gathercole and Baddeley 1993) suggest that our capacity for processing and storing linguistic information directly determines the accuracy and efficiency with which we process language for meaning. They go on to speculate that it is the speed and efficiency with which such cognitive operations are executed, rather than individual variations in total available resources, that are responsible for working memory differences in individuals.

Isham (1994) in his experimental comparison between two groups of bilinguals and professional interpreters arrived at the conclusion that there are two types of interpreters: Type I interpreters translated input on a sentence-by-sentence basis and paid attention to the surface form of these sentences, which aided verbatim recall. Type II interpreters, on the other hand, exhibited quite different processing behavior: they apparently were oblivious to the presence of syntactic boundaries and thus seemed to process incoming sentences in a way that drew attention away from their surface form, thus leaving little trace in memory of the original parsing of words into clause or sentence units. Isham concludes that deverbalization is only one possible stage of interpretation, and not necessarily a required one (between English and French). He qualifies, however, that a strictly word-for-word transcoding of the SL is not possible, and thus coined the term "form-based approach" for the interpreting strategy chosen by Type I interpreters, and "meaning-based approach" for that of Type II interpreters.

Whether we should term these approaches strategies, which would imply that they are consciously chosen, or processes, remains to be determined. Experience has shown that some interpreters may choose one approach for certain materials and for working under certain conditions and another in different working conditions and for different types of text. External factors such as listening conditions, accents, density of incoming material, fatigue, familiarity with subject matter, etc., all seem to influence the choice of approach of these interpreters. The loose use of terms such as automatisms, strategies, translation problems in much of the literature on processing issues in translation and interpretation has not contributed at all to a careful delineation of processes and sub-processes and has, if anything, masked some of the essential underlying issues.

Research into the degree of automaticity of processes in interpreting is currently underway at the University of Geneva. Within the framework of a large, interdisciplinary project on acquisition of language processing strategies, work focuses on the acquisition of translation and interpretation strategies. In the first phase of this long-term project language fluency of incoming students is evaluated as a potential determiner for successful acquisition of translation and interpretation skills. By making a clear distinction between base-line skills of students beginning their studies and trained professionals, the goal is to shed more light on strategy acquisition, development of automatisms and individual processing differences. There should be some cross-fertilization between this line of research and computer modeling of the interpreting process.

Recent research in speech perception (see Massaro 1994 for a review) indicates that humans use multiple sources of information (auditory, visual and tactile) in the perceptual recognition and understanding of spoken language. Experiments in bimodal (auditory and visual) speech perception (Cohen and Massaro 1994; Massaro et al. 1993a; Massaro et al. 1993b) across languages lend further support to the notion that individuals evaluate and integrate information from multiple sources and that the underlying mechanisms for speech perception are similar across language and culture (English, Japanese and Spanish were the languages/cultures studied in these experiments).

These experiments are currently being replicated with conference interpreters at the University of Geneva to provide experimental support for interpreters' intuitive claim that one has to see the speaker to interpret well, but more importantly, to develop a more comprehensive view of information sources (nonverbal communication; for a review of the role played in conference interpreting by non-vocal signals sent by listeners see Bühler 1985) and their importance for the interpreting process. This should be of interest to machine-assisted interpreting of dialogues, since particularly in small negotiating settings, nonverbal communication and turn-taking appear to assume particular importance.

Conclusions

By distinguishing clearly between three levels of inquiry, that of our phenomenal experience (introspective explanations), that of functional mental processes (information processing states) and that of our physiological brain states (neural states), one line of research in simultaneous interpreting has focused on providing theoretical explanations and experimental proof of certain mental processes. It is this similarity in approach that allows us to group all of the approaches described in this paper under the information-processing paradigm. All researchers operate in an interdisciplinary environment, integrating findings from and collaborating with neighboring disciplines, trying to fit experimental results to existing models.

Certain criticism has been leveled at this line of research, especially in terms of its artificiality, i.e. its insistence on carefully controlled experiments, and in terms of its lack of comprehensiveness, i.e. not integrating all aspects of the interpreting situation (cultural, situational, etc.). We often refer to what is going on in the mind of the interpreter/translator as the black box: within the human information processing framework we want to find out how many boxes there are, how they work and how they interact. This approach has proven fairly productive in studying other kinds of complex human performance (e.g. in reading) and enables us to study methodological, logical, and theoretical issues in a consistent and coherent manner (Massaro 1989). But, as I indicated earlier, no model is meant to correspond exactly to the phenomena under study; if it did, it would no longer be a model but identical to the phenomena.

Without such careful delineation of processing stages and experimental controls we might easily be led to interpret performance differences in interpreting as processing differences, when indeed they might have been due to information differences. It is this attention to detail that is by and large missing in so-called general, all-encompassing theoretical treatises on translatology: the theoretical framework provides only a very coarse mesh that ultimately allows researchers to fit all kinds of empirical data. The conclusions drawn are sometimes quite tempting (Seleskovitch 1975; Pöchhacker 1994) but non-verifiable. A model such as the one developed under Verbmobil may ultimately be able to glean useful information from a variety of approaches (cf. Hauenschild and Heizmann 1997).

References

Baddeley, A. D. (1978) "The Trouble with Levels: A Reexamination of Craik and Lockhart's Framework for Memory Research," *Psychological Review* 16: 139–52.

—— (1986) *Working Memory*, Oxford: Clarendon Press.

—— (1990) *Human Memory. Theory and Practice*, London: Lawrence Erlbaum Associates.

Bühler, H. (1985) "Conference Interpreting – A Multichannel Communication Phenomenon," *Meta* 30 (1): 49–54.

Cohen, M. M. and Massaro, D. W. (1994) "Development and Experimentation with Synthetic Visible Speech," *Behavior Research Methods, Instruments and Computers*, 26 (2): 260–5.

Craik, F. I. M. and Lockhart, R. S. (1972) "Levels of Processing. A Framework for Memory Research," *Journal of Verbal Learning and Verbal Behavior* 11: 671–84.

Daneman, M. and Carpenter, P. A. (1980) "Individual Differences in Working Memory and Reading," *Journal of Verbal Learning and Verbal Behavior* 19: 450–66.

Darò, V. and Fabbro, F. (1994) "Verbal Memory during Simultaneous Interpretation: Effects of Phonological Interference," *Applied Linguistics* 15:4, 365–81.

Dillinger, M. L. (1989) "Component Processes of Simultaneous Interpreting," PhD thesis, McGill University, Montreal.

—— (1994) "Comprehension during Interpreting: What Do Interpreters Know that Bilinguals Don't?," in: S. Lambert and B. Moser-Mercer (eds).

Flores d'Arcais, G. B. (1978) "The Contribution of Cognitive Psychology to the Study of Interpretation," in D. Gerver and H. W. Sinaiko (eds) *Language Interpretation and Communication*, New York: Plenum Press.

Frederiksen, C. (1975) "Representing logical and semantic structure of knowledge acquired from discourse," *Cognitive Psychology* 7: 371–458.

Gathercole, E. and Baddeley, A. D. (1993) *Working Memory and Language*, Hillsdale: Lawrence Erlbaum Associates.

Gerver, D. (1976) "Empirical Studies of Simultaneous Interpretation: A Review and a Model," in R. Brislin (ed.) *Translation. Applications and Research*, New York: Gardner Press.

Hauenschild, C. and Heizmann, S. (eds) (1997) *Machine Translation and Translation Theory*, Berlin: Mouton de Gruyter.

Isham, W. P. (1994) "Memory for Sentence form after Simultaneous Interpretation: Evidence both for and against Deverbalization," in S. Lambert and B. Moser-Mercer (eds).

Lambert, S. (1983) "Recall and Recognition among Conference Interpreters, in Transfer and Translation," in *Language Learning and Teaching*, RELC Anthology Series, Singapore University Press, 12: 206–20.

—— (1989) "Information Processing among Conference Interpreters: A Test of the Depth-of-Processing Hypothesis," in L. Gran and J. Dodds (eds) *The Theoretical and Practical Aspects of Teaching Conference Interpretation*, Udine: Campanotto.

Lambert, S. and Moser-Mercer, B. (eds) (1994) *Bridging the Gap. Experimental research in simultaneous interpretation*, Amsterdam: John Benjamins.

Marslen-Wilson, W. D. and Tyler, L. K. (1980) "The Temporal Structure of Spoken Language Understanding," *Cognition* 8: 1–71.

Massaro, D. W. (1975) *Understanding Language*, New York: Academic Press.

—— (1989) *Experimental Psychology. An Information Processing Approach*, New York: Harcourt Brace Jovanovich.

—— (1994) "Psychological Aspects of Speech Perception. Implications for Research and Theory," in M. Gernsbacher (ed.) *Handbook of Psycholinguistics*, New York: Academic Press.

Massaro, D. W., Cohen, M. M. and Gesi, A. T. (1993a) "Long-term Training, Transfer, and Retention in Learning to Lip-Read," *Perception and Psychophysics* 53 (5): 549–62.

Massaro, D.W., Cohen, M. M., Gesi, A. T., Heredia, R. and Tsuzaki, M. (1993b) "Bimodal Speech Perception: An Examination across Languages," *Journal of Phonetics* 21: 445–78.

Moser, B. (1976) "Simultaneous Translation: Linguistic, Psycholinguistic, and Human information Processing Aspects," unpubl. PhD thesis, Univ. of Innsbruck.

—— (1978) "Simultaneous Interpretation: A Hypothetical Model and its Practical Application," in D. Gerver and H. W. Sinaiko (eds) *Language Interpretation and Communication*, New York: Plenum Press.

Moser-Mercer, B. (1984) "Testing Interpreting Aptitude," in W. Wilss and G. Thome (eds) *Translation Theory and its Implementation in the Teaching of Translating and Interpreting*, Tübingen: Narr.

Norman, D. A. and Shallice, T. (1980) *Attention to Action: Willed and Automatic Control of Behavior*, CHIP Report 99, University of California, San Diego.

Pöchhacker, F. (1994) *Simultandolmetschen als komplexes Handeln*, Tübingen: Narr.

Sánchez Martínez, J. A. (1988) "Barbara Moser: Simultaneous Interpretation: A Hypothetical Model and its Practical Application," unpubl. Master's thesis, Univ. of Heidelberg.

Seleskovitch, D. (1975) *Langage, langues et mémoire*, Paris: Minard.

Shallice, T. (1982) "Specific Impairments of Planning," *Philosophical Transactions of the Royal Society London*, Series B, 298: 199–209.

—— (1988) *From Neuropsychology to Mental Structure*, Cambridge: Cambridge University Press.

Treisman, A. (1964) "Monitoring and Storage of Irrelevant Messages in Selective Attention," *Journal of Verbal Learning and Verbal Behavior* 3: 449–559.

Tulving, E. (1987) "Multiple Memory Systems and Consciousness," *Human Neurobiology* 6: 67–80.

DANIEL GILE IS undoubtedly the most prolific and influential author on interpreting in what he himself labeled the "Renaissance" period of conference
interpreting research after the mid-1980s. Having trained and worked as both a
mathematician and a conference interpreter, he launched into interpreting research in
the early 1980s in contradistinction to the dominant paradigm of Danica Seleskovitch
at his alma mater, the Paris School of Interpreters (ESIT). Appointed Professor of
Translation at the Université Lumière Lyon 2 in 1995, Gile continues to combine
his career as a conference and media interpreter with his active commitment to
promoting research standards and international cooperation in Interpreting Studies,
most notably by publishing the semi-annual *IRN Bulletin* for the dissemination of
information on conference interpreting research.

Apart from his writings on the evolution and methodology of research on interpreting and numerous reports on small-scale empirical investigations, his major theoretical contribution to the field has been his conceptual model of cognitive processing
efforts in interpreting. Developed originally in the early 1980s for simultaneous interpreting (Gile 1985a), the "Effort Models" have since been elaborated and applied to
various types of interpreting and processing constellations. The present paper, published originally in a collective volume on *Cognitive Processes in Translation and
Interpreting* (Danks *et al.* 1997), gives an up-to-date presentation of the models and
discusses their merits and implications. Abridgements to the original text are limited
to the discussion of pedagogical issues, the concluding recapitulation of basic assumptions and model architecture, and the research input desired from cognitive scientists.

Further reading: Gile 1985a, 1992, 1995a, 1995c, 1999a.

Daniel Gile

CONFERENCE INTERPRETING AS A COGNITIVE MANAGEMENT PROBLEM

THE LITERATURE ON conference interpreting is largely devoted to the investigation of the mental processes of interpreting, in particular in the simultaneous mode. Several process models of simultaneous interpretation (SI) have been developed (Gerver 1976; Mizuno 1995; Moser 1978; Moser-Mercer [1997]). Unfortunately, due to the complexity of interpreting and to insufficient interest in the subject, little progress has been achieved in the testing and development of such models. Although efforts in this direction are continuing, other approaches, more goal-oriented and less ambitious, also have potential value.

One such endeavor started out with the recognition that errors, omissions, and weakened linguistic and delivery output were numerous even in the performance of experts. It is striking that most texts on interpreting have paid little attention to performance limitations and failures as a phenomenon *per se*. Professional interpreters have tended to gloss over such failings and to ascribe inadequate performance to poor working conditions or to interpreter incompetence. Psychologists have used errors and omissions as tools to test the influence of other variables (Barik 1969; Gerver 1976), but only rarely has the extent of the phenomenon been investigated in the field. It is easy to understand why practicing interpreters do not wish to draw attention to such weaknesses. The fact is, however, that errors and omissions can be very numerous. Although their precise definition and identification is problematic (Stenzl 1983) in observational and experimental studies, there are also many very clear-cut cases: wrong numbers, wrong names, wrong propositional content occurring up to several times per minute of interpretation (Gile 1984, 1989, 1995a). Of interest, many such errors and omissions are found in the performance of interpreters enjoying a high professional reputation and in environments in which no unfavorable conditions, such as noise, excessive delivery speed, poor pronunciation, technical complexity of speech, complexity of syntactic structure in the source language, and so on, can be identified. In many cases, they cannot be explained by the interpreter's weaknesses in terms of source language or target language proficiency, world knowledge, or interpreting skills. The evidence suggests that there is an intrinsic difficulty in interpreting, which lies in the cognitive tasks involved.

This chapter presents the Effort Models, a set of rather gross cognitive models of interpreting developed in the early 1980s (and first mentioned in writing in Gile 1983) to account for this intrinsic difficulty, and discusses their explanatory power with respect to well-known problem triggers. It then goes on to elaborate on possible implications with respect to fundamental theoretical and practical issues, to discuss methodological issues in their further exploration, and to request input from psychologists and linguists.

The Effort Model of simultaneous interpretation

The efforts

This Effort Model was developed initially to be used as a conceptual framework for interpretation students. Therefore, while drawing on the concept of processing capacity and its finite availability, it was designed with the simplest possible architecture that would yield the required explanatory power. In particular, complex operations were bundled into three "efforts" (the name was chosen to underscore their nonautomatic nature), presented as distinct entities in spite of the probable existence of overlapping cognitive components.

- The listening and analysis effort (L) is defined as consisting of all comprehension-oriented operations, from the analysis of the sound waves carrying the source language (SL) speech that reach the interpreter's ears, through the identification of words, to the final decisions about the meaning of the sentence.

- The production effort (P) is defined in the simultaneous mode as the set of operations extending from the initial mental representation of the message to be delivered, through speech planning, and up to the implementation of the speech plan.

- The memory effort (M) is the high demand on short-term memory during simultaneous interpreting, due to the operation of several factors including (a) the time interval between the moment SL speech sounds are heard and the moment their processing for comprehension is finished, (b) the time interval between the moment the message to be formulated in the target language (TL) speech is determined and the completion of its formulation, (c) tactical moves, which are used, for instance, if an SL speech segment is unclear to the interpreter because of bad sound, strong accent, unclear logic, errors in the SL speech, and so on (the interpreter may decide to wait until more context is available to help understand the unclear segment), and (d) linguistic reasons, as will be discussed in a later section.

Tactical decisions on how to deal with particular problems (coping tactics) will be considered here as part of the production effort, although they are often related to professional, sociological, or psychological factors rather than to linguistic or cognitive factors, and their impact may be largely felt in the memory effort as well.

The Effort Model and its operational requirements

Using these definitions, simultaneous interpretation (SI) can be modeled as a process consisting of the three "efforts" described above, plus a coordination effort (C) (Eysenck and Keane 1990):

(1) SI = L + P + M + C

In the most general case, at any point in time, the three basic efforts are processing different SL speech segments. When interpreting a speech consisting of a succession of segments A, B, C, and so on, production may be working on A, memory on B, and listening and analysis on C. This, however, is not a set rule. For instance, anticipation often results in a production effort being performed on a segment not yet heard in the SL.

   In the most general case, at any point in time, the three basic efforts are simultaneously active (there is now ample evidence that interpreters do indeed listen and speak simultaneously during most of their interpreting time; in addition to the findings of Gerver and Barik, see, for example, Čenkova 1988, for the Russian–Czech combination). Total processing capacity requirements (TR) are therefore presented as a sum (although not necessarily an arithmetic sum, as some resources may be shared) of individual processing capacity requirements:

(2) TR = LR + MR + PR + CR

where LR = capacity requirements for L, MR = capacity requirements for M, PR = capacity requirements for P, and CR = capacity requirements for C.

   At each point in time, each effort has specific processing capacity requirements that depend on the task(s) it is engaged in – a particular comprehension, short-term memory, or production operation being performed on specific information segments. Due to the high variability of requirements depending on the incoming speech flow and on its segmentation into processing units by the interpreter (Goldman-Eisler 1967), processing capacity requirements for each effort can vary rapidly over intervals of a few seconds or even fractions of a second. At any time, if interpretation is to proceed smoothly, the capacity available for each effort (LA, MA, PA, and CA) must be equal to or larger than its requirements for the task at hand:

(3) LA > LR,
(4) MA > MR,
(5) PA > PR, and
(6) CA > CR.

This goes beyond the mere condition that total available capacity (TA) be at least equal to total requirements (TR):

(7) TA > TR

The model becomes meaningful when it is assumed that the total processing capacity available at any time is finite, and that meeting conditions 3 to 7 is not trivial. As explained above, it is precisely the evidence that the interpreter's capacity is often insufficient to perform the interpreting tasks correctly that inspired the effort models.

Interpretation difficulties and failures

The layperson tends to believe that interpretation errors and omissions occur when the interpreter does not know a term or concept in the SL or TL. This does happen, but the effort models explain frequent errors and omissions associated not with such lack of knowledge but with cognitive load. When one or more of the conditions defined by inequalities 3 to 7 is or are not met, one of two things may happen. Either the execution of a task is delayed, which may lead to heavier cognitive load on the processing of the next segments and, ultimately, to failure sequences as discussed below, or the task is not executed, which is not necessarily detected, as both the sensitivity and the linguistic and world knowledge of observers are often insufficient (see Gile 1995a, 1995c).

For instance, if an incoming SL speech segment requires increased capacity for production, the interpreter may have to wait until more processing capacity can be directed toward the production effort, possibly after having been freed from the listening effort that is busy with an incoming segment. This may result in increased load on memory, as further SL speech segments continue to arrive and have to be processed for comprehension and then stored until they are reformulated into the TL or omitted. If additional processing capacity is then allocated to the memory effort, this may in turn deplete the capacity available for the listening and analysis effort, leading to a potential problem in the comprehension of another incoming SL speech segment. Such failure sequences can account for errors or omissions occurring at a distance from a difficulty in the SL speech and affecting SL speech segments that pose no problem *per se*.

In fact, distal failures need not come from a problematic segment at all. The short delay needed to change processing capacity allocation to the various efforts as SL speech processing tasks are completed, and new tasks have to be undertaken, may be enough to generate capacity shortages at various points in the processing of sentences containing no particular difficulty. Figure 1 gives a hypothetical example, with a sentence having one comparatively dense segment, for instance, "Ladies and Gentlemen, *the International Association of Frozen Food Manufacturers* is happy to welcome so many of you in Paris for this meeting." The dense segment (in italics) goes from t2 to t3, while total requirements resulting from an addition of the requirements for L, P, and M reach their maximum value between t6 and t7.

Sometimes no significant waiting is possible, for instance, when identifying a word from sounds, which are known to disappear rapidly from memory. In such a case, the relevant SL segment is not understood, which may result in an error or omission.

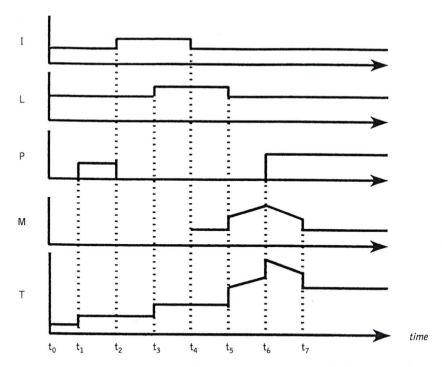

Figure 1   A theoretical and schematic representation of the processing capacity involved during the simultaneous interpreting of a simple sentence with a single informationally dense segment.

The Effort Model of consecutive interpreting

The model

In consecutive interpreting (CI), the interpreter alternates with the speaker, translating SL speech segments of at least several sentences after the speaker has completed them and has paused for translation. CI can therefore be viewed as a two-phase process: a listening phase, during which the interpreter listens to the SL speech, and generally takes notes, and a reformulation phase, during which the interpreter makes a TL speech from memory and from notes. The listening phase can be modeled as follows:

(8) CI (listening) $= L + M + N + C$

L is the listening and analysis component already referred to for SI. N refers to note-taking, which differs from note-taking in other circumstances in several ways. In particular, CI notes do not cover all the information contained in the SL speech, but essentially serve as reminders to help the interpreter retrieve said information from memory (Rozan 1956). The effort N therefore involves decisions on which information should be noted and how it should be noted (as full words or abbreviations, in the SL, the TL, or another language, as symbols, drawings, and so on), as well as the implementation of these decisions. M is the same short-term memory component as in SI, which in this case occurs between the time SL information is received and the moment it is taken down, or the moment the interpreter decides not to note it, or the moment it disappears from working memory. C is the same coordination component as in the Effort Model for SI.

The reformulation phase can be modeled as follows:

(9) CI (reformulation) = Rem + Read + P

The Rem component refers to the operations involved in recall from memory, and notes of the SL speech segment being translated. The Read component refers to the reading (or deciphering) of the notes taken during the listening phase. The P effort is the same as in SI.

Processing capacity requirements in consecutive interpreting

When the processing capacity requirements of CI are analyzed in the same way as in the Effort Model for SI, three features stand out.

First, in terms of processing capacity, only the listening phase is critical. In the reformulation phase, processing capacity allocation is done by the interpreter at his or her discretion, and there is no risk of overloading due to a high density of the speech over time. In particular, if some difficulty arises in the execution of one task by one effort, the execution of tasks by other efforts can be delayed without risking information loss, as no further information comes in during that time. Whereas in the listening phase, the three efforts may be viewed as highly competitive, in the reformulation phase, there seems to be much more potential for cooperation, in particular between note-reading and remembering. Incidentally, this could explain why many interpreters accept work into a B language (active, but nonnative) in consecutive, but not in simultaneous, interpreting. The presumably higher cost of speech production in the B language could be accommodated in the reformulation stage of consecutive, but not under the heavier pressure of simultaneous, interpreting.

Second, processing capacity requirements associated with the note-taking effort are largely determined in the time it takes to write notes, during which incoming information accumulates in working memory. Memory failure may therefore be more frequent in CI than in SI.

Finally, processing capacity requirements in consecutive interpreting depend to a large extent on the way the interpreter takes his or her notes, in other words, on a technical skill not found in SI.

Sight translation and SI with text

In sight translation (ST), the translator or interpreter translates an SL text aloud while reading it. The listening and analysis effort becomes a reading and analysis effort; the speech production effort remains, but there is no memory effort as in simultaneous or consecutive interpreting because the SL information is available on paper at any time.

(10) ST Reading + Production

Sight translation is not paced by an SL speaker. Its rhythm depends on the translator, and as is the case with the reformulation stage of CI, he or she has some margin of freedom in allocating processing capacity to the reading and analysis effort or to the production effort.

On the other hand, in consecutive interpreting, notes are used only as an aid to trigger memory of an SL speech that was heard and understood previously. In sight translation, however, the reading effort also carries the burden of the initial comprehension of the text. Moreover, whereas notes represent only part of the information and are laid out to help visualize the logical structure of the speech (see Rozan 1956), written texts carry all of the information content of the author's message, plus language components associated with rules of syntax and style that carry little information (in particular, function words, forms of politeness, and so on). Their layout is determined by graphic presentation conventions, and not by the need to see the logic of the discourse at a glance; their information density and linguistic style make instantaneous oral translation more difficult.

Yet another difference lies in the fact that, while in consecutive, and to a lesser extent in simultaneous, interpreting, the memory of the SL words fades away to a significant degree before the reformulation of their content in the TL (generally 1 to several seconds after they were heard), in sight translation, they continue to be visually present throughout. It follows that the risk of linguistic interference is probably higher in sight translation than in SI – and higher in SI than in CI because of the rapid fading of SL words from memory. Finally, in SI and in the listening phase of consecutive interpreting, the information is retrieved mainly from sound (but also from the speaker's body language and from visual information displayed on a screen as slides or overhead transparencies as well as in handouts). In the reformulation stage of consecutive interpreting, it is retrieved from memory and from the interpreter's notes. In sight translation, it is retrieved solely from the writing in the text. What implications this might have in terms of effort requirements, and in particular in terms of cooperation or interference between the SL reading input and the spoken TL output, is not clear.

SI with text (the speaker is reading a text that the interpreter also has in the booth) can be performed as a mixture of SI and sight translation going from "pure" SI (without any reference to the text) to "pure" sight translation (without any reference to the sound). The one extreme (pure simultaneous) deprives the interpreter of the visual help. The other extreme (sight translation) is considered risky for two reasons in addition to the linguistic interference factor. First, by neglecting the actual speech, the interpreter may miss possible deviations by the speaker from the written text (side comments, additions, and other changes). Second, when focusing on the text, the interpreter is tempted to translate all of it even when the speaker is reading very fast, and "compression" tactics involving selected omissions would be required. As a result, the interpreter may lag further and further behind and eventually be forced to omit a large speech segment.

The explanatory power of the Effort Models

A series of problematic speech-segment types, well known to professionals and often mentioned in the literature, can be classified and explained using the Effort Models.

Problems arising from an increase in processing capacity requirements

High information density in the SL increases processing capacity requirements, because more information must be processed per unit of time. This applies to both the listening and analysis effort and the production effort in simultaneous, and the note-taking effort in consecutive, interpreting. High speech density may be the most frequent source of interpretation problems and failures. It is associated with fast delivery of the speech; enumerations (which are devoid of low-density connective segments); external factors, such as poor sound quality (which also increases the processing capacity required for speech comprehension); and prepared speeches, in particular when read from polished texts. Not only are prepared speeches more densely formulated than spontaneous speech (Halliday 1985), they are delivered with fewer false starts and hesitations, which have a low information content and account for a large proportion of the total speech time. Moreover, it is argued by some authors (see, for instance Déjean le Féal 1978) that the intonation pattern of speeches read from texts is not as helpful for comprehension as that of spontaneous speeches (although this has been challenged by a recent study by Shlesinger 1994).

There are also information-reordering-associated problems. Names composed of several words may require a reordering of their components in the TL. For instance, *Association internationale des interprètes de conférence* becomes *International Association of Conference Interpreters*. As long as there is no automated response to the name as an entity, this increases the memory effort requirements in a twofold mechanism. First, because of the high information density of such names, depending on the specific language pair, the interpreter may have to wait until they have unfolded completely before starting to translate, with no possibility of unloading memory gradually. Second, the reordering process requires repeated scanning and comparison of the SL name and its gradually developing TL translation, as opposed to direct word-to-word or meaning-to-word reformulation. This slows down the process even further and therefore increases the load on memory. Compound technical terms pose a similar problem, as in *water cooled double-walled high integrity stainless steel tank*.

Differences between the syntactic structures of the SL and the TL can increase the memory effort's processing capacity requirements because of the waiting involved before being able to reformulate the SL segment into the TL.

A language-specific difficulty identified in Japanese is associated with the high proportion of homophones in its vocabulary, due to the importation of Chinese words and morphemes into the more restricted Japanese phonological space, which reduces the redundancy of speech signals – hence the potentially higher vulnerability to processing capacity mismanagement (see below) and increased processing capacity requirements for comprehension. In a study by Gile (1986), words read aloud to Japanese listeners often invoked several different lexical units, and sometimes none. In Japanese, not only are homophones numerous, there is little grammatical and other redundancy. It is not clear to what extent the linguistic and situation context can offset these difficulties, as no testing was done on actual speeches.

Problems associated with signal vulnerability

Some SL speech segments are not necessarily difficult to process but are more vulnerable to a momentary shortage of processing capacity in the listening effort because of their short duration or low redundancy. This in particular is the case with numbers and short names, including acronyms. In an experiment involving the simultaneous interpretation of a speech, the proportion of names incorrectly understood and/or reformulated was very high (Gile 1984). The same difficulty should also apply to a significant proportion of the vocabulary of some languages such as Japanese and Chinese, where the difference between many words lies in a single phoneme. Such signal vulnerability makes proper and precise processing capacity management critical, as a very brief shortage of processing capacity in the listening and analysis effort may be enough to cause significant loss.

The models imply two types of trigger mechanisms for failure: saturation, that is, a situation where the sum of capacity requirements is larger than the total available capacity; and individual deficit, where the interpreter's total available capacity covers total requirements but the capacity available for one or more effort(s) (L, M, P, and so on) at a particular moment is not enough to cover its/their requirements for the task(s) at hand.

Saturation inevitably results in individual deficits. Individual deficits not mediated by saturation are more a matter of capacity management. They may occur when the interpreter devotes more capacity than necessary to TL speech production (trying to formulate an idea very elegantly when the speech is informationally dense and much capacity needs to be devoted to the listening and analysis effort), when he or she writes too many notes in consecutive interpreting, and so on. Individual deficits may also occur because of a short attention gap in the listening and analysis component occurring at the time a vulnerable SL segment is uttered by the speaker (numbers, short names, and so on). Such management problems are partly associated with faulty techniques and tactical decisions (see below), and partly related to inappropriate subconscious, automated processes acquired during initial interpretation training at school or during one's professional experience in the field.

As explained earlier, saturation and individual deficits may lead to immediate failures, or to failures at a distance from a difficult SL segment, often with the result that it is not the difficult SL speech segment that is omitted or translated erroneously, but another segment, which is not problematic *per se*. It seems that, to date, the Effort Models' failure sequences are the only explanation put forward for this rather frequent type of failure.

Interpretation strategies, tactics, and other issues

Interpretation strategies and tactics

The explanation of failure mechanisms through saturation and individual deficits leads to the obvious quest for means to reduce effort requirements. The advantages of many strategies adopted in interpreting can be analyzed in such terms. For instance, advance preparation of conferences may be assumed to increase the availability of the relevant lexicon of the SL and TL, of technical terms, and other relevant linguistic knowledge and world knowledge, and therefore to reduce the processing capacity requirements both in the listening and analysis component and in the production component. Regulation of the ear–voice span – that is, the time between the moment a segment is heard and the time it is reformulated in the TL – can be assumed to aim at optimizing the balance between short-term memory load and speech production requirements. The further an interpreter lags behind the speaker, the clearer the understanding of his or her message, hence the easier its reformulation but the heavier the burden on working memory. The same can be said of the "segmentation" strategy advocated in SI from German into French, that is, reformulating successive short segments of the SL into the TL without waiting for all of the idea to be uttered (see Ilg 1978).

In consecutive interpretation, using many symbols in note-taking (Matyssek 1989) helps reduce the time required to note ideas. However, until they are mastered, retrieving them from memory and/or recognizing their meaning from the notes in the reformulation phase may require more time and processing capacity than would be the case when writing plain words. Also, as mentioned above, laying out the notes in a particular way can reduce capacity requirements of the Rem component (i.e., recalling the content of the speech).

In sight translation, preparing the SL text by dividing it into "translation units" using slashes makes it possible to focus eye movements on shorter text segments, and thus reduce the time and processing capacity required for comprehension. Writing glosses in the SL text and numbering words in the order in which they will be translated into the TL reduce production capacity requirements.

In addition to strategies, interpreters use coping tactics to prevent or contain damage when a problem occurs or threatens to occur (Gile 1995b). Each tactic has a price in terms of potential information loss, credibility loss, impact loss, and time and processing capacity cost. For instance, consulting documents in the booth and explaining or paraphrasing a term for which the interpreter has no TL equivalent requires much time and processing capacity. Taking notes during SI so as not to forget proper names or numbers can be costly in time, and it introduces further processing capacity requirements because of the added writing activity. In both cases, there is a risk of memory overload. The advisability of each coping tactic in a given situation can be analyzed on the basis of such parameters. The Effort Models underscore the importance of time and processing capacity in such assessments.

Theoretical and pedagogical issues

The Effort Models also provide a convenient conceptual framework for a discussion of fundamental theoretical questions. Chief among these is the issue of language specificity. It has been argued vocally by proponents of the *théorie du sens*, which prevailed in the 1970s, that interpretation is language-independent, on the alleged grounds that competent interpreters understand any language in exactly the same way as other listeners in their respective mother tongues, and that speech production in the TL is spontaneous and effortless (Gile 1995a). Other authors believe that syntactic differences between the SL and TL do make a difference (Fukuii and Asano 1961; Ilg 1978; Kunihiro, Nishiyama and Kanayama 1969; Wilss 1978).

The debate was limited to claims and counterclaims. The Effort Models would suggest, as explained earlier in the chapter, that syntactic differences that force interpreters to wait longer before starting to formulate their TL speech tend to increase the load on the memory effort. One might even go further and talk about the intrinsic requirements of specific languages in terms of the listening effort and/or in terms of the production effort. As mentioned above, languages with many short words and homophones and few grammatical indicators, such as Chinese and Japanese, could be more vulnerable in the listening effort because of the lack of redundancy. Languages with a limited vocabulary and a rather rigid grammar that imposes strict conditions on the order of elements in the sentence as well as grammatical agreement conditions could be associated with higher production effort requirements. Specific information density patterns may also have implications on processing capacity requirements. Many Japanese sentences have a rather long predictable ending (Gile 1992), which might reduce significantly the processing capacity requirements of the listening and analysis effort over enough time to have an impact on interpreting strategies.

[. . .]

Discussion

[. . .]

Validating and fine-tuning the Effort Models

If the assumptions underlying the Effort Models' architecture are found to be compatible with state-of-the-art knowledge of cognitive psychology and psycho-linguistics, it will still be necessary to test the hypotheses underlying the hypoth-esized processes. Such testing is difficult for some of the following reasons.

Processes occurring during interpreting involve, simultaneously, speech perception and production, content analysis, decision making, storage, retrieval, and comparison of sounds and other information in various components of memory. Moreover, it may reasonably be assumed that because of their simultaneousness and the cognitive load involved, they interact with and modify each other. Hence the possibility that research findings on single processes conducted in cognitive psychology and psycholinguistics in non-interpreting environments do not apply fully.

The complexity of interpreting is compounded by the important part highly variable strategies play, as evidenced by the above-mentioned wide interindividual distribution pattern of errors and omissions.

Because of the probable high degree of interaction between the processes occurring in interpretation, it is difficult to isolate them in an experimental setup, except possibly for rather gross bundles such as speech comprehension or note-taking in consecutive interpreting. Setting aside some manipulations of the SL speech (Dillinger 1989; Gerver 1976) and of noise and other environmental conditions (Gerver 1976), strict selective control of independent variables is tricky.

Indicators for quantitative evaluation are a problem. Many indicators used in psychological experiments are difficult to use because they require breaking down interpretation into isolated tasks. More holistic indicators such as errors and omissions are tricky (Stenzl 1983). They can be useful but lack sensitivity, reliability, and precision. Noninvasive on-line physiological indicators would be most helpful if they could measure cognitive load directly. Not only would they provide a means of testing many hypotheses described above, they could serve as guiding tools in interpreter training. No adequate indicators seem to have been found. Pupil dilation measurements required that the interpreter's head be maintained in a certain posture (Tommola and Hyönä 1990), and EEG measurements imposed "mental interpretation," without TL sound (Kurz 1996).

Some of the difficulties of empirical testing could be partly offset by increasing sample sizes and by multiplying replications. The sheer effect of large numbers would reduce the effect of random variation and there would be more possibilities for comparing actual interpretation occurrences using specific differences in selected variables (e.g., language combination, speed, previous knowledge of the subject) retrospectively. For professional, psychological, and practical reasons, however, access to subjects and material is difficult, and the use of students as subjects is problematic. Neither their processes nor their strategies can be safely assumed to reflect those of professional interpreters, if only because very few pass their final exams and become interpreters. The large sample size, multiple replication paradigm is therefore not a realistic one.

Conclusion

The concept of processing capacity and the Effort Models have proved useful for explanatory purposes. However, they have to be validated both against state-of-the-art knowledge in the cognitive sciences and with experimental methods before any fine-tuning and further development can be done. One of the main difficulties in such validation lies in the identification of precise, reliable, and sensitive indicators. It is precisely because of these difficulties that the input of researchers from the cognitive sciences is highly desirable.

References

Barik, H. C. (1969) "A Study of Simultaneous Interpretation," unpublished doctoral dissertation, University of North Carolina.

Čenkova, I. (1988) *Teoretické aspekty simultánního tlumočení* [Theoretical aspects of simultaneous interpreting], Prague: Charles University.

Déjean le Féal, K. (1978) "Lectures et improvisations: Incidences de la forme de l'énonciation sur la traduction simultanée," unpublished doctoral dissertation, Université Paris III.

Dillinger, M. (1989) "Component Processes of Simultaneous Interpreting," unpublished doctoral dissertation, McGill University, Montreal.

Eysenck, M. W. and Keane, M. T. (1990) *Cognitive Psychology: A Student's Handbook*, Hillsdale, NJ: Lawrence Erlbaum.

Fukuii, H. and Asano, T. (1961) *Eigotsuuyaku no jissai* [An English interpreter's manual], Tokyo: Kenkyusha.

Gerver, D. (1976) "Empirical Studies of Simultaneous Interpretation: A Review and a Model," in R. W. Brislin (ed.) *Translation: Applications and Research*, New York: Gardner, pp. 165–207.

Gile, D. (1983) "Des difficultés de langue en interprétation simultanée," *Traduire* 117: 2–8.

—— (1984) "Les noms propres en interprétation simultanée," *Multilingua* 3: 79–85.

—— (1986) "La reconnaissance des Kango dans la compréhension du discours japonais," *Lingua* 70: 171–89.

—— (1989) "La communication interlinguistique en réunion multilingue: Les difficultés de la transmission informationelle en interprétation simultanée," unpublished doctoral dissertation, Université Paris III.

—— (1992) "Predictable Sentence Endings in Japanese and Conference Interpretation," *The Interpreters' Newsletter*, Special Issue 1: 12–23.

—— (1995a) *Regards sur la recherche en interprétation de conférence*, Lille: Presses Universitaires de Lille.

—— (1995b) "Basic Concepts and Models for Interpreter and Translator Training," Amsterdam: Benjamins.

—— (1995c) "Fidelity Assessment in Consecutive Interpreting: An Experiment," *Target* 7: 151–64.

Goldman-Eisler, F. (1967) "Sequential Temporal Patterns and Cognitive Processes in Speech," *Language and Speech* 10: 122–32.

Halliday, M. A. K. (1985) *Spoken and Written Language*, Victoria: Deakin University Press.

Ilg, G. (1978) "L'apprentissage de l'interprétation simultanée de l'allemand vers le français," *Cahiers de l'E.T.I.* 1: 69–99.

Kunihiro, M., Nishiyama, S. and Kanayama, N. (1969) *Tsuuyaku: Eigokaiwa kara doujitsuuyaku made* [Interpreting: From English conversation to simultaneous interpreting], Tokyo: Nihonhososhuppankyokai.

Kurz, I. (1996) *Simultandolmetschen als Gegenstand der interdisziplinären Forschung*, Vienna: WUV-Universitätsverlag.

Matyssek, H. (1989) *Handbuch der Notizentechnik für Dolmetscher: Ein Weg zur sprach-unabhängigen Notation*, Heidelberg: Groos.

Mizuno, A. (1995) "The Dynamic Model of Simultaneous Interpretation (II): A Pilot Study on the Convergence of Translation Patterns," *Tsuuyakurironkenkyuu* [Interpreting Research] 8: 9–26.

Moser, B. (1978) "Simultaneous Interpretation: A Hypothetical Model and its Practical Application," in D. Gerver and H. W. Sinaiko (eds) *Language Interpretation and Communication*, New York: Plenum, pp. 353–68.

Moser-Mercer, B. (1997) "Beyond Curiosity: Can Interpreting Research Meet the Challenge?," in J. H. Danks, G. M. Shreve, S. B. Fountain and M. K. McBeath (eds) *Cognitive Processes in Translation and Interpreting*, Thousand Oaks, London and New Delhi: Sage, pp. 176–205.

Rozan, J. F. (1956) *La prise de notes en interprétation consécutive*, Genève: Georg.

Shlesinger, M. (1994) "Intonation in the Production and Perception of Simultaneous Interpretation," in S. Lambert and B. Moser-Mercer (eds) *Bridging the Gap: Empirical Research in Simultaneous Interpretation*, Amsterdam: Benjamins, pp. 225–36.

Stenzl, C. (1983) "Simultaneous Interpretation: Groundwork Towards a Comprehensive Model," unpublished Master's thesis, University of London.

Tommola, J. and Hyönä, J. (1990) "Mental Load in Listening, Speech Shadowing and Simultaneous Interpreting: A Pupillometric Study," in J. Tommola (ed.) *Foreign Language Comprehension and Production*, Turku: AFinLA – Finnish Association of Applied Linguistics, pp. 179–88.

Wilss, W. (1978) "Syntactic Anticipation in German–English Simultaneous Interpreting," in D. Gerver and H. W. Sinaiko (eds) *Language Interpretation and Communication*, New York: Plenum, pp. 343–52.

ROBIN SETTON'S COGNITIVE-PRAGMATIC account of discourse processing in simultaneous interpreting is one of the most significant advances in interpreting research at the close of the twentieth century. Much like his theoretical framework, which brings together linguistic and cognitive approaches, and much like his analytical approach, which links authentic discourse data to mental models, Setton's career has typically been "both–and" rather than "either–or": a 1979 graduate of ESIT in Paris, he has worked as a conference interpreter, both staff (OECD) and freelance, with both French and English as active target languages (AIIC double A); apart from his European working languages (including passive German), he also interprets from Chinese, having earned an MA in Chinese Studies from the Sorbonne VII in the late 1980s; with experience in (technical and literary) translation as well as interpreting, he has held leadership positions in interpreter education at both the Graduate Institute of Translation and Interpretation Studies of Fu Jen University, Taipei (1990–4) and the École de traduction et d'interprétation of the University of Geneva, where he was appointed Professor of Interpreting in 1999 and Head of the Interpreting Section in 2000.

The paper reprinted here, with some abridgements (particularly in the introductory sections, some examples, and the first part of the Discussion section) was originally published in *Interpreting* in 1998. It reflects the essential components of the author's 1997 PhD thesis at the Chinese University of Hong Kong, published in updated and revised form by John Benjamins in 1999.

Further reading: Setton 1993, 1994, 1999a, 1999b.

Robin Setton

MEANING ASSEMBLY IN
SIMULTANEOUS INTERPRETATION

[. . .]

SI THEORISTS ARE aware of the extralinguistic and implicit factors in speech but, lacking a reasoned model of their operation, have had to gloss over the intermediate stages of the translation process. Information-processing (IP) approaches address SI in terms of the limitations on human computing power, but are vague on what is computed or stored . . . While the relationship between linguistic and conceptual processing remains unclear, some accounts make bold assumptions about task modularity, likening SI to "multitasking" on the model of dichotic performance on unrelated activities . . . In modelling the fate of the linguistic material, [. . .] propositional and "information"-based descriptions understate the directive or communicative dimension of discourse, and leave a significant residue of phenomena to be ascribed to the "unusual logic" of the input, stylistic choice, error, or "neutral" padding.

More radical and systematic approaches to representing situated discourse have been opened up with speech-act theory (Austin 1962; Searle 1969, 1983) and Grice's conversational maxims (Grice 1967, 1989), and their development in Relevance Theory (Sperber and Wilson 1986), the latest attempt at a comprehensive theory of cognition in speech communication. This paper addresses the processes of meaning assembly in SI in an RT framework, with particular emphasis on pragmatic factors. A compatible cognitive configuration for SI is proposed elsewhere in the form of a process model (Setton 1997, 1999).

[. . .]

Modern cognitive science recognises the need for intermediate representation of some kind in the brain to process stimuli from the environment, not least those of the complexity of goal-directed speech. Short of admitting telepathy, we must assume that meaning is constructed independently by each individual [. . .]. Translation . . . cannot be satisfactorily explained without, first, an account of how context – defined . . . as a psychological construct – is assembled and managed through the task. [. . .] Second, the "Message" is not exhaustively defined by its informational, or even "cognitive" content. To explain many features of natural data we need some means of capturing the directed, volitional dimension of discourse, or the quality of intentionality (Searle 1983).

Modelling discourse

No-one doubts that other information than what is encoded in the speech forms enters into comprehension, and therefore into translation; a decoded speech stimulus is indeterminate (vague or ambiguous) until enriched and disambiguated with the help of context in the inferential phase. Let us call what can be decoded with a basic grammar and lexicon – from word categories, case marking, word-order, and so on – the semantic representation (SR) of a sentence. "Semantics" is understood not in the loose everyday usage which tacitly refers to word meanings, but in the technical sense which includes both lexical and logical values: a semantic representation is a logically structured set of concepts derived from rules of grammar and lexical meaning. For a string like *Had I known that nothing (I did (would make any difference, . . .))*, for instance, most of the SR would be logical form: tense, quantification, conditionality etc.

In speech, however, ostensibly "logical" words like *and, but, since, although, if . . ., then*, do not transparently encode logical values; interrogatives and imperatives are often not questions or orders (Grice 1989). As for "content" words, no line can be drawn between "basic" meaning and encyclopaedic, conventionalised and contextualised meaning (see e.g. Fillmore 1982). Linguistics has had to reject logical positivism and recognise communicative and contextual factors in speech exchange: the SR is incomplete in both informational and communicational terms (Sperber and Wilson 1986; Garnham 1987; Grice 1989; Searle 1992, and others). Grice proposed a set of tacit conventions to explain how meaning is derived by hearers. Austin (1962) identified *illocutionary force* as an independent characteristic of all spoken utterances, and Searle developed this "speech-act" theory into a theory of intentionality.

Relevance Theory (RT) has developed the Gricean programme into a full pragmatic theory in which speech communication is described as an "ostensive-inferential" process. Ostension is the Speaker's manifestation of his intent to communicate a relevant meaning to a hearer at a proportionate effort, and is further realised locally in devices (like focus and other distributors of emphasis) which guide listeners to relevant contexts for inference. Comprehension therefore requires both decoding and further inference in contexts selected by the hearer with the Speaker's ostensive guidance. In this framework, "context" is defined very broadly from the listener/interpreter's point of view, to include *any and all sources which complement the SR*, i.e. as a psychological construct comprising the body of percepts and assumptions (however recent, however complex) which are involved in interpretation. This definition also includes the associations evoked by words; and admits of no hard and fast line between the implicit and the explicit: explicature and implicature differ only in degree, and are interwoven in the very fabric of discourse.

One must immediately wonder at how comprehension could then be modelled or explicitly tracked on-line. IT theorists [i.e. proponents of the interpretive theory or *théorie du sens*] are sceptical, suggesting that it unfolds in a subjective pattern as successive *déclics* of understanding ("dawnings") specific to each individual listening to the same discourse (Lederer 1981:146). Fodor expresses scepticism (in his "First Law of the Non-existence of Cognitive Science" (1983:107)) about analysing higher cognitive processes in general, on the grounds that the knowledge base for them is open-ended; and studies of interpretation which are sensitive to this variable (e.g. Pöchhacker's 1994 *skopos*-based investigation) are ultimately defeated by it. Relevance Theory claims that speech processing – unlike scientific theorising, for instance – is accessible to analysis. While the *potential* contexts for interpreting utterances may indeed include any of the hearer's beliefs and perceptions, context and inference can be modelled for a particular hearer receiving a particular utterance in a way that inference in independent thinking cannot, since (a) the immediacy of speech exchange places the previous utterance in the forefront of accessible contexts, and, most importantly, (b) communication proceeds from "ostension" on the Speaker's part as well as inference on the hearer's: in other words, Speakers *actively guide* hearers to intended meanings, or contexts for deriving them (Sperber and Wilson 1986:16; 49–54). Once this is recognised, the tracking of comprehension in a circumscribed speech situation like SI becomes viable.

[. . .]

In RT, meaning assembly begins with decoded semantic blueprints, which go through a process of reference assignment, disambiguation, and enrichment to determinate propositional forms; these are related to each other and accessible contexts in order to yield strong implicatures. SI reminds us that this process may advance by fragments. A constructed example (1a–c) can help to illustrate how different types of linguistic information and inference are combined. Suppose that a corporate management guru opens a speech with the words *I want to run –*, then pauses to cough allowing various possible continuations:

> Example (1)
> a. "*– briefly through some of the points discussed so far, before . . .* ":
> b. "*– the most competitive business in my industry. Where do I start?*"
> c. "*– that's what my students always seem to be saying. And I say, first you gotta learn to walk.*"

Falling intonation on *run* (phonology) would suggest sentence-final position (syntax), and therefore intransitive use (syntax, semantics). For an animate subject, this rules out such transitive meanings as "manage", "execute", "maintain", etc., leaving the intransitive "move fast on foot"; but the situation (pragmatics) biases strongly against this literal reading, leaving the possibility of metaphor and/or reported speech, as confirmed in (1c). On the other hand, if intonation on this opening fragment is neutral or not clear, a wide range of potential meanings of *run* remain, two of which emerge in (1a) and (1b). The experienced interpreter will decide at what point to produce viable fragments: here she would be unlikely to say anything after "*run*", except perhaps "*Mesdames, Messieurs, bonjour . . .*"

We may speculate that an item like *run* would remain syntactically "virtual", a mere phonological entity, until its syntactic features become clear, then semantically virtual, a bare selection frame of the form "[Subject RUN (Direct Object) (Indirect Object)]", until a lexical meaning emerges; but that this then instantly triggers a spreading web of semantic associations, possibly bootstrapped as whole scripts or frames (Fillmore 1982, 1985), which intersect with and bias each other, and enter into compositional meaning assembly along with features of incoming text, evoked aspects of prior knowledge, the situation, etc. This fits the model of selective suppression which has been proposed for access to the monolingual or bilingual lexicon (Marslen-Wilson 1987; Moser-Mercer *et al.* 1997:138).

On the strength of these observations we prefer to see the traditional parser as only one component of an "Assembler", whose function is to prepare propositional representations. The range of linguistic and contextual input involved means that, to derive a model of meaning assembly in SI, we need a detailed synchronised transcript of a corpus, including phonological features; and a model of the contexts available to the interpreter and salient at different points.

Corpus analysis

This section reviews a structural, semantic and pragmatic comparison of input and output in a small corpus (Setton 1997). A wide net has to be cast for sources of meaning, since it is generally recognised that understanding makes use of *all* available information. The method adopted was to reconstruct all the relevant information – syntactic, lexical, prosodic, conceptual, visual, etc. – available to the interpreter at critical points and compare it to the information necessary for her ensuing formulation. This required (a) a rather thorough representation of input and output: transcripts were made from dual-track recordings, timed and synchronised to < 0.5s accuracy, marked for pauses, primary pitch contour, stress and speech errors, and labelled for syntax and prosody; and (b) knowledge of other relevant information available to the interpreters (documentation, preparation, etc.), which was possible in five out of six cases.

We attempted first to match the propositional content in the parallel texts (compositional meaning arising from lexemes and syntax), and examined them for any correlation. Meanings expressed in output which could not be traced to local or other input-text sources in strictly lexico-syntactic terms were analysed for sources in extratextual knowledge or pragmatic inference, and the processing hypothesis was developed on this basis.

"Bottom-up" theories of speech processing have assumed that contextual and pragmatic factors are applied in a second phase distinct from the decoding of semantic meaning(s) for the sentence, whereas in some AI simulations, the frame or "script" information is allowed to bias a reading strongly "top-down". Recent work in RT has shown how a range of features in an intentional discourse (i.e. not sentences fabricated for an experiment), such as connectives, modals, particles, and some marked word-orders, do not encode conceptual content but are rather *procedural* devices which point the hearer to the context in which to derive the intended explicit and implicit meaning (Blakemore 1987; Wilson and Sperber 1993). These may contribute to the semantics of the proposition itself, by facilitating reference assignment and disambiguation (e.g. pronouns), or may clarify the attitude or illocution embedding the proposition, or – by signalling "dependent" relevance between propositions – connectives like *after all, anyway*, German *nämlich* or *doch* may constrain the implicatures which the Speaker intends his audience to derive.

This is compatible with the finely incremental and "weakly interactive" model of speech comprehension proposed by Altmann, Crain, and Steedman (Altmann and Steedman 1988) to replace problematic serial and parallel parsing models. "Weakly interactive" means that decoding is prior, i.e. context eliminates certain readings but does not generate them. "Finely incremental" means that information from lexical association, intonation and so on is used to assemble meaning word by word. Taken with the RT analysis, this means that even as the parser delivers logically assembled fragments, and conceptual meanings are activated, numerous features in the discourse string contribute to building determinate propositions from these blueprints, relating them to each other and processing them in the activated contexts, and hence building meaning from the explicatures and strong implicatures derived. This analysis has the advantage of assigning a clear role in communicating meaning to a range of features in discourse which were neglected in the traditional syntax-and-lexicon-based semantics, without generating the proliferation of nomenclature (with limited explanatory power in terms of communication) of Hallidayan discourse analysis. For SI research it suggests that we will find a wealth of on-line contributions to meaning which probably outweigh the inconvenience of purely syntactic asymmetries between languages like left-branching and verb-last structure; and, since formulation can be driven more incrementally by this on-line information, some explanation for the formal "distance" between SL and TL structure usually described as paraphrase and "free" translation. Of course, this calls for demonstration in a corpus, beginning with a comparison between input and output purely in terms of syntactic structure considered without its pragmatic dimension.

Structural patterns

To test the significance of sentence structure in meaning assembly, it is necessary to compare SI between "asymmetrical" languages, and to compare performances from spontaneous (at most semi-rehearsed) discourse and from recited text. Several samples were analysed in two language combinations, German–English (3 interpreters) and Chinese (Putonghua)–English (2 and 3 interpreters). Contrasting source and target languages were chosen to explore the possible effect of typological differences. German and Chinese are both partly SOV, contrasting with rigid SVO English. German as SL (a "free word-order" language with final verbs) has been a main focus of opposing claims about the significance of SL–TL structural asymmetry (Wilss 1978; Lederer 1981; Stenzl 1983). Chinese, which has further typological peculiarities, has been little studied as an SI language, and no corpus study had previously been attempted. English was chosen as the common target language for its accessibility and for comparability on the TL side. The corpora consist of semi-rehearsed, discursive speech[1] representative of conference discourse, with comparable subject-matters and levels of technicality.

[. . .]

Previous studies of SI data have adopted various units of segmentation, including syllables, words, pauses (Goldman-Eisler 1972; Barik 1973, 1975), speech bursts, syntactic constituents (Goldman-Eisler 1972; Davidson 1992), units of understanding formed irregularly in the interpreter's mind on line (units of *sens*: Lederer 1981), or other units defined heuristically by the researcher (e.g. Davidson 1992). To test for structural correlations between input and output, we first examined the treatment of SL structures which could not be rendered phrase by phrase into acceptable English, then of those which could be so transposed with only minimal adjustments at phrase level. SL features which contrast with English, e.g. verb-last sentences, heavy left-branching NPs with embedded participials, and Chinese Topic-Comment structures, were compared with the structures used by interpreters to carry the same propositional content, to see whether (a) a pattern of segmentation could be found and described in terms of a minimum sequence of constituents required before beginning formulation, as suggested by Goldman-Eisler (1972), who claimed a NP–VP structure as the minimum unit, and Davidson (1992), who found different patterns in terms of his units for beginners and seasoned interpreters; and (b) whether any input–output correlation could be found which might reflect conscious or unconscious "strategies" capable of being described in structural terms.

This comparison confirmed some observations found in the literature, corresponding roughly to syntactic, extratextual and communicative processes respectively: simultaneous interpreters often expand or insert structure with respect to the original discourse; use text-external knowledge of the situation or conference event; and use connectives, conjunctions, conatives and other interclausal elements rather liberally with respect to the original. All these transformations might, indeed, be found in written translation. The particular interest of SI for theories of speech processing lies in the time factor. The fluent synchronicity of professional SI suggests that the linearity constraints which might be expected from language structure might be largely overcome by attunement to a semantic-pragmatic level at which there are sufficient clues to construct meaning at a much finer degree of incrementality than dependence on Subject–Predicate structure would allow.

[. . .]

The aim of the present study was to find the appropriate level of discourse description to account for the transformations observed in SI, by determining whether some regular pattern of syntactic restructuring could be found, or if not – and if paraphrase is rather the rule than the exception even in the presence of compatible phrase-order – whether some more realistic and general principle can be found than the postulation of learnable strategies or the subjective parameter of stylistic preference.

To simplify, as an interpreter receives each successive sentence in SI, one of four conditions obtains: either

A.   her current output takes her beyond the whole of an incoming sentence ("consecutive in SI"), or it does not and she either

B.   pauses or waits until the new predicate is available; or

C.   begins afresh with "neutral" material, thus "stalling" until this predicate appears; or

D.   commits herself to a Subject and/or Predicate independently of the incoming structure (*saucissonnage* or "anticipation").

Before looking at the fate of whole sentences available for "consecutive" treatment (A), we examined cases where the interpreter begins before the current sentence is complete. Interpreters do not usually wait (B) during left-branching constituents, although short silences are sometimes noticeable if an earlier segment has been dealt with quickly. Where they encounter a left-branching structure signalled early in a sentence they usually "enter" (begin or continue a sentence) as soon as the first left-branching phrase begins (C or D); this was particularly clear from German, where sentences were an average 12s in length. In the Chinese speech, the average clause length was 5.8s, and interpreters could usually process whole clauses "consecutively" (A). These clauses must often be restructured, since Topic-Comment will not necessarily go into English; but, as in German–English, no regular restructuring pattern could be found: the contents of pre-verbal phrases, like Topic and "if" phrases . . ., emerge in the output in every possible syntactic guise. Even TL *Subjects* only matched those of the corresponding Chinese sentences structurally and semantically about 40% of the time (37 out of 90). In short, the evidence did not support any generalisation framed in terms of a sentence structure strategy, of the kind "where you encounter an embedded structure, wait for the head noun/ predicate" or "produce your own"; or for an initial Chinese proposition whose status is unclear, "produce as a self-contained clause".

Second, propositional matching was frustrated by the fact that interpreters often introduce connectives and/or conative rhetorical phrases of the type described in the literature as "neutral" or "filler" material. Input–output correspondence for these items was even more elusive than for the core propositions. Some look like stalling devices, but they occur throughout the discourse, not just at sentence openings and asymmetric structures. Some are purely performance variations of spoken discourse – slow, deliberate articulation, with drawling on vowels and schwa-suffixing on consonants, semantically redundant structures (*and this is something which..*), and elements which would normally be candidates for ellipsis. But others carry meaning, including more or less gratuitous expanded qualifications (*in this particular seminar*), and notably, a class of sentence-scope items – some of which have no overt origin in the source discourse – such as modal or conative phrases or adverbs (*obviously, of course, I think, in particular*), conjunctions (*and, but*), parenthetical additions, and discourse connectives (*Secondly, . . .; however*). In the Chinese–English corpora, which were more spontaneous and informal, both Speakers and interpreters used abundant such material, with only incidental formal correspondence: of the interpreters' 86 sentence- or clause-initial "responses" in the main corpus, over half involved additions, deletions, expansions or enrichments, simplifications, abridgements, or meaning-changing paraphrases. Over the recited written text, which lacked these lubricants, interpreters supplied a few of their own.

We thus have several apparently disparate phenomena at odds with a formal structural or semantic match between the SL and TL versions, including

(a)   insertions, additions, and omissions;
(b)   restructurings often described in terms of strategies, like anticipation or "chunking";
(c)   other deviations from formal syntactic-semantic correspondence, such as unexplained reordering or paraphrase, and holistic or "free" renderings.

At this point we must state another assumption of our analysis, although it may seem self-evident: that everything produced by the interpreter (as indeed by any speaker) that is input to the hearers' decoding and inferencing process – i.e. which is not filtered out at stimulus level, like an involuntary cough – has potential *meaning* and, in any event, some source in the interpreter's cognitive processes. Insertions and openings described as "padding" often carry meaning which must be sourced somewhere, regardless of whether they are felt to be natural or dismissed as translation errors (cf. Barik 1975). The "bolder" gambits produced independently of the source syntax (b or c above) also require some source. The next step was to identify these sources and capture them in an overall account.

Semantic sources in SI

The more ambitious (less neutral) structures produced at left-branching strings and elsewhere were found to fall into three classes in semantic terms (underlined strings had no overt source in input):

> 1. Expansion of a Subject, e.g. "*European subsidy fraud is a crime which . . .*"; "*this is something that . . .*"; "*rejoining the UN is a task which . . .*"; or insertion or expansion of parentheticals, e.g. "*as has already been said – in this particular semi/nar*"

> 2. Creation of a presentative (copula) or existential Main or Relative Clause which in effect simply asserts a presupposition of the embedded input structure, e.g. on hearing "**. . ., das unter dem grossen Feld, das unter dem Generalthema . . .**", "*there is a very large range of questions*".

> 3. "Anticipation", i.e. early output of a Head Noun or Main Verb.

Expansions as in (1) are usually described in the literature as padding or stalling devices. Their source can often be found in encyclopaedic knowledge, usually general attributes which avoid adding significant specification – e.g. *fraud "is a crime"* – or even a dummy attribute (*this is something that . . .*). The attribute is sometimes contextualised: "*is a task*" is only pertinent to "*rejoining the UN*" in this context. Evoked frame information of this type is likened by Fillmore (1985:245) to a form of lexical presupposition. Taking these with the existential and presentative statements exemplified in (2) allows us to generalise to a common source of SI production as simple presuppositions of different types licensed by elements of input text while syntax is still unfolding.

Frame or presupposition-based responses are illustrated in Table 1, where symmetrical translation into English is not possible, as the Subject **zwei Komplexe** ("two groups-of-issues") is delayed by a long PP and relative clause.

At the fronted phrases "**unter . . ., das unter . . .**" Interpreter L practises *saucissonnage*. She can predict a downstream Subj-V-O structure, qualified by "within

Table 1   SI processes.

Input	Interpreter L	Interpreter A	Interpreter B
In Ihrer Tagung hat In [NPyour meeting [has	*/by way of intro* *DUCtion*	+	*and THAT's basic ally* *what I shall try and* *do/HERE*
sich bereits **her'ausgestellt –** [IP[NP *refl* [already [emerged	+ *I think*	*in. the.* *-symPOSium*	*y-*
daß sich #Fe# unter **dem 'großen Feld** [CPthat[IP[NP*refl* # [PP under the large field	*during the course-* *of. this seminar-* *it- has@*	*so /far*	*/Y_OUR- -* *m\MEEting* +
das unter dem **Generalthema - er'faßt** **ist –** [IP that[VP[PPunder the general- theme [subsumed is -	*become. quite* *\clear 7.3 - that.* *there is a very @*	+	*h-has @* *alREADy -*
insbesondere zwei **Komplexe** **her'auskristallisieren –** [₁especially [two groups[out- crystallize]]]] -	*LARGE. RANGE* *of QUEStions*	*it has emerged.* *that there are*	*disCUSSed@ +* *@TWO - speCIFic*
das Eine ist [CP[IP the one is.	*@m -*	*TWO MAIN -*	*issues@ - IN - the* *OVERall*
	under- the-	*ISSues -*	*ISSue that*
	@ main topic - of @ *subsidy \fraud*		*you're - re/FERRing -*

Key: @ filled pause (schwa, "er" sound); - pause; + longer pause; # error or solecism; CAPS: stress; ' intonation peak (German); /,\ rising, falling pitch (English). Full stop within sentence: clipped word boundary (quarter-pause).

the broad domain . . .", but not its content. But she can simply assert the existence of this domain: *there is* a *very@ LARGE. RANGE* [*of QUEStions@m*], the minimal presupposition licensed by its status as Definite.[2] (She can also enrich it with her own knowledge about the identity of this "general theme", i.e. that it is in fact the main topic [*of the meeting*]: . *under- the- main topic - of subsidy \fraud.*) When the SL Subject **zwei Komplexe** appears she continues in this "presentative" mode: "*and there are TWO - MAIN - points of con\cern (- firstly. .)*".

Interpreter B ventures "*Your meeting . . .*" as a Subject, forcing her to generate her own independent sentence, requiring a predicate expressing some action, state or attribute, on the Subject "meeting", with no help from either the input grammar or content (". . . it has emerged that – within the broad domain covered by the overall theme . . ."). But the "meeting" frame contains a prototypical activity – discussion – and the next words fit its likely objects ("subject-matter": theme, field . . .), so that generating "discussed" as predicate is a fair gambit, by which time the vague "subject-matter" is specified as "two complexes".

The extract also shows how the choice of outputs is constrained by the interpreter's ongoing sentence. Interpreters A and B use the referent of **zwei Komplexe** ("two complexes") according to the status of their current sentences, A in a presentative ("*there are two main issues*"), B as an Object ("*has discussed two specific issues*"). B then attaches the earlier qualifying phrase (". . . *in the overall issue* . . ."), while A discards it (whether as a result of a relevance judgement or due to processing or memory failure cannot be established).

In "stalling" or *saucissonnage*, interpreters draw on inferred or associated knowledge to produce structure autonomously. In "anticipation", predicates or other downstream elements appear to be guessed by the interpreter. Traditionally the basis for such guesses is classified as either linguistic (e.g. probable collocations) or "logical" (e.g. from previous discourse). In this corpus, a wider range of cognitive and pragmatic sources was identified, including anticipation of the conclusion of an argument, where some premises and conclusions must have been supplied internally by the interpreter; anticipation from an early clue to a propositional attitude; and anticipation based directly on pragmatic principles (Setton 1997: 177–9). This latter is exemplified in (2), where the rapid inference allowing anticipation of both the final verb and its negation reflects pragmatic inference as well as knowledge of social conventions:

Example (2)
(Speaker's previous sentence: Professor Odersky is going to speak on this theme . . .)
als Präsi'denten - des 34.7 - deutschen 'Bundes
as President [Acc] -   of the   German   Federal
Int. A: . . . going to address precisely that / THEME 35.4 -
gerichtshofs 36.3 - brauche ich Herrn -   Professor
Justice Court -   need   I   Mr [Acc] - Professor
- he 36.9 - hardly 37.7 needs any
Odersky 38.1 - hier - NICHT VORzustellen 40.1
Odersky   here - *not introduce*
introDUCtion 38.9 I think ah for 40 as you know he's. the. President of the. Federal High Court

When she produces "*hardly needs any introduction*", the interpreter knows the Chairman is about to introduce Prof. Odersky, but in terms of semantic input for this particular utterance she has only the Accusative phrase "**als Präsi'denten . . .**" (and just possibly, "**Herrn**") and the verb "I need". According to RT, the "marked" fronting of the Accusative phrase signals the availability of a contextual effect by virtue of the additional processing effort it requires; and **als** ("given that [the Object] is . . .") points to the context for deriving it: Odersky occupies an exalted position whose incumbent must be known to all. The deduction that the moderator does *not* need to introduce him is made and formulated in less than 2 seconds.

Other transformations

Interpreters' caution with Chinese initial Topics is understandable, since their semantic dependency is obscure. But we also need to explain why interpreters should paraphrase and recast when presented with clearly marked logical and syntactic forms in transposable sentence structures. These corpora show frequent such recasting, both on line without hesitation, and in consecutive renderings of strings whose word-order could easily be followed in TL. Where several clauses are available, they are often fused or otherwise rationalised. Most significantly, apparently unproblematic (transposable) structures, such as subordinates clearly marked by initial conditionals or causative complementisers (*If. . ., Since . . ., Although . . .*), or interrogatives, are regularly recast:

1. a right-branching string of Nouns may be converted to verb and complement structure:
Example (3)
dürfte - der - der Schutz   - der-   des Finanzsystems -
might -   the - the protection - of-the - of-the -finance system
Int. A: + + +
des   des   Mißbrauchs der   Subventionen -
ofthe ofthe abuse   of the subsidies -
+ *the point being to -*
ah der europäischen Ge'meinschaften - in unserem Land -
of the   European   Communities -   in our country -
ah pro/DECT - European community's finances . . .
in Kern -
in core
from being misused

2. an interpreter may be offered a clear, unambiguous Subject – an initial Nominative-case Noun Phrase – but prefers to use it as an Object in her own formulation:
Example (4)
Der europäische Subventionsbetrug -
The European   subsidy fraud -
Interpreter A: . . . . .I'm going to address fraudulent obtention[5] of
SUBsidies - IN Europe.-

3. the only direct interrogatives in the corpora, the rhetorical question-and-answer forms in the Chinese corpus (**Weishenme (ne) ? yinwei . . .** "Why (is this)? Because . . . ") are ignored by the interpreters, who replace them with simple causal connectives (. . . . *as* . . ., / *because* . . .) or conative openings (*because we know that* . . .).

4. a fronted subordinate clause is rendered as a Main clause by all three interpreters even when the semantic relation (here, a causative) seems to be clearly marked [entry points in superscript]:
Example (5)
Da einer der Schwerpunkte - dieser - 'Tagung - auf[L] diesem[A]-
[since [one of-the focal-points   -[of this   - meeting] - [[on   [this -
Be'REICHdes[B] - Subventionsbetruges. liegen soll
area [of the   subsidy fraud   [lie should]]]]]
L: *which is. as I have said. one. of- the-main ah points ah. . . .*
A: *one of the - M MAIN points of our symposium - WAS. . . .*
B: *and that is- ah one of the important points - of . . .*

Why these departures? Either interpreters are deliberately and unnecessarily rejecting parallel structure, or discourse is not logically transparent. To attribute these extensive SL–TL changes to "stylistic preference" is something of a theoretical dead-end, and suggests an implausibly high degree of spare attentional capacity, control and sustained motivation. To attribute them to some strategy for managing cognitive resources, or efforts (e.g. Gile 1995, 1997) also requires an account of the conceptual and linguistic processing involved before corresponding efforts can be conjectured. In fact, these transformations can often be explained by pragmatic indeterminacy in input, or as ostensive packaging for output.

Pragmatic structure

A pragmatic feature which may garden-path or delay an interpreter has been described by Sweetser (1990) as the functional polysemy, or pragmatic ambiguity, of many elements of discourse which were once assumed to be logically transparent, including causatives, conditionals, interrogatives, modals and connectives, as seen in this contrast between a real causative use and an epistemic use of "must" and "because":

Example (6)
John must go to all the department parties
a. . . . because he's agreed to be bartender
b. . . . because he's always out on those nights

The pragmatic values of devices like connectives and modals are language-specific. In French, for instance, as Sweetser notes, these two functions of *because* may be distinguished by *puisque* and *parce que*. "Conditional" markers are also subtly different: "if" in English is only rarely concessive (*if he was a good Governor, he was a better President*), while French *si* often simply attaches a scalar epistemic value to a premise in this way rather than marking the subordinate clause as antecedent in a true conditional. Chinese "antecedent" clauses marked with "if" (**ruguo, . . . de hua, yao(shi)**) in our corpus, were not usually rendered as real conditionals, but treated as rhetorical openers ("givens"), or integrated into the sentence as adjuncts. In German, by contrast, although **wenn** is polysemous as between *realis/irrealis* (when/if), which may not be resolved until later, it has no "speech-act" use – i.e. meaning "while it is the case that" – so an initial *wenn* clause can be safely followed at a "logical" level as a real conditional – as it is, immediately, by all three interpreters – even when it turns out to be rhetorically hypothetical (the "representative" is the Speaker himself):

> Example (7)
> (Ladies and gentlemen . . .)
> **mm   wenn - ein Repräsentant eines Ge'richts . . .**
> er . . . when - a   representative of a   court
> [is to give a speech . . .]..

[. . .]

Holistic renditions

Finally, input–output correspondence is elusive in holistic or "idiomatic" renditions, and lubricant connective and conative items. "Free" translation poses a challenge to psycholinguistic modelling, and invites an ambitious stab at describing the boot-strapping and composition which must go on in central processes. A rendition like (8) illustrates the redistribution of lexical meaning in translation – "basically" con-veys the generality in the meaning of **Leitlinie** – but also the recognition and reproduction of (a) procedural features, like perspective ("that is what . . .") and the cohesive-resumptive function of the connective **auch**, rendered with "and" and the stress on THAT; and (b) conceptual metarepresentations of Speaker intent, as extracted from features like modals, needed to explain how "I shall try and do" translates **(das) soll**:

> Example (8)
> **Das soll auch die Leitlinie - für meine -einführenden**
> That shall indeed the directing-line - for my - introductory
> **Worte hier sein..**
> words here be
> *B: and THAT's basically what I shall try and do/HERE*

The idea that cognitive processes use a language of intermediate representation is now fairly uncontroversial. We shall suggest that it comprises a "vocabulary" to (meta)represent concepts, intentions and attitudes, and a "syntax" of deduc-tive procedures for inference, with an unspecified influence of affect and instinct on both. The jury is still out on how an associative network (connectionist) formalism could "cognize" conceptual and procedural meaning[4] and directed inten-tionality, but a *functional* model of processing for SI, independent of its neural implementation, must somehow embody these distinct dimensions of meaning as realised in language communication: since they are conveyed via different linguistic devices in different languages (and different cultures, and Speakers), they must be apprehended and encoded independently of form for "re-ostension" to the interpreter's audience.

Modelling on-line meaning assembly

It remains to see how intermediate propositions are assembled, how they are enriched or biased by conceptual input from memory, or by recent perceptual input; and how they acquire the quality of directedness or intentionality which drives the presentation of the content in the target discourse, while contributing to the incremental formulation observed in SI. Over long sentences, logical structure must be held even while the words have begun to evoke complex associations and contextual matching is in progress: in other words, logical (from syntax) and thematic structure (from content words and associations) must be built in parallel; a simultaneous interpreter cannot always wait for complete propositional forms, but sense may emerge from words and prosody before any syntactic or logical structure is available.

Previous accounts have distinguished a short-term phonological "scratchpad" memory from a conceptual or cognitive memory not clearly distinct from the store of world knowledge: IT models SI as alternating between these bases depending on the amount of context available. Our data is consistent with the hypothesis of a *medium-term* conceptual working memory (independent of the decaying phonological echo) which holds a construct of contexts relevant to the task at hand, couched in the intermediate language which – since it must integrate perceptual and previous conceptual information – is at one remove from linguistic form.

Adaptive working memory: the mental model

A mental model (MM) in adaptive working memory (Johnson-Laird 1983; Garnham 1987), offers a good account of the organisation of useful contextual support to utterance interpretation in SI. The MM can be seen as a dynamic, self-organising thematic-relational structure which supplies the premises and contexts for the deduction and inference in meaning assembly, and maintains an updated record of the entities, relations and propositions most salient and relevant to the discourse, whether their origin is explicit or implicit in the text, evoked or invoked as part of a frame, confirmed by direct perception (e.g. objects in the room), or assumed by the interpreter or Speaker on evidence of different strengths.

In the MM hypothesis, representations have different inherent strengths depending on whether they originate as percepts, concepts or attitudes. Percepts, as direct evidence for entities and relations from the audiovisual sphere, offer the highest degree of certainty. Situation-related elements of the mental model are kept salient by analogy with perceptually sourced imagery (e.g. positions in the conference room). All deictic indices, including time, place (visually verifiable) and personal (verifiable for the participants present) are monitored automatically. A mental model deriving from perception is assumed to be simpler and more determinate than one built from discourse (Johnson-Laird 1983: 407–8): indeed, among the elements used most autonomously by interpreters in their output are social or spatio-temporal deictics rooted in the situation, which enjoy the highest degree of strength (verifiability) in that they are backed by percepts.

A crucial point about the MM is that it does not "receive" concepts, percepts, or affect from a Speaker, but builds analogue representations with its own percepts, concepts and affect. Communication depends on the quality of this simulation, which in turn depends on the richness of this resident stock of experience. An MM is limited only by conceptualising ability: it can embody tokens linked by spatial, temporal or causal relations (events), and in general "content and form adapted to function" (*ibid*. 1983: 411).[5]

The MM might also be called a contextualiser. More than in the case of most ordinary conversation, contextualisation for SI begins before input: the interpreter starts assembling pieces of the model before entering the booth (perhaps weeks before), adding features at an accelerating rate as she gets the agenda, the minutes of the previous meeting, and the list of participants, then arrives at the meeting room; finally, if her colleague ("booth-mate") starts working first, she is fully contextualized by the time she begins. The overall course of discourse interpretation is therefore "top-down" insofar as some context is already available to interpreters in advance of input, forming a background for the operation of the parser on successive utterances; so that the interpreter's promptness and confidence in formulating directly from the Assembler's semantic output will depend to a considerable extent on its familiarity or compatibility with the constructed context in the mental model.

Contextualisation on line is unconscious to the extent that, as probably in all cognitive activity, relevance (coherence) is sought as a matter or routine. Context can be seen as a nested set of assumptions: a background about the world and the situation, then assumptions based on previous discourse, on the previous utterance, and finally those taking shape from utterance-initial cues about the illocution or modality of the impending utterance, the authority the Speaker wishes to attribute to it, its intended weight in the ongoing argument, or other indications of how it should be processed. This Speaker-related level of contextualisation may be supplied by a connective (conjunctive or subordinate), by a sentence-adverbial (e.g. *Furthermore* or French *Certes*), a prosodic feature, or indeed by the Speaker's body-language or facial expression. These verbal and other cues may prefix the new utterance or be interwoven with it, usually in the opening words.

The MM presents to the Assembler a set of probable referents and salient candidates for the main roles in the next proposition, with their evoked frame information, including local combinatorial lexical meaning and associated encyclopaedic knowledge which has been accessed. Information generated, assembled or retrieved in the process of comprehension may remain and be integrated into the model, so percepts and transitional inferences (including implicatures) may all potentially be reflected in the output.[6] MM-supported interpretation is illustrated in the continuation to the passage in Table 1:

Example (9)

(In Ihrer/ Tagung hat sich bereits herausgestellt - daß sich #Fe# unter dem großen Feld das unter dem Generalthema - erfaßt ist - insbesondere <u>zwei Komplexe</u> herauskristallisieren - <u>das eine</u> ist das Anliegen das verständliche Anliegen der europäischen Gemeinschaft - nach wirksamen strafrechtlichen Schutzzusicherung ihrer - ah ah ihre- -s eigenen Finanzsystems - <u>das andere</u> - vielleicht mehr von der Mitgliedstaatsseiten ah betonte Anliegen ist das- der- ah Ver- der Verbesserung ah der der Zusammenarbeit in der Kriminalitätsbekämpfung)
Meine kurzen /Worte - ah gliedern sich deshalb auch
My short words are - articulated hence also
in <u>diese beiden \Teile</u>
in these two parts
L: *and I \hope that my - brief presentation will deal with both of these \aspects*
A: *and what I have to say - fits - under BOTH of those - concepts and \ISSues*
B: *and therefore I will make -m my- divide my statement into- two \PARTS*

The phrase "**Meine kurzen /Worte . . .**" is assembled compositionally (**Worte** is a body of discourse, though its extension in time remains vague) as a representation for which the interpreters select different formulations: "*my statement*"; "*my presentation*"; and "*what I have to say*". Demonstratives direct a hearer to search for a recent/accessible referent in working memory (Givón 1984:398 ff.; Chafe 1994), in this case a "doublet" compatible with **diese beiden Teile**, "these two parts". This was installed in the MM by "**zwei Komplexe**" 30 seconds previously, and then developed in the two macro-propositions: "two problem areas in particular . . . the first . . . the second . . ." (underlined). The interpreters' formulations reflect the attributes which have meanwhile accrued to this entity (*those aspects; those concepts and \ISSues*) as much as those attached to its latest realisation (*two \PARTS*).

The connectives **deshalb** and **auch** are procedural items which point to dependent relevance between these propositions. This connectivity is recognised in the interpreters' use of sentential *and*, rather than the VP-attached readings "*also" or "*too" licensed by the logical and lexical values of **auch**. But the interpreters' use of *I \hope that. . .*, *what I have to say* and *I will make . . .*, suggests that an intentionality is perceived, which we can ascribe partly to **auch** and partly to the inference that **meine kurzen Worte** refers to the future discourse. While we have suggested that such elements already mark the MM representation, they may also contribute to a longer-term representation at a higher, coordinating level sensitive to the coherence and intentionality of the whole discourse.

On this basis a first approximation to a cognitive model can be outlined, in which conceptual representations are organised for relevance in the mental model, supporting the assembly of successive propositions from input in the Assembler, while secondary pragmatic processing is centred on a coordinating Executive, on which all inputs converge (propositional, instinctive etc., and self-monitoring): this Executive makes any necessary further overall fidelity judgements and prepares for production. "Macro" timing and choice intervene at this stage, where the interpreter may choose to formulate from more or less enriched Assembly products, fuse, summarise, elaborate, etc. The Executive in our SI model differs from most supervisory centres conjectured in the cognitive psychology literature in that, in addition to task coordination, it performs secondary pragmatic processing on the propositions supplied to it from the MM or Assembler, including the interpreter's own self-monitored speech.

To conclude our analysis of meaning assembly, we shall briefly describe phenomena suggesting Addressee-oriented processing, in which linguistic resources are mobilised by the interpreter as *speaker*, at the point of production, to restore the communicative integrity of the speech, and hence its pragmatic fidelity. This notion is based on Gutt's (1991) RT-based definition of the aim of direct translation (as opposed to adaptation): to allow Addressees access to the same contextual effects at the same processing effort. This requires the preservation or restoration of all communicative clues (roughly, the procedural dimension).

Production: compensation and re-ostension

At production, two additional operations are necessary: compensation for semantic dilution or garden-pathing forced by the SI conditions; and re-ostension.

First, it would be implausible to suggest that while utterances are still incomplete a simultaneous interpreter routinely finds formulations which may stand uncorrected – even sovereign Speakers do not always get it right first time – and the processes of inference and translation upset the implicit–explicit balance as well as the informational content. Simplification and dilution arise from (a) pressure for efficiency in MM assembly, in which like arguments may be fused and logical structure simplified; (b) "afterthoughts" or other elements belatedly modifying meaning in a complex sentence; and (c) a superordinate or generic "placeholder" being produced to stand in for a word or sense as yet unresolved. Even if experienced professionals produce fluent, natural-sounding speech, corpus analysis clearly shows approximation and compensation at both sentence and text level.

Second, speech communication requires ostension and encoding on a Speaker's part, and decoding and inference on the hearer's. An interpreter becomes a Speaker at the point where her own speech-acts are formed. While an ordinary hearer is *guided* to content by the pragmatic dimension of input, which he does not therefore normally notice, an interpreter must apprehend this pragmatic guidance and *reapply* it in TL for her Addressees. This additional level probably develops with the trainee's experience of her role. Re-ostension is required in TL since the illocutionary indicators and other devices which guide hearers are language-specific (Fillmore 1984; Sweetser 1990), and include focus, stress, word-order effects and other pragmatic pointers: expressions like *however, as I have said, of course, I hope that* are only the most tangible layer of ostension. Whether this dimension is essentially computed, or carried by affect or instinct (or telepathy), it must be reconstructed in the target discourse, and corpus analysis shows that much of it can be tracked from the Speaker's to the interpreter's speech (Setton 1997), as for example in (10), where the cohesive link achieved in German by fronting a phrase is realised in English by inserting an adverbial:

Example (10)
Zu diesem Thema wird - Herr Prof. Odersky - sprechen
On this   topic   will - Mr   Prof. Odersky - speak:
L: . . . on *precisely* this topic
A: . . . *going to address* precisely *that* / THEME

Pragmatic fidelity can be restored through commands to production, the most autonomous part of the SI cycle. In the theoretical framework proposed here, the intermediate "seme" is conceived of as a feature in the language of thought (we can call it "backlink", "focus", "relevance pointer", etc.), inferred from a word-order choice in German, then expressed as an adverbial in English. Simultaneous interpreters, as one might expect, favour expressive resources which do not rely on word-order: stress, speed, volume, or voice modulation, and local or relatively "portable" items like adverbials and parentheticals. Local stress can be used to restore an emphasis marked in SL by word-order; or something which would normally be left to inference can be omitted in TL, following Relevance principles (or indeed, the Gricean Maxim of Quantity). In the extract in Table 1, L's simple conjoining of the two statements *there is a very @ LARGE. RANGE [of QUEStions @m]* . . . *and there are TWO - MAIN points of con\cern* simplifies the semantic structure of the German, which specifies that "two complexes emerge (**herauskristallisieren**) *within* the broad range of issues *under* the general theme". In some cases, the interpreter may post-edit to supplement this kind of advance approximation, but here it is unnecessary: the conjunction is sufficient for listeners to infer, for what it's worth, that the latter (points of concern) are ranked "under" the former (main topic); in other words, the inferential processing of the interpreter's Addressees is taken into account, and *pragmatic* fidelity is adequate.

Summary

Some salient features of SI discourse processing can now be summarised in a number of principles:

1. Comprehension and Assembly follow a fine-grained **Incrementality**, inasmuch as words may introduce potential contexts even as the logical structure of a sentence is unfolding: options to formulate are available at all times, from attributes of text items to clues to attitudes. To produce speech before an utterance is complete, a simultaneous interpreter may draw either on a contextualized mental model, or on a logical or propositional form, which are more or less enriched stages of representation of a recent utterance; or produce a pragmatically justified utterance-scope expression such as a connective, a phrase of saying or believing, a phrase reflecting a modality or propositional attitude, or one with wider text scope, such as a parenthetical reference to previous discourse. Different types of meaning (logical, thematic and pragmatic) may come in any order, and pragmatic or prosodic

features relevant to the interpretation of a string can inform formulation before parts of its semantic representation.

2. The semantic simplification observed in SI may be explained by a principle of **Efficiency**, or parsimony, of the mental model representing the discourse-in-situation for the SI task in working memory: it integrates propositions, with their relevant associated referents and their attributes, and their presuppositions and implicatures, as concisely as possible; for example, the currency of referents fades unless strengthened by repeated reference. A mental model may represent propositional content vaguely (with more or less attribution) but not as ambiguous or unresolved.

3. Formulation begun in the absence of a full proposition involves **Approximation** or placeholding. Incomplete or partly unresolved logical forms can be used for formulation as provisional "placeholders" standing in for referents, relations, or attitudes and illocutions which have not yet been adequately contextualized or resolved. These devices may include

(a) existential quantifiers and pro-forms (e.g. *this, something, what*), as placeholders for referents;

(b) presuppositions, presentative constructions or Aboutness functions (e.g. *(there) is a . . .; I'd like to discuss . . .; as far as . . . is concerned*), as placeholders for attributes and relations;

(c) declaratives and assertions, as placeholders pending the clarification of mood or modality.

In this case, output structure can be provisionally generated or expanded from something confidently evoked from input: logical (recursive expansions with dummy variables and connections), thematic (expansion of attributes, superordinates) or pragmatic (expressions of illocution and attitude).

4. Pragmatic fidelity is achieved by a process of **Compensation**, which is directed by the Executive and implemented in production, for temporary semantic loss or dilution which arises at word or proposition level; and **Re-ostension**, to replace the ostensive and directive features lost in translation and/or supply those appropriate to the target language (and Addressees).[7]

Finally, the assumption that indeterminacy may be resolved by recourse to a *combination* of different kinds of information (perceptual, memory-based, and parser output) entails the translation of these primary inputs into a compatible central "language" which can also be read for formulation, a kind of language of thought (LOT: Fodor 1975, 1987). This *lingua franca* of central representations, from Assembler to Executive, might comprise a vocabulary of both semantic and intentional quanta (or qualia), representing concepts (entities–properties–relations) indexed for deixis and thematic role, and metarepresented under illocutions and attitudes derived from the basic intentional states of Belief and Desire; and a "syntax" of logical operators and inference procedures. The linguistic knowledge acquired in L1, L2, etc. is indexed, in each case, to this intermediate language, more or less richly and intimately depending on the age of acquisition and subsequent practice. An experimental LOT of this kind is used to represent central processing in a tabulated blow-by-blow corpus analysis in Setton (1997, 1999).

Discussion

We have analysed the "Message" for translation as comprising not only propositional content, and the attitudes under which it is presented, but also procedural directions to Relevance, all of which must be re-expressed for the Addressees. We have tried to show how these elements are intertwined in discourse in such a way as to allow the finely incremental assembly of Speaker meaning, and hence incremental formulation in advance of full propositions, with the result that SI output often resembles lexical and syntactic structure of input only remotely. The corpora, taken from professional practice, suggest that the result can nevertheless achieve pragmatic fidelity subject to the interpreter's ability to compensate for on-line approximations and re-inject the appropriate ostension. [. . .]

This analysis may also shed some light on the significance of language typology. [. . .] In SI from an SOV to an SVO language, pragmatic and contextual resources can allow confident entry over a formally complex structure, or, if lacking, cause hesitation over a simple one. [. . .]

Generalisations about psychodynamics and performance in SI must remain tentative on the basis of a limited corpus designed to explore local and medium-term processes. At least four important variables could not be directly addressed: discourse-type, Speaker, language, and the interpreter's motivation or choice. However, the framework offers a theoretical accommodation of these parameters. Variations in the interpreter's readiness, the depth of conceptual assimilation on-line, the effects of varying clarity of Speakers . . . and the voluntary effort put into the cohesion of the product, can all be expressed in terms of activity in the MM (conceptual cohesion) and/or Executive (pragmatic processing, "communicative management").

Anticipating two possible objections, it may seem that an unnecessarily complex processing model is being proposed to justify what is ultimately another declaration of faith in the interpreter's ability to achieve complete fidelity. On the matter of complexity, first, the model is meant to account for the whole process, not just the parts which are accessible to conscious introspection by a practitioner; the process as we have modelled it only enters a potentially conscious phase (roughly) from Principle 3 ("Approximation") onwards: as researchers, we will find interpretive and constructive processes to be pervasive in speeches which interpreters felt to be quite straightforward.

Second, the model is designed to account for SI tasks involving maximal inference and/or pragmatic reformulation. It is clear that for some interpreters in some task conditions the bilingual lexicon may play an overwhelming role, while less activity is required in the mental model. Professionals undoubtedly build up and refine a huge "phrase-book", which may contain entire formulas (Levelt 1989), refined by habits of inter- and intralinguistic association and selective suppression. An experienced staff interpreter in an international organisation, for example,[8] where phraseology is relatively standardised and her basic MM is valid from one meeting and Speaker to the next, may draw systematically on such ready-made elements (which are probably not distinguishable in a corpus from spontaneously assembled structure), and very little complex inferencing or sovereign formulation may be necessary. This does not mean that meaning assembly and executive supervision are not there; simply that comprehension is facilitated by rich top-down support from the mental model, and formulation fully exploits the phrasebook if it contributes to efficiency. Discourse type and subject variables, in other words, are reflected in variations on routing and contributions from different components of the model.

Does SI require special skills, and can we teach SI "strategies"? The recommendation that trainee interpreters should learn as many "automatic" skills as possible is questionable for various reasons. The first argument is psycholinguistic. Current theory suggests that activation is automatic, while selective suppression is not and requires training; and that simultaneous interpreters probably have an additional burden of suppression due to self-monitoring and the presence of two languages (Moser-Mercer *et al.* 1997:138). If this is so, and meaning assembly in novel situations (as usually encountered by beginners) involves integrating syntax, procedural indicators, lexical meaning, and context, then reliable *automatismes* are probably confined to the retrieval of phrasal forms, especially in very different languages; whereas in cognate languages, it would be dangerous for the novice to rely on them, not having fully developed either selective suppression or the expert phrase-book.

It is possible that some local "strategies" and tactics can be described to pedagogical effect, but unlikely that they can be usefully implemented without being generalised into the *habit* of exploiting cognitive resources and pragmatic sensitivity on-line. These two general skills needed for interpretation can be inferred from the two functions which are tested more than in everyday communication: the temporary construction of large new contexts, and the ability to recreate the intentionality of a third party in one's own discourse. Experience and corpus findings suggest that survival, then quality in SI, depend on three conditions: (i) reducing obstacles to perception, decoding and encoding (sound quality, language competence); (ii) the quality of the intermediate representation (preparation, general knowledge); and (iii) communicative or pragmatic competence. Any recommendation on more specific techniques should be subordinate to development in these areas.

Finally, in purely theoretical terms, the account needs closer specification in those areas currently being explored in cognitive linguistics: the boundaries between primary decoding and the inferential phase of comprehension, and between the assembly of conceptual representations (MM) and the apprehension of intentionalities; for example, it may ultimately make more sense to collapse propositional and intentional representation into a single process. Theoretical explanations in "soft" science are of course as difficult to validate as to falsify empirically: to test a model in which pragmatic factors are central, and a complex cognitive configuration is proposed, would require multivariate analysis (for instance: information density, interpreter's preparation and discourse connectivity) on *situated* data. Given a sufficiently broad data base, one might compare pragmatic features of speeches which interpreters have graded for difficulty (or users for quality); explore variables such as ostensive or illocutionary clarity (in spontaneous vs. recited text), or the position of the discourse in the event; or experimentally manipulate variables such as the interpreters' degree of preparation. Certainly it is difficult to see how SI research can progress without more, larger and more varied corpora. [. . .]

Notes

1   Semi-rehearsed speech is perhaps the most common register in international conference practice, lying between spontaneous dialogue, as in the negotiations in Lederer's (1981) corpus, and speech recited from text, which is also quite common. Furthermore, conference discourse typically belongs to the discursive or argumentative genre; hardly ever is it primarily descriptive or narrative.

2   A definite NP is identified by Strawson as the most basic type of "presupposition trigger" (Levinson 1983:181).

3   "Obtention": lexical interference from the interpreter's L2 (French) during L3–L1 interpretation.

4   We must beware of the potential confusion between terms like procedural, declarative, implicit and explicit, as used in *psychology* to describe different types of memory, and the meaning of these terms in *linguistics* to describe types of meaning; in view of the tight intertwining of procedural and conceptual encoding in language, it is difficult to see how they could be assigned to distinct memories.

5   Schematics of putative MM states and contents at different points in unfolding discourse are given in Setton 1997 and Setton 1999 (Ch. 6).

6   Memory retains the representations made at the time of comprehension, not the exact words (Johnson *et al.* 1973 in Garnham 1987). We can therefore expect to find inference products in the output.

7   More research is necessary to discover to what extent interpreters actually take specific Addressees into account.

8   Steven Pearl, a former UN chief interpreter, has recently questioned the need to rethink and reformulate discourse in SI to the extent claimed by IT writers (Pearl 1995).

References

Altmann, G. and Steedman, M. (1988) "Interaction with Context in Human Sentence Processing," *Cognition* 30: 191–238.

Austin J. L. (1962) *How to Do Things with Words*, Oxford: Clarendon Press.

Barik, H. C. (1973) "Simultaneous Interpretation: Temporal and Quantitative Data," *Language and Speech* 16: 237–71.

—— (1975) "Simultaneous Interpretation: Qualitative and Linguistic Data," *Language and Speech* 18: 272–97.

Blakemore, D. (1987) *Semantic Constraints on Relevance*, Oxford: Blackwell.

Chafe, W. (1994) *Discourse, Consciousness and Time*, Chicago: University of Chicago Press.

Davidson, P. (1992) "Segmentation of Japanese Source Language Discourse in Simultaneous Interpretation," *The Interpreters' Newsletter* [Special Issue no. 1]: 2–11.

Fillmore, C. (1982) "Frame Semantics," in The Linguistic Society of Korea (ed.)

Linguistics in the Morning Calm [vol. 1.] Seoul: Hanshin Publishing Co., pp. 111–37.

—— (1984) "Remarks on Contrastive Pragmatics," in J. Fisiak (ed.) *Contrastive Linguistics: Prospects and Problems*, Amsterdam/Philadelphia: Benjamins, pp. 119–41.

—— (1985) "Frames and the Semantics of Understanding," *Quaderni di Semantica* VI/2, Dec.: 222–54.

Fodor, J. (1975) *The Language of Thought*, Cambridge, Mass.: Harvard University Press.

—— (1983) *The Modularity of Mind*, Cambridge, Mass.: MIT Press.

—— (1987) *Psychosemantics*, Cambridge, Mass: MIT Press.

Garnham, A. (1987) *Mental Models as Representations of Discourse and Text*, Chichester: Ellis Horwood.

Gile, D. (1995) *Regards sur la recherche en interprétation de conférence*, Lille: Presses Universitaires de Lille.

—— (1997) "Conference Interpreting as a Cognitive Management Problem," in J. Danks, M. Gregory, B. Shreve, S. Fountain and M. McBeath (eds) *Cognitive Processes in Translation and Interpreting*, London: Sage, pp. 196–214.

Givón, T. (1984, 1990) *Syntax – A Functional-Typological Introduction*, Amsterdam/Philadelphia: Benjamins.

Goldman-Eisler, F. (1972) "Segmentation of Input in Simultaneous Translation," *Journal of Psycholinguistic Research* 1 (2): 127–40.

Grice, P. (1967) *Logic and Conversation*, unpublished manuscript of the William James Lectures, Harvard University.

Grice, P. (1989) *Studies in the Way of Words*, Cambridge, Mass.: Harvard University Press.

Gutt, E.-A. (1991) *Translation and Relevance: Cognition and Context*, Oxford: Blackwell.

Johnson, M, Bransford, J. and Solomon, S. (1973) "Memory for Tacit Implications of Sentences," *Journal of Experimental Psychology* 98: 203–5.

Johnson-Laird, P. (1983) *Mental Models*, Cambridge: Cambridge University Press.

Lederer, M. (1981) *La traduction simultanée*, Paris: Minard Lettres Modernes.

Levelt, W. (1989) *Speaking – From Intention to Articulation*, Cambridge, Mass.: MIT Press.

Levinson, S. (1983) *Pragmatics*, Cambridge: Cambridge University Press.

Marslen-Wilson, W. (1987) "Functional Parallelism in Spoken Word Recognition," *Cognition* 25: 71–102.

Moser-Mercer, B., Lambert, S., Darò, V. and Williams, S. (1997) "Skill Components in Simultaneous Interpreting," in Y. Gambier, D. Gile and C. Taylor (eds) *Conference Interpreting: Current Trends in Research*, Amsterdam/Philadelphia: John Benjamins, pp. 133–48.

Pearl, S. (1995) "Lacuna, Myth and Shibboleth in the Teaching of Simultaneous Interpreting," *Perspectives: Studies in Translatology* 3 (2): 161–90.

Pöchhacker, F. (1994) *Simultandolmetschen als komplexes Handeln*, Tübingen: Gunter Narr.

Searle, J. (1969) *Speech Acts*, Cambridge: Cambridge University Press.

—— (1983) *Intentionality*, Cambridge: Cambridge University Press.

Searle, J. (1992) *The Rediscovery of the Mind*, Cambridge, Mass.: MIT Press.

Setton, R. (1997) "A Pragmatic Model of Simultaneous Interpretation," unpublished doctoral dissertation, Chinese University of Hong Kong, UMI no. 9819120.

—— (1999) *Simultaneous Interpretation: A Cognitive-Pragmatic Analysis*, Amsterdam/ Philadelphia: John Benjamins.

Sperber, D. and Wilson, D. (1986) *Relevance: Communication and Cognition*, Oxford: Blackwell.

Stenzl, C. (1983) "Simultaneous Interpretation – Groundwork towards a Comprehensive Model," unpublished Master's thesis, Birkbeck College, University of London.

Sweetser, E. (1990) *From Etymology to Pragmatics*, Cambridge: Cambridge University Press.

Wilson, D. and Sperber, D. (1993), "Linguistic Form and Relevance," *Lingua* 90 [Special Issue on Relevance Theory, vol. 2, D. Wilson and N. Smith (eds)]: 1–24.

Wilss W. (1978) "Syntactic Anticipation in German–English Simultaneous Interpretation," in D. Gerver and H. W. Sinaiko (eds) *Language Interpretation and Communication*, Proceedings of the NATO Symposium on Language Interpretation and Communication, Venice, 1977, New York: Plenum Press, pp. 335–43.

Part 4

Broadening the View

INTRODUCTION

IN THE FIRST decades of systematic study directed at the phenomenon of interpreting, what commanded most researchers' attention was the description and
explanation of the cognitive processes involved in simultaneous (conference) interpreting, for which psychological and psycholinguistic experiments were regarded as the
method of choice. The wider situational, interactional and sociocultural contexts,
within which the activity of interpreting is carried out, were seen rather as a diffuse
backdrop to the cognitive dynamics at center stage. The work of the three authors
presented in this Part broadens the analytical focus on interpreting in several different
directions to cover the social constellations in which interpreters appear in their
unique, albeit ill-defined, role; the interaction settings in particular sociocultural and
institutional environments as well as their interplay with numerous parameters defining the communicative process; and the various semiotic relations which obtain in
different channels of interaction when communication is mediated in the consecutive
or simultaneous modes of interpreting.

A classic of the IS literature, which was "re-discovered" more than a decade
after its original publication, is the sociological account of the interpreter's role by
R. Bruce W. Anderson. Though not part of a sustained involvement in interpreting
research, the analysis put forward by Anderson (1976, and in this volume) from a
social science perspective introduces many of the key concepts and issues which IS
researchers, particularly when studying interpreting in non-conference settings, have
found particularly salient. These include: the degree of the interpreter's bilingualism,
with the spectrum extending from "natural translators" (Harris and Sherwood 1978)
to fully balanced bilinguals (Thiéry 1975); prototypical interaction constellations,
as analyzed by Feldweg (1996: 178) for conference interpreting and, more
broadly, by Alexieva (1997, and in this volume); the status and power differential
between the interpreter's two clients, which is virtually the essential ingredient of

community-based interpreting, though certainly not limited to it (cf. Baker 1997); the interpreter's impact on the course of the interaction in a "gatekeeping" function (cf. Wadensjö 1998: 67–9), as studied, for instance, with reference to turn-change behavior (e.g. Roy 1996; Apfelbaum 1999); and, as the epitome of the issue of role, conflicting loyalties and expectations (e.g. Kaufert and Koolage 1984; Niska 1995; Morris 1999; Pöchhacker 2000a).

Most of the issues introduced in Anderson's seminal essay, and reflected also in his follow-up effort to establish "cross-cutting typologies" of interpreter roles and interpreting situations (1978), are taken up in a more systematic and more closely communication-oriented perspective by **Bistra Alexieva** (1997, and in this volume). Her "Typology of Interpreter-Mediated Events" is one of the most comprehensive frameworks available to IS scholars for categorizing and differentiating their object of study. Drawing on her rich personal experience of the Bulgarian interpreting market as well as on her scholarly expertise in linguistics, Alexieva demonstrates the descriptive potential of her multiple parameters, which cover aspects of the message, as expressed in the source and target texts, as well as the situational environment. Research on the textual (and intertextual) dimension of interpreting, to which Alexieva contributed several innovative studies of her own (e.g. 1985, 1992, 1994), is the focus of Part 5 of this volume; the variables of the communicative situation, on the other hand, which Alexieva covers along the lines of the Lasswell formula ("Who speaks, to Whom, Where," etc.), have been dealt with by a number of scholars in Interpreting Studies, such as Namy (1978), Gile (1989a), Cokely (1992), Salevsky (1993a, 1994), Pöchhacker (1992, 1994a, 1995a) and Mikkelson (1999, with reference to the typology by Alexieva).

As one might expect in a part devoted to particularly broad perspectives on the phenomenon of interpreting, there are many areas of interface not only between the sociological analysis by Anderson and the communicational typology by Alexieva, but also between the latter and the comprehensive semiotic account by **Fernando Poyatos** of the (nonverbal) communication channels in simultaneous and consecutive interpreting. Apart from two early papers by Bühler (1980, 1985) on the significance of nonverbal information in conference interpreting, it was Poyatos (1987, and in this volume) who provided the first, and by far the most comprehensive, account of the broad range of semiotic phenomena extending between the verbal and the situational dimension. As a leading scholar in the field of nonverbal communication studies, Poyatos is in a position to apply his own highly developed conceptual framework, especially on the manifestations of paralanguage (Poyatos 1993), to the communicative activity of interpreting. Though he became acquainted with the study and teaching of interpreting during lectures at the (conference) interpreter training schools in Heidelberg and Germersheim, Poyatos nevertheless maintains a broad focus and, not surprisingly perhaps, addresses many issues which are especially relevant to the analysis of face-to-face interpreting in various institutional settings.

In the research literature on conference interpreting in particular, Poyatos's work has proved influential for a number of IS scholars: it is prominent in Pöchhacker's (1994a, 1994b) model of the text in simultaneous conference interpreting, in the study by Ahrens (1998) on nonverbal indicators of processing load in consecutive interpreting, in the PhD thesis by Collados Aís (1998) on nonverbal communication in the simultaneous mode, and in Alonso Bacigalupe's (1999) experiment on the impact of visual contact on simultaneous interpreters' performance. The latter represents perhaps the most salient issue in this context, given the great professional challenge of remote interpreting, whether in the form of video conferencing (e.g. Mouzourakis 1996; Heynold 1995; Kurz 2000), conventional telephone interpreting (e.g. Wadensjö 1999) or remote simultaneous interpreting in healthcare settings (Hornberger 1997; Hornberger *et al.* 1996). Since research on this subject (e.g. Balzani 1990; Lebhar Politi 1989; L. Anderson 1994; Tommola and Lindholm 1995; Alonso Bacigalupe 1999; Niska [*et al.*] 1999) has produced little conclusive evidence, the topic of information transmitted through the visual channel remains as significant to interpreting research as when Poyatos first made it a subject of systematic analysis. A closely related issue, which is touched but not dwelt upon, in Poyatos's (1987) essay, is the complex role of visual cues in signed-language interpreting. With or without the added difficulties of remote interpreting, this is surely one of the most relevant points of interface between IS research and a broadly semiotic approach to communication studies. The same holds true, of course, for the posture and position of spoken-language interpreters in face-to-face interaction (e.g. Harris 1981) – another object of study which remains wide open for empirical investigation.

A number of the sociological, situational, discoursal and semiotic issues raised by the systematic analyses presented in this part are dealt with elsewhere in this volume. The main implication of this exercise in "broadening the view," however, is the realization that a comprehensive, multi-dimensional understanding of the phenomenon of interpreting requires more in-depth research from a variety of theoretical approaches than one could ever hope to collect – or even represent by a balanced sample – within a single anthology. With the view thus broadened, the remaining parts can do no more than single out a limited number of studies and select a few major themes for drawing them together.

THE PROBLEMATIC NATURE of the interpreter's role, now a dominant theme of research on community-based interpreting, was virtually unexplored until R. Bruce W. Anderson's 1976 paper – and largely remained so for well over a decade. Indeed, as Sturge (1997) has shown, reflection on the role of translation and translators in cross-cultural contacts was hardly more sophisticated up to the 1990s. In both respects, Bruce Anderson, a sociologist with degrees from Northwestern and Duke universities, deserves credit as a pioneer. In 1966, his interest in methodology and things cross-cultural prompted him to give a paper on translation as a methodological problem in bilingual surveys at a meeting of the American Sociological Association. Two years later, in the same forum, he extended his theoretical focus to a sociological account of language and translation and thus laid the foundation for what was to become a seminal paper for the study of interpreting as a social activity in cross-cultural interaction.

The paper reprinted here with some abridgements, mainly concerning contemporary issues in bilingualism, and some diagrams, was originally published in Richard W. Brislin's volume *Translation: Applications and Research*, alongside chapters by Gerver and Seleskovitch which are among these authors' most-cited works. While the book (Brislin 1976a), with whose editor Bruce Anderson shares a long-standing commitment to cross-cultural communication, is long out of print, and while Anderson, during his twenty-six-year tenure as Associate Professor at the University of Texas at Arlington, ultimately shifted his focus to the sociology of health, the crucial issues he raised back in the 1970s – of power and role conflict in interpreting – are finally here (in IS) to stay.

Further reading: Brislin 1976b; Anderson 1978.

R. Bruce W. Anderson

PERSPECTIVES ON THE ROLE OF INTERPRETER

IN THE PAST, sociologists have shown little interest in translation or in the behavior of interpreters or other translators. Several sociologists have recently focused attention on methodological problems arising from translation in comparative research. Among these are statements by Grimshaw (1969a, 1969b), Deutscher (1968, 1969), and Anderson (1967, 1969) which attend to translation problems in both *inter*national and *intra*national investigations. One gains the clear impression from these reports that translation is potentially a methodological issue whenever the investigator and his subjects differ with respect to cultural background or the subjects differ from one another. Though the methodological problems resulting from (the need for) translation are virtually ubiquitous, their visibility is clearly greater when cultural differences are paralleled by language, rather than dialect differences.

Probably as a result of the dominance of survey research in sociology, much of the concern with translation as a methodological issue has focused on problems of comparability between paper-and-pencil instruments. Translation of such instruments is primarily undertaken by bilinguals working more-or-less in isolation, and it is essentially nonsocial behavior. One need only read Phillips' (1960) account of his experiences in working through an interpreter while interviewing in Thailand to realize that translation also occurs in *social* situations – situations amenable to sociological analysis. In any such setting the role played by the interpreter is likely to exert considerable influence on the evolution of group structure and on the outcome of the interaction. For a sociologist conducting interviews through an interpreter, the problem of maintaining rapport with him may give greater bearing upon data quality than the time-honored problem of maintaining respondent rapport!

International negotiations concerning trade agreements, peace treaties, and the like constitute another area of potential sociological interest in the role of the interpreter. Here sociological interest in the evolving social structure of a small group of negotiators merges with the interests of social psychologists, political scientists, and legal scholars in analysis of problem-solving behavior. Whether one is interested in . . . the politics of international crises (Young 1967, 1968), attitudes of various ethnic groups toward each other in multilingual societies (Gumperz 1962; Ferguson 1962; Lambert 1967) or problems of integration of ethnic and linguistic minorities (Ervin-Tripp 1967; Macnamara 1967), <u>understanding the role and behavior of interpreters</u> is likely to prove relevant. [. . .] Understanding the role of the interpreter may also aid understanding of interaction between people of different statuses and backgrounds within a single-language community. For example, paraphrasing, which may be viewed as a special case of translation, commonly obtains in labor negotiation, doctor–patient interaction, parent–child interaction, and resolution of disputes between dominant and minority groups. In each case the parties to the interaction differ in their vocabulary (e.g., technical versus nontechnical) and in their understanding of the meanings of terms known in common. Frequently, the services of an intermediary are needed for effective communication. The remainder of this chapter explores *some* factors that describe and determine the role of the interpreter in relation to others involved in bilingual (or multilingual) interaction.

Basic elements of translation situations

To facilitate analysis of the role of the interpreter a brief outline of a set of minimal conditions that are necessarily present in translation situations follows.

1. Typically, translation occurs in <u>social situations</u> involving interaction among at least three persons.

2. These actors may be identified as producer, interpreter,[1] and consumer. In some cases "producer" and "consumer" are roles adopted interchangeably by a single participant. In others they are played by unique individuals. The dual role situation may be illustrated by a multilingual conference, whereas the separate role situation might be exemplified by a translated lecture. At times it may be convenient to refer to <u>both producer and consumer together as clients of the interpreter,</u> since both use his services.

3. It follows that <u>the role of the interpreter is pivotal to the entire social process.</u> In the type case of three participants, two may be assumed to be monolingual. The interpreter is, by definition, bilingual. The two monolingual actors would be unable to communicate with each other without his aid – except through a primitive set of gestures.

Roles of the interpreter and some hypotheses about his behavior

The interpreter as bilingual. There is a growing body of literature dealing with the nature and types of bilingualism. For example, studies by Lambert (1955) and his associates have shown that the linguistic behavior of bilinguals is influenced by the order in which they learned the languages at their command, the relative dominance of their languages, and the extent to which the language systems merge. A bilingual's characteristics with respect to each of these dimensions seem to have implications for the role of the interpreter. [. . .]

Most bilinguals learn one language first ["mother tongue"] – although second-language learning may take place quite early in childhood. [. . .] For the interpreter the consequence is a somewhat greater probability that he will identify with mono-lingual speakers of his mother tongue than with speakers of other languages, *ceteris paribus*.

Of course, all other things are unlikely to be equal. Another matter that must be considered is linguistic dominance. [. . .] For the interpreter, linguistic dominance has two consequences [. . .]. First, it is generally easier to understand a language than to speak it with facility. It follows that a bilingual translating to his dominant language may be expected to meet with more success than when he is translating from it, *ceteris paribus*.

The second consequence of linguistic dominance relates to the interpreter's likely identification with his clients. The situation is similar to that encountered in the case of primacy. Dominance, however, must be treated separately from primacy, because its effects may either reinforce or counteract those of primacy. In general, it is expected that the greater the linguistic dominance the more likely an interpreter will identify with the speakers of the dominant language, rather than with clients speaking his "other" language.

[. . .]

Ambiguities and conflicts of the interpreter role. The interpreter commonly serves two clients at the same time. He is the "man in the middle" with some obligations to both clients – and these obligations may not be entirely compatible. Phillips (1960), for example, describes both positive and negative consequences of this situational dilemma for his anthropological research in Thailand. Social psychologists have explored the implications of such situations in terms of role conflict.[2] Juxtaposition of a good summary of this research with Ekvall's (1960) account of his experience as interpreter reveals the relevance of several role-theoretical constructs for the inter-preter's dilemma.

For example, Ekvall discusses a number of situations in which the details of his role as interpreter had to be worked out on an *ad hoc* basis. These illustrate the fact that the interpreter's role is always partially undefined – that is, the role prescrip-tions are objectively inadequate.[3] The interpreter's position is also characterized by role overload. Not only is it seldom entirely clear what he is to do, he is also frequently expected to do more than is objectively possible. This situation obtains under several conditions noted by Ekvall:

1   When everyone talks at once – the interpreter is simply unable to translate the entire flow of speech.
2   When the translation activity is carried on over too long a time period, introducing fatigue and mental strain.
3   When a client talks extemporaneously with too few breaks and/or with too long between breaks.

The two types of role ambiguity discussed above are essentially problems of inconsistency within a single role. In the first instance the precise nature of that role is unclear. Should the interpreter be a mere echo, or should he be an advisor and ally? Should he inform his client of whispered, off-the-record remarks made by the other party to the interaction, or should he stick to the text? In the second instance, the issue is not what, but how much behavior is expected. In either event, a sociology of interpreter behavior should include propositions about the likely effects of the interpreter's efforts to cope with these ambiguities upon the ongoing interaction. Although there are insufficient empirical data available to allow specification of hypotheses, factors that should be examined may be identified. Among these are the relative power of the interpreter vis-à-vis his clients and his perceived hierarchy of obligations, both of which would influence the legitimacy of alternative means of ambiguity reduction. For example, a powerful interpreter could solve the role overload problem simply by insisting that his clients take turns talking, pause often, and break off the exchange after an hour or two.

The interpreter, like the foreman, is occupationally vulnerable to counter pressures from his two clients. No matter what he does, one of them is apt to be displeased. Ekvall (1960) notes that in most situations involving international negotiations, such as the recent Paris Peace Talks, each party provides its own translator(s). This serves the purpose of eliminating many aspects of role strain by making the interpreter responsible to a single client. His identification with his principal then becomes possible without the complications of role conflict, and his linguistic ability becomes a part of the negotiating team's arsenal. In other cases, in which the interpreter is not so closely linked with a single client, role conflict is apt to present considerable difficulty.

In general, the interpreter's role is characterized by some degree of inadequacy of role prescription, role overload, and role conflict resulting from his pivotal position in the interaction network. Research is needed to allow specification of the conditions under which each of these characteristics obtains.

Power and the interpreter. Because the interests of three parties may be discovered in all translation situations, this section focuses on the power relations in the type case, and structural forms that deviate from the triad are not considered here. The previous section attended to the ambiguities of the interpreter's position as the man in the middle. The resulting weakness of his position is mitigated considerably by the fact that the interaction obtained would be impossible without his participation. Bilingualism constitutes a rare skill which the other parties to the interaction are unable or unwilling to acquire. To the extent that qualified interpreters are hard to find, and replace, the interpreter is cast in a highly important role vis-à-vis his clients. Thus his position in the middle has the advantage of power inherent in all positions which control scarce resources. This advantage, when combined with the relative ambiguity of the interpreter's role, allows him considerable latitude in defining his own behavior vis-à-vis his clients. His behavior may, therefore, be expected to have an unusually great impact on the structure of the entire situation.

The interpreter's control over the interaction pattern that develops, and thereby over the structure of the triadic relationship, is founded in his ability to translate selectively. He may translate all that is said by both clients with as great fidelity as he can muster – or he may choose not to. His monolingual clients will be unable to ascertain the difference unless he oversteps rather wide bounds.

If the interpreter acts as a "faithful echo" of the remarks of *both* clients, he is in effect casting himself in the role of the nonpartisan. This, of course, is a difficult task – complicated by the considerations of bilingualism discussed above. There is reason to believe, however, that some interpreters have a neutral self-image, which appears most likely to occur when bilingualism and biculturalism are relatively well balanced. It would also seem reasonable to expect relatively greater impartiality on the part of multilinguals, or other persons for whom *neither* of the languages spoken is primary or dominant.[4]

If the interpreter assumes the nonpartisan role, what would be expected regarding group structure and process and translation fidelity? Simmel's (1964) classic essay on the triad offers some interesting insights into what might reasonably be expected. [. . .] His formulation of the mediator's role serves well to describe what we might expect of the nonpartisan interpreter. He would be likely to orient himself toward his listener as if he were echoing the other client with utmost fidelity. This orientation would presumably be the same when translating in either direction – always characterized by apparent personal detachment from the content of his translations. Under this façade would be considerable manipulation of communicative content in the direction of moderation and rationality. Hidden losses in fidelity would blunt angered words and soften rigid stances.

Simmel further develops this argument to note that nonpartisanship may be of different sorts. If the interpreter's nonpartisanship results from equal interest in the ends of both other parties, then we would expect modified transmittal as described above. In this case the interpreter would probably attempt to manipulate the interaction in the direction of a "just" outcome[5] whereby both clients would believe that they had maximized their own gains.

On the other hand, the interpreter's nonpartisanship might result from his total personal detachment from the situation. Rather than being equally pulled in both directions, he might be pulled in neither.[6] In such instances, instead of pseudofidelity, we should expect maximal attention to faithful interpretation – even to reproduction of intonation and gestural signs. The value-laden aspects of any utterance would likely come through with minimal filtering. His detachment would force his clients to work out their own differences, because any outcome would be acceptable to him. Thus the nonpartisan interpreter can either function as a fair, but covert manipulator, utilizing the power inherent in his monopoly of the means of communication, or he can remain a passive element in the interaction network. Factors leading translators to adopt one rather than the other of these orientations merit investigation.

The power of the interpreter need not be used impartially in the interests of both clients. Again, Simmel has anticipated some relevant considerations. It is clear that the interpreter may choose, for whatever reasons, to ally himself with one rather than the other client. The discussion of *Tertius Gaudens* contained in Simmel's (1964) essay on the triad stresses reasons for and implications of an opportunistic motivation. Simmel is concerned with the situation where the man in the middle derives advantage from choosing sides *per se*. An example of a client "competing for the favor of" (Simmel 1964: 155) the interpreter is found in Phillips' (1960) report that informants sometimes confided in his Thai interpreter with the request that their remarks *not* be conveyed to the outsider. It is unclear from Phillips' account if there was hostility directed toward him in any of these situations, but it is unquestionable that anthropologists have occasionally been greeted with suspicion if not overt hostility. It is clear that the anthropologist, working through a native interpreter, must encourage his translator to ally with him if he is to accomplish his ethnographic task. Equally obvious is the fact that members of the society under study are likely to view the interpreter as something of a deviant – and may seek to "save" him from the outsider's corrupting influence. The interpreter is then called upon to take sides – and benefits of one sort or another are probably offered to entice him to do so.

The successful anthropologist breaks down suspicion and eventually gains a measure of acceptance into the host society. Simmel (1964: 160) has observed that this will inevitably result in the destruction of the favorable position of the *tertius*. Phillips (1960) discusses this in terms of his eventual learning of Thai, after which he was able to obtain information which the interpreter was denied.[7] [. . .] This is but one of several examples . . . that illustrate the way in which the structure of the situation changes, and the power of the interpreter disappears, if a client happens to be bilingual. Thus it appears that there are at least three possible ways in which the power of the interpreter might influence the interaction, and their frequency of occurrence and the attendant antecedents and consequences merit empirical investigation.

Summary and conclusions

This chapter is offered as an initial indication of the relevance of the role of the interpreter for sociolinguistic and sociological theory and research. It has sought to shed some light on determinants of that role and to illuminate some aspects of translation situations. The role of the interpreter in face-to-face interaction has been explored through examination of some implications of selected literature relevant to three aspects of that role:

1   The interpreter as a bilingual.
2   The interpreter as a man in the middle, subject to client expectations that are often conflicting.
3   The interpreter as a power figure, exercising power as a result of monopoliza-tion of the means of communication.

There are undoubtedly other aspects of the interpreter's role and of translation situations that merit consideration. Three broad groups of potentially relevant factors are mentioned here, although adequate discussion of them would require expansion of this chapter beyond reasonable bounds. One group of variables that is particularly well known to sociologists as exerting influence on interaction in varied contexts includes the relative statuses of the participants with respect to social class, education, sex, age, and so forth. Other variables that may prove relevant are the situational factors, some of which have been noted in passing here. In addition to variations in the number of participants and in the distribution of language skills among them, one would expect the arena of interaction (whether political, military, academic, religious and so on) and the level of tension (cf. Young 1967, 1968) to influence emergent role relations. Finally, the relative prestige of the national or ethnic groups involved and the associated attitudes toward the languages spoken are of potential interest (cf. Tucker and Lambert 1969; Lambert *et al.* 1965; Lambert 1967). The addition of these three groups of variables to those discussed in this chapter as factors influencing the role of the interpreter brings us to the clear, if clichéd, conclusion: further investigation is required.

Notes

1   Clearly the interpreter is both "consumer" and "producer" at once. He "consumes" the utterance in the source language, and "produces" an utterance in the target language. This is true for any item that is conveyed in the interaction, while his clients *either* produce *or* consume any single item – hence the distinction drawn here.

2   Excellent summaries of this literature are found in Secord and Backman (1964) and Newcomb *et al.* (1965).

3   On the objective inadequacy of role prescriptions, see Newcomb *et al.* (1965: 399). Ekvall (1960: 34) describes an experience during World War II when he was assigned the task of interrupting "official" interpretation whenever it seemed to him to be in error. He notes that "It was a thankless job . . . yet slowly the value of a check and recheck of what was transposed from language to language became established." Other instances when the interpreter's role was worked out on the spot are described throughout the book.

4   Some evidence of the occurrence of such neutrality may be extrapolated from Useem (1963) and Useem *et al.* (1963). Bohannan (1965) has remarked that "secondary ethnocentrism" is common among biculturals, and suggests the learning of a third culture as a means of counteracting this tendency and attaining a neutral perspective.

5   "Outcome" is used here to mean "result of the interaction." The term seems appropriate in most cases in which an interpreter is employed – with the possible exception of instances in which interaction is based on sociability alone. The "justice" of any outcome may, of course, be differentially perceived by the several participants to the interaction. To the extent that the manipulative translator, through biculturalism and other mechanisms, is able to perceive the interaction adequately from the perspectives of *both* clients, a shared perspective may obtain.

6   The situation of bidirectional pull seems akin to the psychological concept of approach–approach conflict (Barker 1942, 1946). The contrasting situation in which there is pull in neither direction is similar to Parsons' (1951) notion of affective neutrality.

7   These instances clearly indicate the destruction of the translator's power. For example, "I did not tell Kham Sing because he is a Thai and an expert at gossiping but . . ." (Phillips 1960: 298).

References

Anderson, R. (1997) "On the Comparability of Meaningful Stimuli in Cross-Cultural Research," *Sociometry* 30: 124–36.
——— (1969) "Hidden Translation Problems in Mono-Cultural Research," *Sociological Focus* 3: 33–42.
Barker, R. (1942) "An Experimental Study in the Resolution of Conflict by Children," in Q. McNemar and M. Merrill (eds) *Studies in Personality*, New York: McGraw-Hill, pp. 13–34.
——— (1946) "An Experimental Study of the Relationship between Certainty of Choice and the Relative Valence of Alternatives," *Journal of Personality* 15: 41–52.
Bohannan, P. (1965) Personal communication.
Deutscher, I. (1968) "Asking Questions Cross-Culturally: Some Problems of Linguistic Comparability," in H. Becker *et al.* (eds) *Institutions and the Person*, Chicago: Aldine, pp. 318–41.
Deutscher, I. (1969) "Asking Questions (and Listening to Answers): A Review of Some Sociological Precedents and Problems," *Sociological Focus* 3: 13–32.
Ekvall, R. (1960) *Faithful Echo*, New York: Twayne.
Ervin-Tripp, S. (1967) "An Issei Learns English," *The Journal of Social Issues* 23: 78–90.
Ferguson, C.(1962) "The Language Factor in National Development," in F. Rice (ed.) *Study of the Roles of Second Languages in Asia, Africa, and Latin America*, Washington, DC: Center for Applied Linguistics.
Grimshaw, A. (1969a) "Language as Obstacle and as Data in Sociological Research," *Items* 23: 17–26.
——— (1969b) "Some Problematic Aspects of Communication in Cross Racial Research in the United States," *Sociological Focus* 3: 67–85.
Gumperz, J. (1962) "Language Problems in the Rural Development of North India," in F. Rice (ed.) *Study of the Roles of Second Languages in Asia, Africa, and Latin America*, Washington, DC: Center for Applied Linguistics.
Lambert, W. (1955) "Measurement of the Linguistic Dominance of Bilinguals," *Journal of Abnormal and Social Psychology* 50: 197–200.
——— (1967) "A Social Psychology of Bilingualism," *Journal of Social Issues* 23: 91–109.
——— *et al.* (1965) "Evaluational Reactions of Jewish and Arab Adolescents to Dialect and Language Variations," *Journal of Personality and Social Psychology* 2: 8–90.
Macnamara, J. (1967) "The Bilingual's Linguistic Performance – A Psychological Overview," *Journal of Social Issues* 23: 58–77.
Newcomb, T. *et al.* (1965) *Social Psychology*, New York: Holt, Rinehart, and Winston.

Parsons, T. (1951) *The Social System*, Glencoe, Ill.: The Free Press, pp. 393–427.

Phillips, H. (1960) "Problems of Translation and Meaning in Field Work," *Human Organization* 18: 184–92.

Secord, P. and Backman, C. (1964) *Social Psychology*, New York: McGraw-Hill.

Simmel, G. (1964) "The Triad," in K. Wolff, trans. and ed. *The Sociology of Georg Simmel*, New York: The Free Press.

Tucker, G. and Lambert, W. (1969) "White and Negro Listeners' Reactions to Various American-English Dialects," *Social Forces* 47: 463–8.

Useem, J. (1963) "The Community of Man: A Study of the Third Culture," *Centennial Review* 7: 481–9.

—— et al. (1963) "Men in the Middle of the Third Culture: The Roles of American and Non-Western People in Cross-cultural Administration," *Human Organization* 22: 169–79.

Young, O. (1967) *The Intermediaries: Third Parties in International Crises*, Princeton: Princeton University Press.

—— (1968) *The Politics of Force: Bargaining During International Crises*, Princeton: Princeton University Press.

APART FROM A few exceptional institutions in Western Europe and the US, interpreting research is all too often confined to the work of a handful of individuals working on their own within one of the language departments of their university. The work of Bistra Alexieva is a case in point. Her early work on interpreting, such as "Some Issues Related to Simultaneous Interpreting" (published in the Bulgarian journal *Izkustvoto na prevoda (The Art of Translation)*, vol. 3), appeared in the late 1970s. After completing her PhD ("Implicitation and Explicitation in English and Bulgarian") at St Kliment Ohridski University of Sofia in 1982, Alexieva went on to specialize in the study of interpreting, and her research agenda soon extended to the cognitive, linguistic, text-linguistic and semiotic aspects of the interpreting process and product (e.g. Alexieva 1985, 1988, 1992, 1994, 1998, 1999).

This paper (presented here in abridged form, as the original also includes numerous examples to support the writer's hypotheses) follows on the initial classification introduced by Salevsky (1982). It first appeared in *The Translator* in 1997, and is based on a corpus culled from the author's twenty-two years (1967–89) of work as an interpreter, from numerous recordings and from the diploma theses of her graduate students. Taking on the formidable challenge of mapping the field of interpreter-mediated events in all its diversity, Alexieva adopts a prototype rather than a taxonomic approach, and attempts to categorize events in terms of two broad parameters: mode of delivery and elements of the communicative situation.

Bistra Alexieva

A TYPOLOGY OF INTERPRETER-MEDIATED EVENTS

THE COMMUNICATION EXPLOSION in the twentieth century, particularly its second half, has given a new impetus to the study of translation and interpreting, on which much of our lives now depends. Today, translator- and interpreter-mediated encounters vary tremendously in terms of their settings, modes, relationship among participants and other factors, posing a major challenge to the theory, practice and didactics of interpreting in particular.

[. . .]

The demarcation lines proposed by Salevsky (1982: 80–86) are particularly interesting and worth summarizing briefly in our current context. Salevsky . . . distinguishes types of translation and interpreting on the basis of the way in which these three activities relate to a set of seven parameters:

- Repeatability/non-repeatability of the activity;
- The object of the activity, in terms of whether the translator has at his or her disposal the whole text or portions of it;
- The unfolding of one of the constituent activities with respect to another: whether reception, for example, is performed relatively independently of the other two activities or whether it runs parallel to realization;
- Temporal conditions: whether the speed of the process and the time allotted for its completion are subject to any restrictions;
- Spatial conditions, in terms of the physical location of the communicants in space;
- Mode of reception of the original text: via the visual or auditory channel, and with or without the use of technical equipment;
- Mode of realization: whether the translated text is written or spoken, and whether it is relayed with or without the help of technical equipment.

On the basis of these parameters, Salevsky goes on to define twelve varieties of written translation (which do not concern us here) and six varieties of interpreting. The latter are based on an initial distinction between Consecutive Interpreting (CI – two sub-varieties) and Simultaneous Interpreting (SI – four sub-varieties).

CI may be (a) with note-taking, or
            (b) without note-taking.
SI may be (c) in a booth, without a written source text – this is "SI proper", with unrepeatable reception of the source text via the auditory channel alone, and with the use of technical equipment,
            (d) in a booth, with a written source text; the text is thus received via two channels: the auditory and the visual,
            (e) with the interpreters in the conference hall rather than in the booth but provided with the necessary technical equipment (headphones, microphones, partitions, etc.), or
            (f) in "half-voice" (chuchotage); this type is described as being closer to CI, because it is carried out without technical equipment and ensures immediate contact and feedback (Salevsky 1982: 85).

We may well want to question the validity of one or two of these categories, but Salevsky's attempt at categorization is useful overall because it goes beyond the traditional reliance on mode of delivery as the basis for elaborating a typology of interpreting events and makes use of a variety of relevant parameters.

1 Towards a "multi-parameter" typology of interpreter-mediated events

Interpreter-mediated events have traditionally been categorized in the literature on the basis of single parameters. One such parameter is the communicative situation or context in which the event occurs. Thus various writers have used such classifications as "conference interpreting" (irrespective of whether it is conducted in consecutive or simultaneous mode; see, for instance, Glémet 1958: 105–22, Gile 1990: 2–5), "court interpreting" (Berk-Seligson 1990, González et al. 1991, Edwards 1995), "community/dialogue interpreting" (Wadensjö 1992, Schweda Nicholson 1994, Zimman 1994), and even "TV interpreting" (Delabastita 1989: 193–218, Gottlieb 1994: 271–73, Gambier 1994: 275–76, Alexieva 1996).

Other "single-parameter" categories are based on the nature of the input text in interpreting. Such texts may be distinguished in terms of (a) their "substance" (phonic in the case of a spoken utterance, phonic and graphic in cases where the interpreter has access to a written version of a speech, or graphic only in the case of sight translation; see Salevsky 1982: 85, Alexieva 1978: 61–63), (b) their position on a continuum of orality vs. literacy (i.e. whether the text is more oral-like or more written-like; see Shlesinger 1989: 11–46), and (c) the intertextual relationships obtaining between a speaker's contribution (an SL micro-text) and the whole body of texts delivered at a conference (the macro-text); see Alexieva (1985: 195–98, 1994: 181–82).

[. . .]

I would like to argue here that it is more productive to adopt the "multi-parameter" approach exemplified by Salevsky's model and that more parameters should be included in order to account for the greater variety of interpreter-mediated events that take place today. The additional parameters that I would like to see included concern (a) the various elements of the communicative situation: *Who* speaks, to *Whom*, about *What, Where, When* and *Why* (and for what purpose, see Chernov 1978: 139–44, Gile 1990: 16–18), rather than simply the temporal characteristics of delivery and the spatial coordinates of communicants, and (b) the nature of the texts involved in the event, not just in terms of topic (in answer to *What* above) or the "whole" vs. "segment" distinction proposed by Salevsky, but also in terms of the way the text is built, whether it is more oral-like or written-like, and the intertextual relationships obtaining between the individual texts which constitute the macro-text of an interpreter-mediated event.

The attempt to account for all or even most of the variables involved in real-life interpreter-mediated events confronts us with a major methodological difficulty. The huge range of phenomena to be accounted for and the difficulty we have so far experienced in attempting to classify them suggest that the boundaries between these phenomena are likely to remain fluid and that we cannot expect to delineate clear-cut categories. It is therefore my contention that prototype theory offers the most reliable model for our current attempt to develop a typology of interpreter-mediated events. Rather than attempt to describe these events as rigid categories, we should approach them as "families", with central members (prototypes) and peripheral members (blend-forms) being identified on the basis of their position on a scale or continuum (Lakoff 1987: 57). This approach has already been applied to the categorization of written translations (Snell-Hornby 1988: 29–36) and the initial results look promising.

In attempting to develop a typology of interpreter-mediated events, it is also important to bear in mind that interpreters mediate across cultures, and not just across languages. Thus "the communicative situation involving the interpreter is always and by necessity an instance of intercultural communication" (Kondo and Tebble 1997: 150). It might therefore be useful to think of interpreter-mediated events in terms of the degree of their cultural embeddedness, and to attempt to locate them on a scale of "universality" vs. "culture-specificity". In the discussion which follows, I will be making frequent reference to the question of universality vs. culture-specificity and the way this feature interacts with various parameters in determining the nature of an interpreter-mediated event.

2 Parameters of categorization

We may proceed to develop our proposed typology by grouping the parameters we wish to investigate under two broad headings:

- Mode of delivery: this allows us to distinguish between (i) a non-stop delivery of the source text and simultaneous production of the target text, and (ii) a consecutive delivery of the source text (in chunks of varying lengths) followed by the production of the target text. This distinction also involves differences in the use, or non-use, of ancillary equipment, the specificity of the setting and the nature of the contact and distance between participants.

- Elements of the communicative situation, namely: the primary participants (Speaker and Addressee), the secondary participants (Interpreter, Organizer, Moderator), the topic discussed and the way it relates to the communicative context, the type of texts used in the communication, the spatial and temporal specificities of the communication, and the purpose of communication or goals pursued by the participants.

Some of these parameters may of course be refined by introducing more subtle distinctions between, for example, language-only texts and texts containing non-linguistic or visual material such as formulae, graphs, tables, etc., or indeed texts which rely heavily on accompanying non-verbal signs such as facial expressions and gestures.

The above broad distinction is useful as a starting point, but we now need to take each of the proposed parameters and attempt to elaborate it in more detail, relating it both to the other parameters and to the question of universality vs. culture-specificity of interpreter-mediated events.

2.1 Parameter 1: mode of delivery and production

A prototypical **simultaneous interpreting** event (or SI proper) is characterized by non-stop delivery of the source text and parallel production of the target text; this simultaneity can only be achieved with the mediation of ancillary equipment (headphones, microphones, partitions, etc.). Hence, communication between the primary participants – speaker and addressee – as well as between the primary and secondary participants – mainly the interpreter(s) – is not direct. A corollary of this is a greater distance, in terms of physical space, between speaker and addressee(s). The distance between these primary participants and the interpreter is usually greater still, because the booths can be outside the conference hall and the inter-preters may not even be able to see what is going on inside the hall: monitors meant to provide visual contact are often out of order.

The indirect nature of the communicative act and the physical distance between the participants inevitably diminish the role of kinaesthetic and proxemic factors and affect the non-verbal behaviour of all communicants. This is particularly the case with the speaker, since the very awareness of the necessity to use a microphone activates his or her self-monitoring mechanism for obvious reasons, resulting in a more formal, less culturally-marked communicative style, certainly when addressing a large international audience. [. . .]

Chuchotage, or "whispering" (or interpreting in "half-voice"), is a peripheral type of simultaneous interpreting. It is usually resorted to when it is not feasible to use ancillary equipment, for instance when interpreting has to be provided for one or two speakers of a minority language. The very fact that the interpreter has to whisper means that the physical distance between him or her and the recipient of the translation cannot be too great. Physical distance between communicants usually reflects social and personal distance (Hall 1972a: 278–82), and in this case instead of the "social-consultative distance" it ought to be, the distance between interpreter and addressee becomes more like a "casual-personal distance", varying between 18 and 30 inches. By contrast, the distance between addressee and speaker is usually greater, and – if accompanied by a culturally marked verbal and/or non-verbal behaviour on the part of the addressee (usually a member of a minority group) – may hamper communication between the primary participants themselves.

The limited distance between interpreter and addressee clearly has a bearing on the significance of kinaesthetic and proxemic factors, and more specifically the proxemic dimensions of posture and the touch, thermal and olfactory (smell) codes. There are cultures, for example the American culture, in which "the olfactory sense is culturally suppressed to a greater degree than any of the other senses" (Hall 1972b: 263). The touch code similarly varies among different cultures: it is very different in the Mediterranean region and the Balkans vis-à-vis, say, Northern Europe. Chuchotage is therefore an interpreter-mediated event in which culture-specific factors tend to play an extremely important role, particularly in terms of communication between interpreter and addressee.

Consecutive interpreting displays more variation in terms of the use of ancillary equipment and physical distance between participants. Although it is a direct, face-to-face communicative act, the use of ancillary equipment is not precluded: for example, a consecutive interpreter may have to use a microphone in larger meetings and rallies. Communication in consecutive interpreting can therefore be equipment-mediated. In terms of distance, the direct nature of the communication, particularly where it is not mediated by microphone, implies the co-presence of speaker, addressee(s) and interpreter(s). The physical distance between participants is therefore not great, though it remains much greater than in the case of chuchotage. The wide tables usually used in political and business negotiations can provide optimum proxemic conditions that reduce the impact of cultural differences in the way people share space. [. . .]

Norms relating to the location of the speaker in space, for example whether he or she is standing away from other participants or sitting with them around a table, may also vary across cultures and inevitably influence the dynamics of communication. [. . .]

Liaison interpreting may be classified as a peripheral member of the CI family of interpreter-mediated events. As in CI, there is a consecutive pattern of delivery of the source text and production of the target text. However, in liaison interpreting the communication tends to consist of spontaneous, improvised pieces of spoken discourse and the setting and communicative intention tend to be more "personal": LI tends to be used, for instance, in doctors' practices and welfare appointments rather than conferences and large business meetings. The nature of the communicative situation precludes the use of note-taking (which is common in consecutive interpreting) and the turns are therefore shorter.

The most important features of liaison interpreting, from our point of view, concern the nature of contact and distance between the primary participants. Contact here is direct: it is not mediated by ancillary equipment and is characterized by a greater intensity of interaction, involving the engagement of all (or almost all) senses. Each participant pays a great deal of attention not only to what the other participant says but also to the way he or she behaves (eye contact, body language, etc.). Feedback in this context is immediate due to the frequent interchange of roles (speaker and addressee). The interpersonal nature of this type of event (Yudina 1982: 117–28) is perhaps its most important feature and determines the function of all linguistic and non-linguistic codes employed in the exchange.

Unlike in chuchotage, the distance between participants, including the inter-preter, has to be close in social/personal terms ("casual personal" rather than "social-consultative" in Hall's terms). Thus all the issues discussed under chuchotage acquire even greater significance here: in the case of chuchotage, failure to recognize culturally relevant differences may affect the relationship between the addressee and the interpreter, but in liaison interpreting such failure may lead to irreparable disruption in the communication between all participants.

To sum up, the mode of delivery (non-stop vs. consecutive) determines the value of two extremely important factors in terms of the cultural specificity of the verbal and non-verbal behaviour of primary and secondary participants, namely: (a) directness of contact (whether the event is mediated by ancillary equipment), and (b) distance/proximity between the primary participants themselves, as well as between them and the interpreter(s). I suggest subsuming "directness of contact" under "distance vs. proximity" and will come back to this important dimension of cultural specificity in the conclusion.

2.2 Parameter 2: participants in interpreter-mediated events

This parameter may be investigated in terms of five factors: degree of command of the source and target languages, involvement in the textual world, status, role and number.

The first factor, **command of languages**, concerns the degree of the speaker's command of the SL and the addressee's command of the TL and the familiarity of both participants with the two cultures. Where the source language is the mother tongue of the speaker, the communicative act usually involves contact between only two languages and cultures. However, there are cases where the source language is not the native language of the speaker and the speaker's first language and culture may therefore affect his or her verbal and non-verbal perform-ance. Non-native speakers of English, for example, often use literal translations of metaphoric expressions known in their culture; such expressions may not mean anything in English or, worse, they may mean something entirely different.

The addressee's command of the target language and familiarity with the target culture are also highly relevant: conference participants often receive the speaker's message via an interpreter in a language other than their mother tongue. This is extremely important because non-native speakers of the target language, in the role of addressees, may partly or totally misinterpret a message. Knowledge of the target language on the part of the speaker may also be culturally relevant, not only in terms of sensitivity to the background of his or her addressees but also because such knowledge gives the speaker greater power over the interpreter, whose performance he or she is then able to monitor.

The second factor concerns the primary participants' **involvement in the textual world**. Participants in an interpreter-mediated event may be involved in the discussion (explicitly or implicitly) as text entities, i.e. they themselves or the countries, organizations or institutions they represent may form part of the textual world. Alternatively, the participants may not be part of the textual world: at a conference on anthropology, "man" may be, and usually is, a textual entity, while the author of the paper is not, i.e. the subject of research is not identical with its object. The position of an interpreter-mediated event on this scale of "involvement" vs. "non-involvement", like its position on the "distance" vs. "proximity" scale, can help us determine the degree of its cultural embeddedness. Closeness to the "involvement" end will imply deeper cultural embeddedness. For example, critical remarks on the organization a participant belongs to, made by another speaker, may trigger various reactions on the part of representatives of different cultures, showing different degrees of explicit, culturally marked emotive involvement in the argument.

The third factor has to do with the **status** of participants, or the power relationships involved in an interpreter-mediated event. In this context, the major bases of power derive mostly from the social status of the primary participants institution-wise (their institutional affiliation and position within the hierarchy) and expertise-wise (their prestige as authorities on the issues discussed). The speaker's command of the target language, particularly in consecutive and liaison interpreting settings, also lends him or her more power, not only vis-à-vis the interpreter (by monitoring the latter's performance), but also vis-à-vis other primary participants who are not familiar with the source language. Knowledge of both languages gives a participant the advantage of hearing each utterance twice, as well as more time to plan his or her next move in the negotiations. Age and gender may also influence power relations and this may vary across cultures. Research has shown that male speakers generally tend to dominate female speakers, especially in terms of control of topics, and to interrupt in turn-taking (claiming a turn and holding the floor).

An atmosphere of equilibrium and solidarity is likely to pertain where speaker and addressee enjoy equal status; where they do not, varying degrees of tension may result, depending on source and target cultural norms of behaviour (Brown and Gilman 1960/1972: 109). This is highly relevant in "facework", i.e. what we do in order "to have our ego recognized and taken account of, to have one's views heard, and to some extent accepted by others, or at least have others accept one's right to have them" (Mulholland 1991: 68). Face-saving strategies may vary substantially across cultures (*ibid*: 92–93), because they depend to a large extent on the rigidity of the social stratification system, the need for deference towards participants who hold a superior position, age and gender differences, and a variety of other factors. For example, using titles and honorifics to acknowledge the status of the addressee while downgrading one's own (*ibid*: 92), or using the "first name" move, may be interpreted differently across cultures.

Also of particular significance here is the difference between individualistic and collectivistic ethos, i.e. between what Hall (1973) describes as "low-context" and "high-context" cultures, with the former assigning greater power to the individual and the latter to the group. As Ting-Toomey suggests, "interactions across the divide between low-context and high-context cultures are particularly prone to confusion" (1985; in Cohen 1991: 25). However, Cohen himself points out that such a dichotomous model "involves simplifications and stark contrasts" (1991: 25). In line with the prototype model adopted here, we should perhaps treat the two cultural prototypes as extreme points on a continuum rather than in terms of a clear-cut dichotomy.

Finally, the social status of the interpreter, as well as his or her level of education, age and gender may also contribute to the level of equilibrium or tension in an interpreter-mediated event, depending on the cultures involved. The greater the imbalance in power between the primary participants, and between them and the interpreter, the higher the risk of increased tension.

The **role** of the participants in an interpreter-mediated event is particularly relevant in cases where it does not coincide with their social status outside the conference hall, that is, when people of unequal power have to participate in a conference as equals. This kind of situation may generate a great deal of tension, especially when representatives of high-context cultures are involved. The roles set for the primary participants (speaker and addressee), as well as those of the chairperson (organizer or moderator), may conflict with their claims to power in a number of ways. [. . .]

Interpreters may be tempted to exceed their brief, or definition of their role, where they feel superior to either speaker or addressee in terms of age, gender, knowledge of topic (this applies mostly when a specialist in the field is acting as an interpreter), communicative skills, or command not only of the source and target languages but also of the respective cultures and specific norms of behaviour relevant to the communicative situation. [. . .]

For the sake of simplicity, the two dimensions of status and role discussed above may be conflated into a single scale of "equals/solidarity" vs. "non-equals/power", along which we may attempt to locate culturally marked ways in which the primary and secondary participants in an interpreter-mediated event typically attempt to exercise power in a given culture.

Finally, the **number** of participants in an interpreter-mediated event is also relevant, since smaller gatherings create a cosier atmosphere which is conducive to a lower degree of self-monitoring. This, in turn, tends to result in a higher incidence of culture-specific verbal and non-verbal behaviour. We may use a further scale here for profiling interpreter-mediated events: "formal setting" vs. "informal setting". Larger conferences and televised events will occupy a position closer to the "formal" end of the scale, while liaison interpreting, chuchotage and smaller gatherings will be closer to the "informal" end.

2.3 Parameter 3: the topic of an interpreter-mediated event

The nature of the issues discussed at an interpreter-mediated event constitutes another important parameter which determines the location of the event along the "universal" vs. "culture-specific" continuum. The major distinction to be drawn here is between the textual world of scientific knowledge and that of human interaction.

Topics related to science and technology tend to revolve around relatively more objective and universal issues and are therefore less culture-specific. Discussion of such topics entails little or no involvement of the participants as text entities:

participants do not normally form part of the textual world in this context. By contrast, the textual world of human interaction consists of issues which directly address the way people (individuals or organizations) interact with one another; such issues are usually discussed in an attempt to arrive at a group decision and find solutions which are important to the participants themselves or to the institutions they represent. Interpreter-mediated events which address such issues are inevitably characterized by a higher degree of subjectivity and greater involvement on the part of participants in the textual world where they figure explicitly or implicitly as text entities. [. . .]

The topic of an interpreter-mediated event therefore contributes to its location along the "involvement" vs. "non-involvement" scale discussed under 2.2. above (the primary participants' involvement in the textual world).

2.4 Parameter 4: text type and text building strategies

In addition to the topic of an interpreter-mediated event, the participants' text building strategies – the way they use language to express their communicative intentions – will also have a bearing on the degree of culture-specificity of the event. In particular, differences can be seen at work with respect to the degree of reliance on oral vs. literate strategies (Shlesinger 1989: 10–15) and the observation of what is known as the "Cooperative Principle" (Grice 1975).

Interpreting is generally associated with the spoken mode, but research has shown that mode is not the only determinant of text type. Even texts delivered orally can have varying degrees of orality or literacy, and this distinction has already proved useful in interpreting research (see Shlesinger 1989). Shlesinger uses five criteria to determine the position of a text on the orality/literacy scale:

- Degree of planning: whether a text is improvised/spontaneous or has been prepared prior to delivery; this has an impact on coherence and semantic density;
- Shared knowledge: knowledge that the addressee is assumed to bring to the discourse; this has a bearing on the autonomy of the text. A high level of autonomy is associated with the literacy end of the scale;
- Lexis: use of literary, colloquial or unmarked words and expressions;
- Degree of involvement: i.e. the degree to which a speaker may feel personally involved in the discussion of a particular topic with a particular group of people as interlocutors. Texts positioned towards the literacy end of the scale exhibit less ego-involvement, less addressee-involvement and less involvement with the topic of discussion (Shlesinger 1989: 33); and
- The role of non-verbal behaviour: this is particularly important in the way "spoken-like" texts are produced (*ibid*: 35–42).

The degree of planning, i.e. whether the speaker "reads" a written text or delivers it more or less spontaneously, reflects a text-building strategy which, to a certain extent, seems to be dependent on culture-specific norms. [. . .]

The degree of planning influences the speaker's choice of lexis and syntactic structures (Shlesinger 1989: 10–61); it may also determine the cultural embeddedness of the text and the entire event, mainly with regard to the following parameters:

- Use of culture-specific imagery, making the text more difficult to interpret. The speaker may not be aware that he or she is using culture-specific imagery, particularly in the case of a lower degree of planning, or complete improvisation;
- Use of paralinguistic (non-verbal) means of expression, including facial expression, gestures and tone of voice. These means of expression can be highly culture-specific and therefore difficult to interpret;
- Use of, or reference to, culture-specific knowledge which is only available to members of the source-language community. More difficulty is experienced when the source language is not the speaker's mother tongue, and the culture-specific knowledge therefore relates to a third language and culture community. This makes interpretation of the source text heavily dependent on cross-cultural intertextual relationships (Alexieva 1994: 181). [. . .]

Apart from the orality vs. literacy dimension, there is also the question of norms of communication [. . .]. Different cultures seem to vary in the way they interpret the details of the cooperative principle and the notion of relevance. For example, the maxim of quantity can have a variety of instantiations, since what the speaker may consider "required" in a given context could be different from what his or her interlocutors deem to be the case. This has an impact on negotiating strategies employed in different cultures (Mulholland 1991: 68–93). Thus a speaker may withhold some piece of information at a given point in order to manipulate the outcome of the negotiation; this strategy is quite common in some cultures. If the addressee belongs to a culture in which this strategy is not used, he or she will not consider the speaker's contribution adequately informative and this could naturally lead to problems. [. . .]

Interpreter-mediated events may be located on a "cooperative/direct" vs. "non-cooperative/indirect" scale in terms of negotiation strategy. This should help us capture differences in the interpretation of Grice's maxims and the notion of optimal relevance in such events.

2.5 Parameter 5: spatial and temporal constraints

Spatial constraints seem to be more significant and culturally relevant than temporal constraints, particularly with respect to the location and setting of an interpreter-mediated event.

The location of an event can be discussed in terms of proximity to or distance from the speaker's home country. If the two locations coincide, the speaker tends to feel more at home and his or her performance may be characterized by the use of more culture-specific lexis and strategies: there tends to be less self-monitoring on the part of the speaker in these contexts. By contrast, where the event is located away from the speaker's home country, he or she will tend to be less complacent and to use lexis and strategies that are likely to be understood by an international audience. Interpreters who have interpreted for the same person at home and abroad confirm that where the event is situated outside the speaker's country, the speaker tends to use less body language and to show more modesty in sharing space.

The setting of an interpreter-mediated event is also important in terms of whether the "space" in which the event takes place is reserved for the primary and secondary participants alone (as in community interpreting in health care institutions) or shared by other people (as in media events and press conferences). In the first instance, the participants will enjoy greater privacy and a more relaxed atmosphere, which is conducive to less self-monitoring and greater use of culturally marked behaviour. In the second case, there is less privacy, more self-monitoring and hence less culturally marked behaviour on the part of participants.

Distance and privacy both contribute to the degree of formality of an event and may be used to locate it along a continuum of "formal" vs. "informal" setting.

2.6 Parameter 6: the goal of an interpreter-mediated event

Individuals, groups of people and representatives of institutions may want to get together for a number of reasons and with a view to accomplishing a great variety of goals. In spite of such variety, we can factor out three main parameters which may help us group interpreter-mediated events in terms of the goals pursued by the individual speakers, other participants and the event as a whole:

- Knowledge exchange: some events are organized to allow exchange of knowledge, to impart information, or to demonstrate the validity of something which is external to the speaker in the sense that he or she is not personally involved in the textual world as a text entity. Participants in events of this type can be expected to share the same or at least similar goals.

- Arriving at group decision: some events are organized in order to work out a common strategy or arrive at solutions for problems shared by all participants, whether individuals or institutions. The implementation of proposed solutions, however, may depend on institutions or authorities external to the participants. A shared goal facilitates discussion, reduces in-group conflict and makes it easier to arrive at a decision. In this context, simpler negotiation strategies, usually of the more direct type, tend to be used.

- Conflicting goals: some events are organized to discuss issues that are of vital importance to all participants, but resolving these issues may involve curtailing the rights and/or harming the interests of some of the participants. This naturally creates conflict and complicates negotiations. Cultural differences in terms of choice of negotiation strategy tend to become more prominent, especially if the division of participants into "interest groups" coincides with their division into "cultural groups". International political negotiations and interviews with political leaders provide typical examples. Baker (1997) describes a televised interview during the Gulf War between Trevor McDonald and Saddam Hussein, where "the gulf that separates the two cultures involved . . . [wa]s so wide, and the political positions of the parties concerned so irreconcilable, that each participant set out not to communicate a point of view or to reach some form of compromise but to destroy the other party's position, to expose him, and to reassert his own position". It is of course possible to mitigate the conflict of some events of this type, but only if the concessions required from some of the participants are minor and the outcome is expected to benefit all participants, as in the case of conferences which address global issues of war and peace, environment, health, and so on.

The location of an interpreter-mediated event along a scale of "shared goals" vs. "conflicting goals" is highly relevant in shaping its internal structure, predicting levels of stress, and understanding the nature of the tasks that the interpreter has to perform.

3 Conclusion

An interpreter-mediated event may be located along a continuum of "universality" vs. "culture-specificity" using a number of scales that I have suggested in the previous discussion, namely:

- "distance" vs. "proximity" (between speaker, addressee and interpreter);
- "non-involvement" vs. "involvement" (of the speaker as text entity);
- "equality/solidarity" vs. "non-equality/power" (related to status, role and gender of speaker and addressee, as well as the interpreter in some cases);
- "formal setting" vs. "informal setting" (related to number of participants, degree of privacy, and distance from home country);
- "literacy" vs. "orality";
- "cooperativeness/directness" vs. "non-cooperativeness/indirectness" (relevant to negotiation strategies);
- "shared goals" vs. "conflicting goals".

Of these, I would argue that the most important scale in terms of determining the degree of culture-specificity of an event is "distance" vs. "proximity", which relates to the distinction between simultaneous and consecutive interpreting and the role of kinaesthetic and proxemic factors. "Non-involvement" vs. "involvement", "equality" vs. "non-equality", and "shared goals" vs. "conflicting goals" come next and determine the location of an event on the other scales. For example, the position of an event on the scale of "shared goals" vs. "conflicting goals" can help us predict those features which will determine its position on the scale of "cooperativeness" vs. "non-cooperativeness" in terms of negotiation strategy.

Identifying the degree of culture-specificity associated with a given type of interpreter-mediated event should allow us to make more reliable predictions about the role that the interpreter typically has to play in such an event. For instance, events located towards the "universal" end of the continuum (those closer to the lefthand side of the scales listed above) require the interpreter to act simply as an interlingual mediator, what Kopczyński describes as a "ghost" (1994: 192–5): the interpreter does not have to perform any "repair" operations in order to avoid hitches in communication, and his or her presence may even remain largely unnoticed. This type of situation is particularly common in events located closer to the "distance" end of the first scale, that is in simultaneous rather than consecutive or liaison interpreting.

By contrast, the task of the interpreter in events located towards the "culture-specific" end of the continuum (those closer to the righthand side of the above scales) is more difficult to perform, and the interpreter therefore has a more important role to play: he or she has to actively intervene in the communication to prevent misunderstanding and smooth cultural differences, for instance to explain differences in the use of body language, as in the case of the head movements denoting "Yes" and "No" in English and Bulgarian. In other words, the more an event is embedded in a particular culture (speaker's, hearer's or both), the greater the role of the interpreter as intercultural mediator and "repairer" and the more visible he or she becomes.

[. . .]

References

Alexieva, Bistra (1978) "Za nyakoi problemi na sinhronnia prevod" (Some Issues Related to Simultaneous Interpreting), in *Izkustvoto na prevoda* (The Art of Translation), vol. 3, Sofia: Narodna Kultura, pp. 60–74.

—— (1985) "Semantic Analysis of the Text in Simultaneous Interpreting", in Hildegund Bühler (ed.) *Proceedings of the Xth World Congress of FIT*, Vienna: Braumüller, pp. 195–8.

—— (1994) "Types of Texts and Intertextuality in Simultaneous Interpreting", in Mary Snell-Hornby, Franz Pöchhacker, and Klaus Kaindl (eds) *Translation Studies. An Interdiscipline*, Amsterdam and Philadelphia: John Benjamins, pp. 179–87.

—— (1996) "Kinaesthetic and Proxemic Factors in Consecutive Interpreting", unpublished manuscript.

Baker, Mona (1997) "Non-Cognitive Constraints and Interpreter Strategies in Political Interviews", in Karl Simms (ed.) *Translating Sensitive Texts. Linguistic Aspects*, Amsterdam: Rodopi, pp. 111–29.

Berk-Seligson, Susan (1990) *The Bilingual Courtroom: Court Interpreters in the Judicial Process*, Chicago and London: The University of Chicago Press.

Brown, R. and Gilman A. (1960/1972) "The Pronouns of Power and Solidarity", in John Laver and Sandy Hutcheson (eds) *Communication in Face-to-Face Interaction*, Middlesex: Penguin, pp. 103–27.

Chernov, G. V. (1978) *Teoria i praktika sinhronnogo perevoda* (Theory and Practice of Simultaneous Interpreting), Moskva: Mezhdunarodnie Otnoshenia.

Cohen, Raymond (1991) *Negotiating Across Cultures*, Washington DC: United States Institute of Peace Press.

Delabastita, Dirk (1989) "Translation and Mass Communication: Film and TV Translation as Evidence of Cultural Dynamics", *Babel* 35 (4): 193–218.

Edwards, Alicia (1995) *The Practice of Court Interpreting*, Amsterdam and Philadelphia: John Benjamins.

Gambier, Yves (1994) "Audio-Visual Communication: Typological Detour", in Cay Dollerup and Annette Lindegaard (eds) *Teaching Translation and Interpreting 2. Insights, Aims, Visions*, Amsterdam and Philadelphia: John Benjamins, pp. 275–83.

Gile, Daniel (1990) *Basic Concepts and Models for Conference Interpretation Training*, Paris: INALCO and CEEI (ISIT).

Glémet, R. (1958) "Conference Interpreting", in *Aspects of Translation. Studies in Communication 2*, London: Secker & Warburg.

González, Roseann Dueñas, Vásquez, Victoria and Mikkelson, Holly (1991) *Fundamentals of Court Interpretation: Theory, Policy and Practice*, Durham, North Carolina: Carolina Academic Press.

Gottlieb, Henrik (1994) "Subtitling: People Translating People", in Cay Dollerup and Annette Lindegaard (eds) *Teaching Translation and Interpreting 2. Insights, Aims, Visions*, Amsterdam and Philadelphia: John Benjamins, pp. 261–74.

Grice, H. P. (1975) "Logic and Conversation", in P. Cole and J. L. Morgan (eds) *Syntax and Semantics, Vol. 3. Speech Acts*, New York: Academic Press, pp. 41–58.

Hall, Edward T. (1972a) "Silent Assumptions in Social Communication", in John Laver and Sandy Hutcheson (eds) *Communication in Face-to-Face Interaction*, Harmondsworth: Penguin, pp. 274–88.

—— (1972b) "A System for the Notation of Proxemic Behaviour", in John Laver and Sandy Hutcheson (eds) *Communication in Face-to-Face Interaction*, Harmondsworth: Penguin, pp. 247–73.

—— (1973) *The Silent Language*, New York: Anchor Books.

Kondo, Masaomi and Tebble, Helen (1997) "Intercultural Communication, Negotiation and Interpreting", in Yves Gambier, Daniel Gile and Christopher Taylor (eds) *Conference Interpreting: Current Trends in Research*, Amsterdam and Philadelphia: John Benjamins, pp. 149–66.

Kopczyński, Andrzej (1994) "Quality in Conference Interpreting: Some Pragmatic Problems", in Mary Snell-Hornby, Franz Pöchhacker and Klaus Kaindl (eds) *Translation Studies. An Interdiscipline*, Amsterdam and Philadelphia: John Benjamins, pp. 189–98.

Lakoff, George (1987) *Women, Fire and Dangerous Things. What Categories Reveal about the Mind*, Chicago: University of Chicago Press.

Mulholland, Joan (1991) *The Language of Negotiation*, London and New York: Routledge.

Salevsky, Heidemarie (1982) "Teoreticheskie problemi klassifikatzii vidov perevoda" (Theoretical Problems of the Classification of Types of Translation), *Fremdsprachen* 26 (2): 80–6.

Schweda Nicholson, Nancy (1994) "Training for Refugee Mental Health Interpreters", in Cay Dollerup and Annette Lindegaard (eds) *Teaching Translation and Interpreting 2. Insights, Aims and Visions*, Amsterdam and Philadelphia: John Benjamins, pp. 207–10.

Shlesinger, Miriam (1989) "Simultaneous Interpretation as a Factor in Effecting Shifts in the Position of Texts on the Oral–Literate Continuum," unpublished MA thesis, Tel Aviv University.

Snell-Hornby, Mary (1988) *Translation Studies. An Integrated Approach*, Amsterdam and Philadelphia: John Benjamins.

Ting-Toomey, Stella (1985) "Toward a Theory of Conflict and Culture", *International and Intercultural Communication Annual* 9: 71–86.

Wadensjö, Cecilia (1992) *Interpreting as Interaction – On Dialogue Interpreting in Immigration Hearings and Medical Encounters*, Linköping University, Department of Communication Studies.

Yudina, G. G. (1982) "Mezhlichnostniy Aspekt Dvustoronnogo Perevoda" (Interpersonal Aspects of Bilateral Interpreting), in *Sbornik Nauchnih Trudov, Vipusk 203* (Collection of Research Papers, no. 203), Moscow: Maurice Thorez Foreign Language Institute, pp. 117–28.

Zimman, Leonor (1994) "Intervention as a Pedagogical Problem in Community Interpreting", in Cay Dollerup and Annette Lindegaard (eds) *Teaching Translation and Interpreting 2. Insights, Aims, Visions*, Amsterdam and Philadelphia: John Benjamins, pp. 217–24.

THE MOST EMINENT representative of nonverbal communication as an inter-disciplinary field of study, Fernando Poyatos has contributed his insights and models to a number of disciplines. Apart from two decades of teaching his subject in the departments of anthropology, psychology and sociology at the University of New Brunswick, Canada, he has published an impressive number of books, some of them in Spanish and in several volumes, and lectured widely throughout the world. Following some of those lectures at the translation and interpreting schools in Heidelberg and Germersheim, Germany, in the mid-1980s, Poyatos resolved to analyze the nonverbal systems in simultaneous and consecutive interpreting as well as in the translation of a literary text. His work in this field is represented most comprehensively in his edited volume on *Nonverbal Communication and Translation*, published in 1997. In the section on interpreting, Poyatos presents his detailed analysis of "the reality of multi-channel verbal–nonverbal communication in simultaneous and consecutive interpret-ation," which is largely based on his original 1987 paper reprinted here.

Written after his lectures in Heidelberg, Poyatos's first article on the subject of nonverbal communication and interpreting was published in the German journal *TEXT-conTEXT* and gradually came to the attention of the interpreting studies community. Nevertheless, it proved highly influential and formed the conceptual basis of a number of specific studies. In fact, Poyatos's treatment of the complexity of nonverbal systems in interpreted communication is so rich and extensive that some sections of his paper had to be abridged or even left out in the version made available here.

Further reading: Poyatos 1983, 1993, 1997a, 1997b.

Fernando Poyatos

NONVERBAL COMMUNICATION IN SIMULTANEOUS AND CONSECUTIVE INTERPRETATION
A theoretical model and new perspectives

0 Introduction

[. . .]

BEING SENSITIZED TO the complex functioning of somatic systems beyond verbal language in oral translation reveals not only how messages are often completed only through nonverbal signs, but how many times they are transmitted exclusively in nonverbal ways, two facts that cannot be neglected by the sensitive translator and which respond to different reasons that must also be understood, often even rendered "understandable" in the translation. In the sections that follow, besides an outline of language, paralanguage and kinesics as the true reality of speech, two specific models are presented: one which affords an exhaustive and systematic observation and analysis of speaker and listener behaviors, and another which reveals the extreme intricacy of the structure of conversation. The specific consequences of the interactive characteristics of speaker and listener must also be acknowledged, as well as the translator's own responsibilities in the interpretation situation, which will become more apparent as we progress through the former sections. Finally, it has been my interest, as in earlier publications, to call attention to a very neglected area, namely, the importance of achieving interactive fluency in what I have called "reduced interaction," in this case in interpretation . . . mainly when blind or deaf interactants are involved.

1 Sign systems and forms in the interpretation situation

A progressive and systematic analysis of the interpretation situation that would disclose in an exhaustive way its possibilities, limitations and problems would require that we first establish which sign-conveying systems are available to the speaker, which of those are perceived by his listener, which are perceived by the latter through the interpreter, and in what ways the interpreter perceives them from both speaker and listener and transmits them between the two, considering simultaneous and consecutive interpretation as basic forms, and differentiating in each one which of the three participants are in co-presence and which are visually absent.

Table 1, "Speaker's and Listener's Perception and Interpreter's Emission of Verbal and Nonverbal Systems," attempts to show at a glance what actually constitutes the material and forms of interpretation, which the reader should be able to use as a basic schematic reference and enlarge greatly upon it, developing an entire theoretical and methodological framework. On the left side are shown the sign-conveying systems which, together with chemical (e.g. tears, artificial or natural body odors), dermal (e.g. blushing) and thermal (e.g. rises and falls in body temperature) messages would complete what elsewhere (Poyatos: 1983: 55; see also 1988) I have discussed as intersomatic communication: verbal language, paralanguage and kinesics, discussed below, part of which are audible gestures and the facial gestures of speech. We can assume that in the interpretation situation chemical, dermal and thermal signs and proxemic attitudes (see Poyatos: 1983: 204–10) are normally absent because the situations the interpreter must engage in are typically social or public encounters, although, as will be mentioned later, certain reduced-interaction encounters and extreme situations, such as those of people in distress, must be acknowledged and seriously considered by the interpreter. But that which constitutes the main body of the interpretation material is undoubtedly the basic triple structure language–paralanguage–kinesics. Based then on this triple audible-visual reality of speech – and from an interactive point of view – the table presents the two ways of rendering the speaker's deliverance (verbal or nonverbal) into the target language: *simultaneous*, that is, without the speaker's flow being interrupted, as in a lecture or speech, during which the listeners can follow the speaker in their respective languages through earphones; and *consecutive*, which is the case in a conversational speaker–listener encounter (e.g. a diplomatic meeting), or also in the one-to-many situation of the public speech, lecture or sermon, during which the speaker pauses every few sentences for his side-to-side interpreter to translate.

A few comments on the abbreviations and symbols used in the table may suggest to the reader some of the aspects of interpretation which continue to be rather neglected and which certainly merit much closer attention. S, L and I stand for Speaker, Listener and Interpreter. The arrow pointing toward either speaker or listener denotes the verbal or nonverbal signs he may or may not perceive from his cointeractant (i.e. language, paralanguage, etc.), indicated with [+] or [−] in that column. The arrow pointing away from the interpreter indicates whether or not he conveys a given type of signs, symbolized also with [+] or [−] and either a question mark [?] when it is doubtful that the interpreter would convey the speaker's paralanguage and kinesics, but perhaps desirable, or [his own], which means of course that he accompanies his translated verbal language with his own native paralinguistic features and kinesic behaviors, or, as is very often the case (typically when he is visually absent), with very low key paralanguage and no kinesics. The fourth column under each form of interpretation suggests that the interpreter may or may not

Table 1 Speaker's and listener's perception and interpreter's emission of verbal and nonverbal systems.

	Simultaneous interpretation								Consecutive interpretation								Speaker aud.–visual present for Listener absent Interpreter			
	Speaker–Listener in aud.–vis. copresence absent Interpreter				Speaker visually present for Listener absent Interpreter				Speaker–Listener–Interpreter in aud.–visual copresence				Speaker–Listener in aud.–visual copres. absent Interpreter							
	$S<$	$>L$	$<I$	$I≥$	$S<$	$>L$	$<I$	$I≥$	$S<$	$>L$	$<I$	$I≥$	$S<$	$>L$	$<I$	$I≥$	$S<$	$>L$	$<I$	$I≥$
Acoustic Systems																				
Verbal Language	+	+	+	+ − ?	−	−	+	+ − ?	+	+	+	+ − ?	+	+	+	+ − ?	−	+	+	+ − ?
Paralanguage	+	+	+ − (his/own)	+ − ?	−	−	+ − (his/own)	+ − ?	+	+	+ − (his/own)	+ − ?	+	+	+ − (his/own)	+ − ?	−	+	+ − (his/own)	+ − ?
Audible Kinesics	+	+	−	−	−	−	?	?	+	+	+ − (his/own)	+ − ?	+	+	−	−	−	+	−	−
Visual Systems																				
Speech facial gestures	+	+	−	−	−	+	−	−	+	+	−	−	+	+	−	−	−	+	−	−
Kinesics	+	+	+	−	−	+	+	+ − ?	+	+	+ − (his/own)	+ − ?	+	+	+ − (his/own)	+ − ?	−	+	−	−

perceive and try to convey secondary-channel activities, mainly the listener's feed-back behaviors and the speaker's own counterfeedback ones.

We will limit our study of what is entailed in the interpretation situation to language, paralanguage and kinesics, but never below that basic triple structure which represents total speech. And yet, the communicative complexity of those three cosystems as they operate in interaction (and, therefore, during interpretation) and the problems and responsibilities of the interpreter, will be quite obvious as we progress through the various sections.

2 Limitations of words and interchangeability of language, paralanguage and kinesics

2.1 The first problem the interpreter must face is the expressive limitations of the words he depends on far too much at times to convey to the listener or listeners what the speaker is truly communicating with words, paralinguistic features and kinesic behaviors that possess that indivisible semantic and grammatical value char-acteristic of speech. Words lack the capacity to carry the whole weight of a conver-sation or speech, that is, all the messages encoded in the course of it, because our lexicons, our "dictionaries" (even if the impossible interpreter knew them all!), are extremely poor in comparison with the capacity of the human mind for encoding and decoding an infinitely wider gamut of meaning which at times (and the inter-preter will face them more than once) we refer to as "ineffable." If that conversation or speech we are trying to translate were to be formed by means of "stripped" words only there would be not just an intermittent series of semiotic gaps, but some overriding vacuums as well; but there are no such vacuums in our speech, for they are actually filled with nonverbal activities, either clearly separable among other parts of our deliverance (e.g. a click of the tongue, a meaningful silence, an ironic chuckle, an audible exhalation of hesitation) or stretching over varying portions of it, from single phonemes to sentences to the complete encounter (e.g. quavery voice, high pitch, orotundity). [. . .]

2.2 Furthermore, what makes language–paralanguage–kinesics a functionally cohesive structure is undoubtedly their common kinetic (not yet kinesic) generator, and then their combined semanticity and lexicality and their capacity to operate simultaneously, alternate with or substitute for each other as needed in the inter-active situation. But, can we as interpreters preserve that cohesiveness as we render one language (realizing only too well by now what we mean by "language") into another? To make matters worse – and, again, that is only the reality of speech – we are faced with the fact that paralanguage and kinesics may appear in a complete sentence in three basic different ways in relation to verbal language: *simultaneously* to it, that is, superimposed, as in "But . . . I don't think we can do it" where there is first a prolonged drawling and frowning, then a quickened tempo that betrays irritation, and finally a sort of pleading higher pitch and tension of voice with a slight questioning tone; *as a syntactical replacement* for verbal language, that is, alternating with words in the same sentence, as when the sentence is actually begun with a long narial intake of breath and pursed lips (which would be enough for many to understand), followed then by a palatal click + slight smile, followed by a light chuckle and finally the words "I think we can do it," which, of course, have been eloquently qualified by the paralanguage and kinesics that preceded them; and *independently* of verbal language, that is, paralanguage and kinesics constituting an unambiguous sentence-like construct, as in an expression of approval and satisfaction whose only signs are "Mmmmm, uh-huuu," while smiling + raised brows + repeated head nodding + intently looking the listener in the eye. How the interpreter should handle such an expressive, albeit wordless, intervention on the part of the speaker should also constitute a subject of serious thought (which the reader can find suggested in Table 1), for the following alternatives are possible: he could reproduce the speaker's paralanguage and kinesics as originally encoded, there being perhaps the same foreignness in them as there would be in his words; he could translate them verbally; or perhaps, to be faithful to the speaker's style, he could translate the speaker's paralanguage and kinesics into the target language's paralanguage and kinesics. The possibilities are certainly there, and the appropriate use of each of them as applicable would result in specific interpreting styles and, in turn, in different ways of perceiving the speaker on the part of his single listener or audience.

3 The basic functions of paralanguage and kinesics in speech and the concepts of redundancy and complementarity

3.1 The widely ascribed roles of nonverbal communication, that is, replacing, supporting, repeating, or contradicting what is being said verbally, should be seen as within the three basic functions and, again, considered in the light of the speaker's and listener's perception and the interpreter's emission, as shown in the table. Elsewhere (Poyatos 1993) I have discussed at length the kinesic-audible (i.e. visual-audible) basis of speech. Paralanguage and kinesics are audible and visible, respectively, but, as has been indicated in Table 1, there is an important visual aspect of the facial gestures of speech which should be acknowledged when considering their functions. First of all, paralanguage and kinesics can provide *additional information* to what is being said verbally, by *repeating* what has been said in words (e.g. a negating gesture after saying "No"), by *supporting* it (e.g. the smile superimposed to affectionate words), or by *contradicting* it (e.g. the smile that may accompany hypocritical words). All this shows – and its importance in interpretation should be apparent – that kinesics can be also an *economy device*, as it "says" something else in the same length of time when it is simultaneous to words, and so can paralanguage (e.g. when a tone of disbelief is added to the statement "Oh, yes, he'll do it for you!"), in both instances instead of verbalizing further. Finally, paralanguage and above all kinesics are observed to be used quite often for lack of words, that is, out of *verbal deficiency*, as when someone refers to objects or abstract concepts he cannot name by using descriptive gestures and even meaningful paralinguistic utterances (e.g. a "chandelier," a very "sleek" car, a very "elaborately carved" piece of furniture, when the speaker lacks those words), which in some cases can become true *nonverbal periphrases* longer than the verbal expressions.

3.2 Only the identification of the various functions generates immediately a number of important questions for the interpreter and as many challenges. For instance, how to handle each of the examples just given. When our speaker used additional nonverbal information which may just repeat, but may also very well support, what he is saying verbally or, even more, intentionally emphasize it, are we going to convey to his listener or listeners only his verbal message, or are we going to add his conspicuous paralanguage (perhaps also translate verbally if it corresponds only to his culture) and, if we are visible, his kinesics as well? Won't our interpreting style be regarded as much more articulate and rich if we do? What if his facial kinesics clearly contradicts (perhaps through what has been called verbal leakage) what he is saying verbally, as happens typically on some occasions with the overriding smile of the Japanese, which we westerners are bound to decode as a positive sign all the time? I feel that is a very useful example, among many others, worth pondering. The same would hold true for the paralanguage and kinesics that acts as an economy device: can we, in our target language, use exactly the same signs, or should we also translate, or perhaps get one or two words in edgewise because economy is not possible? And what about verbal deficiency? Shouldn't we just supply the word the speaker lacks (or cannot remember) as the logical solution, thus making up for his lexical deficiency? And, as for that nonverbal periphrasis, won't it seem the best solution in most cases to replace it with a more efficient verbal (perhaps also nonverbal) expression?

3.3 One comment should be added to these thoughts on the functions of nonverbal communication and how to deal with them in interpretation. I have discussed many times how, in the light of the interchangeability of language, paralanguage and kinesics within the same stretch of discourse, the concept of *redundancy* should be revised, as it is so many times misused, for what appears to be redundant is most of the time only *complementary*, that is, supporting, emphasizing or contradicting the essential message. But even true redundancy must not be given a negative connotation of purposelessness either, for it might express precisely a personal style, or a given culture, and although it might be redundant from a communication point of view, it would hardly be so on the social or cultural level (e.g. the more gesticulating Mediterranean peoples).

4 Paralanguage: audible communication beyond words

[. . .] Paralanguage, despite twenty-five years of research – or rather, of repeating some poorly fundamental ideas about it, for instance, that paralanguage serves to convey emotion, as if that were its only function – mainly in psychology, occasionally in cultural studies, and in linguistics, has not as yet exploited its many possibilities for systematic study in so many areas. [. . .] I will offer a realistic definition of paralanguage as: the nonverbal long-term qualities of the voice, the many modifiers of it which result in marked formal and semantic changes, and the many independent word-like sound constructs, which we use consciously or unconsciously supporting, contradicting, accompanying or replacing the linguistic and kinesic messages . . . either simultaneously to or alternating with them.

Four important categories can be differentiated in our daily paralinguistic repertoires. *Primary qualities*, fundamental constituents of human speech, which first of all allow us to differentiate individuals, include personal timbre, voice resonance, loudness, tempo of speech, pitch level, pitch registers, pitch intervals, intonation range (melodious to monotone), syllabic duration (drawling or clipping), and rhythm, and will therefore modify other paralinguistic features as well. While some, like timbre, or certain malfunctions, depend on biological or physiological factors, others – more important in the interpretation situation at times – respond to psychological, sociocultural and occupational determinants. *Qualifiers* are sound effects which, beyond the many nuances of meaning made possible by primary qualities, constitute the most complex type of voice characteristics, intimately related to facial and even bodily expression, as they actually appear very often in combination with congruent kinesic behaviors, in other words, as an inherent part of the "speaking face," an audible-visual reality that cannot be neglected. [. . .]

Differentiators are actually part of paralinguistic-kinesic constructs which are differentiated in various degrees according to sex, age, culture, socioeducational status and normal or pathological personal features. I would say that (leaving aside coughing, sneezing, etc.) laughter deserves the most attention in the interpretation situation for the nuances of meaning it can carry. In fact, laughter accompanied by facial expression – and also by itself – may occupy the space a verbal sentence would take without leaving out for the average listener any important message, were it not because different forms of laughter may carry different meanings according to culture. The same can be said of crying, and we know that there are cultures where weeping in distress, for instance, or in highly emotional circumstances (arrivals, goodbyes, weddings, funerals, before the law, etc.) is more to be expected than in others, and the interpreter in those situations may want to render the speaker's crying verbally, for leaving it out might prevent listeners from understanding its true meaning. Finally, *alternants*, word-like single or compound utterances occurring either isolated or alternating with verbal language and kinesics, can be loosely described as sighs, meaningful throat clearings, tongue clicks, audible breath intakes, narial (nostril) frictions (e.g. of contempt), closed- or open-mouth sounds (e.g. "Uh-hu," "Mm-hm!"), meaningful silences, etc. Each language, each culture or social community possesses a great number of perfectly encoded and decoded alternants which constitute a true lexicon used constantly in personal interaction as systematically as dictionary items (which some are already, e.g. "Uh!," "Psst!," "Pooh!"). Because they play important roles in the mechanism of interaction with as high a frequency rate as words and often with a clearer semantic and regulatory function, alternants should be given serious thought, not only in linguistics and communication research, but specifically as regards how the interpreter ought to treat them as they come up in the speaker's discourse as well as in the listener's feedback reactions. [. . .]

Again, whether or not we acknowledge the presence of these nonverbal signs will make the difference between a faithful and exacting interaction and one in which the translator's liberties by omission or commission hinder greatly the conveyance of the speaker's actual messages. [. . .] The speaker, it is true, may support them with kinesic behaviors that may be understood by interpreter and listener, but what if the interpreter cannot understand them himself? – for instance, the misleading accompanying slight head nods of the Japanese male listener's "Eeeh" or "Nn," which is meant only to convey polite attention, and not agreement. What could the fluent interpreter do about it? To let the other cointeractant believe that his statements always meet with his Japanese listener's agreement, which is not true? To initiate the listener's new turn as speaker with some clarifying verbal form? This latter thought is not just a gratuitous one, for in the give and take of a translated conversation one must strive to minimize the occasions for misunderstanding or for utter lack of decoding of elements which should be decoded by each party.

[. . .]

Finally, within paralanguage, mention should be made also of truly paralinguistic silences, which actually can be included within alternants as meaningful nonactivities never to be neglected as mere gaps. [. . .] There will be silences in the speech being translated by an interpreter which will "say" what the speaker is not saying in any other way. Should the interpreter, then, remain silent, too? If he does, his own silence will be most likely a true meaningless gap, unless he conveys verbally what the speaker is expressing silently. Yet, is that legitimate on the part of the translator, since the speaker did not disclose his thoughts verbally? Or shall we say that one must discern the difference between the silence that wants to express and the silence that wants to conceal, and thus respect that concealment?

What should remain clear at this point is that the translator . . . needs to know the paralinguistic cultural repertoires of the source language, weigh their coding problems, and act accordingly.

5 Kinesics: visual communication with and beyond words

5.1 We can define kinesics as: the conscious or unconscious psycho-muscularly based body movements and intervening or resulting positions, either learned or somatogenic, of visual, visual-audible, and tactile or kinesthetic perception, which, whether isolated or combined with the linguistic and paralinguistic structures and with other somatic and objectual behavioral systems, possess intended or unintended communicative value. [. . .]

Three types of behavior should be distinguished within kinesics: *gestures* (unfortunately the only type included in otherwise very worthy cultural inventories, e.g. Saitz and Cervenka 1972; Barakat 1973; Morris *et al.* 1979; Rector and Trinta 1985; Rector 1986), conscious or unconscious movements made mainly with the head, the face alone (including the eyes), or the limbs, dependent or independent of verbal language, simultaneously to or alternating with it and serving as a primary communicative tool (e.g. smiles, gaze movements, a hand gesture for emphasis); *manners*, more or less dynamic and mainly learned and socially ritualized according to specific situations, either simultaneously to or alternating with verbal language (e.g. the way we greet others, cough, cross arms or legs to adopt those postures); and *postures*, equally conscious or unconscious, but more static and also codified by social norms and used less as communicative behaviors, although they may reveal culture, sex, mental attitudes like sulkiness, willingness, boredom, tenseness, etc. [. . .]

5.2 An in-depth study of kinesic behaviors in the realm of translation in visual-acoustic interaction would suggest immediately the need for correctly decoding at least both the speaker's significant gestures and, again, the listener's significant feedback movements. This means simply that the translator must have acquired sufficient interactive fluency in the foreign culture, becoming aware of the intercultural encoding and decoding problems. [. . .] In view of the various ways in which kinesics combines with language and paralanguage, as seen in the next section, it would seem that the translator would have to "keep an eye" on the speaker's total speech, lest he should miss something which has been said kinesically only. This amounts to saying that an interpreter can translate visually and not only audibly, in other words, that he is not only the translator of verbal language, but of the whole triple structure, with a selective criterion that would be anything but easy to determine [. . .].

6 Morphological and functional categories of nonverbal behaviors: a model for the identification and study of interactive repertoires

[. . .]

6.1 *Emblems* are mostly nonambiguous gestures, but also certain paralinguistic utterances, that have their equivalence in a word or phrase (e.g. "So-so," "Okay," "Stop," "Ssh"); besides those which have become quite universal through intercultural borrowing, each culture has a rich repertoire of them. [. . .] In the context of simultaneous or consecutive translation one could establish as a norm that emblems that accompany their verbal equivalents are dispensable and do not have to be conveyed in any way to the listener, while those that are displayed alone may be quite indispensable for the translation of the speaker's message, according to the translator's criterion.

6.2 *Language markers* constitute the most culture differentiating category and the subtlest one, as they are conscious or unconscious behaviors that punctuate and emphasize the acoustic and grammatical succession of words and phrases according to their location and relevance in the speech stream and coincide with written punctuation symbols, which are grammatical and attitudinal themselves and can reveal verbal and nonverbal cultural peculiarities. [. . .] The kinesic markers always present in discourse more or less noticeably (they generally do not show in a Swede as much as in an Italian!) include, for instance: *pronoun* markers (e.g. personal, pointing at present and even absent persons with head nods and gaze, head tilts, etc.; reciprocal, as in "We always write to each other"); *prepositional* markers (e.g. brief face and hand gesture with "until," "in order to," "without"); *conjunctional* markers (e.g. gestures with "so," "which," "however," "therefore"), *verbal* markers (indicating both temporal and modal differences (e.g. "there was," "there will be," "if there were any," symbolizing something past and real, immediately preceding, expected with certainty or only possible); *stress* markers (e.g. emphasizing with head, brows or hands the stresses in "Well, the Russians don't seem to think there is any danger, but *we* do!").

6.3 *Space markers* and *time markers* illustrate, on the other hand, size, distance and location (e.g. "Over there" with a hand-and-gaze nod among North Americans and chin-and-gaze among Latins), and on the other, the distant or immediate past, the present, and the immediate and distant future, as well as the duration of events (e.g. "Veeery sloowly"). These, of course, may be used with nonverbal accompaniment (actually emblems, for these categories are not mutually exclusive).

6.4 *Deictics* are movements, sometimes utterances, which truly point to the location of a person, object or place in space, even if the referent is not present, and to an event in time (e.g. "This conference is a great success!").

6.5 *Pictographs, echoics, kinetographs*, and *kinephonographs*. These are the imitative nonverbal behaviors, and only pictographs and kinetographs are likely to appear in the interpretation situation under normal circumstances. With pictographs we draw in the air or on a surface a picture of the shape or contour of someone or something (e.g. the so-called hour-glass gesture signifying an attractive woman), while kinetographs imitate any type of action, whether bodily, mechanical or natural. Echoics are imitations of sounds done either paralinguistically, kinesically or with both movement and sound, while kinephonographs are combined imitations of movement and sound kinesically and paralinguistically.

6.6 *Ideographs* and *event tracers* are movements, sometimes accompanied by paralinguistic sounds, which trace the direction of a thought or event being described. The former may refer to a pleasant experience, a great deed, a beautiful piece of art, etc., while event tracers follow the development of an event, such as the "comings" and "goings" of a person.

6.7 *Identifiers*, along with language markers and the next category, externalizers, are undoubtedly the most intriguing, fascinating, difficult to master in a foreign culture and the most inherent nonverbal components of discourse cross-culturally. The three together are responsible for the individual expressive style of each person (e.g. "ladylike," "elegant," "very articulate," "vulgar"), betraying sex, age, socio-economic and educational status and culture. They are displayed simultaneously to or alternating with verbal language, which they illustrate, refer to, or literally give bodily form to and identify certain abstract concepts (e.g. "impossible," "absurd"), moral and physical qualities (e.g. "unfriendly," "tough," "stingy," "cautious") and qualities of objectual and environmental referents (e.g. "dirty," "crystal clear," "smooth," "murky").

6.8 *Externalizers*, which make up the most complex of all categories, do not illustrate words, but react to them at the most. They are reactions to other people's past, present, anticipated or imagined reality, to what has been said, is being said or will be said, silenced, done or not done by us or someone else, to past, present, anticipated or imagined events, to esthetic experiences and to spiritual experiences.

Within this category we find, of course – and they are important cross-culturally – those social random behaviors displayed daily by all of us in personal and culture-defining ways as externalizations of hidden states or past, present or anticipated motives, and they would remain outside the interpreter's domain despite their obvious semantic content (e.g. betraying the speaker's tenseness during a political debate or an official ceremony, in spite of his experience and self-control), although it would be important to be sensitive enough to detect them and interpret them for oneself.

6.9 *Adaptors* are an important group of nonverbal categories including activities or positions in which parts of the body (mainly the hands) come in contact with other parts (self-adaptors), another person's body (alter-adaptors), objects (object-adaptors) and substances and objects most immediately associated with the body (body-adaptors, e.g. food, clothing). Of these four, only self-adaptors and object-adaptors are likely to be displayed in the average encounter for a translator. As for *self-adaptors*, apart from the fact that some language markers, identifiers and externalizers may involve touching oneself, the speaker may preen himself slowly while reminiscing, fidget to the point of attracting the attention of both translator or listener, etc., while the listener may stroke his hair out of boredom or rub his chin with incredulity as forms of feedback. *Object-adaptors* are displayed as soon as the speaker or the listener handles a pen, glasses, etc., and when grabbing or pounding on a lectern, stroking the arm of a chair, rearranging paper sheets or flicking imaginary lint (to the point of revealing tenseness as externalizers!), and, as with self-adaptors, they must be identified by the professional interpreter as part of the speaker's and the listener's arsenal of interactive behaviors.

[. . .]

7 Language, paralanguage and kinesics in reduced interaction: its problems and the translator's position and responsibilities

I have defined reduced interaction before (Poyatos 1983: 85–89, and very briefly but with some new thoughts on it, 1988) as the situation in which emission and/or perception of external body behaviors, which may or may not take place face-to-face, is impeded in one or more channels by a somatic malfunction, external physical agents or mutual agreement between the interactants. [. . .] The curtailment of communication in any of the two modalities (language–paralanguage and kinesics) can have a profound significance, not just in terms of the encoding and decoding problems they entail, but as regards the relationships between persons and the affective content of their attitudes. Take, for instance, how the blind speaker may miss the eloquent facial expressions of the speaker, or the speaker the listener's kinesic feedback behaviors, which could affect his own attitude and speech, were he able to perceive them; or the effect that the visual appearance of the seeing interlocutor could have had on him; how the deaf person can never feel the emotional acoustic impact of the speaker's words and paralinguistic modifiers, nor the very sound of a voice he would have liked or disliked [. . .].

When it would seem that all the important facets of the interpretation situation have been at least touched upon throughout the previous sections and that through them many hitherto neglected aspects have been further suggested, the sudden exposure to the situation in which either the speaker or the listener is not fully equipped to perceive or emit the three components of speech, which in turn affects the translator's perceptual abilities, makes one realize two things: first, that, as in linguistics, general communication studies, and even areas such as counselling, social work and medical personnel–patient interaction, the efforts to analyze in depth the problems of reduced interaction and to try to develop the needed interactive fluency with the blind, the deaf, etc., have been minimal; and second, that the interpreter must train himself or herself to acquire that fluency and become a fit instrument of social and affective communication. [. . .]

References

Barakat, Robert A. (1973) "Arabic Gestures," *Journal of Popular Culture* 6: 749–893.

Bouissac, Paul, Herzfeld, Michael and Posner, Roland (eds) (1986) *Iconicity: Essays on the Nature of Culture. Festschrift für Thomas Sebeok*, Tübingen.

Morris, Desmond, Collett, Peter, Marsh, Peter and O'Shaughnessy, Marie (1979) *Gestures: Their Origins and Distributions*, New York.

Poyatos, Fernando (1983) *New Perspectives in Nonverbal Communication: Studies in Cultural Anthropology, Social Psychology, Linguistics, Literature and Semiotics*, Oxford.

—— (1986) "Nonverbal Categories as Personal and Cultural Identifiers: A Model for Social Interaction Research," in Bouissac, Herzfeld and Posner, pp. 469–525.

—— (1988) "New Research Perspectives in Crosscultural Psychology through Nonverbal Communication Studies," in F. Poyatos (ed.) *Cross-Cultural Perspectives in Nonverbal Communication*, Lewiston, NY and Toronto.

—— (1993) *Paralanguage: A Linguistic and Interdisciplinary Approach to Interactive Speech and Sounds*, Amsterdam.

Rector, Monica (1986) "Emblems in Brazilian Culture," in Bouissac, Herzfeld and Posner, pp. 447–67.

Rector, Monica and Trinta, A. R. (1985) *Comunicação Não-Verbal: A Gestualidade Brasileira*, Petrópolis and Rio de Janeiro.

Saitz, Robert L. and Cervenka, Edward J. (1972) *Handbook of Gestures: Colombia and the United States*, The Hague.

Part 5

Observing the Product and its Effects

INTRODUCTION

AS REFLECTED IN the first three parts of this volume, research on interpreting, and on simultaneous interpreting in particular, has largely been concerned with the cognitive intricacies of the interpreting process. The source speech and the interpreter's rendition thereof are thus looked at not as textual entities in their own right but as input conditions and output parameters for studying the intervening process (cf. Seleskovitch 1976: 95; Gile 1991a: 155). Considering the prevailing paradigms in the language sciences at the time when interpreting research was getting under way, this lack of interest in the interpreter's output in terms of its "textuality" is hardly surprising. Even linguists themselves did not begin to venture beyond the lexical and sentence levels into the textual dimension before the 1970s. While some of them, like Dressler (1974), made early attempts to account for translation and interpreting in text-linguistic terms, such theorizing was not followed up with empirical studies. It was only with the procedural approach to text and discourse (Beaugrande 1980; Beaugrande and Dressler 1981; Brown and Yule 1983), together with the socio-semiotic framework of Halliday's systemic-functional model of language (Halliday 1978, 1985; Halliday and Hasan 1976), that interpreting scholars were offered a more dynamic, communication-oriented framework for viewing interpreters' output in terms of text or discourse (e.g. Bühler 1989, 1990).

Among the standards of textuality which have since received particular attention in IS are cohesion (e.g. Gallina 1992; Shlesinger 1995; Mizuno 1999), coherence (e.g. Taylor 1989; Falbo 1993; Pöchhacker 1993; Kusztor 2000) and intertextuality (e.g. Alexieva 1994; Pöchhacker 1994a; Ivanova 1996). Not surprisingly, the textual manifestations of orality (cf. Ong 1982; Tannen 1982; Halliday 1989) have proved particularly significant to the study of interpreted discourse. Apart from early work on oral delivery and text types as presented by Déjean le Féal (1982) and Kopczyński (1982) at the Symposium on *Impromptu Speech* (Enkvist 1982), interpreting researchers have devoted attention to such aspects of oral textuality as prosodic features (e.g. Shlesinger 1994; Williams 1995; Bendik 1996; Collados Aís 1998, and in this volume), structure shifts (e.g. Pöchhacker 1995b) and, more holistically, the relative position of interpretations on the oral–literate continuum (Shlesinger 1989a).

All of this is not to say, of course, that product-oriented studies of interpreting can only be carried out within a particular text-linguistic paradigm. Moreover, as emphasized by Toury (1991, 1995) with regard to Holmes's ([1972/1988]) distinction between process-oriented, product-oriented and function-oriented descriptive studies, research on the translational product can hardly be seen in isolation from processing issues or functional implications. Hence there is considerable heterogeneity in this part on product- (or text/discourse-based) approaches to interpreting, which range from observation of the text surface to the experimental study of the socio-semiotic (pragmatic) dimension of speech.

By way of introduction – and a comprehensive and "didactic" one indeed – **Basil Hatim** and **Ian Mason** present the application of a comprehensive discourse-theoretical model to an analytical differentiation of the principal modes of interpreting. Building upon the terminological foundations laid by Beaugrande and Dressler (1981) and incorporating a number of key concepts from discourse analytical approaches, Hatim and Mason (1990, 1997) dispose of a rich set of tools with which to tackle the analysis of highly diverse samples of discourse. Their basic distinction between texture, structure and context is used to highlight the distinct procedural constraints applying to simultaneous, consecutive and liaison interpreting. While the more text-centered domains of texture and structure link up closely with many of the product-oriented studies cited above, the third, more open-ended domain in Hatim and Mason's tripartite conceptualization points to the numerous socio-semiotic aspects which become particularly prominent in face-to-face interaction. Rhetorical purpose, register, politeness, power and ideology are some of the key notions which have proved particularly applicable to the analysis of bilateral interpreting in non-conference settings. Indeed, Mason has been actively promoting and shaping the study of (dialogue) interpreting in discourse analytical terms (cf. Mason 1999, 2000, 2001), thus establishing a close linkage between the text-linguistic approach in TS and the community of scholars investigating interpreting in community-based settings. While the latter will be represented mainly in Part 7 of this volume, the discourse-based pragmatic approach to liaison interpreting foregrounded in Hatim and Mason's tripartite model is also exemplified by the third paper in the present part.

An approach that remains much closer to the level of the text surface but nevertheless has significant implications for the theory of interpreting informs the work of **Helle V. Dam** (1995), one of the few interpreting researchers to carry out a major empirical investigation into the consecutive mode of interpreting. Surprisingly perhaps, Dam is not concerned with the nature and role of note-taking, as analyzed in text-linguistic terms by Allioni (1989) and documented with a highly innovative methodology by Andres (2000); nevertheless, her work links up, both theoretically and methodologically, with the seminal study of Seleskovitch (1975) on consecutive interpreting: both investigations are based on transcriptions of an experimental corpus of consecutive interpretations, and explore the fundamental issue of meaning-based vs form-based strategies of interpreting. Both studies, one might add, are also plagued by methodological difficulties. For Dam (1998, and in this volume), who is no less aware than Seleskovitch of the problems of generating data in a non-authentic setting, it is the aim of quantifying translational equivalents that poses the greatest method-ological challenge. While Dam's analysis largely circumvents that issue by focusing on formal similarity between the target- and source-text surfaces, the essential problem of measuring meaning is there all the same, albeit implicitly. Elsewhere, Dam (1993) attempted to tackle that issue head on by analyzing omissions in terms of strategic compression ("text condensing") – which leads right back to the classic problem of quantifying translational "deviations" as raised even in the earliest psychological studies (cf. Part 1) and left largely unresolved despite a number of innovative efforts (e.g. Mackintosh 1983; Gile 1989b; Tommola and Lindholm 1995).

Quite apart from the issue of "fidelity," "accuracy" and "completeness," which could be said to loom in the background of any product-based comparative analysis, the study by Dam presented in this volume points to some highly relevant directions for further research. Most obviously, the aim of quantifying the presence and distribution of lexical material suggests the application of corpus-linguistic statistical procedures (e.g. Armstrong 1997; Shlesinger 1998; Lamberger-Felber 1999). Moreover, an ana-lytical focus on the consecutive versus the simultaneous mode of interpreting may help shed light on the relationship between the product – and its "quality" – and the underlying process or processing strategies (e.g. Viezzi 1993, 1996). To the extent that the adoption of a more form-based or meaning-based processing strategy is a matter of deliberate choice (cf. the "Minimax principle" developed by Levý (1967) with reference to literary translation as well as Séguinot's (1989) "principle of least effort" and Riccardi's (1998) "strategy of least commitment"), the resulting product can and should be investigated with respect to its communicative effectiveness as well. An authentic research model for this purpose is the distinction between transliteration and signing in interpreting for the deaf, as employed by Livingston et al. (1994) in their study on comparative cognitive outcomes in an educational setting.

The effect of the interpreter's product on the communicative interaction in another particularly relevant setting was investigated by **Susan Berk-Seligson** as part of her groundbreaking work on interpreting in the courtroom (1990a). Her experi-mental study on the impact of politeness on jurors' appreciation of witness testimony (1988, and in this volume) represents a great enrichment of the literature in IS, both through its innovative methodology and because of its broadly sociolinguistic perspec-tive on discourse in a given situation. In the context of court interpreting research, Berk-Seligson's study highlights the need to study both the product itself – as is done, for instance, in discourse-based analyses of particular features such as register (e.g. Hale 1997a, 1997b), question types (e.g. Wadensjö 1997, Berk-Seligson 1999) and interjections (e.g. Hale 1999) – and the communicative effect of that product in a particular setting. The impact of the interpretation on the process of interaction is closely linked to the issue of the interpreter's role, especially in community-based domains of interpreting, which is given due attention in Part 7 of this volume. In simultaneous conference interpreting as well, though, an essentially pragmatic, i.e.

function-oriented approach is undoubtedly crucial to a full understanding of the phenomenon. Indeed, Gerver (1972), following through on his own suggestion to extend
experimentation from information processing by interpreters to the reception of their
output by the users (cf. Gerver 1971: 114), carried out an experiment comparing
listeners' comprehension of simultaneous vs consecutive interpreting under noisy listening conditions (cf. Gerver 1976: 176–7). Experimental work focusing on reception
and comprehension by the listeners came to the fore only in the 1990s (e.g. Shlesinger
1994; Collados Aís 1998, and in this volume; Steiner 1998); prior to that, the user
perspective had been investigated mainly in terms of quality expectations regarding
the interpreter's product – a socio-translatological issue which will be addressed in
Part 6.

Further reading: Taylor Torsello 1996; Taylor Torsello [*et al.*] 1997; Tebble 1999.

THE CHAPTER PRESENTED here is taken from *The Translator as Communicator* (1997) – the second of two joint volumes by Basil Hatim and Ian Mason. Their collaborative efforts, during the time when both were based in the School of Languages at Heriot-Watt University, Edinburgh, also include *Discourse and the Translator* (1990). In both works, Hatim and Mason adopt an essentially text-linguistic and discourse analytical approach. Trying to avoid any compartmentalization of the field, they have highlighted the broader context in which all acts of translating are essentially acts of communication aimed at enabling the construction of meaning, and text users engage in a form of negotiation which moves in a text-to-context direction.

In addition to their shared endeavors, each of the two authors has contributed extensively to the translational literature. Basil Hatim, who holds a Chair in English and Translation at The American University of Sharjah, United Arab Emirates, has translated numerous works from and into Arabic, and has written a *Practical Guide to English–Arabic–English Translation*. His 1997 monograph *Communication Across Cultures* brings together the three disciplines of contrastive linguistics, text linguistics and translation theory using authentic data, both spoken and written.

Ian Mason is Professor of Interpreting and Translation and Director of the Centre for Translation and Interpreting Studies in Scotland at Heriot-Watt University. His specializations include dialogue interpreting and screen translation, with particular emphasis on text-linguistic and pragmatic issues. He has guest-edited a Special Issue on Dialogue Interpreting for *The Translator* (1999) and published an extended collection of these *Studies in Dialogue Interpreting* in 2001.

Further reading: Hatim and Mason 1997; Mason 2000.

Basil Hatim and Ian Mason

INTERPRETING
A text linguistic approach

[. . .]

THE THREE BASIC domains of textuality . . . are texture, structure and context. The term "texture" covers the various devices used in establishing continuity of sense and thus making a sequence of sentences operational (i.e. both cohesive and coherent). [. . .]

Another source from which texts derive their cohesion and acquire the necessary coherence is structure. This assists us in our attempt to perceive specific compositional plans in what otherwise would only be a disconnected sequence of sentences. Structure and texture thus work together; with the former providing the outline, and the latter fleshing out the details. [. . .]

In dealing with structure and texture, we rely on higher-order contextual factors which determine the way in which a given sequence of sentences serves a specific rhetorical purpose such as arguing or narrating (i.e. becomes what we have called "text"). [. . .] Discoursal meanings influence the way texts are put together (duality of text function, opaqueness of compositional plans and subtleties of the words chosen). [. . .] Texture, structure and text type focus are all involved and together reflect deeper underlying meanings that are essentially discoursal (i.e. serve as the mouthpiece of institutions).

All of the factors mentioned so far – rhetorical purposes, attitudinal meanings, structure and texture – are deployed to meet the requirements of particular social occasions (e.g. the diplomat's ultimatum). Genres are conventionalized forms of language use appropriate to given domains of social activity and to the purposes of participants in them. [. . .] Genres have by common consensus attracted particular forms of linguistic expression and have thus acquired a formulaic status. There are strict do's and don'ts regarding who the participants are, what to say and how to say it within certain formats generally sanctioned by the community of text users.

Through the principle of intertextuality, text users recognize the various texts, discourses and genres, and their linguistic expression, as signs. At the global level, argumentation-disguised-as-exposition would be recognized as a particular text form, the masking of real intentions as a particular discourse function and the diplomat's ultimatum as a particular genre. [. . .]

Interpreting and the standards of textuality

[. . .]

The three principal modes of interpreting (the simultaneous, the consecutive and the liaison) inevitably place different demands on the interpreter. It is true that all well-formed texts, oral and written, possess all of the following characteristics:

1   They are cohesive in texture.
2   They are coherent and exhibit a particular structure.
3   They serve a clear rhetorical purpose as text.
4   They relay specific attitudinal meanings as discourse.
5   They are in keeping with the requirements of certain conventional formats as genres.
6   They serve a set of mutually relevant communicative intentions pragmatically.
7   They stand out as members of distinct registers.

It is also true that, whatever the mode of interpreting, input or output will have to display all of the above characteristics. However, the three modes of interpreting mentioned above seem to focus on different areas of text production and reception. The various domains of textuality – context, structure and texture – are not equally prominent. To reflect this varying degree of prominence we now put forward a set of hypotheses.

A set of hypotheses

1   Bearing in mind the nature of the demands made on the interpreter by the situational constraints normally associated with each of the three basic modes, it may be assumed that the simultaneous interpreter has to settle for a partial view of both context and text structure and has therefore to rely more heavily on the emerging texture in order to make and maintain sense. This is because, in this mode of interpreting, reception and production of text take place at more or less the same time.
2   The consecutive interpreter, whose output comes after the source text has been delivered, tends to focus on information relevant to text structure as this outweighs that yielded by context or texture in what is noted down and used as a basis for delivery.
3   Finally, the liaison interpreter has access only to a partial view of texture and structure, both of which would be unfolding piecemeal in the two-way

exchange. In this case, context would seem to be the main resource which the interpreter draws on in the task of maintaining the continuity of the exchange.

In terms of the demands on the interpreter, then, particular strands of textuality remain partly inaccessible, leaving the interpreter to make fuller use of those which are more readily available. Some might argue that "inaccessibility" is perhaps too strong a word for what must potentially be present, even if it is incomplete. While not wishing to make too much of the issue of accessibility, we can from the interpreter's point of view take the following as a fair representation of what actually happens:

(a)   In the case of simultaneous interpreting, context and structure are revealed only piecemeal and can thus be accessed more effectively via texture, i.e. the words as they are spoken.
(b)   In the case of consecutive interpreting, texture and context are retained only in a most short-lived manner and can thus be stored more effectively via structure.
(c)   In the case of liaison interpreting, texture and structure are manifested only partially and can thus be negotiated more effectively via context.

In short, it is our contention that only the most "local" and hence insufficient information is made available regarding context and structure in simultaneous interpreting, texture and context in consecutive interpreting and texture and structure in the case of liaison interpreting. [. . .]

Let us re-express our initial set of hypotheses . . . :

1   Input for simultaneous interpreting is characterized by context and structure being less readily usable than texture.
2   Input for consecutive interpreting is characterized by texture being less readily usable than structure.
3   Input for liaison interpreting is characterized by structure being less readily usable than context.

A corollary to this set of basic hypotheses is that, whatever the form of the deficit or the compensation strategy, it is our contention that texture may be treated as a privileged category. Texture is necessarily available at all times, providing the interpreter with a point of departure. It is the mainstay of the simultaneous interpreter's activity; it is there to help the consecutive interpreter retrieve the sought-after structure; and it is there to help the liaison interpreter reconstruct the required context for the one or two utterances dealt with at any given time. This is the basic position which we will now try to elaborate, using examples of authentic interpreting data.

The prominence of texture in simultaneous interpreting

In simultaneous interpreting, the input is received piecemeal, and the interpreter's task is basically to react and interact with utterance 1, then utterance 2 and so on, allowing for the inevitable overlap between the various elements of the sequence. [. . .] Of course, experienced interpreters use all kinds of anticipation strategies which enable them to formulate in advance plausible hypotheses regarding both context and structure. But, even when prior expectations are sufficiently focused, the processing is still tentative and the various hypotheses must be confirmed or disproved by the forthcoming textual evidence. Thus the rich variety of texture signals have to be relied upon as the most tangible point of reference.

To illustrate how texture comes to the fore, guiding the interpreter's efforts in negotiating meanings, let us consider an example drawn from a real interpreting situation. Sample 1 is a formal translation of an extract from the original text of a speech delivered in Arabic at the United Nations by King Hussein of Jordan. Sample 2 is a verbatim transcript of the simultaneous interpretation into English of the extract.

Sample 1

King Hussein (formal translation from Arabic):

> [It is a great honour for me to take part in celebrating the fortieth anniversary of the establishment of the United Nations as the greatest international organization which set its goal in the very first words of the Preamble to its Charter: "to save succeeding generations from the scourge of war and to push social progress ahead and to raise the standard of life in an atmosphere of freedom that is larger". (. . .)
>
> In the past 40 years, the world has, in the nature of things, witnessed a number of developments and changes which were distinguished from those of previous times by their speed and tremendous diversity. With every social or scientific advance emerged a new reality, carrying within it remarkable ironies. The great aspirations stemming from development soon collided with the negative aspects and the apprehensions arising from that development.
>
> During the past 40 years, the world knew the nuclear era with its destructive bombs and its power-generating plants. Mankind enjoyed the fruits of massive progress in science and technology to live in constant terror of lethal weaponry made possible by this progress. And distance between states and nations shrank as a result of the communications revolution. And international terrorism in turn prospered. The degree of consciousness among peoples of the world regarding their common concerns rose to be met by the division of the world into a north largely affluent and pioneering and a south largely impoverished and recipient.]

Sample 2

King Hussein (interpretation from Arabic):

> It is a great honour for me to take part in celebrating the fortieth anniversary of the United Nations. Established as the paramount international organization, its goals were set in the very first words of the Preamble to its Charter, namely: "to save succeeding generations from the scourge of war and to promote social progress and better standards of life in larger freedom". (. . .)
>
> In the past 40 years, the world has inevitably undergone a number of developments and changes characterized by unprecedented speed and diversity. Every social or scientific advance has brought with it a new reality, fraught with striking ironies. Great aspirations inspired by a particular development soon collided with apprehensions and negative effects arising from the same development.
>
> During the same period, the world was thrust into the nuclear era with both its destructive devices and its power-generating plants. Mankind enjoyed the fruits of massive progress in science and technology only to live in constant terror of lethal weaponry made possible by the same progress. Similarly, the communications revolution has brought states and nations dramatically closer, but has also enabled international terrorism to prosper. The nations of the world have become more conscious of their common concerns, but at the same time have been forced to face the reality of a world divided into a largely affluent and pioneering North and a largely impoverished and recipient South.

Readers may assess for themselves the aspect of texture which relates to lexical choice in this highly competent interpreting performance. Consider for example the English *inevitably* for what is literally in Arabic "in the nature of things", *unprecedented* for "distinguished from those of previous times", *fraught with* for "carrying within it", and so on. These are important manifestations of texture and show how collocation is crucial in establishing lexical cohesion.

Of more immediate interest for our purposes is how the interpreter relies on what the text offers by way of textural clues, that is, devices serving anaphoric (backward) and cataphoric (forward) reference, substitution, ellipsis, conjunction and indeed lexical cohesion, and how these devices are then used as clues to the way the text is developed. To illustrate this, a few examples may be drawn from Sample 1 above:

Example 1

Arabic:

> [. . . celebrating the fortieth anniversary of the establishment of the United Nations as the greatest international organization which set its goal in the very first words of the Preamble . . .]

English:

> . . . *celebrating the fortieth anniversary of the United Nations. Established as the paramount international organization, its goals were set in the very first words of the Preamble . . .*

Having disposed of the formulaic expression of "honour", the interpreter identifies the concept of "establishment" as somehow superfluous in sentence 1. This item is not discarded, however, but used as the starting point of sentence 2 which cataphorically relates "establishment" to "goals", thus propelling the text forward. The cataphora is also an ideal way of breaking up a long awkward sentence. All this is done without altering the sequence of source text elements. This close monitoring of texture has the advantage of generally upholding idiomaticity in English and of avoiding the increased pressure which would have been entailed by reordering the parts.

Example 2

Arabic:

> [. . . enjoyed the fruits of massive progress in science and technology to live in constant terror . . .]

English:

> [. . . *enjoyed the fruits of massive progress in science and technology only to live in constant terror . . .*]

Obviously the Arabic "to live" is not a straightforward infinitive of purpose. The restriction (*only to*) is a cohesive device equivalent to an adversative ("but", "however"). This emphasizes the contrast between "progress" and "terror" and anticipates what is to follow (a series of similar contrasts).

Example 3

Arabic:

> [And distance between states and nations shrank as a result of the communications revolution. And international terrorism in turn prospered.]

English:

> *Similarly, the communications revolution has brought states and nations dramatically closer, but has also enabled international terrorism to prosper.*

Faced with two "and" connectors (one genuinely additive, the other in fact an adversative) the interpreter has responded to the contrast perceived earlier between "progress" and "terror" by maintaining it here as intended.

Example 4

Arabic:

> [The degree of consciousness among peoples of the world regarding their common concerns rose to be met by the division of the world into a north largely affluent and pioneering and a south largely impoverished and recipient.]

English:

> *The nations of the world have become more conscious of their common concerns, but at the same time have been forced to face the reality of a world divided into a largely affluent and pioneering North and a largely impoverished and recipient South.*

Drawing on textural clues, the interpreter has now successfully established the contrastive pattern and used this as a basic anticipation strategy. In this way, the initially inaccessible structure and context gradually materialize but only through the piecing together of a variety of textural devices.

The prominence of structure in consecutive interpreting

The input processed by the consecutive interpreter is a text that can be said to be complete and autonomous. Consecutive interpreting thus affords the interpreter the advantage of not having constantly to wait for or anticipate the next fragment of input. Conversely, whereas in simultaneous mode, the interpreter has at least something to embark upon, the consecutive interpreter has to wait before he or she can deliver. There is, in other words, an added pressure and an extra load on memory, which have the result that information relating to texture and, perhaps to a lesser extent, context becomes rather too detailed to be retainable. In note-taking, it is not words in themselves that are recorded but rather arrangements of ideas in relation to each other. In this way, consecutive interpreters seem to use manifestations of texture and of context not as ends in themselves but as the means to gain access to structure.

In consecutive interpreting, then, effective reception and storage of information will involve focusing on the way a text is put together in response to context, and to the way texture is utilized to implement this. Effective consecutive output thus exhibits a clear outline of the way a text is structured. This compositional plan of the text will be the overall arrangement within which only relevant details of texture and context are to be found. Certain kinds of contextual and textural information are liable to be jettisoned if they do not fit within the compositional plan in a way which contributes to making a sequence of sentences operational.

To illustrate this reliance on indications of structure, we reproduce as Sample 3 a short sequence from a speech used as a consecutive interpreting test. Successful negotiation of this difficult passage would depend upon recognition of the counter-argumentative structure it contains and note-taking which clearly reflected this, in particular, the identification of "codification" with "legislation" and the contrast of these to "institutions".

Sample 3

> Dans ce contexte, la première des réponses, c'est la transparence. Et la transparence ne résulte pas seulement de dispositions législatives. Bien sûr, la codification est très importante. Mais il n'y a pas que la codification. Je voudrais profiter de ce débat pour dire que je crois qu'il y a aussi une lisibilité des institutions elles-mêmes . . .

> [In this context, the first response is transparency. And transparency does not result just from legislative measures. Of course, codification is very important. But there is not just codification. I would like to use the opportunity of this debate to say that I believe that there is also a [problem of] legibility of the institutions themselves . . .]

Candidates in the test were clearly divided between those who had relied over-much on the texture of "I would like to use the opportunity . . ." and thus allowed themselves to be diverted from the structural arrangement (making an entirely new point out of "also . . .") and those who had picked up the counter-argumentative signal *bien sûr* ("of course") and used it to structure their output. This clue to structure is all the more important in that the source text is elliptical, saying "there is also legibility . . ." but meaning "there is also a problem of legibility (i.e. transparency)". Only through perception of the structure of the text can this meaning be retrieved.

The prominence of context in liaison interpreting

Liaison interpreting input bears an interesting resemblance to that of simultaneous: in both cases the interpreter receives a first instalment of a longer text and more or less immediately embarks upon delivery. But the resemblance ends here: while the second instalment of simultaneous input is never long in coming, providing the interpreter with more textural information to be processed, the liaison interpreter has to treat the first portion as a self-contained unit. Although the situation improves as the interaction develops, the fact that liaison interpreters are left to work out how the exchange has reached a given point and, perhaps more importantly, where it is likely to go next has serious implications for the way they go about their business. Textural clues would at best be incomplete, restricted to what may be described as "local" cohesion (i.e. covering a sequence of not more than two or three sentences, if not less). Similarly, indications of structure will hardly reveal a coherent and complete design. Yet, it is the task of liaison interpreters to make sense of whatever texture they are provided with, and it is also their task to negotiate with an interlocutor a text design of some kind. That is, on the basis of the separate instalments of input, linked with each other only at the highest level of text organization (i.e. that of the entire interaction), each chunk of output is expected to be coherent in its own right contextually.

To cope with this incompleteness of texture (continuity of sense) and structure, liaison interpreters seem to put to best effect whatever clues are encountered in these domains. For this limitation to be properly overcome, interpreters resort to a more readily accessible strand of textuality and one that ultimately determines how the text is developed. This, we suggest, is context (register membership, pragmatics and semiotics). But why should contextual input be so prominent in comparison with other strands of textuality?

To answer this question, let us consider the situation of the liaison interpreter. Whether the session involves questions and answers or negotiation of some sort, there will be unpredictability at the outset as to how the dialogue will develop and what the long-term significance of current lexical choice or local cohesion will be. Of course, the interpreter has some awareness of the issues involved, of the participants concerned and usually of the topic tackled. But these are not necessarily reliable clues to the way the two-way interaction will develop and conclude. Consequently, contextual clues tend to assume greater importance as long-term guides.

Furthermore, even at the most local level of linguistic expression, context seems to be a much richer category than texture or structure. There are important indications as to register membership, intentionality and intertextuality, with the latter encompassing a variety of relevant genres and discourses. But, perhaps more significantly, it is the intertextual potential of text type that is the prime determinant in the production and reception of texts. Here, a focus emerges that, on the one hand, brings together contextual information from a number of different contextual sources and, on the other, almost causally determines the way both structure and texture appear in texts.

Let us illustrate this with an example from a real-life situation. Although involving a communication breakdown, it is hoped that the following example will demonstrate not only what can go wrong but also what should ideally happen, underlining in the process the role of context in liaison interpreting. For whereas context is, we are suggesting, the key domain in liaison interpreting, it may, by the same token, become the main source of problems [. . .].

Sample 4

Interviewer: What were the contents of the letter you handed
                                    to King Fahd?
Tunisian Government minister: This matter concerns the Saudis.
(as relayed by interpreter)

In Sample 4, the interviewer asks a very pointed question. The minister is reported to have replied rather curtly in Arabic, in terms which the interpreter has relayed verbatim into English. The wrong impression has been conveyed, however, and the intended sense should have been relayed as:

   This is a matter solely for the Saudis' consideration!

The error may be attributed to lack of awareness of contextual specifications which surround utterances and dictate the way they should be interpreted. Relevant contextual factors include:

1   the register membership of the text (journalese, diplomacy, etc. as fields; formality of tenor; etc.);
2   the pragmatic force of the utterance (what is intended and not explicitly stated – here, unwillingness to give a direct answer to a question);
3   the culture-specific genre requirement that journalists do not overstep the mark; the discourse of rebuttal; and the text-type focus on managing a situation.

   In addition to these factors, much contextual information lies outside the text, in the area of prior expectations – about the line of questioning pursued and even beyond this about the whole speech event which ultimately culminates in the form of words used (i.e. in the utterance proper). True, the word *concern* carries a considerable amount of textural information, but in the absence of contextual indications from both within and outside the currently unfolding interaction, this particular word could mean anything and could thus function in a variety of speech acts, one of which is the "representative statement" erroneously opted for. The utterance was obviously intended to function as:

(a) a diplomat's way out of journalists' awkward questions;
(b) an intended "telling-off": do not pursue this line of questioning, or else!;
(c) a socio-cultural sign carrying a specific attitudinal meaning (resenting nosi-ness), a certain genre specification (the familiar parrying of nosy journalists' questions) and a particular rhetorical purpose (steering the text reciever in a direction favourable to the text producer's goals).

The English journalist who asked the question would no doubt have appreciated the kind of meanings yielded by the register membership of the utterance ((a) above), its pragmatic meaning (b) and its semiotic significance (c). However, lured by the kind of "inviting" answer which he received through the interpreter, the journalist pursued the initial line of questioning, only to be rebuked a second time.

[. . .]

The way forward

In this chapter, the process of interpreting has been viewed from the vantage point of a discourse processing model within which we distinguish three basic domains of textuality: context, structure and texture. These are seen to correlate in subtle and meaningful ways with the three basic types of interpreting: liaison, consecutive and simultaneous. The basis of the relationship is the need on the part of the interpreter to focus on the particular strand of textuality that is made prominent by the requirements of one skill and not of another. In liaison interpreting, it has been suggested that, given a necessarily least readily accessible structure and texture, the interpreter needs to acquire facility in reacting to and interacting with the various vectors of context. The simultaneous interpreter, on the other hand, would seem to handle less readily available context and structure by heavily relying on texture, maintaining text connectivity through interacting with the various aspects of cohesion, theme–rheme progression, etc. Finally, less readily available context and texture in the kind of short-term storage of input that is characteristic of consecutive interpreting entails the category of structure being utilized to best effect.

In conclusion, it may be appropriate to enter one or two notes of caution to restrain the scope of what our proposals could be taken to suggest. First, the atomism that might strike one in the neatness of the various trichotomies (less readily available X and Y, with Z predominating) should be viewed as a methodological convenience and not an accurate reflection of the real situation. As far as interpreter performance and the training required are concerned, the reality is far more involved than could be accounted for by the kind of idealized theory outlined. As far as text processing is concerned, on the other hand, the reality is even fuzzier. The variables of context, structure and texture intermesh in subtle and intricate ways, and the interdependence of the various interpreting skills is normally too complex to be discussed in definitive terms.

But theorizing has a role to play in the maze of the various processes involved. Certainly, most of the statements we have made in the course of the above discussion are hypothetical at this stage and are in need of further corroborative evidence. Nevertheless, research into the nature of the interpreting process, which in certain quarters is already underway, must start somewhere, and it is in this spirit that we have advanced what in our judgement are plausible hypotheses in need of further investigation.

F ROM ITS INCEPTION, research on interpreting in conference settings has reflected a privileged interest in the simultaneous mode. One of the most notable exceptions is the 1975 study by Seleskovitch (in this volume), whose concern with the process of consecutive interpreting had far-reaching implications for the theory as well as the pedagogy of interpreting. The work of Helle Vrønning Dam addresses these in terms of the dichotomy between sense-based and form-based interpreting on the basis of a product-oriented analysis of an experimental corpus.

A graduate of translation and interpreting from the Århus School of Business (Faculty of Modern Languages), where she went on to become Associate Professor in the Department of Spanish (1999), Helle Dam forms part of what could be described as the Århus School of Interpreting Research. Together with Friedel Dubslaff and Anne Schjoldager she participated in the 1993 session of the CERA Chair Summer School at Leuven with incumbent Daniel Gile. The PhD research carried out by these three in the mid-1990s, while not reflecting or aspiring towards a particular theoretical framework, clearly shares a methodological focus on product-oriented corpus analysis.

The article reprinted here is based on Dam's 1995 PhD thesis on text condensation in consecutive interpreting. It was originally published in 1998 in *The Translator* and has been abridged mainly in the introductory part and the section exemplifying the categories of analysis.

Further reading: Dam 1993, 1996.

Helle V. Dam

LEXICAL SIMILARITY VS LEXICAL DISSIMILARITY IN CONSECUTIVE INTERPRETING
A product-oriented study of form-based vs meaning-based interpreting

THE PURPOSE OF the present paper is simple: to provide a pilot description of the degree of lexical similarity vs lexical dissimilarity between source and target texts in consecutive interpreting. However simple, the issue of lexical similarity and dissimilarity is part of the broader question of how much influence the linguistic form of the source text exerts over the target text and, as such, it may ultimately contribute to shedding some empirical light on one of the most fundamental and persistent but as yet largely undocumented claims regarding interpreting in general: that an interpreted text is produced mainly on the basis of an essentially non-verbal representation of the *meaning* of its source text and only exceptionally on the basis of its linguistic *form*.

While this idea may be traced back to the first authors within the field of interpreting (e.g. Herbert 1952; Rozan 1956; van Hoof 1962), its formalization may primarily be ascribed to Danica Seleskovitch [. . .] and other representatives of the so-called Paris School. [. . .]

Though the Paris philosophy is generally said to have been predominant mainly in the 70s and the 80s and to have had little impact on present-day interpreting studies (e.g. Gile 1994), there is no doubt that some of the fundamental ideas of this philosophy still prevail – also among scholars outside the Paris School. Thus, the Seleskovitchian distinction between transcoding and interpreting proper is often resorted to by scholars who represent the new generation in interpreting studies (e.g. Gran and Fabbro 1988; Fabbro *et al.* 1990, 1991; Darò and Fabbro 1994; Isham 1994, 1995; Gran and Bellini 1996), although these concepts are commonly referred to as **form-based** (or word-based) and **meaning-based interpreting**, respectively, and are generally viewed with less dogmatism by these scholars. But in spite of the rejection of normativity and speculation characteristic of the new

generation of interpreting scholars, it is still not uncommon to come across statements regarding the superiority of meaning-based interpreting, "interpreting
proper" in Seleskovitch's terminology, over form-based interpreting or "transcoding" (e.g. Gran 1989: 98), or statements claiming that meaning-based interpreting is
more frequent than form-based interpreting (Fabbro et al. 1990: 75; Gran and
Bellini 1996: 105), even if these claims remain undocumented.

[. . .]

In the present study, I propose to examine the distribution of form-based and
meaning-based interpreting from an entirely different angle. Whereas the studies
mentioned above focus on the cognitive processing in the two procedures of interpreting, the focus of the present study is on the interpreting product. In other
words, the question here is not how interpreters process a source text, but what
kind of target text they produce.

In a product-oriented study of the distribution of form-based and meaning-
based interpreting, the relevant question to be asked is how a target text relates to
its source text in terms of form: is it, in essence, formally similar to the source text
or is it, in essence, formally dissimilar? On the one hand, we may expect the direct
passage from source to target text involved in form-based interpreting to lead to a
target text that displays a high degree of *formal similarity* in relation to its source text.
On the other hand, we may expect the deverbalization process hypothesized for
meaning-based interpreting to lead to a target text in which there are very few
traces of the linguistic form of the source text, i.e. a target text that exhibits a
high degree of *formal dissimilarity* in relation to its source text. In other words, in
a product- or text-oriented study, the concepts of formal similarity and formal
dissimilarity may be used as tools to identify form-based and meaning-based
interpreting, respectively.

The concept of form is, in itself, multi-faceted and will not be examined in all its
aspects in the current study. Rather, I have chosen to focus on lexis, thus excluding
for instance syntax, which was the aspect of form studied in the experiments by
Fabbro *et al.* (1991) and Isham (1994). This decision is motivated by the choice of
the type of interpreting to be studied, namely consecutive interpreting [. . .]. Consecutive interpreting differs from interpreting in the simultaneous mode in that the
target text utterances are not produced immediately upon reception of the corresponding source text utterances, but with a time lag of up to several minutes. This
temporal distance makes it unlikely that the interpreter is able to remember the
linguistic form of the source text at the time of target text production, since verbal
memory, i.e. memory for verbatim surface forms, lasts only a few seconds, as has
been amply demonstrated in psycholinguistic research (Kintsch 1974; Kintsch and
van Dijk 1978; Isham 1994). However, during source text reception, the consecutive interpreter takes notes which are afterwards used as a guide in constructing the
target text. Due to their necessarily sketchy nature, interpreters' notes generally
capture very few syntactic and morphological features, but consist essentially of
words or word-representations such as symbols or abbreviations. The crucial question in this context therefore concerns the quality of the words noted down
and, notably, their subsequent representation in the target text:[1] are they reflections of the source text words, as can be expected if the procedure applied is

form-based interpreting, or are they different from the source text words, as can be expected for meaning-based interpreting, and as is often claimed to be the case (e.g. Seleskovitch 1968, 1975). It should therefore be clear why the formal feature that is most relevant in a study of consecutive interpreting is lexis, rather than syntax for instance. Consequently, the concepts used to identify form-based and meaning-based interpreting in the present study are those of **lexical similarity** and **lexical dissimilarity**, respectively.

The concepts of lexical similarity and lexical dissimilarity obviously pose certain problems when comparing texts that are expressed in two different languages. Clearly, it is not possible to determine whether the lexical items of a text expressed in one language are similar or dissimilar to those of a text expressed in another language, unless we introduce some kind of *tertium comparationis* against which the two texts can be matched. In the present study, the identification of lexical similarity and dissimilarity is based on the notion of **formal equivalence**. A relation of formal equivalence is considered to exist between source and target text when a particular lexical target text item can be identified as the *closest possible contextual equivalent*, or an inflectional or derivational form thereof, of a particular lexical source text item; in that case, the relation between the two items in question is considered to be one of lexical similarity. If, on the other hand, it is not possible to identify a given target text item as the closest possible contextual equivalent, i.e. as the formal equivalent, of a given source text item, the relation between that target text item and the source text is determined as one of lexical dissimilarity.

Identifying the "formal equivalent", or the "closest possible contextual equivalent", is of course considerably more problematic than is suggested here. As we all know, no two languages describe reality in exactly the same way. We therefore also know that for some words in one language there are no direct equivalents in some other languages, whereas for other words two or more quite close equivalents may be identified. I have, however, chosen to take a pragmatic approach to this problem, not problematizing it more than necessary.[2] For one thing, I have chosen to base the present study on a source text that consists of lexical items for each of which there is at least one target language equivalent in the given context (see section 1 below). Furthermore, when there are several target language equivalents – with approximately the same degree of equivalence – for a given source text word, each of those equivalents is considered as "the closest possible" one here. [. . .]

1 Data

The study is based on an experimental corpus which consists of recordings of a Spanish speech (the source text) and five consecutive interpretations of this speech into Danish (the target texts). The source text was delivered by a native speaker of Spanish on the basis of a written manuscript. The target texts were rendered by five different professional interpreters with Danish as their A-language and Spanish as their B- or C-language. The duration of the source text is 7.5 minutes, and it was presented to the subjects without interruptions at an average rate of 144 words per minute. The topic is drug policy, and the overall function of the text is argumentative, the aim being to convince the audience of the advantages of legalizing drugs.

The source text was elaborated so as to ensure that a fairly literal – or word-for-word – interpretation into the target language, i.e. Danish, would be structurally possible, though such an interpretation would far from always comply with the conventions of Danish language usage. In particular, the choice of cohesive ties was markedly Spanish and deviated considerably from Danish conventions, but a literal interpretation of these ties would still lead to a target text that would be both in accordance with the structural rules of Danish and comprehensible to a Danish-speaking audience.

For the purpose of the analyses, the recordings of source and target texts were transcribed, essentially in accordance with orthographic standards. The transcribed texts were then divided into smaller and more manageable units, hereafter referred to as **segments**. As a rule, a segment consists of a series of words grouped around a verb. [. . .] The segments, then, constituted the units of analysis in the comparative analyses of source and target texts.

2 Model of analysis

Since the phenomenon under study, namely lexical similarity vs lexical dissimilarity, is defined in binary terms, the model of analysis designed to investigate it is also binary in structure. Thus, according to their formal-lexical relation to the source text segments, the target text segments may be allocated to one of two opposing categories: parallel segments or substituting segments. **Parallel segments** are target text segments that are exclusively characterized by lexical similarity in relation to the source text. **Substituting segments** are target text segments that are exclusively characterized by lexical dissimilarity in relation to the source text. Apart from these two categories of pure target text segments, a series of mixed categories are included in the model of analysis in order to allow for a possible co-presence of lexical similarity and lexical dissimilarity in one and the same target text segment. Thus, the category of **parallel (substituting) segments** is included to designate target text segments that are mainly characterized by lexical similarity, but also by some degree of dissimilarity. Furthermore, the category of **substituting (parallel) segments** is included to designate target text segments that are mainly characterized by lexical dissimilarity, but also by some degree of similarity. Finally, a 50–50 category of **parallel/substituting segments** is included to designate target text segments in which the distribution of lexical similarity and lexical dissimilarity is approximately even. [. . .]

2.1 Parallel segments (P-segments)

A Parallel segment, hereafter referred to as a *P-segment*, is a target text segment in which all the lexical items can be identified as the formal equivalents, or inflectional or derivational forms of such equivalents, of particular lexical items in the source text segment on the basis of which the target text segment appears to have been constructed. The formal-lexical relation between a P-segment and the corresponding source text segment is, in other words, one of similarity.

The degree of similarity between a P-segment and the corresponding source text segment may vary. In some cases, the similarity is complete, which means that it extends to morphological, syntactic and lexical aspects of the linguistic material used. The relation between a P-segment of this type and a literal translation of the corresponding source text segment is therefore one of identity [. . .]. In most cases, however, P-segments are not completely identical to their source text segments but contain morphological and/or syntactic changes in relation to these. It therefore follows that morphological and syntactic changes do not prevent a target text segment from being categorized as a P-segment, if the lexical items used to construct it are otherwise basically the formal equivalents of the lexical items of the source text segment. [. . .]

. . . Some P-segments do not reproduce the totality of the source text items, but only some of them. In spite of the deletion(s), the lexical items of such P-segments are still the formal equivalents of the lexical items of the source text segments, i.e. lexical similarity remains the characteristic feature also in this type of P-segments, as in the following example:

> ST: *por un lado* en el mercado negro los consumidores no tienen posibili-
> dades de . . . (*on the one hand* on the black market the consumers have no
> possibilities of . . .)
>
> TT-2: på det sorte marked har forbrugerne ikke mulighed for . . . (on
> the black market the consumers have no possibility of . . .)

In sum, in spite of possible morphological and syntactic changes or deletions, P-segments are considered to be manifestations of similarity in the present analyses.

2.2 Substituting segments (S-segments)

A substituting segment, hereafter referred to as an *S-segment*, is a target text segment in which no lexical item can be identified as the formal equivalent, or an inflectional or derivational form of such an equivalent, of any lexical item either in the source text segment on the basis of which the target text segment appears to have been constructed or, if no source text segment can be identified as the basis of the target text segment, in any other source text segment. The formal-lexical relation between an S-segment and the source text is, in other words, one of dissimilarity.

It follows from the above definition that, in terms of content, an S-segment may either relate to a particular source text segment, in which case it is a complete reformulation of this segment, or not relate to any source text segment, in which case it is an addition.

[. . .]

Since only the formal relation between source and target texts is studied here, no distinction is made between reformulations . . . and additions . . .: as they both introduce formal differences in relation to the source text, both are categorized as S-segments, i.e. as the type of target text segments that are considered to be pure manifestations of dissimilarity.

2.3 Parallel (substituting) segments (P(s)-segments)

A Parallel (substituting) segment, referred to here as a *P(s)-segment*, is a target text segment in which most of the lexical items can be identified as formal equivalents, or inflectional or derivational forms of such equivalents, of particular lexical items in the source text segment on the basis of which the target text segment appears to have been constructed, whereas no such identification can be made for the rest of the lexical items of the target text segment. The formal-lexical relation between a P(s)-segment and the corresponding source text segment is, in other words, mainly one of similarity, but dissimilarity is also represented.

[. . .]

2.4 Substituting (parallel) segments (S(p)-segment(s)

A Substituting (parallel) segment, referred to here as an *S(p)-segment*, is a target text segment in which most of the lexical items cannot be identified as formal equiva-lents, or inflectional or derivational forms of such equivalents, of particular lexical items in the source text segment on the basis of which the target text segment appears to have been constructed, whereas such an identification can be made for the rest of the lexical items of the target text segment. The formal-lexical relation between an S(p)-segment and the corresponding source text segment is, in other words, mainly one of dissimilarity, but some similarity is also present.

[. . .]

2.5 Parallel/Substituting segments (P/S-segments)

A Parallel/Substituting segment, hereafter referred to as a *P/S-segment*, is a target text segment in which approximately half of the lexical items can be identified as formal equivalents, or inflectional or derivational forms of such equivalents, of particular lexical items in the source text segment on the basis of which it appears to have been constructed, whereas no such identification can be made for approxi-mately the other half of the lexical items of the target text segment. The formal-lexical relation between a P/S-segment and the corresponding source text segment is, in other words, characterized by an even distribution of similarity and dissimilarity.

[. . .]

3 Results and discussion

All the target text segments in the corpus – a total of 482 – were categorized according to the model described above, whereby the results summarized in Table 1 were obtained. In the table, the figures without brackets indicate the absolute number of occurrences of target text segments as distributed over the different categories, whereas the figures appearing in brackets indicate percentages.

Before commenting on the results, I shall briefly discuss the conceptual status of each of the categories in relation to the distinction between form-based and meaning-based interpreting. As argued in the introduction, lexical similarity may be conceived of as evidence of form-based interpreting, whereas lexical dissimilarity may be taken as evidence of meaning-based interpreting. As we have seen, the target text segments categorized as *P-segments* represent pure manifestations of lexical similarity and may therefore be regarded as evidence of form-based interpreting. On the other hand, target text segments categorized as *S-segments* represent pure manifestations of lexical dissimilarity and may therefore be taken as evidence of meaning-based interpreting. The rest of the categories, i.e. *P(s)-*, *S(p)-* and *P/S-segments*, present a less clear picture, because they are not pure manifestations of either lexical similarity or lexical dissimilarity. Nevertheless, the *P(s)-segments* are essentially what can be expected to result from a form-based approach to consecutive interpreting. Only in theory would it be possible to represent every source text word in the notes, as would be required if a strictly word-for-word interpreting were to be performed. In practice, consecutive interpreters take notes at a speaker-imposed pace, which does not allow them to write down each and every source text word, even if they attempted to do so. When constructing the target text, they would therefore sometimes have to insert words that replace the missing ones in order to create coherent target text sentences, and these "inserted" words are likely to turn out differently from the words originally uttered by the speaker. So, even if the approach to consecutive interpreting is form-based, one has to realistically expect quite a number of target text segments to exhibit small lexical changes [. . .]. Conversely, the *S(p)-segments* exhibit a pattern which, to a large extent, can be expected to result from meaning-based interpreting. Even if interpreters generally dissociate meaning from words and interpret only on the basis of the former, we cannot expect there to be absolutely no lexical similarities between source and target texts; we may for instance expect proper nouns and numbers to be rendered by their formal target language equivalents in most cases. *S(p)-segments* may therefore be considered evidence of meaning-based interpreting simply because of their high degree of dissimilarity in relation to the source text. Only *P/S-segments* are neutral as regards the distinction between form-based and meaning-based interpreting, because they contain an even distribution of similarity and dissimilarity and therefore do not represent one particular formal-lexical relation between source and target texts.

We can now revert to the results summarized in Table 1 above. If we contrast the target text segments which provide evidence of form-based interpreting with those which provide evidence of meaning-based interpreting, it is obvious that the former type is represented with a higher frequency than the latter in the corpus analyzed here. Thus, the category of *P-segments* accounts for almost twice as many

Table 1   Occurrences of target text segment categories in the corpus.

	TT-1	*TT-2*	*TT-3*	*TT-4*	*TT-5*	*TOTAL*
P-segments	16 (18%)	21 (20%)	22 (22%)	26 (25%)	15 (17%)	100 (21%)
S-segments	6 (7%)	9 (9%)	16 (16%)	8 (8%)	12 (14%)	51 (11%)
P(s)-segments	20 (23%)	29 (28%)	31 (30%)	41 (40%)	25 (29%)	146 (30%)
S(p)-segments	27 (31%)	25 (24%)	22 (22%)	10 (10%)	23 (26%)	107 (22%)
P/S-segments	18 (21%)	19 (18%)	11 (11%)	18 (17%)	12 (14%)	78 (16%)
Total	87	103	102	103	87	482

target text segments overall (21% in total) as does the category of *S-segments* (11% in total). Also, if we group the *P-* and *P(s)-segments* together and contrast them with the *S-* and *S(p)-segments*, the former group remains dominant with a total representation of 51% against only 33% – or approximately one third less – in the latter group.

The same pattern can be observed in the interpreters' individual performances. Thus, all five target texts have a higher representation of *P-segments* than of *S-segments* (18% vs 7% in TT-1; 20% vs 9% in TT-2; 22% vs 16% in TT-3; 25% vs 8% in TT-4; and 17% vs 14% in TT-5). Likewise, all five interpreters represent more source text segments as *P-* or *P(s)-segments* than as *S-* or *S(p)-segments* in their target texts (41% vs 38% in TT-1; 48% vs 33% in TT-2; 52% vs 38% in TT-3; 65% vs 18% in TT-4; 46% vs 40% in TT-5).

It is therefore clear that lexical similarity is a more salient feature than lexical dissimilarity in the corpus analyzed here. And, insofar as lexical similarity and lexical dissimilarity can be regarded as general yardsticks of form-based and meaning-based interpreting, respectively, the evidence indicates, by analogy, a dominance of the former interpreting procedure over the latter. This means that the general hypothesis according to which interpreted texts are produced mainly on the basis of a non-verbal representation of source text meaning, with only exceptional reference to source text form, cannot be confirmed by the findings of the present study; in fact, only 11% of the target text segments analyzed here, namely the *S-segments*, had been constructed without any apparent recourse to the linguistic form of the source text. This suggests that interpreters pay considerable attention to formal source text features when working in the consecutive mode.

This observation does not in any way exclude meaning as such from the interpreting process: all it does is suggest that the source text representation on the basis of which target text production occurs – whatever the nature of this representation – is, at least partly, verbal, as opposed to non-verbal or deverbalized. Thus, if we assume, as is generally done, that this representation basically constitutes the meaning of the source text, the findings of this study simply suggest that this meaning representation should be qualified as (partly) verbalized, since the high degree of formal-lexical similarity observed throughout the corpus would be unlikely to have occurred if the interpreters had performed a complete deverbalization of the source text prior to note-taking and, subsequently, target text production.

In much the same way as form and meaning cannot be taken to be mutually exclusive, but may in fact be complementary, so do form-based and meaning-based interpreting appear to go hand in hand, judging from the corpus analyzed here. Thus, all five target texts contain instances of each of the five categories of target text segments, even if their relative weight varies from text to text. Even more salient is the overall dominance of the mixed categories of target text segments, i.e. *P(s)-, S(p)-* and *P/S-segments*, in which evidence of form-based and of meaning-based interpreting may be said to co-occur: of the 482 target text segments analyzed here, as many as 331 – or approximately 69% – were allocated to one of the mixed categories. This suggests that target text production in consecutive interpreting is based on a constant alternation between verbal and non-verbal source text features. This observation allows us to identify the sharp distinction that is normally drawn between form-based and meaning-based interpreting (or transcoding and interpreting proper) – as if they were in fact completely binary and mutually exclusive – as a theoretical construct, which may be empirically useful only if the two procedures are viewed as extremes on a continuum that is likely to be subject to constant changes.

4 Conclusion and perspectives

The formal-lexical relation between the source and target texts analyzed in the present study was found to be dominated by similarity rather than dissimilarity, a finding that runs counter to the hypothesis that interpreting generally proceeds on the basis of a non-verbal representation of the source text.

It should be stressed, however, that this finding can only claim validity for the data analyzed here, which is clearly subject to a number of limitations and weaknesses. Thus, the representativeness of the corpus is restricted as a function of the limited number of subjects, the non-authentic setting in which the data was collected and the fact that only one mode of interpreting, only one language pair and interpretations of only one text were studied. [. . .]

The results of the present study serve to point out the potential usefulness of comparative studies of source and target texts aimed at identifying linguistic differences and similarities – a type of study that is sometimes dismissed as irrelevant to research in interpreting due to the assumed lack of direct contact between the two linguistic products involved in the process.

Limited as it is to distributional observations based on the corpus as a whole, the present study can do no more than address such general issues. Specific questions relating to the distribution of form-based and meaning-based interpreting have not been addressed and therefore cannot be answered at this stage. For instance, the study provides no answers as to which factors influence the position of a target text on the form-meaning continuum. It may be influenced by the nature of the source text material, the mode and direction of interpreting, the languages involved, the interpreters' level of experience, etc., but no attempt to identify the effects of these variables has been made here. While this paper therefore clearly raises more questions than it answers, the proposed methodological framework may provide a useful basis for a future search for answers to a series of clearly relevant questions.

Notes

1   Studying the interpreters' notes, instead of the target texts, would be another possible way of approaching the present topic. This method cannot, however, be extended to the study of interpreting that is performed without notes, notably to simultaneous interpreting, whereas the one proposed here can.

2   In support of this non-problematizing approach, I might mention the very existence of concepts such as literal, direct or semantic translation – abundantly present in the literature on translation – which may be taken as evidence of a consensus of intuition that for most lexical items in one language it is indeed possible to identify rather close equivalents in many other languages, especially when these items occur in a specific context. While this does not eliminate the problems associated with the determination of equivalence, it should refute objections of a more existential nature.

References

Darò, Valeria and Fabbro, Franco (1994) "Verbal Memory during Simultaneous Interpretation: Effects of Phonological Interference", *Applied Linguistics* 15 (4): 365–81.

Fabbro, F., Gran, B. and Gran, L. (1991) "Hemispheric Specialization for Semantic and Syntactic Components of Language in Simultaneous Interpreters", *Brain and Language* 41: 1–42.

Fabbro, F., Gran, L., Basso G. and Bava, A. (1990) "Cerebral Lateralization in Simultaneous Interpretation", *Brain and Language* 39: 69–89.

Gile, Daniel (1994) "Opening up in Interpretation Studies", in M. Snell-Hornby, F. Pöchhacker and K. Kaindl (eds) *Translation Studies. An Interdiscipline*, Amsterdam and Philadelphia: John Benjamins.

Gran, Laura (1989) "Interdisciplinary Research on Cerebral Asymmetries: Significance and Prospects for the Teaching of Interpretation", in L. Gran and J. Dodds (eds) *The Theoretical and Practical Aspects of Teaching Conference Interpretation*, Udine: Campanotto Editore.

—— and Bellini, Beatrice (1996) "Short-term Memory and Simultaneous Interpretation: An Experimental Study on Verbatim Recall", *The Interpreters' Newsletter* 7: 103–12.

—— and Fabbro, Franco (1988) "The Role of Neuroscience in the Teaching of Interpretation", *The Interpreters' Newsletter* 1: 23–41.

Herbert, Jean (1952) *Le Manuel de l'Interprète*, Genève: Georg.

Isham, William P. (1994) "Memory for Sentence Form after Simultaneous Interpret-
ation: Evidence both for and against Deverbalization", in S. Lambert and
B. Moser-Mercer (eds) *Bridging the Gap. Empirical Research in Simultaneous
Interpretation*, Amsterdam and Philadelphia: John Benjamins.

—— (1995) "On the Relevance of Signed Languages to Research in Interpretation",
Target 7 (1): 135–49.

Kintsch, Walter (1974) *The Representation of Meaning in Memory*, Hillsdale, New
Jersey: Lawrence Erlbaum.

—— and van Dijk, Teun A. (1978) "Toward a Model of Text Comprehension and
Production", *Psychological Review* 85 (5): 363–94.

Rozan, Jean-François (1956) *La Prise de Notes en Interprétation Consécutive*, Genève:
Georg.

Seleskovitch, Danica (1968) *L'Interprète dans les Conférences Internationales. Problèmes de
Langage et de Communication*, Paris: Minard.

—— (1975) *Langage, Langues et Mémoire. Étude de la Prise de Notes en Interprétation
Consécutive*, Paris: Minard.

van Hoof, Henri (1962) *Théorie et Pratique de l'Interprétation*, München: Max Hueber.

THE EFFECT OF socio-pragmatic elements and discourse markers on listeners' perceptions of the message, and of the person who produces it, is a key concern of sociolinguists like Susan Berk-Seligson, of the Department of Hispanic Languages and Literatures and the Department of Linguistics of the University of Pittsburgh.

Using an array of empirical tools, her work uncovers differences in pragmatic force due to seemingly minor shifts. Berk-Seligson's research began with phonological variation and with code-switching and became increasingly forensic: her work on the social dimension of interpreting culminated in *The Bilingual Courtroom: Court Interpreters in the Judicial Process* (1990a) – a volume which won the 1991 "Outstanding Book" Award from the British Association of Applied Linguistics. A cornerstone in the literature on court interpreting, Berk-Seligson's research monograph comprises both ethnographic analyses based on more than 100 hours of tape-recorded judicial proceedings, and experimental work as presented here. Her investigation of the interpreter's impact on jurors' perception of witness testimony was first published in 1988 in *Multilingua: Journal of Cross-Cultural and Interlanguage Communication*, and is reprinted here with some abridgements.

More recently, Berk-Seligson contributed papers to the specialist journal *Forensic Linguistics* on such topics as the impact of interpreting on leading questions (1999) and interpreting for the police (2000). In these studies, as in the present one, she captures the complexities of language use in adversarial proceedings, where the manner in which utterances are formulated may be as significant as their propositional content.

Further reading: Berk-Seligson 1989, 1990a, 1990b, 1999, 2000.

Susan Berk-Seligson

THE IMPACT OF POLITENESS IN WITNESS TESTIMONY
The influence of the court interpreter

Introduction

IT HAS BEEN known for some time now that listeners react subjectively to numerous aspects of a person's speech. Listeners attribute different sorts of social/psychological attributes to a speaker depending on that speaker's dialect, delivery style, and voice quality. The present study examines the subjective reactions of persons listening to witness testimony, in particular, courtroom testimony given in Spanish and interpreted in English. It will be shown that one aspect of a witness's speech, politeness, plays an important role in the formation of impressions of witnesses. Furthermore, it will be demonstrated that the court interpreter has the power to alter the politeness of a witness's testimony, and in so doing, influences the impression that mock jurors have of that witness.

[. . .]

Scholars interested in sociolegal questions, particularly the relationship between law and language, have begun to notice the relevance of the relationship between speech cues and perceived personality characteristics. O'Barr (1982) and his colleagues at Duke University have isolated a number of recurring testimony styles in the speech of witnesses, among them being the dichotomy "powerful" and "powerless" style. After extensive observation in criminal trial courts, O'Barr noticed that some witnesses spoke in a style very similar to the one described by Lakoff (1975) as being typical of American women. This style, which O'Barr has called "powerless" testimony style, consists of a constellation of linguistic features, one of which is the use of polite forms. Specifically, these polite forms comprise the terms "please," "thank you," "sir," and "ma'am." The consequences of using powerless versus powerful speech style are not trivial. In a series of experimental studies O'Barr and his colleagues demonstrated that each style has a different impact on persons serving as mock jurors. To testify in the powerful style is to leave the listeners with the impression that one is more convincing, more truthful, more competent, more intelligent, and more trustworthy than if one testifies in the powerless mode. Thus, the use of powerful versus powerless testimony style counts in court.

The experimental design employed by O'Barr and his colleagues, the one adapted for use in the study reported on here, involves the use of a "matched guise technique" type of subjective reaction test. Typically the matched guise technique involves playing two audio recordings to different groups of subjects. [. . .] Subjects are always asked to rate the speaker they have heard on the recording along various social/psychological dimensions (such as intelligence, strength, honesty, passivity, and so on). In the interest of comparability with the subjective reaction test used by O'Barr and his colleagues, the social/psychological traits chosen for use in the present study were competence, intelligence, trustworthiness, and convincingness.

Rationale: politeness in the bilingual courtroom

[. . .] The present study sets out to determine how important verbal politeness is for mock jurors listening to interpreted testimony.

The reason why politeness was chosen as a focus of investigation, aside from the fact that it represents one constitutive element of powerless testimony style, is that politeness was observed to be an important variable in the witness/interpreter/lawyer verbal relationship. This observation comes as a result of an ethnographic study I had previously carried out on the bilingual courtroom (Berk-Seligson 1990), which produced a total of 114 hours of tape-recorded judicial proceedings involving the use of eighteen Spanish/English court interpreters.

[. . .]

What was observed in the ethnographic study of interpreted judicial proceedings is that the court interpreter frequently initiates a cycle of mutual polite address when she directs her interpretation at the witness. This usually happens when the interpreter is trying to put the witness at ease, particularly when the witness is obviously frightened or nervous. When the interpreter is someone who has been brought up in Latin America, and arrives in the U.S. as an adult, she will behave culturally with another Hispanic the way she would in a Hispanic setting, that is, with a higher use of polite verbal tokens than would an Anglo in the same context. The use of polite address by the interpreter begins a cycle of reciprocal polite address. Thus, once the interpreter has begun addressing the witness with *señor*, or *señora*, the witness will tend to use a polite address term in answering the interpreter. What is clear is that most witnesses who testify through the mechanism of a court interpreter very quickly begin to answer the interpreter directly, as if it were she who was asking the question, rather than answering the attorney, who in fact is the person posing the question. That this is certain is reflected by two common patterns: (1) in answering a question the witness tends to maintain eye contact not with the attorney, but with the interpreter, and (2) the polite address term frequently correlates with the sex of the interpreter rather than with that of the lawyer. The second pattern becomes easily noticeable in the commonly occurring situation where the interpreter is a woman and the attorney is a man. It should be pointed out that the rules of working with a court interpreter require that the witness speak directly to the examining attorney or judge, and not speak to the interpreter as a person. Thus, in theory, the two common occurrences just mentioned ought not happen. However, they do, repeatedly. When a mismatch occurs in the polite address term used by the witness and the sex of the examining attorney, interpreters are faced with the choice of (1) interpreting the witness's address term accurately, and thereby possibly embarrassing the attorney; (2) interpreting the address term incorrectly, so that the gender of the address term matches the sex of the lawyer; (3) dropping the address term altogether in the interpretation of the answer; and (4) raising the problem with the judge and lawyer. The first route is not very often taken. The second and third are the more common approaches taken by interpreters. [. . .]

The most prevalent pattern of interpreter addition of politeness is the situation of defendants answering the question of judges. The speech situations which call for defendant/judge interaction are initial appearances, arraignments, changes of plea, and sentencings. In such judicial proceedings, the judge typically asks the defendant a predesignated series of questions, many of which are yes/no type questions. Often when the defendant answers with a simple *Sí* or *No* answer, the interpreter will render the responses as "Yes, sir" or "No, sir." Clearly, the interpreter wants the answer to be more polite. The question is whether the politeness she is striving for is for the defendant's sake or for her own. Court interpreters, particularly those employed fulltime in a courthouse, are highly sensitive to the fact that they are employees of the court, and that they are expected to act just as obsequiously before the judge as any lawyer, defendant, or clerk. Thus, court interpreters feel the need to speak politely to the judge in their capacity as court employees. The addition of politeness markers to defendants' answers may simply be part of the sense that interpreters have that judges are listening to them as persons in their own right, and not merely as mechanical vehicles for converting speech from one language into another. And even though ideally the interpreter is supposed not to have her own persona in the proceeding, in fact she is spoken to directly by witnesses, as was demonstrated above, and she often is addressed by lawyers and judges, even though she is there merely to be a medium through which court officials can communicate with the non-English speaking and hearing impaired (see Berk-Seligson 1990). Since she is given a persona by the various parties present at a judicial proceeding, it is not surprising that she carries over the sense of persona when she facilitates communication between defendants and judges. It is the judge who more than any other party in the courtroom is delegated with the authority to evaluate her performance. It is no wonder, therefore, that she wishes to address the judge politely.

Research design

[. . .]

A research design was devised that would be capable of testing if the presence or absence of politeness markers in the English interpreted testimony of

Spanish-speaking witnesses would leave a significant impact on persons playing the role of jurors. If such a differential impact could be found to exist, then it would show not only that politeness makes a difference, but that the interpreter herself makes a difference, in so far as she constitutes a crucial factor in the formation of juror impressions of non-English speaking witnesses.

An experimental research design was set up along the lines of the matched guise technique. Two audio recordings were made of a witness testifying in Spanish through an interpreter, the recordings being identical in every way except that in one version the interpreter interpreted in English every instance of the polite address marker *señor* "sir" that occurred in the speech of the witness, whereas in the other version the interpreter failed to interpret the polite marker in every instance (see Appendix for the text of the polite version). Thus, the interpreter's interpretation of the witness's testimony in one tape-recording was systematically polite, whereas her interpretation in the other version was devoid of politeness.

It should be stressed that the text of the recordings was based on the transcription of an actual case that I had recorded in the previous research project, the ethnographic study of the bilingual courtroom. Thus, the text on the tapes used for the present study is drawn from an actual examination by a lawyer of an undocumented Mexican alien. The actors who played the roles of witness, interpreter, and lawyer were in real life similar socially and occupationally to the persons whom they were portraying on the recordings: the witness was a Mexican immigrant living in a Chicago *barrio* (neighborhood with a high concentration of Hispanics), who knew very little English; the woman who played the interpreter was a Mexican-American woman who was a fulltime court interpreter at the Cook County Circuit Court, Chicago's principal state-level criminal court; and the lawyer was played by an Anglo male who had graduate level university education.

[. . .] The explanation that preceded the playing of the examination sequence was relatively brief. The explanation, which was done on the tape-recording itself so as to standardize the explanatory input that each mock juror in the study would be exposed to, consisted of the following facts: (1) they, the mock jurors, were about to hear a case involving the transporting of illegal aliens across the U.S./Mexico border; (2) they would be hearing the voices of three people, a male lawyer, who would be asking questions in English, a male witness, who would be testifying in Spanish, and a woman, the court interpreter, who would be interpreting the lawyer's questions into Spanish, and the witness's testimony into English; (3) the person who was testifying was not the defendant in the case, that is, he was not the one being accused of anything in this particular proceeding, but he was being asked to testify in regard to the man who was the defendant, that is, the person who was being accused of smuggling him and other people across the border for a fee; (4) they would be asked to pretend that they were members of the jury in this case, and to give their impressions of the witness based on what they had heard.

NOT INTELLIGENT 1 : 2 : 3 : 4 : 5 : 6 : 7 INTELLIGENT

Figure 1   Intelligence scale

Each participant in the study was given a standardized questionnaire, on which four lines represented four seven-point scales. At one end of each line appeared an adjective ("convincing," "competent," "intelligent," "trustworthy"). At the other extreme lay the polar opposite of the evaluative term (see Figure 1). In order to enable Hispanic respondents with greater proficiency in Spanish than in English to perform the task easily, everything written on the questionnaire, including general instructions, was in Spanish as well as in English.

The sample

A total of 551 persons in the greater Chicago and Pittsburgh areas participated in the study. The sample consisted of 55 percent women and 44 percent men. Their mean age was 27.3 years, 55 percent of the sample being of college age (17–22). A deliberate effort was made to include in the sample as many adult non-four-year college student respondents as possible, that is, persons who were already in the work force or who had life experience beyond that found in educational settings. For this reason, church groups and adult education classes were included in the sample, as were community-based vocational training classes and high school equivalency classes for adults who for various reasons had never earned a high school diploma. Consequently, educational attainment among the 551 participants varied widely. Twenty-nine percent of the respondents had no more than twelve years of education (i.e., U.S. high school). Interestingly, 30 percent of the sample had attended school outside of the U.S. One-third of this group had completed high school abroad, and 7 percent had attended college in their native country. Since nearly the entire group of persons who had attended school abroad was Hispanic, this meant that at a minimum the 17 percent who had completed at least high school in Latin America would be somewhere between Spanish dominant and balanced bilingual in their Spanish/English proficiency. As is explained below, comprehension of Spanish is an important variable in this study, since it turns out to be an important predictor in determining listener evaluations of the testifying witness.

Ethnically, the sample was 52.3 percent Anglo-American, 39.4 percent Hispanic, 6.7 percent Afro-American, .7 percent Oriental, and .04 percent native American Indian. [. . .]

Comprehension of Spanish was considered to be a potentially crucial variable in the outcome of the experiment, since it was hypothesized that having access to the meaning of the witness's Spanish testimony would cancel out whatever effect the interpreter might have in creating in the minds of the mock jurors one sort of impression of the witness rather than another. Therefore, it had to be determined to what extent the non-Hispanic population had understood the Spanish of the witness, and to what extent the Hispanic population had. For this reason, subjects were asked (1) if they had ever studied Spanish in school, (2) if they had, how many years had they studied it, and (3) if they had, how well had they understood the Spanish on the recording, on a 5-point scale ranging from "very well" to "hardly at all."

Hispanic subjects were asked an additional series of questions aimed at measuring their degree of bilingual proficiency. The answers to these questions revealed that 96.7 percent of those who identified themselves as Hispanic reported that they spoke Spanish.

Findings

The major hypothesis of this study is that politeness in the testimony of a witness makes a difference, that is, has an impact on the impression that jurors form of that witness. It was expected, given the findings of O'Barr and his colleagues regarding the negative impact of powerless speech style upon mock jurors and the fact that politeness is one feature of powerless speech, that the interpretation of politeness markers into English by the court interpreter would cause mock jurors to evaluate the witness more negatively than when the interpreter did not interpret the witness's Spanish politeness markers.

Table 1 presents a summary of the findings in this regard, and summarizes the output of a difference in means test (t-test) of the answers of the entire sample of 551 subjects. The t-test was applied to the subjects' impressions regarding the degree to which the witness seemed convincing, competent, intelligent, and trust-worthy, comparing the mean answers of those who heard the "polite version" of the English interpretation with the means of those who heard the interpretation lacking in politeness. It should be recalled that the higher the number of the evaluations (numbers approaching 7), the more positive were the mock jurors; the lower the numbers (approaching 1), the more negative were the impressions. Looking down the column labeled "Mean" we see that in every case where the witness's testimony was interpreted faithfully to the original, that is, with the polite markers present, the means reflected a more positive evaluation, on each of the four social/psychological attribute continua. More importantly, the difference between the means for the polite version and those for the non-polite versions is statistically significant, for all four attributes. In other words, it is highly unlikely that the mock jurors reacted this way by chance.

Two important substantive conclusions emerge from an examination of Table 1. First, even though politeness has been considered to be one of the characteristics of powerless testimony style, and hence should have a negative impact on jurors, this study finds that just the opposite is true: politeness gives a witness an enhanced image. Second, what has made the difference between one version and another is the role played by the interpreter. The witness answered politely in Spanish in exactly the same way in both versions of the experimental tapes. It was merely the inter-preter who rendered the testimony differently. And this difference, the absence of "sir" following an answer to an attorney's question, was sufficient to cause mock jurors to evaluate the witness more negatively. This pivotal role of the interpreter is not surprising.

[. . .]

To determine whether Hispanic mock jurors are affected in any way by the English interpretation of the witness's testimony, a t-test was computed on the responses of those Hispanics who had listened to the polite version of the testimony, comparing them with those of Hispanics who had heard the non-polite version. The results of

Table 1   Difference of means (*t*-test) for entire sample.

Attribute	N[1]	Mean[2]	Std. Dev.	Sig.[3]
Convincingness				
polite interpret.	257	3.2	1.8	<.001
non-polite interp.	286	2.6	1.8	
Competence				
polite interpret.	257	3.2	1.7	<.001
non-polite interp.	286	2.4	1.5	
Intelligence				
polite interpret.	256	2.9	1.7	<.001
non-polite interp.	287	2.2	1.5	
Trustworthiness				
polite interpret.	255	3.1	1.8	<.001
non-polite interp.	288	2.5	1.8	

[1] N varies because of non-response.
[2] Scores for each attribute range between 1 and 7, 7 being the most positive evaluation and
1 being the most negative.
[3] Values of .05 or less are considered to be statistically significant.

the *t*-test are presented in Table 2, which shows that for two of the social/ psychological attributes, convincingness and trustworthiness, there was no significant difference in the scores of those Hispanics who had heard the polite interpretation and those who had heard the non-polite version. This was as expected. That is, it was expected that being able to understand the original language of the testimony would enable Hispanics to ignore the English rendition of the court interpreter.

What came as a surprise, however, is that on two of the four social psychological attributes, competence and intelligence, the English interpretation clearly had an impact on the formation of evaluations by the Hispanic mock jurors. That is, on the attributes of competence and intelligence there were statistically significant differences in the means of those who had heard the polite version and those who had heard the non-polite version.

Interestingly, but not unexpectedly, the Hispanic sample rated the witness whose interpreted testimony was polite as more competent and more intelligent than the witness whose testimony was interpreted without the politeness markers. If there was going to be any differential impact of the interpretation on the Hispanic subjects, it was anticipated that Hispanics would view polite speech more positively than speech lacking in politeness, because of the generally higher use of politeness in Hispanic verbal interaction compared to that in Anglo-American speech. Even the mean scores on convincingness and trustworthiness, although not statistically significant, were in the expected direction: the scores on the polite interpreted testimony were somewhat higher than those on the interpretation lacking politeness.

The fact that the difference in means was significantly different on the qualities

Table 2   Difference of means (*t*-test) for Hispanic sample.

Attribute	N[1]	Mean[2]	Std. Dev.	Sig.[3]
Convincingness				
polite interpret.	106	3.3	1.9	NS
non-polite interp.	103	3.1	1.9	
Competence				
polite interpret.	106	3.3	1.8	.002
non-polite interp.	103	2.6	1.6	
Intelligence				
polite interpret.	105	3.1	1.9	.003
non-polite interp.	104	2.4	1.6	
Trustworthiness				
polite interpret.	104	3.4	1.8	NS
non-polite interp.	105	3.1	1.8	

[1] N varies because of non-response.

[2] Scores for each attribute range between 1 and 7, 7 being the most positive evaluation and 1 being the most negative.

[3] Values of .05 or less are considered to be statistically significant.

of competence and intelligence, but not on the attributes of convincingness and trustworthiness, would seem to indicate that for Hispanics politeness in a witness's speech does not have much bearing on the evaluation of that witness in terms of his being convincing or trustworthy, two somewhat related characteristics that might be underlain by some common semantic dimension, possibly honesty. However, Hispanics apparently do give great weight to the factor of politeness in determining the competence and intelligence of a testifying witness, two traits that also seem to have some common semantic underpinning. Most importantly, even for a subgroup that understands the language of the testifying witness, the rendition of the court interpreter makes a difference in the impression formed of the witness by that bilingual subgroup.

[. . .] Table 3 demonstrates that for non-Spanish comprehending non-Hispanics politeness in the interpreted testimony of the witness makes a significant difference. On all four social/psychological attribute scales, persons who had to rely entirely on the English interpretation of the testimony found the witness who had produced English politeness markers to be significantly more convincing, competent, intelligent, and trustworthy than was the witness whose testimony as rendered in English was lacking in such tokens of politeness.

An interesting difference between the non-Spanish comprehending subsample and the entire sample of 551 subjects is that even though both groups rated the witness in the English polite version more positively on all four social/psychological scales, the means of the non-Spanish comprehending group are generally lower than those of the sample as a whole. Thus, even though politeness in testimony clearly

Table 3 Difference of means (*t*-test) for non-Hispanic informants who have never studied Spanish.

Attribute	N[1]	Mean[2]	Std. Dev.	Sig.[3]
Convincingness				
polite interpret.	64	3.0	1.7	.036
non-polite interp.	66	2.3	1.5	
Competence				
polite interpret.	64	3.0	1.7	.028
non-polite interp.	66	2.3	1.4	
Intelligence				
polite interpret.	64	3.0	1.7	.001
non-polite interp.	66	2.1	1.4	
Trustworthiness				
polite interpret.	64	2.8	1.7	.036
non-polite interp.	66	2.2	1.7	

[1] N varies because of non-response.

[2] Scores for each attribute range between 1 and 7, 7 being the most positive evaluation and 1 being the most negative.

[3] Values of .05 or less are considered to be statistically significant.

counts for the subgroup, some other factor is making its evaluations somewhat less positive than those of the larger group, which comprises non-Hispanics who had studied Spanish in school and Hispanics. A guess as to why the non-Spanish comprehending are somewhat more negative to the polite witness is a hidden factor associated with not taking Spanish in school: either these subjects found something in the Spanish language and/or Hispanic culture sufficiently unappealing so as to opt for a different language of study, or else the fact that they had not learned about Hispanic culture through a study of the language makes them now unsympathetic to Spanish-speakers when they hear them. [. . .]

The analyses presented above demonstrate that politeness in the speech of a testifying witness makes a significant difference in mock juror evaluations of that witness. What they do not show is the relative importance of politeness compared to other factors that may be affecting those evaluations. In order to determine how important politeness is in light of other possible predictors of social/psychological attribution, a stepwise multiple regression analysis was carried out. Included in the regression analysis were the following predictors: the subject's age, sex, income, years of education completed, whether he or she had ever been in a court of law in the U.S., the subject's degree of comprehension of Spanish, and, finally, whether the subject had listened to the polite or the non-polite interpretation of the Spanish testimony. [. . .]

A separate multiple regression analysis was performed on each of the four social/psychological attribute scales of interest to this study. A look at the predictors of evaluation scores for each scale demonstrates that polite versus non-polite interpretation of testimony is the only variable that is a predictor on all four social/psychological attribute scales. In fact, in two of the regression analyses, those of competence and intelligence, politeness is the sole predictor of mock juror evaluations. [. . .] The regression analysis reveals, therefore, that hearing the polite version of the testimony is associated with attributing more favorable evaluations on each trait.

What is interesting is that sex, education, income, and personal experience with the courts have no predictive power at all in accounting for mock juror evaluations of a witness testifying in a foreign language. [. . .] The only demographic variable that emerged as significant in any of the multiple regression analyses was age. Age turned out to be the third significant predictor of evaluations of trustworthiness: the older the respondent, the more favorable were his/her evaluations of the witness.

[. . .]

Discussion

The preceding analysis of the findings of this study has demonstrated that politeness in the testimony of a witness is associated with more favorable evaluations of that witness in terms of his convincingness, competence, intelligence, and trustworthiness. [. . .]

This principal finding is not surprising if one takes into account the multiple functions of verbal politeness. As Ide (1982, 1983; Ide et al. 1986) has shown, politeness has a dual function: one is to give deference by demonstrating the speaker's subservient position vis à vis the addressee, and the other is to show the speaker's demeanor by using a linguistic form which indicates that the speaker knows his or her place. In the context of courtroom interaction, one can conclude that the regular use of politeness markers on the part of a witness would be a reflection of both of these functions.

It should be noted that the concept of politeness used in this paper limits itself to overt politeness marking. That is to say, although verbal politeness can be manifested in numerous ways, as Brown and Levinson (1978) have shown, the manifestation of politeness that is focused on in this paper is but one of these ways: the use of "sir" and "ma'am" in direct address. In Brown and Levinson's (1978: 183–192) framework, it constitutes one of the many strategies for achieving what they call "negative face," that strategy being "give deference." In using "sir" and "ma'am," a witness who is testifying is giving deference not only to his or her addressee, the attorney, but also, and perhaps more importantly, to the judge and to the Court as an institution.

The second major finding of this study, that politeness in the testimony of a witness can be controlled through the workings of a court interpreter, demonstrates that the interpreter is a powerful filter through which a speaker's intended meaning is mediated. In effect, it was the interpreter who was producing the polite and non-polite versions of the testimony. The witness's Spanish language testimony was a constant: it was identically polite in both versions of the experimental tapes. Thus, the different reactions to the witness were due entirely to the role of the court interpreter. It was she, in effect, who controlled the impressions of the witness, since for those mock jurors whose knowledge of Spanish was nil or quite limited, it was the interpreter's English rendition that had to be relied on for comprehension of the witness's testimony. Thus, the interpreter can be seen to play a pivotal role in how a jury perceives a non-English testifying witness.

[. . .]

Appendix: text of experimental tape-recording (polite interpretation of testimony)

Pros. atty: Sir, would you state your name, please?
Interp: Señor, dé su nombre por favor.

Witness: Roberto Quesada Murillo.
Interp: Roberto Quesada Murillo.

Pros. atty: Where were you born?
Interp: ¿En dónde nació?

Witness: En Saltillo.
Interp: In Saltillo.

Pros. atty: And of what country are you a citizen?
Interp: ¿De qué país es usted ciudadano?

Witness: ¿Cómo?
Interp: Uh, what's that?

Pros. atty: Of what country are you a citizen?
Interp: ¿De qué país es usted ciudadano?

Witness: De México, señor.
Interp: Of Mexico, sir.

Pros. atty: I call your attention to the night of March 23rd and the morning of March 24th. Were you in the United States at that time?
Interp: Le llamo su atención a la noche del veintitrés de marzo y la mañana del veinticuatro de marzo. ¿Estuvo usted en los Estados Unidos en ese día?

Witness: ¿El veinticuatro de marzo?
Interp: March 24th?

Pros. atty: Yes.
Interp: Sí.

Witness: No, señor.
Interp: No, sir.

Pros. atty: Do you recall entering the United States during the month of March at
           all?
Interp: ¿Recuerda haber entrado a los Estados Unidos durante el mes de marzo?

Witness: No, señor.
Interp: No, sir.

Pros. atty: When did you last enter this country?
Interp: ¿Cuándo fue la última vez que entró usted a este país?

Witness: Esta es la primera vez.
Interp: This is the first time.

Pros. atty: When was that, sir?
Interp: ¿Cuando fue esto, señor?

Witness: Um, no recuerdo, como el veintidós.
Interp: I don't remember, around the twenty-second.

Pros. atty: Did you have any documents or papers to authorize your entry?
Interp: ¿Tenía sus documentos, o papeles autorizando su entrada?

Witness: No, señor.
Interp: No, sir.

Pros. atty: Were you inspected by immigration officials when you entered the
           United States?
Interp: ¿Fue usted inspeccionado por un oficial de inmigración cuando entró
           usted a los Estados Unidos?

Witness: ¿Inspeccionado? No entiendo, señor.
Interp: Inspected? I don't understand that word, sir.

Pros. atty: Did you enter through a port of entry?
Interp: ¿Entró usted por la garita?

Witness: No, señor.
Interp: No, sir.

Pros. atty: Did you enter illegally?
Interp: ¿Entró usted ilegalmente?

Witness: Sí.
Interp: Yes.

Pros. atty: Would you explain for the court the circumstances surrounding that
           entry?
Interp: ¿Puede usted explicarle a la corte las circunstancias de por cómo entró
           usted?

Witness: Sí, señor, pues entré, . . . [pause] ¿Cómo entré?
Interp: Yes, sir. Well I entered, . . . [pause] Uh, you mean the way I came in?

Pros. atty: Yes, sir. Did you cross through a fence or . . . ?
Interp: Sí, señor, ¿Cruzó usted por un cerco?

Witness: Sí, por uno.
Interp: Yes, through a fence.

Pros. atty: Had you made any arrangements for a ride before you left Mexico?
Interp: ¿Había hecho usted, ah, arreglos para obtener un raite antes de salir de
           México?

Witness: Sí, señor.
Interp: Yes, sir.

Pros. atty: How did that come about?
Interp: ¿Cómo fue que sucedió eso?

Witness: Bueno, pues, es como no traía yo dinero, busqué en raite.
Interp: Well, since I didn't have any money, I, I asked for a ride.

References

Berk-Seligson, Susan (1990) "Bilingual Court Proceedings: The Role of the Court
    Interpreter," in Judith N. Levi and Ann Graffam Walker (eds) *Language in the
    Judicial Process*, New York: Plenum Press.
Brown, Penelope and Levinson, Stephen C. (1978) "Universals in Language
    Usage: Politeness Phenomena," in Esther N. Goody (ed.) *Questions and
    Politeness. Strategies in Social Interaction*, Cambridge: Cambridge University
    Press.
Ide, Sachiko (1982) "Japanese Sociolinguistics: Politeness and Women's Language,"
    Lingua 57: 357–85.
—— (1983) "Two Functional Aspects of Politeness in Women's Language," in Shiro
    Hattori and Kazuko Inoue (eds) *Proceedings of the XIIIth International Congress of
    Linguistics*, Tokyo: CIPL.
—— Hori, Motoko, Kawasaki, Akiko, Ikuta, Shoko and Haga, Hitomi (1986) "Sex

Differences and Politeness in Japanese," *International Journal of the Sociology of Language* 58: 25–36.

Lakoff, Robin T. (1975) *Language and Woman's Place*, New York: Harper & Row.

O'Barr, William M. (1982) *Linguistic Evidence: Language, Power, and Strategy in the Courtroom*, New York: Academic Press.

Part 6

Examining Expectations and Norms

INTRODUCTION

MUCH WORK ON interpreting has been devoted, first and foremost, to the interpreters themselves and their processing efforts and products, with the other actors in the socio-communicative constellation receiving relatively little attention. The genesis of the rather productive line of interpreting research usually referred to as user expectation studies (see Kurz 2001b) is a case in point: when Bühler (1986) reported her pilot study among conference interpreters on the most desirable qualities in interpreters and interpretations, she hypothesized that the findings from her survey among experts would generally hold true for the quality expectations of users as well. It was only when Kurz (1989, 1993, and in this volume) gathered data from conference participants themselves that a more differentiated pattern of preferences began to emerge. And yet, the perspectives of interpreters and users need not be as separate as they might appear – at least with regard to the theoretical framework for studying them. Both interpreters and users (and indeed any other parties to the communicative interaction) rely on some sort of social consensus as to what is "right," correct or desirable in interpreting activity and its result. This is what Toury (1980, 1995) has conceptualized as "translational norms" and posited as a fundamental concern of Translation Studies.

As with concepts from translation theory in general, the notion of translational norms has been slow to attract attention among researchers in IS. It was first discussed from an interpreting research perspective in an MA thesis (under Toury's supervision) by Shlesinger (1989a) and put up for a wider debate in the first issue of *Target* (Shlesinger 1989b). Following a response from Harris (1990) from the perspective of the interpreting profession, empirical studies explicitly based on the search for norms were carried out in the mid-1990s by Jansen (1995a) and Schjoldager (1996). Other authors who have taken up this approach include Diriker (1999) and Pöchhacker (2000b). Shlesinger (1999, 2000a, 2000b) took up the topic yet again in a cognitive-science-based experimental study which demonstrated that interpreters' performance on ecologically valid experimental tasks is not merely a function of processing requirements and effects, but shaped to a significant extent by their norm-driven choices, e.g. the "norm of condensation" or compression underlying "strategic macroprocessing" (Shlesinger 1999: 69).

The close, if not inseparable linkage between interpreters' performance norms, acquired in the course of professional training and experience, and their ability to meet the cognitive processing requirements of the task at hand in a given situation, has powerful methodological implications for process-oriented research on interpreting, as demonstrated in the pioneering study by **Anne Schjoldager** (1995a, and in this volume). Her PhD research (1996), based on an ambitious research design involving both translation theoretical and processing-related objectives, led her to the realization that interpreters may be guided by operational norms which legitimize deviations from the normative standard of an "exact and faithful reproduction" (Jones 1998: 5) in the interest of maintaining fluency of output and, ultimately, their professional credibility (cf. also Gile 1995c: 201–4). Thus, the interpreter's performance norms, or "professional norms," to use Chesterman's (1993) term, can in fact override what others may expect the interpreter's product, performance or behavior to be like.

While it is easy nowadays to accept that there is considerable interdependence between interpreters' professional norms and the "expectancy norms" (Chesterman 1993) which are brought to bear by others on the translational product and behavior of interpreters (cf. Shlesinger [et al.] 1997), the dimension of user expectations in interpreting really began to be taken more seriously only in the 1990s, when the issue of "quality" came to the fore, and (conference) interpreters, stressing their service function, showed a greater interest in fulfilling their clients' expectations. Before then, it had generally been assumed that interpreters – as well as interpreter trainers and interpreting scholars – would know what was good. Cartellieri (1983), for instance, suggested that, under certain circumstances, less (quantity) might be more (quality) in interpreting, and Viezzi (1993) similarly gives explicit preference to a more synthetic rendition over a "saying-it-all" approach. (See also the literature on strategic compression (e.g. Alexieva 1983; Kutz 1990) and the position of other authors (e.g. Dam 1993; Pearl 1995; Setton 1999a; Viaggio 1992) rationalizing the legitimacy of omission.)

As mentioned above by way of introduction, the shift of emphasis from what interpreters consider good to what interpretation users actually expect, was ushered in by **Ingrid Kurz**, who had questioned whether Bühler's (1986) findings for the ideal interpretation from an interpreter point of view could be generalized to the expectations of users. In her first replication study with Bühler's product-related criteria (Kurz 1989) and several follow-up surveys among different groups of conference participants (Kurz 1993, and in this volume) as well as TV interpreting clients (Kurz and Pöchhacker 1995), Kurz found a differentiated pattern of preferences. The latter was explored further, with different survey instruments, by a number of IS researchers (e.g. Vuorikoski 1993; Kopczyński 1994; Mack and Cattaruzza 1995; Collados Aís 1998) and in the study by P. Moser (1995, 1996) commissioned by AIIC. The main insight which emerges overall from these findings is the considerable variability of expectations, depending on a broad range of variables such as the size and type of the meeting, the languages involved, the occupation and age of the participants, and the extent of their previous exposure to interpreting. A rather clear-cut distinction is found only between the expectations for conference versus media settings, with the latter demanding higher standards of fluency and other delivery-related features, with somewhat less emphasis on completeness (Kurz and Pöchhacker 1995).

An innovative contribution to this line of research is the study by Kopczyński (1994), who also questioned conference participants on their conception of the interpreter's role, both from their perspective as listeners and in their capacity as speakers. While in the former condition conference participants would tolerate a greater extent of intervention by the interpreter, in the latter they showed a stronger preference for the "ghost role" of the interpreter, and favored a close rendition of the speaker's words and even mistakes (cf. Kopczyński 1994: 195). This duality of perspectives as well as the focus on the interpreter's more or less active role point to the common ground between user surveys in research on conference and on community-based interpreting. In the latter, the distinction is usually between the perspective of the service provider (institutional or professional client) and the individual client, with survey instruments tailored to each (e.g. Mesa 2000). Much more so than for conference settings, client surveys in community interpreting center on expectancy norms regarding the interpreter's role, particularly in actively bridging culture-related communication gaps (cf. Pöchhacker 2000a, 2001).

Beyond hypothetical preferences, the research literature on quality-related issues in interpreting also includes work on users' actual assessment of a given performance (e.g. Gile 1990b; Strong and Fritsch-Rudser 1992; Marrone 1993; Garber and Mauffette-Leenders 1997). The fact that these two approaches are highly complementary has been shown convincingly by **Ángela Collados Aís**, whose PhD research (1998) involved surveys on quality expectations as well as actual quality assessment of (experimentally manipulated) interpretations. Her questionnaire-based survey on quality criteria, addressed both to a group of (fifteen) professional interpreters and to some forty specialist users of interpretation (in the field of legal studies), yielded an expectation pattern which largely confirmed previous studies, particularly as regards the priority of "sense consistency with the original" and "logical cohesion" of the interpretation over paralinguistic features such as voice and intonation. Notwithstanding their rather lower expectations regarding the interpreter's delivery, that same group of legal scholars, when confronted with a realistic simulation of a simultaneous interpretation with monotonous intonation, gave a poor assessment, not only of the interpreter's delivery but also of the overall quality of the interpretation and even the interpreter's perceived reliability and professionalism (Collados Aís 1998: ch. 7.2, and in this volume).

The work of Collados Aís reaffirms the fact that multiple perspectives need to be taken into account when studying the issue of quality in interpreting (cf. also Gile 1991b). While research on hypothetical expectations yields data on what users think they want, quality assessment studies are needed to demonstrate what really shapes users' appreciation of an interpreter's performance. When based on observation rather than experiments, concrete assessment of the product or service quality from the client perspective must in turn be complemented by objective evidence of the performance under study, given the high variability of subjects' perceptions of quality-related output features (e.g. by Gile 1985b, 1995d, 1999c). All of these efforts to learn more about the expectancy norms brought to bear on the translational product and behavior of interpreters have to be related back to the professional norms internalized by interpreters themselves, in particular their conception of what they need to do, and how, in order to best fulfill their professional mission of enabling communication. Crucial to this is the issue of the interpreter's role, which is raised in particular by Kondo (1990), Kopczyński (1994) and Collados Aís (1998) for interpreting in conference settings, and brought to the fore as perhaps the most fundamental issue in face-to-face interpreting in Part 7 of this volume.

ANNE SCHJOLDAGER, a 1990 graduate of translation and interpreting from the Århus School of Business, where she is an Associate Professor in the Department of English, is one of the few interpreting scholars who have founded their research on concepts from translation theory. Specifically, she was the first to undertake a search for translational norms (Toury 1995) in a sizeable corpus of interpreted texts. Her motivation to tackle what Shlesinger (1989b) had first raised, rather skeptically, as an issue in Interpreting Studies, was obviously boosted by her participation in the 1993 CERA Chair Summer School at Leuven and her exposure there to leading representatives of the paradigm of Descriptive Translation Studies.

The article reprinted here reflects the main substance of her 1996 PhD thesis at the Århus School of Business, which had been designed rather ambitiously as an experiment to contrast the performance of novice and advanced interpreting students as well as advanced students and professionals of translation with respect to handling the linguistic feature of progressive aspect. The fact that Schjoldager ended up shifting the focus away from her original assumptions and using her experimental corpus for a norm-oriented analysis of target-text/source-text relations is explicitly reflected and discussed in her thesis as well as in the present paper, originally published both in Jansen (1995b) and in *Hermes*, the *Journal of Linguistics* of the Århus School of Business (No. 14, 1995). With the aim of foregrounding Schjoldager's work on translational norms in interpreting rather than the evolution of her research project, the paper has been abridged and, rather exceptionally, restructured for the purpose of this Reader.

Further reading: Schjoldager 1995b.

Anne Schjoldager

AN EXPLORATORY STUDY OF
TRANSLATIONAL NORMS IN
SIMULTANEOUS INTERPRETING
Methodological reflections

0 Introduction

THOUGH THE THEORY of translational norms, first proposed by Toury (1980), has been influential in translation studies for quite some time now, this methodological and theoretical framework seems to have had little impact on interpreting research. Most theory-forming work on interpreting, which did not start till the late 1960s (Gile 1994:149), seems to have been preoccupied with the activity as a process of reformulation or as an extraordinary capacity for shared attention. An example of the former is *la théorie du sens*, the theory of "sense" or "intended meaning", proposed by Seleskovitch in 1968 (Seleskovitch 1978). An example of the latter is Gile's Effort Models (e.g. Gile 1991).

Thus, to my knowledge, descriptive work on translational norms in interpreting is rare. Until recently, very few scholars had touched upon the topic at all. Shlesinger (1989) and Harris (1990) were probably the first interpreting scholars to discuss the concept of translational norms in interpreting – both in *Target*, a journal that has as one of its explicit aims to focus on translational norms. Shlesinger gives a brief account of methodological problems that one might encounter when trying to extend the theory of translational norms to interpreting research. Though she definitely appreciates that norms must play a part in the interpreting process, she concludes that, due to the numerous difficulties involved in their extrapolation, it is too early to start speculating about the nature of such norms. In a response to these views, Harris argues that it is indeed possible to pinpoint existing norms in the interpreting community, but whereas Shlesinger's discussion is mainly concerned with methodological problems, Harris merely supplies a list of normative formulations.

Recently a few scholars seem to have found the concept of norms useful in studies of interpreters in institutional settings. Taking his starting point in

Descriptive Translation Studies (DTS), Jansen (1995) describes a small-scale empirical study of the "interaction between institutional structures and actual translation strategies" in a Dutch courtroom. A different, but related, example seems to be Wadensjö (1992, 1995). Though her theoretical framework is sociology and anthropology – especially Goffman's (1981) analysis of intermediary roles – rather than translation studies, she, too, takes the concept of norms into account in her analysis.

1 The concept of translational norms in interpreting research

According to Toury (1980: 51), translation is subject to various kinds of constraints. These constraints may be described in a continuum between two extremes: objective, relatively absolute rules and fully subjective idiosyncrasies. Translators seem to be influenced mainly by the middle ground of this continuum. Thus, they behave according to constraints which are neither completely codified nor completely arbitrary. These constraints in the middle ground of the normative scale are norms.

Toury (1980) distinguishes between preliminary, initial and operational norms. Preliminary norms concern "the very existence of a definite translation 'policy' along with its actual nature and those questions related to the 'directness' of the translation" (Toury 1980: 53). Initial norms govern the translator's overall strategy: s/he can either opt for adequacy, which emphasizes adherence to source-system norms, or acceptability, which emphasizes adherence to target-system norms. Operational norms concern actual decisions made during the process of translating.

One obvious question in this connection must be: is interpreting a norm-governed activity? I think there can be no doubt that, as a behavioural activity, interpreting must also be governed by norms. Naturally, interpreters, too, need norms to help them select appropriate solutions to the problems they meet. There is, of course, no reason to think that all interpreting performances would be totally predetermined, with no room for personal decision-making. Just as it would be absurd to assume that they would be totally unique and ungoverned by norms. Clearly, there is no such thing as to "just interpret", because this would merely be a case of adopting the "standard norm" (Hermans 1991: 165).

According to Hermans (1991: 167), there are at least three major models that supply the translator's norms: (1) the source text, (2) the relevant translational tradition, and (3) the existing set of similar originals in the target culture. These models seem to be equally true for interpreters: (1) some norms may depend mainly on the source speech itself, as well as its context and purpose. (2) Some are drilled into students while still at school, or are developed out of professional experience, for instance when the interpreter listens to a colleague at work. This situation is very likely, as professional conference interpreters are supposed to work in pairs. (3) They may also depend on the nature of speeches (i.e. originals) that the interpreter has heard in similar contexts.

According to Toury (1980: 57), for the scholar searching for these underlying norms, there are two major sources: textual norms, which are found by means of a source-target comparison, and extratextual norms, which are found in explicit, normative statements in the literature about translation. As far as the identification of textual norms is concerned, various methodological difficulties may be encountered that are peculiar to interpreting research. The main difficulty probably lies in the lack of accessible interpreting performances. [. . .] One consequence of this inaccessibility is that it may be difficult for the researcher to procure a corpus large enough to distinguish general from idiosyncratic tendencies (Shlesinger 1989: 113).

Another methodological problem lies in the fact that, when investigating interpreting performances, the scholar may invariably interfere with the process. [. . .] Interpreters who find themselves the object of scientific analysis may start to behave contrary to their habits. This, again, affects the representativity of the corpus – be that in a real conference where output is recorded or, which is even more artificial, in an experimental and didactic study such as mine.

As far as the identification of extratextual norms is concerned, this is only a little harder in connection with interpreting than with translation. Though there are more books on written translation than on interpreting, it should not be too difficult to find normative literature on interpreting. An example of this is Harris' norm of the "honest spokesperson". In accordance with this norm, interpreters should: ". . . re-express the original speakers' ideas and the manner of expressing them as accurately as possible and without significant omissions, and not mix them up with their own ideas and expressions" (Harris 1990: 118).

However, when investigating interpreting – especially simultaneous interpreting – we should probably also account for the high degree of complexity involved in the task. One way to do this would be to consider processing conditions such as time pressure, the oral medium and the fact that interpreting requires a capacity for attention-sharing. [. . .] If the interpreter does not possess the required amount of processing capacity, the task becomes difficult or even impossible.

Quite clearly, we shall always find it difficult to ascertain to which degree processing conditions determine the interpreting performance. Thus, perhaps the interpreter opts for one solution, following one set of norms, but cannot carry it through because of capacity saturation. One way of dealing with this methodological problem could be to introduce a different kind of norm – one that is peculiar to interpreting. This norm could for instance govern what the interpreter ought to do – or is allowed to do – when the task becomes difficult or impossible. An example of this is mentioned below (5.5).

The rest of this article deals with my own project on simultaneous interpreting and translation.

[. . .]

2 Preliminary objective and assumptions

The preliminary objective of this collection of data was didactic: What had beginners of simultaneous interpreting learned to do and what did they still need to learn in order to live up to professional standards? What had advanced student interpreters learned and what did they still need to learn? How did the behaviour of these two groups compare with that of translators, both beginners and professionals? This preliminary objective was based on three interlinked assumptions. I shall now discuss each of these in turn, and I shall show why they had to be modified or even abandoned.

2.1 First assumption: similar objective, different process

[. . .]

Many scholars seem to share the idea that translation and interpreting are related activities. A good example of this is the existence of a German inclusive term, *Translation*, for both interpreting and translation, first suggested by Kade in Leipzig in the 1960s, and since used by many German scholars – notably Vermeer, Reiss, and Holz-Mänttäri (see for instance Pöchhacker 1992, 1995). In continuation of this, Pöchhacker (1993: 54) suggests that a science of translation and interpreting (*Translationswissenschaft*) would consist of two subdisciplines: (1) translation studies (*Übersetzungswissenschaft*) and (2) interpreting studies (*Dolmetschwissenschaft*). Whereas some specific models and concepts would apply exclusively to either of these two areas, at least some theoretical concepts must be thought to apply equally to both of them. Pöchhacker refers to this shared theoretical framework as a general theory of translation and interpreting (*allgemeine Translationstheorie*).

2.2 Second assumption: less-than-perfect interpreters

The second assumption was that different working conditions would invariably lead to differences in quality – both in terms of source-text fidelity and in terms of target-language acceptability. Thus, as interpreters are disadvantaged by strenuous working conditions (time and medium) and by an extremely complex process, I expected my interpreter-subjects to produce less-than-perfect target texts, whereas I expected the translators to produce all-but-perfect results. [. . .]

There are two reasons why my assumption concerning differences in quality was hasty. The first one has to do with the impossibility of comparing oral and written performances directly. The second reason concerns the risk involved in defining one type of interlingual transfer as inferior to another. [. . .] The point to note is of course that interpreting performances need to be assessed according to different criteria from those of translation.

2.3 Third assumption: progressive aspect as focus of analysis

The third assumption was that it would be possible to concentrate on one linguistic problem whose successful or unsuccessful solution could then be used for generalizations about the nature of the performances. In formulating this third assumption, I was inspired by three empirical investigations carried out at the Copenhagen Business School. In all these investigations, syntactic differences between English and Danish were used as the starting point for generalizations about interpreting and/or translation. [. . .] I, too, decided to focus on syntactic differences between English

and Danish. In my case, the focus was on various incidents of progressive "meaning".
[. . .]

The grammatical notion of aspect concerns the manner in which a verbal action is experienced or regarded. By choosing either progressive or simple verb forms, English speaker/writers signal whether they see the action as being in progress or as completed. Usually Danish speaker/writers do not have to make this choice. Therefore, as the marking of aspect in Danish is mostly optional, many Danish sentences may refer to progressive actions without any formal marking.

Furthermore, whereas English makes use of morphological means, i.e. the aspectual contrast between progressive and simple verb forms, markers of progressive aspect in Danish are fixed, lexicalized phrases. [. . .]

[. . .] The intended methodology was as follows. As all my subjects were advanced speakers of English, I expected their de facto mastery of English grammar, including the reception and production of progressive aspect, to be almost perfect. Thus, I hypothesized, problems encountered in connection with the translation of progressive "meanings" in Danish and English would not be due to lacking proficiency in the two languages, but would mainly be indicative of the translational process. I could then use these incidents as the starting point of my analysis.

[. . .]

3 Procedure

Two late 1990 newspaper texts were selected. The contents of these formed the basis of the source texts of the investigation. The Danish text was an article published on 30 December 1990 in *Jyllands-Posten*, a major quality paper in Denmark. In this article, the journalist critically assesses the situation in the Soviet Union and expresses fears that Mr Gorbachev, the then President of the Soviet Union, might be losing control. The English text was a full-page advertisement in the *Observer*, published on 18 November 1990. In this advertisement, *Amnesty International* tries to persuade readers to become members. Citing horrid details, it describes how the Iraqi government systematically gasses the Kurdish region in Iraq.

For the purpose of the investigation, a simulated situation was constructed: a Danish "society for ordinary people wanting to discuss important issues in the world today" has invited two guest speakers. The idea is that the views expressed by these guest speakers should function as the starting point of the ensuing discussion. Both speakers have chosen their own topics. The first speaker, a Danish journalist from *Jyllands-Posten*, has chosen to talk about the situation in the Soviet Union. The second speaker represents *Amnesty International* in London and has chosen the Kurdish predicament in Iraq as her topic. The audience consists of Danish members of the society as well as English-speaking guests. That is why the speeches are interpreted simultaneously into Danish and English, respectively.

Mid-January 1991, the two source speeches were given "live" – with few deviations from the manuscript – to the group-I subjects (beginner interpreters) in the interpreting laboratory of the Århus School of Business. The interpreting performances were recorded, and so were the source speeches. Then, in the interpreting laboratory of the Copenhagen Business School, the tape recording of the source speeches was played to the group-II subjects (advanced student interpreters), who also interpreted simultaneously. Finally, in March 1991, the source speeches were transcribed. A few oral-language features, such as false starts and throat-clearing sounds, were erased. The written form of the speeches was then given to the group-III subjects (beginner translators) and the group-IV subjects (professional translators) to translate. The translators, who were asked not to use dictionaries and reference books, worked at home and in their own time. All subjects were informed of the simulated situation (i.e. a Danish society with guest speakers), but none of the subjects were given explicit instructions as to target-text purpose. Actually, they were simply asked "to just translate".

4 Methodological problems

. . . I soon discovered that the preliminary objective of my investigation was too ambitious: first, my empirical material was not really suitable for generalizing about differences in the proficiency and behaviour of my subjects. The grouping was not sufficiently well defined for that, and the task probably suited some groups better than others. I would therefore be better advised to place less emphasis on the differences between the two groups and adopt a more exploratory approach in order to look for regularities and irregularities in the corpus as a whole. Second, though my aim was to observe and not to assess the behaviour of the subjects, my choice of parameters was admittedly normative in Toury's sense. The whole methodology was probably too much characterized by an urge to assess quality, and my three assumptions were generally too categorical.

As the methodological framework of my investigation seemed insufficient and unsuitable for what I wished to achieve – namely to describe similarities and differences in the behaviour of my subjects – I was now in need of a different set of analytical tools. I then decided to use the concept of translational norms as a methodological tool. [. . .]

5 An exploratory study of translational norms in simultaneous interpreting

As my investigation is carried out in an experimental and mainly didactic setting, I take it to be self-evident that preliminary norms (translation policy) should be disregarded in the analysis. I therefore assume that the norms employed by my subjects are initial norms (overall strategy) and operational norms (actual decisions during the translational process).[1] I shall search for these by means of a textual comparison between source and target texts. Furthermore, I explore the possibility that some norms may be peculiar to simultaneous interpreting and that they occur in connection with capacity saturation. The results of such a comparison of simultaneous-interpreting performances with their source speeches and with written translations of "identical" source texts[2] may generate hypotheses for further research involving real-life performances by professional conference interpreters.

5.1 Methodological framework

In my search for textual norms, I follow the pattern of Toury's (1980) tripartite model. According to this model, there are three relationships between target and source texts: "Competence", which denotes theoretical, possible ways of translating a text, "performance", which is a description of existing translations, and "norms", which, as we have seen, is the intermediary level of more or less codified guiding principles. Thus, the analytical methodology of my investigation is as follows:

(1)   Suggestion of theoretical models (competence).
(2)   Source-target comparison (performance).
(3)   Reconstruction of guiding principles in the translational process (norms).

5.2 How to translate "gravøl" into English

In the rest of this article, I shall concentrate on possible and actual renditions of one small source-text item: the Danish word "gravøl", which stems from the source-text sentence in example 1:

(1)
Mens jerntæppet brasede sammen i øst, kunne man i alverdens medier se Gorbatjov drikke gravøl i vest.

[While the Iron Curtain was collapsing in the East, you could in all the world's media see Gorbachev drinking grave beer *in the West]*

The Danish word "gravøl" refers to a tradition of grieving over the death of a person after his/her burial. Typically a spouse or another close relative invites the mourners home for refreshments. As the literal meaning of this word is "grave *beer*", one would expect the mourners to drink beer, but other refreshments (especially coffee) are also considered traditional on these occasions. As a prevailing metaphor in the co-text of this source-text item is that the Cold War has "died", the choice of "gravøl" is clearly significant. Furthermore, the choice is probably also ironical: Rather than mourning the "death" of the Cold War, Mr Gorbachev seems to be rejoicing at it.

To produce a target-text item which renders all these connotations is certainly no easy task. In English-speaking countries, there are at least two ceremonies which resemble the Danish custom of drinking "gravøl", a "wake" and a "funeral reception", but none of these seem to cover all the connotations of the Danish term. [. . .]

In his/her rendition of "drikke gravøl", the translator/interpreter may consider the following factors.

(1)   Potential meaning: An informal gathering after the burial, which involves drinking (beer).
(2)   Co-textual factor: A series of funeral metaphors.
(3)   Intended meaning: Ironical.

5.3 *Theoretical model of translational relationships*

Inspired by Delabastita (1989: 199 and 1993: 33), I employ five main categories of translational relationships or transformation categories. [. . .]

A/ **Repetition**
Target-text item bears formal relation with relevant source-text item.
  – "drink grave beer"

B/ **Permutation**
Target-text item(s) is(are) placed in a different textual position from relevant source-text item(s).
  – "beer drinking at the grave"

C/ **Addition**
Target-text item constitutes an addition to information given in relevant source-text item.
  – "[drink grave beer] in the honour of the Cold War"

D/ **Deletion**[3]
No target-text item bears direct relation with relevant source-text item.
  – (No relevant example)

E/ **Substitution**
Target-text item bears no formal relation with relevant source-text item.

E1/ **Equivalent Substitution**
Source-text item is translated functionally.
  – "at the wake"; "at the funeral reception"

E2/ **Paraphrastic Substitution**
Source-text item is translated functionally, but in an expanded and/or segmental way.
  – "having a funeral celebratory drink"

E3/ **Specifying Substitution**
Source-text item is translated functionally and implicit information is made explicit.
  – (No relevant example)

E4/ **Generalizing Substitution**
Source-text item is translated functionally, but conveys less information than relevant source-text item.
  – "at the funeral"

E5/ **Overlapping Substitution**
Source-text item is translated functionally, but with a different viewpoint, so that target-text item conveys different information.
  – "was sad"

E6/ **Substitution Proper**
Target-text item bears little or no resemblance to relevant source-text item.
  – "was orientating himself towards [the West]"

5.4 Source-target comparison

I shall now give a few examples of actual renditions in my corpus. Example 2 is an indication that the rendition of "gravøl" is indeed a problem. The subject, a beginner interpreter (group I), clearly has severe difficulties – presumably not only with the rendition, but also with the simultaneity of the task, i.e. a case of capacity saturation (e.g. Gile 1991). At first, she opts for an overall strategy of A/ Repetition, but then, in connection with "gravøl", she decides on a strategy of D/ Deletion. The left column illustrates how the source speech proceeds, the other the group-I interpreter's performance. The figures in parentheses and bold print indicate real time.

(2)

Mens jerntæppet brasede	. . . .
sammen i øst	. . . .
. . . .	While the iron car..pet
kunne	. . . .
man i alverdens medier	was
se Gorbatjov	ruined in the east
drikke gravøl i vest. (**6.21**)	. . . .
. . . .	you could see-erm
(**6.25**) Det var tydeligt	Gorbachev
at Mikhail Gorbatjov [..]	err_____. (**6.26**)

The next example is taken from the group of advanced interpreters (group II). Again, at first, the interpreter opts for an overall strategy of A/Repetition, and then, in connection with "gravøl", she decides to employ a different strategy. This time the strategy is E2/ Paraphrastic Substitution. In her rendition, she seems to be aware of (1) the potential meaning of "gravøl" (informal gathering after the burial, which involves the drinking of something), possibly (2) that the co-text comprises a series of funeral metaphors, and (3) that the intention here is ironical.

(3)

	. . . .
Mens jerntæppet brasede sammen	. . . .
i øst	As the Iron Curtain fell in
kunne man i alverdens medier se	eastern Europe
Gorbatjov drikke gravøl	it was possible
i vest. (**6.21**)	to see Gorbachev drinking
. . . .	the funeral celebratory drink in
(**6.25**) Det var tydeligt at Mikhail	the west.(**6.29**)
Gorbatjov var tilfreds [..]	

5.5 Looking for norms

In examples 2 and 3, the underlying norm seems to dictate that interpreters should copy the formal features of the source text if at all possible, i.e. adequacy as initial norm. This is so even if the group-I interpreter is unable to carry it through. However, the following performance (by another group-II interpreter) seems to suggest that this initial norm of adequacy is sometimes superseded by a different kind of norm. In the following case, perhaps the reason is capacity saturation.

The norm activated in example 4 may be formulated as follows: an interpreter is allowed to say something which is apparently unrelated to the source-text item in question, i.e. to employ the strategy of E6/ Substitution Proper, provided that s/he can say something which is contextually plausible. The existence of such a norm is probably peculiar to simultaneous interpreting.

(4)

Mens jerntæppet brasede sammen	. . . .
i øst	. . . .
. . . .	As the Iron Curtain
kunne man	collapsed in the east
i alverdens medier se Gorbatjov	. . . .
<u>drikke gravøl</u> i vest. (**6.21**)	it could be seen
. . . .	in the media throughout the world
. . . .	that Gorbachev
(**6.25**) Det var tydeligt at Mikhail	<u>was orientating himself</u>
Gorbatjov var tilfreds	<u>towards</u> the west. (**6.29**)

6 Concluding remarks

After a critical review of the set-up of my project, I have shown some of the possibilities that the theory of translational norms may offer in connection with interpreting research. Using my own project as an example, I have exemplified that this methodology may indeed work on interpreting. Needless to say, though, a lot of work in the field is still necessary before we acquire an extensive knowledge of norms governing interpreting processes. By way of conclusion, I would like to emphasize that the question of norms in interpreting research is both intriguing and worth our attention. Indeed, once we have become aware of the concept of norms in the translational process, it seems hard not to take it into account.

Notes

1   In studies of authentic interpreting, all kinds of norms may be interesting. As regards the identification of preliminary norms, the scholar could for instance investigate what is selected for interpreting and in what ways.

2   "Identical" in linguistic and informational content, but of course not in the medium and immediate context.

3   Dam has thoroughly investigated condensing in consecutive interpreting, a strategy that bears some resemblance to my category D/Deletion. See for instance Dam (1993).

References

Dam, Helle Vrønning (1993) "Text Condensing in Consecutive Interpreting", in Yves Gambier and Jorma Tommola (eds) *Translation and Knowledge: SSOTT IV: Scandinavian Symposium on Translation Theory*, Turku 4–6 June 1992, pp. 297–313, Turku: University of Turku, Centre for Translation and Interpreting.

Delabastita, Dirk (1989) "Translation and Mass-Communication: Film and TV. Translation as Evidence of Cultural Dynamics", *Babel* 35 (4): 193–218.

—— (1993) *There's a Double Tongue: An investigation into the Translation of Shakespeare's Wordplay, with Special Reference to Hamlet*, Amsterdam / Atlanta: Rodopi.

Gile, Daniel (1991) "The Processing Capacity Issue in Conference Interpretation", *Babel* 37 (1): 15–27.

—— (1994) "Opening up in Interpretation Studies", in Mary Snell-Hornby, Franz Pöchhacker and Klaus Kaindl (eds) *Translation Studies – An Interdiscipline: Selected papers from the Translation Studies Congress, Vienna 9–12 September 1992*, pp. 149–58, Amsterdam / Philadelphia: John Benjamins.

Goffman, Erving (1981) *Forms of Talk*, Oxford: Basil Blackwell.

Harris, Brian (1990) "Norms in Interpretation", *Target* 2 (1): 115–19.

Hermans, Theo (1991) "Translational Norms and Correct Translations," in Kitty M. van Leuven-Zwart and Ton Naaijkens (eds) *Translation Studies: The State of the Art: Proceedings of the First James S Holmes Symposium on Translation Studies*, pp. 155–169, Amsterdam / Atlanta: Rodopi.

Jansen, Peter (1995) "The Role of the Interpreter in Dutch Courtroom Interaction: The Impact of the Situation on Translational Norms", in Peter Jansen (ed.) *Translation and the Manipulation of Discourse. Selected Papers of the CERA Research Seminar in Translation Studies, 1992–1993*, Leuven: The Leuven Research Centre for Translation, Communication and Culture, pp. 133–55.

Pöchhacker, Franz (1992) "The Role of Theory in Simultaneous Interpreting", in Cay Dollerup and Anne Loddegaard (eds) *Teaching Translation and Interpreting: Training, Talent and Experience*, pp. 211–20, Amsterdam / Philadelphia: John Benjamins.

—— (1993) "On the Science of Interpretation", *The Interpreters' Newsletter* 5: 52–9.

—— (1995) "Simultaneous Interpreting: A Functionalist Perspective", *Hermes. Journal of Linguistics* 14: 31–53.

Seleskovitch, Danica (1978) *Interpreting for International Conferences*, Washington DC: Pen and Booth.

Shlesinger, Miriam (1989) "Extending the Theory of Translation to Interpretation: Norms As a Case in Point", *Target* 1 (1): 111–15.

Toury, Gideon (1980) *In Search of a Theory of Translation*, Tel Aviv: The Porter Institute for Poetics and Semiotics.

Wadensjö, Cecilia (1992) *Interpreting as Interaction – On Dialogue Interpreting in Immigration Hearings and Medical Encounters*, Linköping: Linköping University, Department of Communication Studies.

I NGRID KURZ, THE first interpreter to complete a doctoral dissertation on interpreting (Pinter 1969), has been a leading representative of interpreting research for many years. Holding a degree in both psychology and conference interpreting from the University of Vienna, she has had a distinguished career as a conference and media interpreter. Since the late 1970s she has taught interpreting at the University of Vienna and has published widely on a variety of topics. Besides earning a reputation as a scholar of interpreting history, she has investigated a number of professional issues (e.g. interpreters' working conditions, job satisfaction) and has applied her intrinsic interdisciplinary expertise to the experimental study of cognitive and neurolinguistic aspects of interpreting activity. The broad range of her research interests is reflected in her post-doctoral thesis (Kurz 1996a), which brings together work on the history of training, interpreters' personality traits, expertise and EEG mapping during mental interpreting as well as the study of user expectations selected for this volume.

Prompted by Bühler's (1986) pioneering survey on quality criteria among conference interpreters, Kurz's fieldwork on the assessment criteria of different user groups triggered a spate of research activity on quality and evaluation criteria in interpreting. The paper reprinted here was originally published in the 1993 issue of *The Interpreters' Newsletter*, produced and circulated by the School of Translators and Interpreters (SSLMIT) at the University of Trieste.

Further reading: Kurz 1989, 1996a, 1996b, 2001b; Kurz and Pöchhacker 1995.

Ingrid Kurz

CONFERENCE INTERPRETATION
Expectations of different user groups

Quality of interpretation – professional standards

IN ORDER TO ensure that their members meet high quality standards, professional organizations like AIIC (Association Internationale des Interprètes de Conférence) have set up a screening system for admitting colleagues to the profession. Five sponsors, who must be experienced interpreters, must observe the applicant in an actual working situation. Besides, AIIC has a special committee for the admission and language classification of applicants (CACL) to process applications for membership.

Déjean le Féal (1990: 155) describes AIIC quality standards as follows:

> While there may be minor individual differences among the standards each interpreter sets for himself, we all share common standards of what we consider to be professional interpretation. These standards can be summarized as follows: What our listeners receive through their earphones should produce the same effect on them as the original speech does on the speaker's audience. It should have the same cognitive content and be presented with equal clarity and precision in the same type of language. Its language and oratory quality should be at least on the same level as that of the original speech, if not better, given that we are professional communicators, while many speakers are not, and sometimes even have to express themselves in languages other than their own.

The Code d'Ethique professionnelle requires all AIIC members to meet stringent quality criteria. Article 3 stipulates:

> Les membres de l'Association s'interdisent d'accepter un engagement

pour lequel ils ne seraient pas qualifiés. Par leur acceptation, ils apportent la garantie morale de la probité de leur prestation.

Situationality and communicative context

From the very beginning, conference interpreters emphasized the significant role played by the listener and by situational factors in interpreting. Herbert (1952: 82ff.) writes:

> It is quite clear that in a diplomatic conference the greatest attention should be paid to all the nuances of words, while in a gathering of scholars, technical accuracy will have greater importance; in a literary and artistic gathering, elegance of speech; and in a political assembly, forcefulness of expression. Similarly, the style and tone cannot be the same in a small group of three or four sitting round a table, in a committee room with a membership of twenty or fifty, and in a big public meeting where many thousands are gathered.

Seleskovitch (1986) points out that interpretation should always be judged from the perspective of the listener and never as an end in itself.

Déjean le Féal (1990: 155) concurs with her in saying that ". . . our ultimate goal must obviously be to satisfy our audience".

Snelling (1989: 142) stresses that a target text must always be targeted upon a specific audience: "It is, therefore, necessary to involve, in the interpretation equation, the audience and the specific quality of that audience". This opinion is also shared by Chernov, a representative of the Soviet school, who writes, "the knowledge of the situational context of the communication being interpreted becomes critically important" (Chernov 1985: 172).

Thiéry (1990: 41) stresses the need for situation analysis on the part of the interpreter, who must always consider "who is talking to whom, to what purpose, and with what possible effect".

Earlier empirical studies

1 Quality criteria assessment by conference interpreters

Bühler (1986) devised a questionnaire containing a total of 15 linguistic and extralinguistic criteria and asked AIIC interpreters to rate these criteria as to their relative importance in sponsoring candidates for AIIC membership. For the purpose of her study she assumed that sponsors applied the same criteria to sponsoring a candidate as to a first-class interpretation.

In trying to find criteria for the ideal interpreter, Bühler (1986: 233) postulates that ". . . he/she is one who supplies an ideal interpretation in a given situation for a given purpose". Following the train of thought of Reiss (1983), she holds that an interpretation is good if it serves its purpose and makes it clear that the ideal interpretation cannot be an absolute value.

Her conclusion, however, that "the criteria as discussed in this paper reflect the requirements of the user as well as fellow interpreter in a (hopefully) well-balanced mixture" (Bühler 1986: 233) is something I cannot immediately subscribe to.

There is no certainty that the ratings given by a sample of AIIC interpreters yield a true picture of user expectations. These can only be determined by asking the users themselves. In fact, such a survey might confirm Cartellieri's assumption that "very often, a good interpreter is two quite different people, being one thing to a conference participant and another to a colleague" (Cartellieri 1983: 213).

Besides, it may be suspected that different user groups attribute different weight to different criteria. Thus, one should preferably not speak of the user but should differentiate between different audiences.

Gile (1989) describes different types of multilingual events (big scientific and technical congresses, seminars, working sessions and plenary meetings of international organizations, parliamentary debates, media events, press conferences, dinner speeches, etc.), which are likely to involve different user expectations and requirements, and concludes:

> . . . peut-être convient-il de considérer l'interprétation non plus comme un système fermé, mais comme un service auxiliaire orienté vers des destinataires extérieures, dont les besoins et les attentes ne correspond-ent pas nécessairement à la définition que donnent les interprètes à leur activité. . . . En tout état de cause, il nous semble que pour avoir une vision plus complète de l'interprétation de conférence, il ne faut plus se cantonner dans un nombrilisme interpréto-centrique, mais étudier également les délégués, leur environnement et leur besoins.
>
> (Gile 1989: 25f.)

Stenzl (1983: 31) notes with regret that with the exception of a study by Gerver (1972), who compared the audience's comprehension and recall in consecutive and simultaneous interpretation, ". . . we have only anecdotal and impressionistic indica-tions of what conference delegates expect from interpreters and how satisfied they are with the service they receive".

2 Quality criteria assessment by delegates

A first empirical study designed to test Bühler's hypothesis that the criteria AIIC members take into consideration when evaluating the performance of candidates for membership also reflect user expectations was carried out by Kurz (1989).

Delegates to a medical conference were asked to rate the first eight criteria in Bühler's questionnaire as to their significance for the quality of interpretation. It was found that some of the criteria which members of the interpreting profession con-sidered highly important, such as native accent, pleasant voice, and correct usage of grammar, were given much lower ratings by the end users participating in this study.

In addition to this first study by Kurz, there are two further investigations in which delegates were asked about the quality criteria they applied to interpretation.

For her paper at the University of Trieste, Meak (1990) used a questionnaire to determine the attitude of ten Italian medical experts representing different disciplines (cardiology, urology, pediatrics, clinical pathology, pharmacology, etc.) towards a number of criteria relevant for the quality of interpretation.

Gile (1990) carried out a case study on the occasion of an ophthalmological conference, asking delegates to assess the quality of the interpretation provided at that conference by rating the following criteria on a five-point scale: 1. general quality of interpretation, 2. linguistic output quality, 3. terminological usage, 4. fidelity, 5. quality of voice and delivery, 6. main deficiencies in interpretation.

One of Gile's findings was that, as in the study by Kurz, quality of voice was considered less important by the respondents in his sample than by the interpreters in Bühler's survey. He ventures the following hypothesis:

> Il est possible . . . de formuler l'hypothèse selon laquelle les scientifiques (et techniciens) seraient moins sensibles à la qualité de la voix, du rythme et de l'intonation de l'interprétation que d'autres publics, pour qui elle a peut-être une plus grande importance.
>
> (Gile 1990: 68)

The first empirical investigations among conference participants showed that not all the AIIC evaluation standards (in Bühler's study) correlated highly with user expectations. Of course, it should be borne in mind that these results, which were obtained in a specific setting, cannot be generalized. It may be expected that different groups of end users have different expectations and needs. In order to test this hypothesis, a comparative study involving different groups of users was carried out.

Expectations of different user groups – a comparative study

Subjects and method

A bilingual (English/German) questionnaire was administered using the first eight of Bühler's quality criteria in order to ensure comparability with her study among AIIC interpreters.

Subjects were asked to rate the following criteria – 1. native accent, 2. pleasant voice, 3. fluency of delivery, 4. logical cohesion of utterance, 5. sense consistency with original message, 6. completeness of interpretation, 7. correct grammatical usage, 8. use of correct terminology – in terms of their significance for the quality of interpretation on a four-point scale.

Three different groups of listeners were examined.

The first survey was carried out on the occasion of an international conference on general medicine (cf. Kurz 1989). Forty-seven completed questionnaires were obtained.

The second study was performed in September 1989 among the participants in an international conference on quality control and yielded 29 completed questionnaires.

The third survey was conducted in 1989 during a Council of Europe meeting on equivalences in Europe. A total of 48 completed questionnaires was obtained.

The answers given by these three user groups were compared with those of the AIIC interpreters in Bühler's study.

The study was designed to answer the following questions:

Is there a difference in the ratings of the above listed quality criteria by conference interpreters on the one hand and delegates on the other hand?

Do different groups of users rate the individual quality criteria differently or do they all share the same expectations with regard to high-quality interpretation?

Can the alleged importance of situationality and communicative context in conference interpreting be empirically verified?

It can be seen that interpreters gave higher overall ratings (X = 3.44) than the three other groups. The second-highest ratings (X = 3.06) were given by the Council of Europe (CE) delegates. Medical doctors (MDs) gave an average rating of X = 3.0, and engineers (i.e. the participants in the quality control conference) gave the lowest ratings (X = 2.8)

The combined ratings of the individual criteria by the four groups are illustrated in Figure 1.

Discussion of results

Table 1 shows the significance attributed to the different criteria by the four groups of subjects.

Sense consistency with original message (criterion 5) was felt to be the most important quality criterion and received an average rating of 3.69. *Logical cohesion of utterance* (criterion 4) ranked second (X = 3.458). It was followed by *use of correct terminology* (criterion 8) with an average rating of 3.44. *Completeness of interpretation* (criterion 6) and *fluency of delivery* (criterion 3) received ratings of 3.2 and 3.1, resp. *Correct grammatical usage* (criterion 7) and *pleasant voice* (criterion 2) were given an average rating of 2.6 only. *Native accent* (criterion 1) ranked lowest with an average

Table 1   Assessment of quality criteria for interpretation by four different groups.

Criterion	Int. N = 47	MDs N = 47	Eng. N = 29	CE N = 48	avg.
1. native accent	2.9	2.3	2.2	2.08	2.365
2. pleasant voice	3.085	2.6	2.4	2.396	2.6
3. fluency of delivery	3.468	2.9	2.966	3.208	3.1
4. logical cohesion	3.8	3.6	3.1	3.3	3.458
5. sense consistency	3.957	3.6	3.655	3.6	3.69
6. completeness of interpretation	3.426	3.0	2.9	3.458	3.2
7. correct gramm. usage	3.38	2.4	2.03	2.688	2.6
8. use of correct terminology	3.489	3.4	3.138	3.729	3.44
average	3.44	3.0	2.8	3.06	3.06

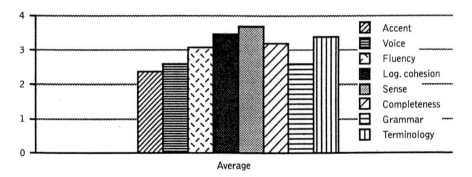

Figure 1   Combined ratings of quality criteria.

rating of 2.365. Figures 2 and 3 illustrate the differences in the rating of the individual criteria by the four groups.

In the following, the eight criteria will be discussed in the order of their average significance.

Sense consistency with original message (criterion 5)

Sense consistency with the original message was given a uniformly high rating. With the exception of CE delegates, who ranked criterion 8 (correct terminology) even higher, all groups considered sense consistency with the original message the single most important criterion, giving it the following ratings: Interpreters: 3.957; MDs: 3.6; Engineers: 3.655: CE delegates: 3.6.

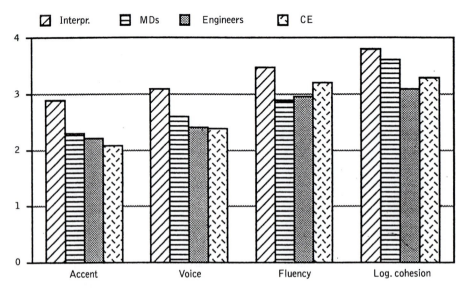

Figure 2   Quality criteria ratings by four different groups.

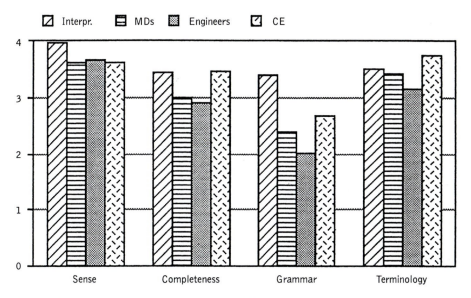

Figure 3   Quality criteria ratings by four different groups.

These results confirm the theory of Seleskovitch and Lederer (1989: 37):

> Il s'agit en interprétation de faire comprendre dans une langue la même réalité que celle qui a été désignée dans une première langue – réalité que nous appelons sens.

Logical cohesion of utterance (criterion 4)

Overall, logical cohesion was regarded as the second most important criterion. However, the ratings given by the four groups differed more widely than they did for sense consistency. MDs considered this criterion to be equally important to sense consistency ($X = 3.6$). Engineers ranked logical cohesion third behind sense consistency and correct terminology ($X = 3.1$). CE delegates gave this criterion a rating of 3.3, ranking it in fourth place (after use of correct terminology, sense consistency with original message and completeness of interpretation).

Logical cohesion more or less corresponds to the standard of coherence in the school of text linguistics of Beaugrande and Dressler (1981: 6), who claim that "a text does not make sense by itself" but that sense is attained by the interaction of the knowledge present in the text receiver's stored knowledge of the world.

Seleskovitch (1986: 39) in this context speaks of "compléments cognitifs", i.e. "les connaissances qui s'ajoutent aux significations des mots".

In general, listeners will be willing to complement discontinuities in the text by bringing in their own world knowledge, and reduced coherence will be tolerated as long as it does not interfere with communication.

The higher degree of tolerance among engineers towards reduced coherence might perhaps be due to the fact that technical papers are very often supported by the presentation of graphic illustrations, tables, charts, etc., which makes it easier for the listeners to maintain coherence.

A possible explanation as to why participants in the Council of Europe conference ranked logical cohesion of utterance only in fourth place may be the specific character of meetings of international organizations, which Gile (1989: 30) describes as follows:

> En générale ces réunions ne comportent pas un flux informationnel unilatéral comme les grandes conférences scientifiques et techniques . . . mais une discussion sur un ensemble d'éléments précis, souvent présentés sommairement à l'avance par le secrétariat de la réunion dans des documents envoyés aux participants . . . L'information ayant été partiellement présentée par écrit et assimilée prealablement à la réunion, les flux d'information en séance sont moins denses et se composent essentiellement de questions, d'explications complémentaires et de commentaires plutôt que d'informations entièrement nouvelles.

It seems that, since spontaneous contributions rather than lengthy prepared (and read) papers tend to prevail in those meetings, the demand for coherence is less stringent. Minor discontinuities frequently go unnoticed, and listeners normally exercise greater tolerance and supply additional material from their own stored knowledge whenever necessary.

Use of correct terminology (criterion 8)

In the combined ratings of all groups, use of correct terminology ranked third. A somewhat unexpected result was the fact that participants in the Council of Europe meeting considered correct terminology to be the most important criterion (X = 3.729). Interpreters and medical doctors ranked this criterion third with ratings of 3.489 and 3.4, resp. Engineers ranked correct terminology second (X = 3.138).

At a first glance, the finding that CE delegates attributed greater weight to the use of correct terminology than medical doctors and engineers is indeed surprising. One might expect the use of correct terminology to play a more important role in medical or scientific conferences.

On the other hand, it has to be borne in mind that, as pointed out previously, the meetings of international organizations are very often devoted to a discussion of documents which delegates have had time to study in advance. Consequently, they are used to a specific terminology which they expect to be hearing during the conference as well. An outsider might not see a big difference between a *committee* and a *commission*, a *president* and a *chairman*. For participants to whom their organization's terminology has almost become second nature, however, it obviously does make a difference. They expect the interpreter to use the technical jargon they are used to and seem to be less tolerant towards any deviations in this respect.

Completeness of interpretation (criterion 6)

On average, completeness of interpretation was ranked fourth. CE delegates and interpreters attributed almost identical ratings to this criterion (3.458 and 3.426, resp.). Medical doctors and engineers gave it somewhat lower ratings (3.0 and 2.9, resp.).

These results were not all too surprising since, according to Gile's typology of conferences, scientific conferences are frequently characterized by high information density, and participants' interests tend to be highly selective (cf. Gile 1989: 27) [. . .].

This may explain why medical doctors and engineers ranked completeness of interpretation fourth and fifth only. One might venture to say that, if they had a choice, they would opt for an intelligent, logical, terminologically correct summary of the original.

Stenzl (1983: 29f.) argues along similar lines:

> . . . a clear and intelligible text with some information loss may be more useful to the audience than a target text that aims at completeness at the cost of clarity and intelligibility. And not every item of information is equally important to the listener.

In addition, one might argue that, as mentioned above, the frequent use of graphic illustrations, diagrams and tables in scientific conferences facilitates understanding on the part of the audience.

The participants in the Council of Europe meeting may have attributed greater relevance to the completeness of interpretation because to them an exchange of information and experience with their fellow conferees constitutes an important aim of the conference. This requires full understanding of the arguments with all their nuances. If details or nuances are omitted in the interpretation, precise comprehension of the argument advanced by another delegate may be impaired.

Besides, it should be added that many participants in the meetings of international organizations are able to understand one or more foreign languages. For them, interpretation is not a necessity but a welcome service. Sometimes they will listen to the interpretation because they expect to get the details and nuances which they might miss when listening to the original. If these expectations are not met, these delegates might prefer to rely on their own, even though imperfect, knowledge of foreign languages. This might be one of the reasons why the CE delegates in this study attributed such great significance to completeness of interpretation.

Fluency of delivery (criterion 3)

In the combined ratings, fluency of delivery was ranked fifth (Interpreters: 3.468; CE delegates: 3.2; Engineers: 2.966; MDs: 2.9).

Here, too, situational factors obviously played a significant role. A possible explanation as to why the Council of Europe delegates participating in this study attributed greater weight to fluency of delivery than medical doctors and engineers may be that they were primarily interested in a lively discussion. A halting interpretation with frequent hesitations, pauses, and an irregular, unnatural rhythm would probably have been regarded as an impairment to a spontaneous exchange of information and experience.

The medical doctors and engineers in this study obviously showed more willingness to apply the "charity principle" (cf. Bühler 1990: 541) to fluency of delivery, provided that the criteria of sense consistency, logical cohesion and use of correct terminology were observed.

It may be expected that in other situations – e.g. when interpreting for the media – listeners will rank fluency of delivery higher.

Correct grammatical usage (criterion 6)

The ratings given to this criterion by the four groups differed considerably. While interpreters attributed a fairly high rating (X = 3.38), delegates considered this quality criterion to be much less important (CE delegates: 2.688; MDs: 2.4; Engineers: 2.03). The engineers in this study regarded correct grammatical usage as the least important criterion.

Correct grammatical usage is closely related with the textuality standard of cohesion (Beaugrande and Dressler 1981: 3), which concerns "the ways in which the components of the surface text, i.e. the actual words we hear or see, are mutually connected within a sequence". Cohesion rests upon grammatical dependencies and syntactic surface structures. A violation of the rules of grammar – a regular feature of spoken language – does not necessarily impair comprehension of a text. Seleskovitch (1986: 236) rightly asks: ". . . what is correct grammatical usage and how significant are minor grammatical errors in an interpretation?" Minor grammatical errors, such as wrong articles or wrong prepositions, sometimes even go unnoticed by the listener.

Moreover, for spoken texts, subsidiary cohesive systems, such as intonation and stress (prosodic features), are available: "Les traits prosodiques transmettent le sens que l'écriture doit analyser en mots et en style, et le ton compense souvent le manque de propriété des termes" (Lederer 1985: 28).

It should be pointed out that these findings were obtained from English- and German-speaking delegates. It may very well be that the members of other language groups, e.g. the French, attribute greater weight to correct grammatical usage. Similarly, this criterion may play a more important role in other situations, such as interpreting for radio and television.

Pleasant voice (criterion 2)

Even though interpreters ranked pleasant voice in second-last place, they gave it a rating of 3.085. The three user groups investigated in this study gave significantly lower ratings (MDs: 2.6; Engineers: 2.4; CE delegates: 2.396).

This finding corresponds to the results of Gile's survey (1990), in which the interpreters' voice did not have a great influence on the overall assessment of their interpreting performance.

Native accent (criterion 1)

Native accent was considered to be the least important quality criterion in the combined ratings (Interpreters: 2.9; MDs: 2.3; Engineers: 2.2; CE delegates: 2.08).

Bühler (1986: 233) assumed that, as delegates do not normally know the original, "[they] are . . . likely to judge the quality of interpretation by such superficial criteria as native accent, pleasant voice, and fluency of delivery". This assumption could not be confirmed in the present study. On the contrary, all three examined user groups gave a lower rating to this criterion than the AIIC interpreters participating in Bühler's study.

Again, it is quite possible that in other situations – particularly in media interpreting, where the interpreter's presentation is judged against that of the TV moderator or newsreader (cf. Daly 1985; Kurz 1985) – listeners will consider pleasant voice and native accent more important quality criteria.

Conclusions

By way of summary it can be said that this study among three different user groups yielded different evaluation profiles. While there was fairly high agreement by all groups on the importance of some of the criteria, conference interpreters and users as well as different user groups among themselves differed in their assessment of other criteria. The demands on the quality of interpretation expressed by the AIIC interpreters in Bühler's survey were generally higher than those obtained from the delegates participating in the present investigation.

The findings confirm the validity of the theories that view translation and interpretation as an intercultural communication process and emphasize the importance of situationality and communicative context (cf. Reiss and Vermeer 1984). They clearly show that the target-language receiver or listener must be seen as an essential element in the process. As Seleskovitch (1986: 236) points out, "the chain of communication does not end in the booth".

It would be interesting to conduct similar studies among other groups of end users so as to develop a broader base of observational data.

References

AIIC (1991) *Code d'Ethique professionnelle*, Genève.

Beaugrande, Robert-Alain de and Dressler, Wolfgang Ulrich (1981), *Introduction to Text Linguistics*, London/New York: Longman.

Bühler, Hildegund (1986) "Linguistic (Semantic) and Extra-Linguistic (Pragmatic) Criteria for the Evaluation of Conference Interpretation and Interpreters", *Multilingua* 5 (4): 231–35.

Bühler, Hildegund (1990) "Orality and Literacy – Theoretical and Didactic Considerations in the Context of Translation Studies", in R. Arntz and G. Thome (eds) *Übersetzungswissenschaft: Ergebnisse und Perspektiven*, pp. 536–44, Tübingen: Gunter Narr.

Cartellieri, Claus (1983) "The Inescapable Dilemma. Quality and/or Quantity in Interpreting", *Babel* 29 (4): 209–13.

Chernov, Ghelly V. (1985) "Interpretation Research in the Soviet Union: Results and Prospects", *Xth World Congress of FIT. Proceedings*, H. Bühler (ed.), pp. 169–77, Vienna: Braumüller.

Daly, Albert (1985) "Interpreting for International Satellite Television", *Xth World Congress of FIT. Proceedings*, H. Bühler (ed.), pp. 203–9, Vienna: Braumüller.

Déjean le Féal, Karla (1990) "Some Thoughts on the Evaluation of Simultaneous Interpretation", *Interpreting – Yesterday, Today, and Tomorrow*, D. and M. Bowen (eds), pp. 154–60, Binghamton, NY: SUNY.

Gerver, David (1972) "Simultaneous and Consecutive Interpretation and Human Information Processing", Social Science Research Council Research Report HR 566/1, London.

Gile, Daniel (1989) "La communication linguistique en réunion multilingue – Les difficultés de la transmission informationnelle en interprétation simultanée", thèse de doctorat, Université Paris III.

—— (1990) "L'évaluation de la qualité de l'interprétation par les délégués: une étude de cas", *The Interpreters' Newsletter*, no. 3: 66–71.

Herbert, Jean (1952) *The Interpreter's Handbook*, Genève: Georg.

Kurz, Ingrid (1985) "Zur Rolle des Sprachmittlers im Fernsehen", *Xth World Congress of FIT. Proceedings*, H. Bühler (ed.), pp. 213–15, Vienna: Braumüller.

—— (1989) "Conference Interpreting: User Expectations", *Coming of Age. Proceedings of the 30th Annual Conference of the American Translators Association*, D. L. Hammond (ed.), pp. 143–8, Medford, NJ: Learned Information Inc.

Lederer, Marianne (1985) "L'interprétation, manifestation élémentaire de la traduction", *Meta* 30 (1), Special Issue: Conference Interpretation, pp. 25–9.

Meak, Lidia (1990) "Interprétation simultanée et congrès médical: attentes et commentaires", *The Interpreters' Newsletter*, no. 3: 8–13.

Reiss, Katharina (1983), "Quality in translation oder Wann ist eine Übersetzung gut?", *Babel* 29 (4): 198–208.

—— and Vermeer, Hans (1984) *Grundlegung einer allgemeinen Translationstheorie*, Tübingen: Max Niemeyer Verlag.

Seleskovitch, Danica (1986) "Comment: Who Should Assess an Interpreter's Performance?", *Multilingua* 5 (4): 236.

—— and Lederer, Marianne (1989) *Pédagogie raisonnée de l'interprétation*, Paris: Didier Érudition.

Snelling, David (1989) "A Typology of Interpretation for Teaching Purposes", *The Theoretical and Practical Aspects of Teaching Conference Interpretation*, L. Gran and J. Dodds (eds.), pp. 141–2, Udine: Campanotto.

Stenzl, Catherine (1983) "Simultaneous Interpretation: Groundwork Towards a Comprehensive Model", MA Thesis, University of London.

Thiery, Christopher (1990) "The Sense of Situation in Conference Interpreting", *Interpreting – Yesterday, Today, and Tomorrow*, D. and M. Bowen (eds), pp. 40–3, Binghamton, NY: SUNY.

I N THE GROWING body of literature on quality in conference interpreting, the contribution of Ángela Collados Aís stands out as a significant conceptual as well as methodological innovation. A 1986 graduate of the Translator and Interpreter School (now Faculty of Translation and Interpretation) of the University of Granada, Collados Aís gathered some ten years of experience as a full-time teacher of interpreting and as a freelance interpreter before taking up doctoral research at her alma mater, where she was appointed professor in 2000.

Inspired by her practitioner's intuition of the importance of nonverbal vocal features of the interpretation, specifically the interpreter's intonation, Collados Aís set out to build on – and add to – the state of the art in research on user expectations and extend the concern with quality criteria to include actual product assessment by different types of listeners. The fact that she also holds a law degree may help explain her success in recruiting both legal experts and professional interpreters as subjects for her main experiment. The latter is described in chapter 7 (of nine) of her 1997 PhD thesis at the University of Granada, published (in Spanish) by Editorial Comares in 1998. The excerpt from that book which was selected by the editors to represent Collados Aís's work in this Reader is an abridged version of the sub-section in chapter 7 on users ("Quality Assessment in Simultaneous Interpreting by Users and Interpreters"), with additional material taken from chapters 4 ("Objectives and Methods") and 9 ("Conclusions"). The translation into English was done by Pamela Faber in cooperation with the editors.

Further reading: Collados Aís 1994, 1998; Pöchhacker 1999a.

Ángela Collados Aís

QUALITY ASSESSMENT IN SIMULTANEOUS INTERPRETING: THE IMPORTANCE OF NONVERBAL COMMUNICATION

Translated by Pamela Faber

Objectives

[. . .] **EMPIRICAL RESEARCH ON** the expectations of interpreters as well as end-users . . . indicates that the former are generally more demanding, but that pleasant voice and/or intonation are not important criteria in the assessment of interpretation quality in either of the two groups (Kurz 1989, 1993). [. . .] Drawing on this research, and on the presuppositions that had guided other empirical work on user expectations of quality in interpreting, we set out to achieve the following objectives:

—   to determine the quality expectations of a specific group of end-users of simultaneous interpretation (SI);
—   to determine the quality expectations of professional interpreters, both in their role as speakers and in their role as listeners;

[. . .]

—   to test the hypothesis whereby monotonous intonation in SI is perceived both by users who are specialists in the subject matter and by professional interpreters;
—   to test the hypothesis whereby monotonous intonation in SI has a negative effect on judgments of quality made both by professional interpreters and by specialist users;
—   to test the hypothesis whereby monotonous intonation in SI has a negative

effect on how users and interpreters evaluate other, more subjective criteria, such as professional performance or the degree of confidence that the interpreter inspires in the users.

In an earlier chapter we suggested that users attribute certain negative aspects of the interpretation either to the original speech/speaker, or to the interpreter. Our idea was to analyze the extent to which monotonous intonation in SI might affect the receptors' assessment of the original discourse. This gave rise to yet another objective of our research:

—   to determine how monotonous intonation in SI may affect the evaluation of the original speech by users and interpreters.

In the course of our study, it also emerged that the actual evaluation of the output does not necessarily correspond with the users' or interpreters' declared expectations. This motivated our decision to analyze how groups of end-users behave when they evaluate the criterion of sense consistency with the original message, particularly in view of previous empirical research on user expectations and evaluation, in which this criterion was unanimously regarded as being the most important. We therefore sought

—   to test the hypothesis whereby certain content errors would go unnoticed by both groups of subjects; and
—   to test the hypothesis whereby unnoticed errors would have no effect on the subjects' evaluations of the interpretation.

[. . .]

Methodology

[. . .]

Preparatory phase

[. . .] Our goal was to measure the effect of the criteria *intonation* and *sense consistency with the original message* on the basis of different versions of the interpretation of the same original text. [. . .] Thus, three video-recordings of SI were made:

1   with monotonous intonation, and fully consistent with the sense of the original discourse;
2   with lively intonation, but not fully consistent with the sense of the original discourse;
3   with lively intonation and fully consistent with the sense of the original discourse.

The three versions were interpretations into Spanish of the same original speech in German [. . .]. Given that our objective was to measure the effects of monotonous intonation in SI, we decided that the original speech should also be delivered monotonously by the speaker. In this way, if our hypotheses were confirmed, the results obtained would allow future research to study if, in the case of a more lively original speech, monotonous intonation might cause the users to evaluate the interpretation even more negatively. It would also be possible to study how monotonous intonation in SI affected the subjects' evaluation of the original speech. This could open a new line of research on the role of the interpreter. These considerations led to the specification of the characteristics of the original German speech [. . .].

The text chosen [. . .] was an example of highly specialized legal discourse with numerous references to the German Constitution and to jurisprudence of the German Constitutional Court. [. . .]

The text had to be shortened since its duration under normal conditions would have been excessive (approximately 40 minutes), and would have prevented some subjects from taking part in the experiment. The length of the text was thus reduced to 10 minutes . . . (2,285 syllables). [. . .] The speech was delivered in German and was situated in a specific context: a seminar on the funding of political parties in Europe, organized by the Department of Constitutional Law. The speaker chosen to play the role of professor of German Constitutional Law was Ludwig Schwarz, a colleague at the Faculty of Translation and Interpretation of the University of Granada and Director of the local Goethe Institute. [. . .]

[. . .]

Whereas the manipulation of the intonation took place when the video was actually being taped, the manipulation of the other criterion – *sense consistency with the original message* – had to be carried out prior to the recording. [. . .] Although we had a published written translation of the original speech, this text was hardly credible as a simultaneous interpretation because of the complexity of its syntactic structure. We therefore had to establish what an actual interpretation of the speech would be like. For this purpose, the speech was read by one of our colleagues in the SI lab of the Faculty, and three professional interpreters interpreted it into Spanish. Their interpretations were recorded and compared. The syntactic structure of the written translation was then modified in all instances where at least two of the three interpretations coincided. The final result was the version of the interpretation used in videos 1 and 3 in which there are no content errors. Because of a slight modification in the text, video 1 comprises 3,011 syllables, while video 3 comprises 3,088 syllables.

[. . .]

[. . .] On the basis of this "oral" version of the translation we produced video 2 by inserting the content errors. This version of the interpretation has a total of 3,009 syllables. [. . .] We basically introduced six types of content errors:

1   errors in the transmission of numbers (e.g. of articles in the German legal code, quantities, and dates);
2   omissions (e.g. of restrictions on donations to political parties);

3   changes in gradation (e.g. describing something impossible as being difficult);
4   incoherence (e.g. saying that the German legal code exhaustively regulates the funding of political parties, and subsequently stating just the opposite);
5   additions (e.g. where the original text states that the German legal code establishes an obligation, the interpreter says that it *clearly* establishes an obligation);
6   incorrect transmission of meaning (e.g. the affirmation that the state cannot limit the free development of political parties was turned into the assertion that the state in fact sets limits to their development; the meaning of the original is thus misrepresented so that the interpretation gives the listeners a totally erroneous concept of how political parties are funded in Germany . . .).

[. . .]

This constituted the video material which served as the basis of our experiments: three different versions of SI superimposed as a voice-over on the video of the original speech.

[. . .]

Assessment by the users

Method

Subjects

The subjects who participated in our experiment were 42 legal experts, who also answered our initial user expectation questionnaire. They were divided alphabetically into three groups of 14.

Material

The material used were the three videos with manipulated versions of SI: (1) video 1: monotonous intonation with no content errors; (2) video 2: lively intonation with content errors; (3) video 3: lively intonation with no content errors.

The questionnaire which the subjects answered after viewing the video-recording was based on the questionnaire regarding their expectations, filled in before the screening of the video.

Actually, both questionnaires contained similar questions (which were to be rated on a five-point scale [1 = worst, 5 = best]). The only differences lie in: (a) their formulation, since the questions in the second questionnaire are not hypothetical but are applied to the evaluation of a specific interpretation, and (b) the inclusion of four additional questions:

—   overall assessment of the interpretation (Gile 1990) [. . .]
—   impression of the interpreter's professionalism [. . .]

–   impression of the interpreter's reliability [. . .]
–   evaluation of the original speech [. . .].

Experimental context

Since it was impossible to have all fourteen members of each group view the videos at the same time and place, the recordings were shown in different departments and offices, mostly on a portable TV with a fourteen-inch screen. [. . .]

Results

The results of this study are presented according to the order of the questionnaire which the subjects answered after viewing the videos. The subheadings thus correspond to the quality criteria used in the evaluation. Results have been calculated as percentages. [. . .] The final section gives a comparative account of the results based on the average ratings for each of the three videos.

1 Overall assessment of the interpretation

The scores show important differences. Subjects gave an overall rating of 3/4 to **video 1** (42.8%: 3, 28.5%: 4) and a rating of 4/5 to **video 2** (50.0%: 4, 35.7%: 5) and **video 3** (50.0%: 4, 42.8%: 5). A Kruskal-Wallis test showed significant differences between **videos 1** and **3** ($p<.05$). No significant differences were observed between **videos 1** and **2**, although results tended towards significance ($p<.10$).

[. . .]

2 Native accent

78.5% of the subjects gave **video 1** a rating of 4/5 (35.7%: 4, 42.8%: 5). 100% of the subjects' ratings for **video 2** fall within the 4/5 range (42.8%: 4, 57.1%: 5). Similarly, a majority of subjects (85.7%) gave **video 3** a rating of 4/5 (35.7%: 4, 50.0%: 5). There were no significant differences between the videos.

[. . .]

3 Pleasant voice

Regarding the criterion of *pleasant voice*, 78.5% of the subjects gave **video 1** a score of 3/4 (42.8%: 3, 35.7%: 4). The same percentage of subjects rated **video 2** as 4/5 (35.7%: 4, 42.8%: 5), and 71.4% assessed **video 3** as 3/4 (28.5%: 3, 42.8%: 4). No significant differences were observed among evaluations of the three videos.

[. . .]

4 Fluency of delivery

78.5% of the subjects gave **video 1** a rating of 4/5 (50.0%: 4, 28.5%: 5). All of the subjects (100%) gave **videos 2** and **3** a score of 4/5. In the case of **video 2**, the percentage was 50.0% each and in **video 3**, the percentages were 42.8%: 4 and 57.1%: 5. No significant differences were found.

[. . .]

5 Logical cohesion of utterance

Both **video 1** and **video 2** were rated 4/5 by 85.7% of the subjects (50.0%: 4, 35.7%: 5 for **video 1** and 21.4%: 4, 64.2%: 5 for **video 2**). The majority of the subjects (92.8%) also assessed **video 3** as 4/5 (42.8%: 4, 50.0%: 5). No significant differences were observed among evaluations of the videos.

[. . .]

6 Sense consistency with original message

Video 1 was rated 4/5 by 84.6% of the subjects (46.1%: 4, 38.4%: 5). One subject did not answer the question because she or he did not feel qualified to do so. The majority of the subjects (85.7%) gave **video 2** a rating of 4 or 5 (42.8% each). Similarly, 92.3% gave **video 3** a score of 4 or 5 (46.1% each). One subject stated that she or he could not evaluate this criterion. No significant differences were observed between the three videos.

[. . .]

7 Completeness of interpretation

All of the subjects (100%) gave **video 1** a rating of 4/5 (75.0%: 4, 25.0%: 5). For this video, there were 12 completed questionnaires. One subject did not answer the question because she or he did not feel qualified, and another subject left the question blank. Since no reason was given, it was possibly due to an oversight. Regarding **video 2**, 92.8% of the subjects gave it a score of 4/5 (28.5%: 4, 64.2%: 5). 84.6% of the subjects gave **video 3** a similar rating (23.0%: 4, 61.5%: 5). There were 13 completed questionnaires. One subject left the question blank because she or he did not feel qualified to answer it. No significant differences were observed.

[. . .]

8 Use of correct terminology

Video 1 was given a score of 4/5 (57.1%: 4, 35.7%: 5) by 92.8% of the subjects. All of the subjects (100%) gave **video 2** a similar rating of 4/5 (42.8%: 4 and

57.1%: 5). A majority of the subjects (85.7%) rated **video 3** as 4/5 (35.7%: 4, 50.0%: 5). No significant differences were observed.

[. . .]

9 Style

Regarding the criterion of *style*, 78.5% of the subjects gave **video 1** a rating of 4/5 (50.0%: 4, 28.5%: 5). **Videos 2** and **3** were given the same evaluation (35.7%: 4, 50.0%: 5) by the majority of the subjects (85.7%). No significant differences were observed.

[. . .]

10 Intonation

Video 1 was given a score of 1 or 2 by 71.4% of the subjects (35.7% each). For **video 2**, the most frequent rating was 4 (42.8%), whereas **video 3** was rated most often as 3 (42.8%). There were significant differences between **videos 1** and **2** ($p < .05$) as well as between **videos 1** and **3** ($p < .05$).

[. . .]

11 Diction

The most commonly assigned rating for **video 1** was 4 (42.8%). As regards **video 2**, 92.8% of the subjects gave it a score of 4/5 (35.7%: 4, 57.1%: 5). **Video 3** was given a similar rating (35.7%: 4, 42.8%: 5) by 78.5% of the subjects. No significant differences were observed.

[. . .]

12 Professionalism

Exactly half of the subjects gave **video 1** a score of 4, whereas 85.7% of the subjects gave **video 2** a rating of 5. Almost all of the subjects (92. 8%) gave **video 3** a 4/5 (42.8%: 4, 50.0%: 5). There were significant differences between **videos 1** and **2** ($p < .05$). No significant difference was found between **videos 1** and **3**, although the results tended towards significance ($p < .10$).

[. . .]

13 Reliability

Video 1 was evaluated as 4/5 (46.1%: 4, 38.4%: 5) by 84.6% of the subjects. (One subject left the question blank.) 92.8% of the subjects gave **video 2** a rating of 4/5 (50.0%: 4, 42.8%: 5), while **video 3** was given a 5 by a majority of the subjects (64.2%). No significant differences were observed.

[. . .]

14 Evaluation of the original speech

Slightly over half of the subjects (53.8%) gave **video 1** a score of 4 (one subject did not answer this question). **Video 2** was rated 3 by 57.1% of the subjects, while exactly half of the subjects gave **video 3** a rating of 4. No significant differences were observed.

[. . .]

Comparison of average ratings

The ratings for each of the criteria analyzed were noticeably lower for **video 1** than for **videos 2** and **3** (Figure 1). **Video 2** obtained slightly higher scores than **video 3**, except for the criteria of *overall assessment of the interpretation* (1), *sense consistency with the original message* (6), and *reliability of the interpreter* (13).

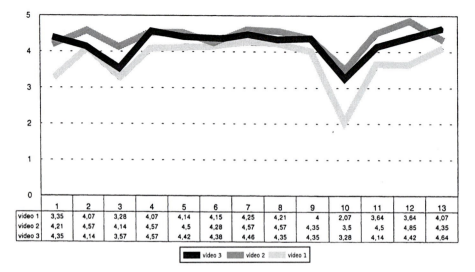

	1	2	3	4	5	6	7	8	9	10	11	12	13
video 1	3,35	4,07	3,28	4,07	4,14	4,15	4,25	4,21	4	2,07	3,64	3,64	4,07
video 2	4,21	4,57	4,14	4,57	4,5	4,28	4,57	4,57	4,35	3,5	4,5	4,85	4,35
video 3	4,35	4,14	3,57	4,57	4,42	4,38	4,46	4,35	4,35	3,28	4,14	4,42	4,64

■ video 3   ▨ video 2   ▫ video 1

Figure 1   Comparison of average ratings.

Discussion

[. . .]

Among the most important findings obtained in our study we would like to highlight the following:

End-user access to certain criteria: Despite the fact that it was impossible for the subjects to provide an objective evaluation of certain criteria which they considered highly important at least on a theoretical level (e.g. *sense consistency with the original message* and *completeness of interpretation*), very few seemed to be aware of this limitation. Only two subjects mentioned it in relation to *sense consistency with the original message* and three in relation to *completeness of interpretation*. The fact that the vast majority did evaluate these criteria indicates that their evaluations are based either on an overall subjective impression of the interpretation or else on criteria other than the ones analyzed in this study.

Evaluation of intonation: [. . .] The monotonous intonation of the interpreter was clearly detected by the users. [. . .]

Evaluation of sense consistency with the original message: The results obtained appear to indicate that the users did not detect the content errors inserted in version 2 of the interpretation. This confirms the findings of Gile (1995) regarding consecutive interpretation. Actually, version 1 received the lowest rating (4.15) with a difference of 0.13 in relation to version 2, and 0.23 in relation to version 3. Although these figures were not statistically significant, they show that monotonous intonation tends to be associated with poorer ratings for this criterion.

Overall assessment of the interpretation: Version 3 received the highest rating (4.35), followed by version 2 (4.21) and version 1 (3.35). Although a significant difference could be established only between versions 1 and 3 ($p<.05$), subjects clearly favored version 2 over version 1. Even though the difference involved ($p<.10$) was only indicative of a tendency, the users' judgments were evidently influenced by the difference in intonation. Since the criterion *sense consistency with the original message* could not be evaluated by the subjects, it did not influence their overall assessment of the interpretation to any significant degree. Nevertheless, video 3 was the one that received the highest ratings, showing a significant difference in comparison to version 1 ($p<.05$), though not in comparison to version 2.

Evaluation of the quality criteria analyzed: The differences between videos 1 and 2 are not significant for any of the eight remaining quality criteria: *native accent, pleasant voice, fluency of delivery, logical cohesion of utterance, completeness of interpretation, use of correct terminology, style* and *diction*. However, in comparison to the other two videos, **video 1** received lower ratings for all of these variables. This seems to show that monotonous intonation has a negative effect on the evaluation of other quality criteria. In all likelihood, the fact that this tendency did not show up in the statistical analysis is due more to the small number of subjects than to a lack of influence. In general, **video 2** obtained the highest scores for all of the individual criteria, followed by **video 3**. The only exceptions were the criteria of *fluency of delivery* and *style*, for which both videos received identical ratings. As **video 2** is the most animated, one can conclude that the less monotonous the intonation, the more positive the users' assessment of the interpretation. [. . .]

Conclusions

[. . .]

The results of our study show a clear separation between quality and the perceived quality or success of a simultaneous interpretation. The users are not good judges of quality, simply because they are not in a position to perform this task. [. . .] If we compare the results obtained in the assessment study with subjects' prior expectations, we find that user expectations clearly relate to the concept of quality, but not to the actual perception of quality or success. The expectations of the subjects did not prove decisive, either for their assessment or for the relative importance and actual weight they attached to the different criteria. In our opinion, this means that users not only desire but in fact demand, albeit implicitly, a certain degree of *intrusion* or active involvement on the part of the interpreter. Even though the speaker's delivery of the original was monotonous, the high ratings obtained by versions 2 and 3 in comparison to version 1 seem to indicate that the interpreter should assume the conscious role of professional communicator, and go beyond the "ghost role" (Kopczyński 1994). Clearly, further research is necessary in order to ascertain the limits to which the interpreter should go in his or her active involvement in the communication process. However, our results show that, as far as intonation is concerned, the interpreter should feel free to improve on the delivery of the speaker, at least at the levels examined in this study.

References

Gile, D. (1990) "L'évaluation de la qualité de l'interprétation par les délégués: une étude de cas," *The Interpreters' Newsletter* no. 3: 66–71.
—— (1995) *Basic Concepts and Models for Interpreter and Translator Training*, Amsterdam and Philadelphia: John Benjamins.
Kopczyński, A. (1994) "Quality in Conference Interpreting: Some Pragmatic Problems," in M. Snell-Hornby, F. Pöchhacker and K. Kaindl (eds) *Translation Studies – an Interdiscipline*, Amsterdam and Philadelphia: John Benjamins, pp. 189–98.
Kurz, I. (1989) "Conference Interpreting: User Expectations," in D. L. Hammond (ed.) *Coming of Age: Proceedings of the 30th Annual Conference of the American Translators Association*, Medford, New Jersey: Learned Information, pp. 143–8.
—— (1993) "Conference Interpretation: Expectations of Different User Groups," *The Interpreters' Newsletter* no. 5: 13–21.

Part 7

(Re)Defining the Role

INTRODUCTION

NORMATIVE EXPECTATIONS REGARDING various features of the interpreter's output, as addressed in Part 6, are a very specific reflection of the more fundamental norms governing the behavior of individuals in the role of interpreter. Viewed in a broad historical perspective, interpreters often appear as all-round intermediaries carrying out a number of variegated and diffuse functions in addition to their translational task (cf. Hermann 1956, and in this volume; Karttunen 1994; Bowen *et al.* 1995). It was only with the emergence of conference interpreting as a profession in the early twentieth century that there appeared sharper boundaries for what interpreters in highly visible international settings would or would not do. As more and more of these high-status professionals found themselves working in the simultaneous mode from a booth, the confines of their role in the communication process tended to become even narrower, with little chance of direct interaction with the communicating parties other than by their audible translational output (cf. Feldweg 1996: 98).

Beyond, or rather below international settings, however, the role of interpreters remained characteristically fluid. Not surprisingly, the issue of the interpreter's role was – and still is – a central concern to practitioners in other domains pushing for greater professionalization. The pioneering efforts of signed-language interpreters in the United States, which date back to the late 1960s, are a case in point. Charged with enabling communication in a situation of inherent inequality, between representatives of mainstream institutions on the one hand and underprivileged, "disabled" individuals on the other, interpreters were naturally cast in a helper role which extended to whatever needed to be done. Signed-language interpreters in the US and elsewhere have made great strides in clarifying and (re)defining their role, particularly by establishing a professional code of ethics, training programs and accreditation (see Frishberg 1990). In the course of their professionalization efforts in the 1980s and

1990s, spoken-language interpreters in community settings also established codes of conduct and standards of practice, particularly for court interpreting (cf. González *et al.* 1991; Edwards 1995) and medical interpreting (e.g. MMIA 1996). Nevertheless, practitioners of community-based interpreting have continued to grapple with role definitions and deontological dilemmas as momentous challenges, given the diversity of sociocultural and institutional constraints shaping their work in any given national environment (cf. Mikkelson 1996a; Pöchhacker 1999b). Against this background, the three papers in this part, all of them written by practicing interpreters and devoted to deontological issues centering on the interpreter's role, reveal a striking degree of cohesion and common ground, and clearly point towards increasing synergies within the broader field of IS.

Perhaps the most comprehensive and vivid overview of the descriptions and meta-phors variously applied to the role of the interpreter was put together by **Cynthia B. Roy** as part of her doctoral research on role issues as reflected in turn-taking behavior (1989). On the strength of her longstanding experience as a practicing (signed-language) interpreter in the US as well as her academic credentials as a scholar in sociolinguistics, Roy (1993, and in this volume) puts her first-hand professional know-ledge in perspective and brings out the broader picture of changing perceptions of the interpreter's role and the ways in which these interact with the process of professional-ization. While she refers mostly to the professional situation and scholarly literature of signed-language interpreting, the socio-psychological dynamics reflected in her account are strikingly similar – and relevant – to the conceptual issues dealt with by spoken-language interpreters working in community settings (cf. Roberts 1997). It is no coincidence, therefore, that Roy's view of the interpreter as an active third party with an intrinsic impact on the communicative event is highly germane to the positions of such key figures in the field of community interpreting as Mikkelson (1996b, 1998) and Wadensjö (1992, 1998).

As if bearing out Roy's belief that interpreting scholars in search of a theoretical underpinning would find inspiration not so much in translation theory but in communi-cation studies, sociolinguistics and other disciplines (cf. Roy 1993: 132, and in this volume), **Cecilia Wadensjö** conducted her pioneering PhD research on interpreting in police and medical settings (1992) in the Department of Communication Studies of Linköping University, Sweden. Herself a professional "dialogue interpreter" (*dialog-tolk*) working between Swedish and Russian, Wadensjö set out to contrast the inter-preter's normative role, as laid down in the official code of conduct or "Guide to Good Practice," with actual interpreter behavior, as documented by transcriptions of authentic discourse data. Bringing together such diverse sources of inspiration as Bakhtin's theory of language and Goffman's conceptual framework for the analysis of talk, Wadensjö's approach to studying the "inter-activity" of interpreting has cast fresh light on the complexity of interpreting behavior. One of the fundamental insights gained from her analysis is the fact that interpreting in dialogue situations exhibits the simultaneous presence and dynamic interplay of "relaying" (i.e. "translating") and "coordinating moves"; in other words, (professional) interpreters are seen as typically going beyond their normative role of "just translating," and as actively shaping the development and outcome of the mediated encounter. This finding clashes with the deontological principle of neutrality, as studied – and shown to be a "myth" – by Metzger (1999) with reference to signed-language interpreters.

Wadensjö's approach to the study of *Interpreting as Interaction* (1998) represents one of the main analytical and methodological orientations of research on interpreting beyond conference settings. Indeed, her active collaboration, e.g. with Roy in the US and Apfelbaum in Germany, reflects the emergence of a broader paradigm of discourse analytical research on interpreting in the course of the 1990s (see Mason 1999). This included a backward link to pioneering work on non-professional interpreting as carried out in Germany in the mid-1980s (Rehbein 1985; Knapp and Knapp-Potthoff 1985; Knapp-Potthoff and Knapp 1986, 1987), which re-emerged in the late 1990s in a major research project on interpreting practices in hospitals (e.g. Meyer 1998). Apart from its currency among scholars investigating community-based interpreting, the discourse-based interactionist paradigm gained visibility also within the more established community of conference interpreting researchers, as highlighted by Wadensjö's role as instructor in the 1997 Århus Seminar on Interpreting Research Training masterminded by Daniel Gile. Moreover, the application of the interaction-oriented discourse analytical approach to such new research areas as automatic dialogue interpreting (Apfelbaum and Wadensjö 1997), telephone interpreting (Wadensjö 1999) and media interpreting (Wadensjö 2000) attests to the potential and productivity of the discourse-based interaction-oriented framework.

Complementing the most widely shared approach among scholars of interpreting in community-based settings, **Granville Tate** and **Graham H. Turner**, both with a professional background in (British) sign language interpreting, came to tackle the fundamental issue of the interpreter's role with research methods from the social sciences. Focusing on the tension between the normative role prescribed by the code of ethics, and the professional dilemmas described by fellow interpreters from personal experience, Tate and Turner set out to establish what some one hundred of their peers would do when faced with particular deontological challenges as posed by a number of hypothetical interpreting scenarios. Their survey yields clear evidence that a code informed by a mechanistic view of the interpreter's role cannot do justice to the demands actually placed on interpreters in concrete situations. The authors' suggestion that a code of practice would need to be brought to life by some sort of complementary case law accords well with Wadensjö's (1998) position regarding the evaluation of professionalism: "In practice, there are no absolute and unambiguous criteria for defining a mode of interpreting which would be 'good' across the board. Different activity-types with different goal structures, as well as the different concerns, needs, desires and commitments of primary parties, imply various demands on the interpreters" (1998: 287). Thus, to cite but a few examples: Is it "professional" for interpreters to use a lower register of language for less educated defendants in court (e.g. Hale 1997a, 1997b)? To promote a client's cause by acting as an "intercultural agent" in an asylum hearing (Barsky 1996)? To follow a service provider in his consistent use of the third person to address the client (Kaufert and Putsch 1997)? To simplify and explain questions and statements directed at limited-proficiency clients? As will have emerged from the papers in this and in the previous part, such questions do not have clear-cut answers, but have to be considered in the light of institutional constraints and individuals' needs as well as the professional norms governing the activity of interpreting.

Clearly, then, the papers presented in this last part of the Reader pave the way – and point to the need – for much further research on what professional interpreters actually do when they interpret; what they should do so as to meet the expectations and needs of their clients; and what they might do in order to optimize the flow and effectiveness of communication for all parties to the interaction.

Further reading: Fenton 1997; Jansen 1995a; Kadric 2000, 2001; Kaufert and Koolage 1984; Lang 1978; Laster 1990; Laster and Taylor 1994; Morris 1995, 1999; Niska 1995; Roberts 1997; Zimman 1994.

PRACTITIONERS AND RESEARCHERS of both spoken-language and signed-language interpreting have been placing ever greater emphasis on the elusiveness and complexity of the interpreter's role in the cross-linguistic interaction. While practiced also in conference and media settings involving "monologic" discourse, most of the day-to-day work of signed-language interpreters is done in situations of face-to-face interaction. Not surprisingly, deontological issues and role definitions have figured prominently in the signed-language interpreters' concerns, as reflected in Cynthia Roy's 1989 PhD dissertation, "A Sociolinguistic Analysis of the Interpreter's Role in Turn-Taking in Interpreted Events," at Georgetown University, and in her book *Interpreting as a Discourse Process* (Roy 2000). In both she presents and develops the view of the interpreter's role as an active participant.

Her metalinguistic analysis of the metaphors and epithets used with reference to interpreting helps explain why the interpreter's role has been perceived as passive and conduit-like, and why we have so rarely been able to grasp fully the nature of interpreted discourse and interaction. The paper reprinted here in an abridged form was originally published in 1993 in the *Journal of Interpretation* of the US Registry of Interpreters for the Deaf (RID).

Roy has been a practicing interpreter since shortly after the introduction of interpreting services for Deaf US citizens in the early 1970s, and has been training interpreters since 1979. She has taught interpreting at Gallaudet University, where she was instrumental in creating the core curriculum for the MA in interpreting, and is currently Director of the American Sign Language/English Interpreting Bachelor's Program at Indiana University, Indianapolis.

Further reading: Roy 1996, 2000.

Cynthia B. Roy

THE PROBLEM WITH DEFINITIONS, DESCRIPTIONS, AND THE ROLE METAPHORS OF INTERPRETERS

1 Introduction

THIS PAPER IS an examination of the ways in which various scholars and practitioners have sought to describe the process of interpreting and the role of the interpreter. I discuss traditional definitions of interpreting and suggest that metaphors and metaphorical descriptions have assisted our understanding of the role of the interpreter. After a brief discussion of the changes in the profession, I describe some of the metaphors that have come about in interpreting and relate a brief history of the metaphorical descriptions that have arisen in sign language interpreting. Unfortunately, these definitions and descriptions have limited the profession's own ability to understand the interpreting event itself and the role of the interpreter within the event. This has led to a belief system about interpreting which is based on the unexamined notion of the interpreter as a conduit. To understand why a change in perspective is necessary, we must first examine these definitions and descriptions to understand why they are unsatisfactory.

2 Definitions of interpreting

As interpreting has emerged as a professional endeavor throughout the twentieth century, individuals have sought to define interpreting in several different ways. Traditionally, interpreting has been subsumed under translation, which, in its broadest sense, has been defined as the transfer of thoughts and ideas from one language (source) to another (target). Proceeding from this general definition of translation, practitioners have created a distinction between spoken messages and written messages. By the time Seleskovitch (1978) wrote the sentence below, the following distinction was commonly accepted: "Translation converts a written text into another written text, while interpretation converts an oral message into another oral message" (1978: 2). Because this distinction neglected to include the act of interpreting between signed and spoken languages, Brislin (1976) suggested the following clarification: "[Interpreting] is the transfer of thoughts and ideas from one language to another, whether the languages are in written or oral form; whether the languages have established orthographies or do not have such standardization; or whether one or both languages is based on signs, as with sign languages of the deaf" (1976: 1). Although mentioning signed languages at that time was new, the definition still retained the distinction between written messages as translation and spoken or signed messages as interpretation. Recently, Ingram (1985) has argued that while this distinction has been of use to practitioners, the difference . . . is not between writing and speech but "between natural language and secondary, or contrived, representations of language" (1985: 91). According to his definition, the distinctions should be between natural languages and secondary representations of language (secondary representations being written language and contrived sign systems), not between written language and spoken language. This approach groups any and all natural languages together, whether they be spoken or signed, and revises the definitions of translation (in its specific sense) and interpretation. Ingram's new definition of interpretation is: "a [form of the translation] process whereby messages encoded as discourse in one natural language are recoded as discourse in another natural language" (1985: 92).

The definitions above are representative of standard definitions which appear in academic writings. They also represent the briefest, most general, and the most widely accepted definitions of interpreting. However, these definitions are so succinct that they lack any true explanatory power about interpreting or the nature of the event. They lend themselves to accounts of interpreting which represent the process in a rather mechanical way which then lends itself to explanations of the interpreter as performing a mapping skill on the tokens of a language.

3 Changes in the profession

Definitions are only one way of explaining the interpreting event; there are also metaphors and metaphorical descriptions that are offered as ways to understand interpreting. However, before those descriptions can be discussed, it is worthwhile commenting on the reasons why such discussions have become necessary and important.

[. . .] The surge of interest, the increasing number of interpreting research studies, and the desire to improve pedagogical strategies have created a cyclical effect upon each other. Together these expanding areas are leading to the active promotion of interpreting as a discipline in its own right by its practitioners and supporters as well as contributing to a growing interest from the practitioners in the research about interpreting.

Thus, this interest and activity are the cause of a re-examination of the theoretical foundations and knowledge bases which potentially form the discipline of interpreting. Up until now, interpreting has relied on the theoretical framework supplied by the domain of translation, which draws most of its theoretical force from its application to written texts. However, as interpreting becomes increasingly differentiated due to the nature of its face-to-face interaction, both practitioners and researchers are considering a theoretical base for interpretation which may not rest on translation theory but rather may construct its own theory through borrowed or adapted notions from communication, sociolinguistics, intercultural communication and other, similar disciplines. [. . .]

4 Metaphors and descriptions of the role of the interpreter

Most of the descriptions of interpreting concentrate on a clarification or explanation of the role of the interpreter. Therefore, this section will discuss the metaphors and the metaphorical descriptions used by practitioners to explain what they do.

People who know more than one language in a variety of situations are afforded the opportunity of pursuing interpreting as a line of work. Interpreter is a role bilingual individuals assume for many reasons, some of which are personal satisfaction and monetary compensation. Professional interpreters often describe their role as the person in the middle by using a metaphor along with metaphorical language which says that they serve as a kind of channel or bridge through which communication between two people can happen. What this channel does is complex: interpreters are required to reproduce a message from one speaker to another faithfully, accurately, and without emotional or personal bias entering into the interpretation. In other words, interpreters must simultaneously render messages without changing the messages' intent and do so with uncommon accuracy, while maintaining a stance of impartiality and neutrality. To be specific, interpreters may not introduce topics, change topics, ask questions of their own, interject their opinion or give advice, and, most importantly, must keep the entire transaction confidential. The performance of this role has been compared to a machine, a window, a bridge, and a telephone line among other metaphors in trying to compress the complexity of the role to a simple, singular analogy.

[. . .] While these metaphors clearly are responding to a need, they also carry double messages. On the one hand, these descriptions attempt to convey the difficulty of the simultaneous tasks in interpreting while reminding everyone that the interpreter is uninvolved on any other level; at the same time, the same descriptions encourage interpreters to be flexible, which usually means be involved. While descriptions and standards of ethical practice extensively, sometimes exhaustively, list what interpreters should not do, they seldom, if ever, explain what interpreters can do, that is, explain what "flexible" means. Consequently, no one really knows where to draw the line on the involvement of the interpreter. This is why Fritsch-Rudser (1988) can say, "Interpreters don't have a problem with ethics, they have a problem with the role," and have a room full of interpreters applaud.

One reason interpreters have adopted this metaphorical usage is due to the fact that the dominant concern in the field, thus far, has been to describe the cognitive processes and the linguistic tokens associated with the act of interpretation. Metaphors used in describing these processes have provided the majority of metaphorical usage when explaining the role of an interpreter. For example, Solow (1980: ix), a practitioner and an educator of interpreters, wrote the following:

> The sign language interpreter acts as a communication link between people, serving only in that capacity. An analogy is in the use of the telephone – the telephone is a link between two people that does not exert a personal influence on either. [. . .]

Most descriptions emphasize that the transfer must be one of meaning, not a transfer of forms. Spoken language interpreters have been at the forefront of explaining this process, which, in and of itself, is not a simple task, and not simply a coding exercise. Seleskovitch (1978) [. . .] explores factors from which meaning is derived, such as background knowledge, familiarity with the speaker, the topic, and the purpose for delivering the message. However, while this is a helpful breakdown of the processing tasks of an interpreter and an acknowledgment of some socio-linguistic factors, it is still a cognitively-based process that leaves out more factors than it includes due to its assumption that conference interpreting represents the fulcrum of interpreting. This is a singular view of a specialized kind of interpreting, conference interpreting, which is limited by its focus on the message of a single speaker as it is received by and then reproduced by a passive and unimportant audience.

In contrast to these two perspectives, what interpreters actually know and do is complex, not only from the perspective of psycholinguistic processes, but also from the perspective of interactive communication systems as a whole. Interpreters are not simply processing information and passively passing it back and forth. Their task requires knowledge of organizational systems, grammatical and discourse systems, language use systems as well as emergent adaptive systems to perform their job successfully and consistently. [. . .]

Any reader of articles, books, or newsletters about interpreting will alternately find words such as communication facilitator, mediator, linguistic intermediary, and, more recently, bilingual, bicultural communicator, all of which are being used to represent the role of an interpreter. The authors explicitly claim that interpreters are much more than conveyors of uttered messages, yet when these writers discuss their terminology and its meaning, the bulk of the attention is on the form of the source or target language and whether or not the content of a target language production adequately approximates the source language message.

The assumption which persists throughout all of these descriptions is that of extreme personal non-involvement by the interpreter which, I believe, is best represented by the metaphorical concept of a conduit. [. . .]

5 A brief history of the descriptions of the role

The descriptions of the role of the interpreter have centered around metaphorical words or phrases and, sometimes, discipline-specific (such as communication and linguistics) terminology. These phrases come to light as academicians and practitioners alike struggle to adequately characterize the role. In spoken-language interpreting articles, the terminology has not undergone substantial changes, other than beginning to include the notion of being culturally sensitive, due to the fact that interpreters have not been perceived as anything other than mediators or channels between languages. And, of course, since their writings focus on the act of conference interpreting, they have not perceived a need to describe the role any differently.

However, the field of sign language interpreting has undergone tremendous changes in terminology due to the recognition of American Sign Language as a natural, independent language used by deaf persons who themselves constitute an ethnic and linguistic minority. [. . .]

In a newsletter of the Registry of Interpreters for the Deaf (RID), a practicing interpreter and instructor reviews the changing terminology of the field and how it affects the profession's view of the work of an interpreter. Witter-Merithew (1986) determined that there have been basically four descriptions to exemplify what interpreters do. The four descriptions [. . .] hinge upon the distinction between extreme personal involvement and extreme to not-so-extreme non-involvement of the interpreter.

5.1 Interpreters as helpers

Family members and friends have been interpreting for deaf persons for a long time. Their only view of themselves was as helpers. Frishberg (1986: 10) explains how sign language interpreting developed:

> Interpretation for deaf people had, of course, always been taking place in the doctor's office, in church and other settings. Few of the "interpreters" were compensated for their time and work; fewer of them had been educated in any formal way for the role they fulfilled. Often the interpreters were family members, neighbors, or friends who obliged a deaf relative or friend by "pitching in" during a difficult personal communication situation.

Thus in the decades before the 1960s, there was no distinction between a helper and an interpreter. Helpers were free to offer advice, translate messages between deaf and hearing persons, and make decisions for one or both sides. Helping out in this way, while it may have seemed admirable to many, reflected attitudes that deaf individuals were not able to take care of their own business, be it personal, social, or professional, without the intervention of the helper. [. . .]

5.2 Professionalism and the emergence of the conduit description

Changing expectations of consumers, and the profession's own need to see itself as rendering professional services, brought about the second description, the conduit model, whereby interpreters portrayed themselves using the concept of a machine. [. . .]

This "machine" idea was useful in a disassociation from the "helper" view. It clarified a wish to be seen as rendering a professional service while refraining from taking over the decision-making responsibilities for either party involved in an interpreting event. For example, the Code of Ethics (1965) states that interpreters "shall maintain an impartial attitude during the course of his interpreting . . .," and "He shall remember the limits of his particular function and not go beyond his responsibility." Although these sentences do not render the concept of a machine, they certainly demonstrate that interpreters did have "particular functions" and that they should refrain from becoming emotionally or personally involved. [. . .]

As could be expected, conflicts arose with the extreme, conduit view of the task, and the conflicting instructions. As Witter-Merithew explains, "Interpreters denied responsibility for unsuccessful interpreted events and clients began to perceive interpreters as cold and self-serving" (1986: 12). She argues that this conduit description allowed interpreters to deny responsibility for any consequences of an interpreting event and led to unsuccessful interpreting events and unflattering perceptions by consumers. For these reasons, interpreters began to search for a clarifying, less radical description of their role.

5.3 Interpreters as communication-facilitators

As the machine description began to fail, interpreters and interpreter educators turned to academic arenas to find alternative views. The profession, accordingly, moved on to a third description, the communication-facilitator, based on theoretical notions provided by the field of communication and promoted by the hierarchy of RID membership whose stated goal was to provide interpreting services to any deaf person no matter what his or her communication "mode"; meaning no matter whether they signed or did not sign, or whether they used ASL or an invented sign system. The facilitator description, building upon the basic notions of communication theory, defined a basic communication event as consisting of a sender, a message, and a receiver. Using this concept, the interpreter is inserted as a channel which facilitates the transfer of messages from a sender to a receiver when they do not speak the same language (Ingram 1974). The facilitator notion caught hold because of the developments in the deaf community and among professionals who worked with deaf persons. Not only did ASL achieve some acceptance as the natural language of deaf persons, but the language attitudes surrounding its use began to change and, for the first time, it was acceptable to use ASL in public, out-group settings. Quickly there was an outcry that not all deaf persons used ASL; that many deaf persons preferred sign-supported speech because of their competence in English; and that many deaf persons did not use signing at all, but no matter what the communication preference of a deaf person, he or she deserved interpreting services. The "channel" now became a "language and communication-mode expert" who made communication easier by adapting to the particular linguistic system desired by each individual deaf person.

These ideas were solidified and codified in an updated version of the primary text of the field, *Introduction to Interpreting*, reissued by the Registry in 1980. [. . .] In addition, the Code of Ethics [. . .] explicitly states: "The interpreter's only function is to facilitate communication. He/she shall not become personally involved because in doing so he/she accepts some responsibility for the outcome, which does not rightly belong to the interpreter" (Caccamise *et al.* 1980: 13). These codes remain in effect today. What is missing are coherent, well-defined parameters of language functions that interpreters must perform to accomplish communication, although it is still clear what functions, specifically, lie outside of the role of an interpreter. [. . .] It is clear that the interpreter while interpreting is still performing the transfer of one form to another form; it is the conduit notion in the disguise of communication-facilitator. [. . .]

5.4 Interpreters as bilingual, bicultural specialists

[. . .]

By the end of the 70s and early 80s most descriptions of interpreters acknowledged the fact that interpreters must be sensitive to the fact that they are communicating across cultures as well as across languages. Cokely (1984) noted: "It is obvious that before an individual can interpret between two languages/cultures s/he must be bilingual and bicultural" (1984: 140). Descriptions of cultural sensitivity include being aware of regional or dialectal differences in language, nonverbal differences, different attitudes toward time, different forms of personal address, and other differences. [. . .]

Sign language and spoken-language interpreters came together at the Conference of Interpreter Trainers (1983) to share their growing recognition of the similarities of the interpreting process, and, consequently, the similarities of educating interpreters. At this conference Arjona (1983) gave a paper in which she claimed that interpreter education was an interdisciplinary endeavor centered around the mastery of communication-based skills. She argued for a task-based analysis approach to the study of interpretation. [. . .]

6 The conduit model persists

[. . .]

This discussion began with a description of the interpreter as a helper. The helper was a role which allowed for the extreme personal involvement of interpreters. This role is inappropriate for it denies the people involved control over their lives and responsibilities. The next three descriptions, while expanding the responsibilities of the interpreter, denied to an extreme any personal involvement by interpreters. But interpreters are involved in a variety of ways, some of which could be termed as personal. Like many situations that involve human beings, interpreting is a complex situation which cannot benefit from such extreme views.

Most practicing interpreters have learned through experience that they are doing more than changing language structures and making cultural adjustments within the language in these encounters. Increasingly, the profession has been subject to conflicting notions of reality. On the one hand, the field, particularly in sign language interpreting, has established comparatively rigid professional standards of behavior and expectations of events, which derive from views built on monologic, public situations where the flow of the message is basically one-way and the receiver is seen as passive. On the other hand, most interpreters now recognize different interpretations of roles and functions that grow from smaller, "real-life" situations in which the interpreter must take an active, participatory stance in the communication between two active participants. Evidence for this can be found in national newsletters, in papers given at conventions, and in a new introductory book on interpreting (Frishberg, 1986: 28), which quotes an interpreter who explains:

> And the interpreter needs to take that on, as part of their role, as "communication cop," because they're the bilingual person in the situation, and they're going to know the timing and the rhythm and the pause sequencing and the languages and know when is an appropriate time.

A model based on the conduit framework leaves out too many factors that play a role in determining meaning.

Another reason such a model is not successful is that [. . .] although we commonly think the primary or basic work of an interpreter occurs in the language exchange, this may be the lesser of interlocutor roles. Condon and Fathi (1975: 206) explain:

> That is, a particular utterance arises from an individual and not from a language in general and it must be re-expressed in a particular choice of words and not just in anything intelligible in that language. It is hard enough to paraphrase within the same language and within the same value system what a speaker meant; it is obviously far more difficult to act within another language that divides reality differently, is related to a different system of values, and is possibly articulated in a different tone of voice.

Assuming that two speakers truly do not know the other's language, the only participant who can logically maintain, adjust, and, if necessary, repair differences in structure and use is the interpreter. Because interpreters are the only bilinguals in these situations, the knowledge of different linguistic strategies and conversational control mechanisms resides in them alone. This means that the interpreter is an active, third participant with potential to influence both the direction and the outcome of the event, and that the event itself is intercultural and interpersonal rather than simply mechanical and technical.

References

Arjona, Etilvia (1984) "The Education of Translators and Interpreters," In M. McIntire (ed.) *Proceedings of the Fourth National Conference of Interpreter Trainers. New Dialogues in Interpreter Education*, Silver Spring, MD: Registry of Interpreters for the Deaf, pp. 111–38.

Brislin, Richard W. (ed.) (1976) Introduction. *Translation: Applications and Research.* New York: Gardner Press.

Caccamise, Frank, Dirst, R., DeVries, R., Heil, J., Kirchner, C., Kirchner, S., Rinaldi, A. and Stangerone, J. (1980) *Introduction to Interpreting*, Silver Spring, MD: Registry of Interpreters for the Deaf.

Cokely, Dennis (1984) "Response to Etilvia Arjona on Evaluation," in M. McIntire (ed.) *Proceedings of the Fourth National Conference of Interpreter Trainers. New Dialogues in Interpreter Education*, Silver Spring, MD: Registry of Interpreters for the Deaf, pp. 139–50.

Condon, John and Fathi, Yousef (1975) *Introduction to Intercultural Communication*, New York: Macmillan.

Frishberg, Nancy (1986) *Interpreting: An Introduction*, Silver Spring, MD: Registry of Interpreters for the Deaf.

Fritsch-Rudser, Steven (1988) Workshop presentation, Region I RID Conference, Boston, Massachusetts.

Ingram, Robert (1974) "A Communication Model of the Interpreting Process," *Journal of the Rehabilitation of the Deaf* 7: 3–9.

—— (1985) "Simultaneous Interpretation of Sign Languages: Semiotic and Psycholinguistic Perspectives," *Multilingua*, 4 (2): 91–102.

Seleskovitch, Danica (1978) *Interpreting for International Conferences*, Washington, D.C.: Pen and Booth.

Solow, Sharon N. (1980) *Sign Language Interpreting: A Basic Resource*, Silver Spring, MD: National Association of the Deaf.

Witter-Merithew, Anna (1986) "Claiming Our Destiny," *RID Views* [Newsletter of the Registry of Interpreters for the Deaf] October, p. 12.

I T IS LARGELY thanks to Cecilia Wadensjö that the discourse-based study of interpreting in community settings has become widely accepted as a major line of research in Interpreting Studies. A 1978 graduate of the diploma course in interpreting at the University of Stockholm, Wadensjö embarked on her doctoral studies in the mid-1980s at Linköping University, Sweden, where she received her PhD in Communication Studies in 1992. Her thesis on dialogue interpreting in immigration hearings and medical encounters, published in 1992 by the local university press as something of a "rough diamond," drew widespread attention and inspired much further research precisely at a time, in the mid-1990s, when community interpreting was "taking off" as a major challenge to those involved in training and research.

Wadensjö has remained active both as a state-certified freelance interpreter and as a researcher affiliated with the Department of Communication Studies at Linköping University. Thanks to her frequent participation in international translation/interpreting studies events and numerous guest lectures in Europe and overseas, her approach has received wide recognition in the Interpreting Studies community and beyond. In 1998 she published an "authoritative" version of her seminal work, and has gone on to apply her research approach also to interpreting in the media.

The paper reprinted here was first presented (with a different title) at the 1991 Elsinore Conference on "Teaching Translation and Interpreting," and thus reflects the pristine quality of Wadensjö's pioneering work. While not included in the proceedings volume of that conference (Dollerup and Loddegaard 1992), it was published in the launching issue of the journal *Perspectives: Studies in Translatology*, edited by Cay Dollerup at the University of Copenhagen.

Further reading: Linell *et al.* 1992; Wadensjö 1992, 1993, 1995, 1997, 1998, 1999.

Cecilia Wadensjö

THE DOUBLE ROLE OF A DIALOGUE INTERPRETER

Dialogue (community) interpreting

THE "DIALOGUE INTERPRETER" (in Swedish: "dialogtolk," or "kontakttolk,") is a factor to be reckoned with in the Swedish social welfare system. She[1] works in institutional settings, such as police stations, social welfare centers, hospitals and courts, where she provides service for laymen and officials, when they speak different languages. Yet, at the same time, she may enable the monolingual interlocutors, conventionally viewed as the primary parties in these kinds of bilingual encounters, to exert a certain mutual *control*.

In a functional sense the Dialogue Interpreter could be compared to what is in English called "community interpreter" (e.g. Shackman 1984). On the other hand, the Swedish Dialogue Interpreter enjoys a professional status, with trade unions and state authorization. The professionality implies that, unlike in countries with community interpreting and the like, the Swedish interpreter's work is regulated by an official code of conduct. The codex states, in short, that the Dialogue Interpreter should *only* interpret, i.e. relay *everything* said, and relay what was said *the way* it was said. In other words, her work is defined by approximately the same professional rules as those applicable for court interpreting in many countries. It follows along with an official principle of interpreters' neutrality.

Interpreting as answering

Interpreting, as well as translating, can be regarded as an "act of communication" (Snell-Hornby 1988: 44). All utterances are understood *in* a communicative context. This goes for everybody, not only for professional interpreters. If the situational context of language interpreting is not taken into consideration in retrospective analyses, there is a great risk of making quite a different sense of what was said, compared to how it was originally understood, both by primary parties and interpreter(s). Originals and renditions are, in equal means, answers to an interactional situation on a turn-by-turn local level, and at a global level of situation type (such as the police interrogation, the diplomatic negotiation, the informal chat, etc.). Given a dialogical view on language and language use, any utterance has the faculty of being an "OTBET" ["answer"] (Bakhtin 1986: 286), but with both retroactive and proactive properties (see also Marková 1990: 1–22). Accordingly, the verbal activity performed by a Dialogue Interpreter on duty could be defined as *answering*, from a culturally and socially established role, in specific cultural contexts. Consequently, more exact than as an individual's "act of communication" the Dialogue Interpreter's work could be described and explored as a role incumbent's *interaction in a social context* of a particular kind – a bilingual face-to-face encounter.

Common-sense understanding of interpreters' activity, as well as many interpreters' official commission, is that they are to render what others say, and that is all. Discussions, among both lay and professional theorists in the field, about what it means to provide just pure, or simply adequate renditions, easily lead on to considerations concerning what such a product and/or activity *ought* to be like.

By definition a copy does not equal the original. What then, are the minimal requirements for arguing that a copy is a copy? What minimal criteria should a rendition fulfill to be counted as a copy? This is one of the major topics underlying a lot of studies on translation. When should a text be considered as a translation or/ and the product of translating activity? What would turn it into something else?

Even a cursory glance at the collected transcriptions of the Dialogue Interpreters' contributions to discourse in the Swedish study "Contact through interpreters"[2] demonstrates that if the criteria were to include a word-by-word transfer, the number of instances would be rather few. This, of course, is just what could be expected. Different languages provide a speaker with different conventional verbal means by which to express herself. Comparing Russian and Swedish, the two languages in question here, there are lots of regular differences in lexical, grammatical and prosodic means as well as in syntactical constructions, phraseologisms, etc. It is also a well-known fact that opinions about standards in one language and their counterparts in others may vary. Thus, if one looks more carefully at the few instances where renditions look indeed very copy-like, as far as e.g. number of lexical items, style and means of emphasis are concerned, it is easily seen that the originals all open up possible alternative renditions, which could be considered at least as adequate, faithful, efficient, or even better, from some other perspective. In many cases one would end up in endless discussions about whether or not a specific rendition of a particular original is really the right, the adequate or the optimal one, no matter whether this is assessed "objectively," or in special regard to a particular context. It is in the nature of language that an utterance is always open for further interpretation (Bakhtin 1986).

One way to get beyond this problem in studies of translation and interpreting is to apply a descriptive approach, as suggested by for instance Toury (e.g. 1980), Hermans (1985) and others. The point in using authentic data is that translators, or, in this case, interpreters, have actually produced what they, their users, and subsequently the retrospect analyst, understood/understand and accepted/accepts as renditions of utterances (originals).

The Dialogue Interpreter's self-image

A Dialogue Interpreter's work consists of enabling exchange of information and experiences. Her identity as Dialogue Interpreter comes from the fact that her contributions are provided in interaction with persons who cannot (or do not wish to) speak each other's language. The Dialogue Interpreter's role, no doubt, is a central one in these persons' mutual communication, due to her unique access to the two languages in which they talk. On the one hand, she relays their respective utterances, and, on the other, she co-ordinates the flow of talk between them.

In a more detailed description of how these tasks are fulfilled one could start in Dialogue Interpreters' self-images, based on the partly codified *normative role*, to use a term from Goffman (1961), that is, what she in principle thinks she ought to be doing when she does a good job. In her thus idealized role, the Dialogue Interpreter could be compared with a copying-machine, who without any personal engagement is *duplicating* what is said in the primary parties' originals in the corresponding form in another language. Another frequent metaphor is the "telephone": the Dialogue Interpreter is thought of as a channel, an instrument *conveying* information, someone who merely technically affects the words, messages, utterances of the monolingual parties. Talking about what the Dialogue Interpreter ought to or ought not to do sometimes calls to the mind the work of a cook, who, striving to *preserve* taste, *prepares* goods to make them digestible for a particular consumer. Not only active dialogue interpreters and their instructors and users express their understanding of an interpreter's work by these metaphors. They are referring both to the relaying aspect of the Dialogue Interpreter's role and to the co-ordinating aspect of her task, even if there are obvious cases where the analogies do not hold water.

The co-ordinating aspect implies that, in interaction, the Dialogue Interpreter normally takes/is given every second turn at talk. A stylized version of a conversation where a Dialogue Interpreter (DI) and two monolingual parties are talking, e.g. a professional (P), speaking the majority language, and a foreign lay person (F), speaking her own language, may be presented as follows:

P: Utterance 1 (in the majority (P's) language)
DI: Utterance 1′ (= rendition of U1 in the foreign language)
F: Utterance 2 (in the foreign (F's) language)
DI: Utterance 2′ (= rendition of U2 in P's language)
P: Utterance 3 (in P's language)
DI: Utterance 3′ (= rendition of U3 in F's language)
etc.

In short, from a normative point of view, the products of Dialogue Interpreter-activity are (or rather, should be) provided in between each and every original utterance, and are copies of these, re-coded in another language. All information explicitly expressed in a primary party's original, including the style and form in which it is expressed, is relayed as closely as possible; i.e. the propositional content explicit in the original utterance (the "what") is relayed, with approximately the same illocutionary force (the "how"). As one notes, this norm concerns only the interpreter as *text-producer*.

A retrospect analysis of the DI-contributions as kinds of texts leads to two mutually compatible typologies. Seen as products of relaying, on the one hand, one must distinguish between *renditions* and *non-renditions*. On the other hand, as products of co-ordinating, Dialogue Interpreter-talk must be categorized according to yet other principles. These will be presented below.

The typologies will be illustrated by reference to data from an encounter at the immigration division of a Swedish local police station. The extracts are from a corpus of all in all 20 meetings, half of which are from this kind of setting, and the other half from health-care institutions.

The Dialogue Interpreter at work: relaying

Among renditions, one could distinguish the following types: *close*, *expanded*, *reduced* and *substituting* renditions. In some cases, the Dialogue Interpreter-contributions following an original cannot be assessed in terms of a one-to-one relation between rendition and original. Thus, in some cases, there will be *summarizing renditions*. In yet others, there is simply *no rendition*.

Expanded renditions

Through expanded renditions the Dialogue Interpreter provides a text which includes some explicitly verbalized information in addition to what is explicitly expressed in the original utterance. This is illustrated in the following extract.

The participants were: **Pia**, a young female police officer, interrogating **Alex**, a speaker of Russian, **a**pplying for a prolonged residence permit. **Iza i**nterpreted between the two.[3] At one stage during the encounter Pia posed a question about summer activities. Alex mentioned some things he had been doing which Iza relayed continuously. Finally the applicant concluded:

Extract (1)

(G 26:6)

    Alex: более или менее я вот **так** проводил.
            *this was more or less **how** I spent [it].*

→ Iza: och det var **ungefär** som jag tillbringade sommaren.
            *and this was **roughly** how I spent the summer.*

This is a simple example of how the Dialogue Interpreter-contribution constitutes an expanded rendition. Iza could assume, inferring from the local surrounding context, that in his original, Alex referred to "the summer." This is made explicit in the subsequent rendition. In this fashion, the Swedish text was also given in a more correct form, a written-language style, compared to the original Russian.

Extract (2)

(G 26:12)
> Pia: e::: (.) ja i allmänhet tror jag att jag fråg- när jag fråga **ni** så
> menar jag . . . alltså både **du** och din fru.
> *e:::(.) yes in general I think that I as- when I asked **you** (plural form)*
> *then I mean . . . that is both **you** (singular form) and your wife.*
>
> → Iza: но если я спрашиваю вас то я нормально е:::
> имею в виду вас обоих. значит вас вместе. вас и-
> с женой.
> *but if I ask you (plural form) then I normally e::: have in mind both*
> *of you. that is you (plural form) together. you (plural form) and-*
> *and [your] wife.*

Extract (2) illustrates how, by expanding, the Dialogue Interpreter *specifies* what is expressed in fewer words in the original. Expanded renditions typically specify and/ or disambiguate the referential and interactional meaning of a given original. Yet, interestingly enough, they also work in the opposite direction. By adding extra information to what is explicitly expressed in the original, the rendition can open up a broader and more complex understanding of what was originally said. This two-fold function is found also in the reduced rendition, the type of Dialogue Interpreter-talk to be illustrated next.

Reduced renditions

Through reduced renditions the Dialogue Interpreter provides a text which contains less explicitly verbalized information than the original utterance.

A simple case of this is illustrated in extract (3), when Pia continued on the theme of summer activities:

Extract (3)

(G 26:7)
> Pia: har ni gjort nånting? speciellt i sommar?
> *have you done anything? special this summer?*
> (1 s)
> Pia: <u>rest eller . . . ?</u>
> <u>*travelled or . . . ?*</u>
> → Iza: <u>вы не занимались?</u> чем-то::: (.) интересным?
> летом.
> <u>*didn't you do?*</u> *something::: (.) interesting? this summer.*

Iza started out relaying, while Pia simultaneously was adding something to the original. The result was overlapping speech. What was overlapped then, "travelled or . . . ?" has no counterpart in the rendition.

Another circumstance leading to reduced renditions is illustrated in extract (4). In the encounter, Pia shortly later took up another question, "what plans do you have for the future?" The applicant replied:

Extract (4)

> (G 26:8)
>
> Alex: (clears throat) (.) на будущее? чтобы. е::: значит желательно поскорее овладеть шведским языком,
> *(clears throat) (.) for the future? to e::: that is preferably as fast as possible master the Swedish language,*
>
> → Iza: för att så snart som möjligt behärska svenska,
> *in order as fast as possible to master Swedish,*

It will be seen then that Alex' question of clarification "for the future?" and the hedges in the beginning of his utterance "to e::: that is" are reduced if one compares the rendition with the original. Hence, Iza's rendition narrows down referential and interactional meaning, relative to Alex' statement.

Extract (5)

> (G 26:8)
>
> Pia: vad har ni för planer för framtiden?
> *what plans do you have for the future?*
>
> → Iza: какие у вас имеются планы на будущее?
> *what plans do you have for the future?*
> (2 s)

It can be noted that the question preceding his answer, "what plans do you have for the future?" in Swedish and Russian, would count as a case of *close rendition*. Yet, interestingly enough, it is discovered much later in the encounter that the monolingual parties had discrepant views on its meaning, i.e. on whose affairs they had actually been discussing at this particular moment. It turns out that Alex believed that the officer was asking about his personal plans. She, on the other hand, assumed that he was speaking about himself as well as his wife. This must be explained by reference to different cultural conventions. In a Swedish–Swedish exchange between people of the age and status of Pia and Alex, the use of second person plural would normally indicate that two or more individuals were being talked to or about. In a Russian–Russian talk, in contrast, the *vous*-form is the regular way to address one person (given a polite conversation between grown-up, unacquainted people).

Substituting renditions

Substituting renditions are found in those cases where the Dialogue Interpreter provides a rendition which is a more complex transformation of the information made explicit in the original utterance, including sometimes both expansion and reduction at the same time.

There was a subtle example of this already in excerpt (1). If the stress on "how" in Alex' original indicated that his story was finished, the emphasis on "roughly" in Iza's rendition rather suggested that more information could be provided/elicited. Extract (2) illustrated another substitution. It is connected to the one exemplified in extract (6) below, drawn from earlier in the encounter at the immigration division.

At this stage, Alex had listed some of his plans for the future. But Pia was not entirely satisfied. She continued asking:

Extract (6)

> (G 26:8)
> Pia: nå din **fru** då?
> *but your **wife** then?*
> Iza: и ваша жена?
> *and your wife?*
> (1 s)
> Pia: nå'ra speciella planer. för det här gäller ju främst **dig**,
> *any special plans. because this concerns first and foremost **you** (singular form),*
> → Iza: это касается конечно в первую очередь вас, (.) но планы вашей жены.
> *this concerns of course first and foremost you, (2 p. plural) but the plans of your wife.*

The following features in this dialogue may possibly have been decisive for the subsequent exchange. For one thing, the emphasis on "you" in the original is underlined both by the stress and by the fact that it is mentioned last. In the rendition, on the other hand, the word order stresses "the plans." This simple example illustrates a tendency which is not unusual with renditions, namely that they start by what the original states last. This would suggest that the Dialogue Interpreter in these cases memorizes and retrieves in a somewhat opposite order. This instance shows that it may result in a slight shift of emphasis.

When Iza finished "but the plans of your wife?," she in a sense connected the beginning of Pia's latest utterance "any special plans" with what she said in the previous turn, "but your wife then?" (which had already been relayed once). Thus, the rendition pointed at in (6) is both expanded and reduced in relation to the immediately prior original. Moreover, the pronoun of address *you*, in the singular, is in the rendition substituted by *you* in the plural. Following the Russian convention, Iza used the *vous*-form, speaking for Pia, instead of the *tu*-form, given by the officer, which is the conventional form in a Swedish context (whereas the *vous*-form in a similar Swedish–Swedish talk would be overtly formal, as was seen above).

If the point of Pia's utterance was to elicit information about Alex' wife's plans, Iza's relaying did indeed work in this direction. However, in the rendition the meaning of "det här," "это" ("this"), gets referred to the answer(s) Alex should give, or to the interrogation as a whole, whereas Pia's original opens up other understandings, such as "what has already been said (and noted)." It turned out that Iza's specification, or disambiguation of meaning on this point, was crucial for the development of a misunderstanding between the primary parties. It was not until the Dialogue Interpreter relayed from the written report that people became aware of this. Checking the text of the report at that stage, Alex pointed to a possible mistake. In the piece of talk where this was discovered, one also may distinguish a case of substituting rendition.

Extract (7)

> (G 26:12)
>
> Alex: я понимаю но она задала вопросы **мне** или **нам**?
> я . . .
> *I understand but did she put the questions to **me** or to **us**? I . . .*
>
> → Iza: *e::: har* du ställt frågan beträffande **mig** eller beträffande **oss**?
> *e::: did you ask the question as regards **me** or as regards **us**?*

In (7) an utterance of Alex' was relayed by a different pronoun of address, "you" instead of "she." Moreover, the rendition does not include any introduction such as Alex' "I understand but." Sometimes substitution implies major changes in address and/or illocutionary force in relation to the original.

Summarizing renditions

By means of summarizing renditions, the Dialogue Interpreter provides a new version of what originally was contributed in more than one original utterance, possibly provided by more than one person. For instance, they might be the result of a dialogue between the primary party and the Dialogue Interpreter herself. These renditions often co-exist with *lack of renditions*, that is cases where originals do not have a counterpart in any unit of Dialogue Interpreter-talk.

In a conversation between two persons speaking the same language some utterances can be heard as off-the-record. In an interpreted conversation, the Dialogue Interpreter is a potential off-the-record interlocutor, and she may, more or less deliberately, engage in that kind of exchange. An illustration is given below in the following extract (8).

Alex' question above (in excerpt 7), about "me or us," concerned traveling in the region. Had the interrogator asked about his, or his and his wife's journeys in the summertime? This was unclear to Alex, and apparently his answer was equally unclear to Pia. She started anew:

Extract (8)

> (G 26:13)
>
> Pia: jo men om jag frågar på nytt *så- beträffande er båda.*
>   *yes but if I ask once again then- concerning you both.*
>
> → Iza: но если я спрашиваю заново.
>   *but if I [may] ask again.*

(Here Iza's rendition again represents a case of reduced rendition. It is most likely conditioned by overlapping speech *and* by the consequent fast response by Alex.)

> Alex: конечно тогда м- я могу это сказать.
>   *of course then c- I can say this.*
>
> Iza: да.
>   *yes.*
>
> Alex: разумеется (light laughter)
>   *naturally (light laughter)*
>
> → Iza: е::: вы ехали совместно просто . . . вокруг е:::
>   области? совместно?
>   *e::: did you travel together just . . . around e::: the region? together?*

Iza's last utterance in this extract (8) was not a rendition of Alex' preceding originals. It was a repeated, summarizing rendition of Pia's question before. Alex' statements, "of course then c – I can say this." and "naturally," were interpreted as off-the-record meta-comments. Consequently, if one wishes to retrieve everything said by the primary parties in the Dialogue Interpreter's renditions, one is left with an empty space.

In the exchange following immediately after the one above, the pattern seemed at first to be repeated, but the status of Alex' and Iza's conversation suddenly changed.

Extract (9)

> (G 26:13)
>
> Alex: вокруг области?
>   *around the region?*
>
> Iza: да да летом.
>   *yes yes in the summer.*
>
> Alex: именно вокруг области?
>   *specifically around the region?*
>
> Iza: да
>   *yes*
>
> Alex: и не допустим ещё дальше?
>   *and not for instance further away?*
>
> → Iza: menar du bara i regionen eller menar du också längre än så?
>   *do you mean only in the region or do you mean further away as well?*

In the Dialogue Interpreter-contribution discussed above, the short exchange between Alex and Iza got the status of on-the-record interaction, in contrast to what had happened just before, in (8). Yet, the rendition was the dialogical outcome of Iza's and Alex' exchange. The Dialogue Interpreter summarized what had just been said and specified, in the interest of Alex, with Pia as addressee, adding the more explicit: "do you mean."

The Dialogue Interpreter at work: Co-ordinating

Micro-analysis of interpreted discourse suggests that the Dialogue Interpreter's relaying activity can result in deviations from originals in either of two directions, in specification or despecification relative to the original utterances. This finding supports recent views of translation as practice.

By necessity the interpreter's contributions to discourse have an organizational function. Some Dialogue Interpreter-utterances, the non-renditions, bring to the fore this *co-ordinating* or gatekeeping aspect. Yet, one should note also that renditions, even the "closest" ones, represent certain ways on the part of the Dialogue Interpreter of handling her co-ordinating task.

How then could Dialogue Interpreter-contributions be categorized in terms of different ways of co-ordinating? There is no such straightforward textual approach available as in the case of relaying. A basic observation, though, is that co-ordinating moves, normally, are provided in only one of the two languages. Thus, they are addressed to the person who understands this. Hence, one principle of classification will be whether the Dialogue Interpreter-contribution is a response to the prior talker or whether it constitutes an initiative, prompting the other person to respond next. Another dimension might be explicitness vs implicitness. This may suggest the following taxonomy:

A Implicitly co-ordinating or gatekeeping contributions

The Dialogue Interpreter is implicitly co-ordinating the conversation as a common activity by carrying out the relaying. As illustrated above, different kinds of renditions function so as to condition the primary parties' exchange of talk. The topical trajectory of discourse is partly determined by the Dialogue Interpreter's rendition (or lack of rendition). This is the case however "close" it is, since a rendition by definition is a reformulation within the linguistic system of another language. However, not all renditions are particularly interesting in the perspective of co-ordinating.

B Explicitly co-ordinating contributions

(a)   Responses to prior speaker, hence also addressed to this primary party. For instance:

—   requests for clarification,
—   comments on substance (or form) of prior speaker's contribution.

The responses tend to produce one-language sequences between the Dialogue Interpreter and the primary party involved, thus temporarily excluding the other from the conversation.

(b)   Initiatives addressed to the other primary party (i.e. not the immediately prior talker). Such contributions give the addressed person the turn she or he would have had according to the unmarked turn-taking scheme of dialogue-interpreted discourse. In effect, these contributions are quite often authored by the Dialogue Interpreter in the interest of the primary party not addressed, trying to elicit information that she or he may need. The Dialogue Interpreter is thus prompting the addressed person to continue discourse from a given point.

These kinds of responses and initiatives, (a) and (b), are normally designed to solicit or invite talk from one of the primary parties, thus, to select the one to become the immediately subsequent speaker. Apart from these, there is a host of Dialogue Interpreter-contributions which are not soliciting so clearly. Their common meta-talk character provides a ground for classification. Hence there are:

(c)   Meta-comments, providing explanations of, for instance:

—   what the other primary party seems to mean,
—   what the other primary party does not understand, or understands in a differ-ent way than the person addressed by the meta-comment,
—   what the other primary party is doing, or going to do in the interaction.

Dialogue Interpreter-contributions which are meta-comments are also addressed to one of the primary parties, either the next-in-turn or the other. However, some-times they are provided twice, once in each language, i.e. they may be two-language contributions much more often than are the Dialogue Interpreter-contributions of the above kinds, (a) and (b).

To illustrate the three main categories under B, explicitly co-ordinating contri-butions, a few more extracts will be provided. They are drawn from the same encounter as those above. To start with, extract (10) below shows a question of clarification from the Dialogue Interpreter.

Extract (10)

(G 26:11)
    Alex: **она** была в Ленинграде. *моя жена*
            she was in Leningrad. *my wife*
→   Iza: *aha.* одна?
            aha. alone?
    Alex: одна. а я . . .
            alone. but I . . .

Iza's contribution in extract (10) functioned as a momentary delay of the ongoing exchange of thoughts between the primary parties. The turn at talk went back to Alex, who started to provide information on a point which Iza considered relevant. Another case of Dialogue Interpreter-response to the immediately prior talker has already been illustrated in extract (9) above.

Extract (9)

> (G 26:13)
>
> Alex: вокруг области?
> *around the region?*
>
> → Iza: да да <u>летом.</u>
> *yes yes <u>in the summer.</u>*
>
> Alex: <u>именно</u> вокруг области?
> *<u>specifically</u> around the region?*
>
> → Iza: да
> *yes*
>
> Alex: и не допустим ещё дальше?
> *and not for instance further away?*
>
> Iza: menar du bara i regionen eller menar du också längre så?
> *do you mean only in the region or do you mean further away as well?*

Iza's contributions here pointed at, "yes yes in the summer." and "yes," did not come out as renditions of what Alex said. She rather provided feedback signals, encouraging Alex to continue talking. Her contributions thus functioned so as to give the turn at talk back to the producer of the preceding original. Selecting him as the next speaker she was concealing for the other primary party what had just been said, at least for the time being.

The next extract, (11), illustrates category (c), meta-comments. When Alex was going to explain how he and his wife spent the summer in different ways, the officer lifted the receiver to answer the phone. As she was listening to the speaker on the phone, Alex turned to Iza:

Extract (11)

> (G 26:12)
>
> Alex: да если это нужно тогда . . .
> *yes if it is needed then . . .*
>
> Iza: <u>да да (xx xx)</u>
> *<u>yes yes (xx xx)</u>*
>
> Alex: <u>и если это</u> . . . она должна-
> *<u>and if this</u> . . . she should-*
>
> → Iza: поправим. поправим.
> *we will correct [it]. we will correct [it].*

In excerpt (11) the Dialogue Interpreter-talk introduced a meta-level. Iza did not relay, but was caught by the illocutionary force of the original in this situation. She responded, and as illustrated in this Dialogue Interpreter-contribution, did so with the authority of a person who is experienced in the situation and in the kind of talk going on. Iza reassured the applicant that corrections to the protocol should be made. Speaking for them both, for the officer and herself, or for the group as a whole, she said: "we will correct [it]. we will correct [it]." This utterance implies a manifestation of the Dialogue Interpreter as a subject involved in discourse.

At this stage, the officer thus answered the phone. When she had put down the receiver, Iza immediately started summarizing her own and Alex' preceding exchange, in the name of the applicant:

Extract (12)

> (G 26:12)
>
> | Pia: | (talks on the phone, puts back the receiver) |
> |---|---|
>
> → Iza: e::: du har frågat **mig** och intervjuat **mig**. då menade- då
> e::: då e::: **tänkte** jag att du åsyftade bara mig **själv**.
> *e::: you have asked **me** and interviewed **me**. then [I] meant- then*
> *e::: then e::: I **thought** that you were only meaning me **myself***
>
> Pia: mhm
> *mhm*
>
> → Iza: du kommer ju att prata med henne. men är det alltså oss
> **båda** du menar då är det lite annorlunda
> *you will talk to her won't you. but [if] you actually mean us*
> ***both** then it is a bit different.*

In terms of relaying, Iza's contributions in excerpt (12) must be characterized as a summarizing rendition. It answers to the prior exchange between Alex and the Dialogue Interpreter herself. Described in terms of co-ordinating, the same utterances illustrate category (b) above, namely an initiative to the other primary party. As such it served to prompt the police officer to continue the exchange on a topic considered relevant from the applicant's point of view. These kinds of Dialogue Interpreter-contributions seem to be quite common when an ongoing conversation is interrupted by something external, in this case a telephone call.

What is simultaneous about consecutive interpreting?

This paper discusses the verbal contributions of a dialogue interpreter on duty in conversation. These have been categorized from two different perspectives, characterizing the two-language talk in terms of the inseparable and intricately interwoven aspects of relaying and co-ordinating. On a macro-sociological level, there is a duality inherent in the function of a dialogue interpreter already in that she, in a sense, exhibits both service and control. In interactions between representatives of the society and laymen, talking to each other in different languages, the Dialogue Interpreter takes/is given a unique, and potentially a powerful, middle position.

The analysis of *authentic Dialogue Interpreter activity* illustrates the theoretical implications of conceptualizing *interpreting as interaction*. This task calls for the application of a new approach to studies in the field. The present article is a plea for a micro-sociological turn in studies of interpreting, and hence for a paradigmatic shift going beyond traditional problems connected to isolating the object of study in the field of translation and interpretation studies.

The empirical data discussed above demonstrate that the Dialogue Interpreter's listenership determines whether the monolingual parties' contributions end up as off-the-record, or as on-the-record talk. Although it is often overlooked in scholarly discussions, listening is obviously an important constituent of conversation. In any kind of interpreting, listening must be carried out simultaneously with talking. But if interpreting a monological speech from an orator at a rostrum implies little or no doubts whether the original(s) indeed is (are) intended to have the status of original(s), the Dialogue Interpreter on duty in conversation is constantly confronted with assessing how, and by whom, interlocutors intend their utterances to be understood. In the course of interaction, the Dialogue Interpreter at work, more or less consciously, evaluates interlocutors' *speakership and listenership*; how the parties relate to the common activities, partly by means of what they say themselves, and partly through how they listen to what others say. In Goffmanian terminology she monitors and contributes to the *participation framework* (Goffman 1981: 226; also Wadensjö 1992). This is one of the important issues for future studies on interpreting.

Notes

1   "She" is the generalized pronoun for Dialogue Interpreters in the present text.
2   [Swedish: *Kontakt genom tolk*], Per Linell and Cecilia Wadensjö, financed by the Bank of Sweden Tercentenary Foundation, (89/44).
3   *Key to transcription:*
     The transcription conventions applied here are a modified version of those invented by Gail Jefferson (Sacks, Schegloff and Jefferson 1974: 731–33). Speech is generally normalized to conventional orthography. Thus, variants of pronunciations are not specified.

     Underlinings in the extracts indicate simultaneous talk.

,	continuing intonation (prosody, possibly also a short pause, indicating that the speaker does not want to drop the turn).
.	terminating intonation (a pause, indicating that the speaker is prepared to relinquish the turn, or, at least, that an informationally completed unit of talk has been issued).
?	rising intonation.

(Note that these punctuation symbols are used to mark intonation terminals, rather than grammatical boundaries as in conventional writing.)

-	sudden cut-off of the current sound.
. . .	open-ended intonation, utterance fading out without an unambiguous intonational terminal.
:	the sound just before has been noticeably lengthened.
(.)	a short silence (micro-pause).
(1 s)	one second silence.
((looks up))	gives a description of a person's nonverbal activity.
boldface	emphasis, which may be signaled by increases in pitch and/or amplitude.
* *	(framing part of an utterance) the framed part is pronounced in low voice.
(xxx)	transcriber heard talk but the words could not be identified.
(something)	transcriber thought she heard a certain word (here: "something") being uttered, but is not completely sure.
italics	the author's translation of utterances into English.
[ ]	(framing part of an utterance) marks words added in the English translation.
→	a righthand arrow marks an utterance to which the author refers in the text.

References

Bakhtin, M. Michail (1986) [originally 1979] *Estetika slovesnogo tvortjestva*, Moscow: Isskustvo.

Goffman, Erving (1961) *Encounters: Two Studies in the Sociology of Interaction*, Indianapolis and New York: The Bobbs-Merrill Company.

—— (1981) *Forms of Talk*, Philadelphia: University of Pennsylvania Press.

Hermans, Theo (ed.) (1985) *The Manipulation of Literature. Studies in Literary Translation*, London and Sydney: Croom Helm.

Marková, Ivana (1990) Introduction, in I. Marková and K. Foppa (eds) *The Dynamics of Dialogue*, London: Harvester Wheatsheaf.

Sacks, Harvey, Schegloff, Emanuel A. and Jefferson, Gail (1974) "A Simplistic Systematics for the Organization of Turn-Taking for Conversation," *Language* 50: 696–735.

Shackman, Jane (1984) *The Right to Be Understood. A Handbook on Working with, Employing and Training Community Interpreters*, Cambridge: National Extension College.

Snell-Hornby, Mary (1988) *Translation Studies – An Integrated Approach*, Amsterdam and Philadelphia: John Benjamins.

Toury, Gideon (1980) *In Search of a Theory of Translation*, Tel Aviv: The Porter Institute for Poetics and Semiotics.

Wadensjö, Cecilia (1992) "Interpreting as Interaction: On Dialogue Interpreting in Immigration Hearings and Medical Encounters," dissertation, Linköping: Linköping University, Department of Communication Studies.

THE PAPER BY Granville Tate and Graham H. Turner, two British Sign Language interpreters, is a paradigm case of action research in a field characterized by dynamic developments in the profession as well as increasing research activity. Granville Tate and others working towards their MA degrees in BSL/English interpreting at the Deaf Studies Research Unit of the University of Durham in the mid-1990s were strongly dissatisfied with the "conduit model" of interpreting underlying their Code of Ethics and collected evidence from interpreters to develop a more realistic account. Tate, who graduated in 1997 and worked as a full-time interpreter before becoming a research associate at the University of Durham in 2000, completed the study in collaboration with Graham Turner, who was then teaching and doing research at the DSRU. Graham Turner, whose first degree was in linguistics, did his postgraduate work at the University of Durham in the late 1980s and early 1990s. Having worked on an award-winning BSL/English Dictionary project (Brien 1992), he became principal researcher in 1993 for a major study of sign language interpreting in the British courts (Brennan and Brown 1997). Following his move to the University of Central Lancashire in 1995, Turner was appointed Senior Lecturer and became course leader of the newly created interpreting program in 1998.

The paper reprinted here was originally published in 1997 in the special issue on interpreting guest-edited by Graham Turner for *Deaf Worlds* (vol. 13, no. 3).

Further reading: Turner 1995, 1996.

Granville Tate and Graham H. Turner

THE CODE AND THE CULTURE
Sign language interpreting – in search of the new breed's ethics

Introduction

ANALYSES OF THE role and responsibilities of sign language interpreters have continued to develop since the "emergence" of the profession (Scott Gibson 1991). The nature of the relationship between service providers and consumers has been of concern in the field (Turner 1995 and 1996). In the UK and elsewhere, Codes of Ethics/Practice have been a principal tool used to guide professional behaviour, and they have been revised to take into account changing experiences in interpreting praxis as well as changing theoretical underpinnings.

What no Code can do is to anticipate all possible situations in which an interpreter may find her/himself and offer an "off-the-peg" solution to whatever dilemmas may arise. So interpreters make sense of problems, and find "spur-of-the-moment" strategies to address them, based upon their best understanding of the *spirit* of the Code, adherence to which is a condition of their registration status. Just as the rules of any sport evolved over time as players and umpires faced newly challenging situations on the field of play, so interpreters in these early years of professionalism have been required to "play the game" in the best way they can.

The question asked in this paper focuses upon one particular aspect of the role of an interpreter, seeking to explore the perspective upon it highlighted in the profession's ethical guidelines and practitioners' interpretations of those guidelines in situated communication events. Our starting point was a sense that in some ethically complex contexts, either the strictures of the Code itself or interpreters' readings of its prescriptions were often at odds with actual practice. The aim, then, was to begin to look a little more carefully, from the interpreter's point of view, at some problem circumstances and thus to get a handle on some apparent discrepancies between the profession's encoded regulatory principles and their practical realisation.

In the following pages, therefore, we first set out briefly some of the underpinning knowledge informing our own approach to the issue; second, sketch the context in which our study was undertaken; third, present the "dilemma" scenarios highlighted and exemplify interpreters' responses to them, offering our perspective on the messages embedded in these responses; and finally, suggest a number of pointers to future developments.

Codes and Models

Interpreting practice in England, Wales and Northern Ireland is subject to regulation by the Council for the Advancement of Communication with Deaf People (CACDP). This body publishes and promulgates the Code of Ethics to which BSL-English interpreters are professionally bound to adhere. The Code is not explicitly wedded to any particular model of interpreters and interpreting, but the *Zeitgeist* in the field inevitably leads to the materialisation at any particular time of a "professional culture" tending towards certain norms. In the UK's case, we would argue – having been involved in providing, coordinating and using interpreting services, as well as in the training of interpreters – that the dominant model of interpreting has been of the "machine" kind (the interpreter is essentially just a device that takes no part in communicative proceedings other than dispassionately to relay messages between individuals not sharing a common language – cf. Roy 1993). Bound up inextricably with this, we believe, the CACDP Code is often *taken both to prescribe and to reflect* this kind of "machine" model.

Broadly speaking, machine interpreting has been seen – in all relevant sectors of the community – as a tool of empowerment for Deaf people. Simply put, machines do what they're told. They're under instruction: no instruction, no action. Machines don't *generate* their own contributions to the job in hand: they simply respond as programmed to external stimuli (levers pulled, buttons pressed, etc.). In part, early versions of interpreting Codes erred on the side of caution with respect to seeking to ensure that the stipulated role of the interpreter was essentially *reactive* and not *proactive*. To a certain extent, this was doubtless a response to the view that, prior to the emergence of interpreting as a defined occupation, Deaf people had too often been preceded through life's doors by hearing people saying "What he/she wants is. . . .". The Code made clear that the aim was for the interpreter to open the door, but first across the threshold, setting and executing their own agenda, would be the Deaf consumer.

This sense that interpreters have a significant but limited part to play in providing access to communication and information for Deaf people continues to be very real and to help define current role-norms. People fear less machine-like models because they risk disempowering Deaf people – anything other than machine can be hard to distinguish from a paternalistic "follow me through the door" approach. However, the ideologically normative strength of the perspective which says that it is only proper for the interpreter to be entirely uninvolved and mechanised – facilitated by its tidy "black-and-whiteness", the unambiguous directives for action which it conveniently supplies – has created a situation where, we would argue, professionals in the field have been reluctant openly to look at what they know *actually*

happens in many situations. This is made difficult since strictures concerning con-
fidentiality within the Code make it hard (if not impossible) to find a professionally
proper space in which interpreters are able to discuss the resolution of role-dynamic
dilemmas. The hegemony of "machine is the only way because its the only way to be
uninvolved" has created a conspiracy of silence – not an actively desired one on the
part of practitioners, but one which they feel duty-bound to observe nonetheless –
about the very real *disempowering* effects of a blanket aspiration to machine-like
behaviour. It has created a reluctance to talk about how interpreters are involved in
interpreting situations and how they do generate action, make choices and exercise
decisive power in hidden and not-so-hidden ways. This very conspiracy forces interpreters into the position of making their discretionary choices and exercising power
covertly with the result that individual interpreters find themselves resolving in
isolation the inevitable role conflicts of their job (Cooke 1995).

Perhaps the barrier to open discussion of this issue has its roots in the early
development of interpreting as a distinct occupational role. At the time, there was a
need, on the one hand, to carve out a distinct area of expertise and, on the other, to
be seen to be operating from a perspective different from that of social/welfare
work, which was often seen as patronising and controlling. The professional position
is, in the UK, now being carved out fairly clearly. Interpreting is now a maturing
occupation. It has broken away from social work. The pressure toward a "machine"
perspective which existed in the early days – and perhaps was a necessary stage to go
through – has diminished. This allows us to seek to explore definitions of roles and
responsibilities in other ways.

Engaging with reality

At this point we would like to take up a number of hypothetical dilemmas. We can
think of them as becoming dilemmas partly because the Code is – in itself – too
stark to tell interpreters how to negotiate the many varied and complex real-life
situations which they encounter. Training and apprenticeship should flesh out this
ethical skeleton and give it a practical dimension – but part of the "conspiracy" to
date has been the unaddressed impoverishment of processes and procedures that
would give substance to any such assurance. The Code by itself, and the mechanistic
role model it has most commonly been taken to endorse, lack the textured richness
or are too one-dimensional always to enable interpreters to act in ways suitable for
the situation. In fact, this Code-role can sometimes seem to *disable* interpreters by
encouraging them to act in one way when they know they could be more effective if
they acted in another way which seems to them to contradict the Code.[1]

The hypothetical dilemmas that follow were put to interpreters[1] for their
anonymous responses. These are dilemmas which may occur at any time in an
interpreter's career. We tried to draw upon situations from our own experiences
and from those passed on to us by other interpreters. We asked respondents to try
to answer in terms of what they felt they really *would* do – rather than what they felt
they were *supposed* to do – if they found themselves in these situations. As an attempt
to begin to grapple with actual professional behaviour, this is, we recognise, in itself
methodologically inadequate; however, all studies have their limitations – if these are

acknowledged for what they are, the results may still be of value. What is most significant in this case, we would suggest, is respondents' articulation of why they have given a particular set of answers.

Given that the approach to questioning adopted here was open-ended (we didn't use a multiple-choice or otherwise readily quantifiable procedure), the statistics we have generated – in each case, we give a figure for those taking relatively mechanistic vs non-mechanistic stances – are based upon *our* interpretative perceptions as analysts of the implications of the response data. Again, we make no attempt to hide any methodological weaknesses.

We originally posed six of these hypothetical questions, but have selected four for this paper. These four all revolve, in our view, around some aspect of the role-model issue: specifically, all four pertain to the mechanistic nature, or otherwise, of interpreter behaviour, the use of professional judgement, and interpreter-generated *input* to the interactional event.

The scenarios and analysis of responses

Tablets scenario

> You are interpreting with a Deaf patient visiting her GP. She is prescribed a drug called Visapan (which the doctor says is powerful) to be taken once a day. In your interpretation you fingerspell the name. The Deaf person nods calmly and signs "Is it okay to take several vitamins at once?" You interpret the question to the doctor and she says "Yes, of course, that's no problem." You are aware that there has been a misunderstanding, i.e. that the Deaf person is referring to the Visapan as vitamins. You have interpreted everything by the book. What do you do, and why?

In this situation some 99% prefer non-mechanistic options. Only one respondent indicated that they would not generate any input of their own.

Two examples which we took to be indicative of non-mechanistic responses:

> *"Forget the book and enable communication."*
> *"I have to live with myself not the Code of Practice."*

Baby scenario

> You are interpreting with a Deaf mother-to-be when she goes for a scan. You know that she doesn't want to know the sex of her baby, but the gynaecologist suddenly comes out with the information that it's a boy! What do you do, and why?

Of the respondents to this question, approximately 77% stated that they would make some kind of non-mechanistic intervention, while some 23% felt that they would not.

Here are two examples of responses from the first group. The first example is representative of the vast majority of responses:

> "I think I would tell her that the doctor has just said the sex but 'you don't want to know, right?' (also explain what I said to the doctor). It's difficult 'cos if hearing the slip would have been heard."
>
> "Don't tell the mum, but explain to the doctor that you are not going to tell her."

Now two examples of replies from the second group:

> "Interpret the info., i.e., do the job."
>
> "I would sign 'it's a boy' because (i) the mother should have made it clear that she did not want to know or (ii) if she had made that clear and the Dr. forgot then a hearing person would have heard and by my signing it the deaf woman would be equal to a hearing woman."

Analysis – tablets and baby scenarios

A key part of the Code at present is its prescription that nothing should be added to or omitted from the meaning of what is uttered by the principal interacting parties. In both of these scenarios a very high percentage of respondents say they would use a non-mechanistic strategy of some kind. How many real-life situations occur, we find ourselves wondering, where this part of the Code is pragmatically sidestepped? It might be argued that the Code as it stands may not be helping or enabling interpreters to function optimally in such situations. It can create anxiety because it is seen as inappropriate in some situations. Certain questions, we feel, arise from this which demand to be aired.

Why do the overwhelming majority of interpreters, many of whom will be qualified and with experience, feel that in these circumstances adherence to the Code guidelines would need to be suspended? Are they misunderstanding the intention of the Code? If so, why are they doing so? Does their feeling actually accord more closely with Deaf consumers' wishes than the alternative would do? And if the Code is not achieving its aim, what is to be done?

With the *Tablets* scenario the reasoning behind the view that adherence to the Code is secondary is easily understood: the gravity of the situation.

> "When you are dealing in any area with crucial results such as this I think the interpreter has a responsibility to ensure all info is clearly understood."
>
> "This could be a serious error that I am not prepared to live with."

What is very clear from many of the responses is that practitioners feel that the Code specifies a particular role from which they must sometimes depart in order to work effectively. From these responses it would appear that interpreters feel their actual practice may not always conform to the Code-model which guides them. As one respondent comments:

> "*Step out of role – sign and speak: 'I believe there has been a misunderstanding – are Visapan vitamins?' Step back into role. This can easily happen. I am responsible for communication.*"

This respondent is appealing to another set of guidelines to inform practice. The interpreter's own "common sense" alternatives have come to the rescue here – developed through knowledge and experience of interpreting and working with the Deaf community. "I am responsible for communication" is almost a definition of an alternative non-mechanistic model (cf. the "dialogue director" model as described in Tate 1996).

But something seems to us to be going wrong if interpreters genuinely feel that to take the above course of action forces them to act in a way that is actually *contrary* to their professional Code: either the Code needs to say something different, or the way that interpreters are enculturated into their professional understanding of that Code needs to change. Either way, we would argue that there is much to be learned from seeking to be aware of and work *with* the best of practitioners' learned experiences.

Those interpreters who chose not to "intervene" appear to see the same boundaries to good practice as prescribed by the Code's account of their role; the key difference is that they present themselves as preferring not to overstep those boundaries, even in these circumstances. Characteristic of these respondents was the person who, citing the exact sections of the Code which he/she felt disbarred him/her from doing anything other than this, said:

> "*NOTHING, because to do something means that I have to step out of my role as an interpreter.*"

Interview scenario

> You are interpreting for a Deaf person at a job interview. There are no other candidates. While interpreting, you realise that the way the Deaf person is presenting himself in BSL is not going to ensure a positive outcome for him. You know for sure that this Deaf person can do the job superbly. You could polish your voice-over to be in line with the interviewer's expectations . . . What do you do, and why?

In this case, some 68% of respondents claimed that they would straightforwardly reflect the Deaf person's signing without any kind of "intervention". Meanwhile, 32% suggested that they would, in the event, look for one or another non-mechanistic strategy, even if doing so left them feeling rather uncomfortable.

Analysis – interview scenario

To us as we set the question, this scenario opened up the possibility of learning something about the extent to which interpreters felt they should, in fact, be "part-advocate" by leaning towards support for Deaf people's interests where possible and appropriate. This is clearly one of the most significant areas for attention in the current search for a *rapprochement* between mechanistic and non-mechanistic approaches to interpreting [. . .]. In addition, there was scope for discovery in relation to practitioners' views of the limits of cultural mediation.

Many respondents in fact answered as if the question were a test of their impartiality, as two examples make clear:

> *"Not my responsibility to ensure candidate presents well."*
> *"If I polish up the voice-over too much the interviewer may be present at a future occasion when the Deaf person is interpreted by another interpreter . . . They will smell a fish."*

The general theme of the responses in this category was, as more than one person stated:

> *"Give the best voice-over you can to reflect the Deaf person . . ."*

However, this offers no explanation of what it would mean to "reflect" the Deaf person in their voice-over. One of the respondents also offers:

> *"But take into account cultural differences – to be fair."*

The issue of what constitutes cultural mediation is one that emerges awash with question marks here. Does the Code enshrine the kind of "polishing" referred to here as "permissible" behaviour, or not? When does smoothing over cultural gaps become an exercise in sheer creativity as opposed to one evolving naturally from the resources of a given situation?

Sixteen people explicitly (and a few more by implication) permitted themselves – using phrases such as "higher level English but without any additions" – to make adjustments to register, although a number equally explicitly stated that they absolutely would not countenance what were perceived as content improvements. Relatedly, a number of comments carried the implication that the voice-over should be formal almost irrespective of what the Deaf person is doing:

> *"Match English register to interviewer voice."*

This seems odd. Of course one goes into a situation expecting to produce language that is appropriate, but judging that appropriacy is a very delicate matter, not at all simply a matter of getting out the "Interview-speak" file before the session and using it come what may. This suggests that a considerable proportion of interpreters do not appreciate the impact of variation of this order. So the person who wrote:

> *"I would possibly consider raising the register although I would not consider interpreting what has not been said. Nor would I embellish."*

patently does not acknowledge that "raising the register" at one's own discretion is embellishment and as such is non-mechanistic.

A proportion of this group of non-mechanistic respondents would intervene in ways where the reasoning is not linguistic/cultural. Some of the comments here suggested a strong desire to act in a kind of advocative capacity. These respondents wanted, for instance, to:

> "Try to encourage the Deaf person to give more personal facts."
> "Explain to employer the candidate's presentation."

Court scenario

> A young Deaf man has been loitering around his old school. He has been warned off many times with increasing severity. The headmaster has finally become fed up and the matter has gone to court. In court, the magistrate sentences the man to be banned from coming within 500 yards of the school. Nobody has pointed out to the court what place a Deaf school has in the cultural life of such a person. The magistrate seems to be a reasonable sort of chap . . . Do you say anything, and why?

The majority of respondents (69%) feel that they would not say anything, either directly in court or indirectly outwith the formal proceedings to the solicitors or the Deaf man. Many of these people make reference to the view that it is not within their role to take any action here. However, almost one third (31%) say that they would say something to someone.

Analysis – court scenario

Once again we see in the responses a clear readiness to reply in terms of a delimited role-bound territory within which the interpreter is empowered to act:

> "No – not my responsibility [. . .] In any case the Deaf person deserves it. There's not a whisper of a dilemma here."

The non-mechanistic respondents here can be divided into direct and indirect "interveners". The latter would offer information but would seek, so far as the court is concerned, to do so in a discreet and diplomatic way, outwith formal proceedings:

> "Yes, I feel it is part of my role to bridge cultural gaps [. . .] I would probably ask to speak to the defence lawyer in the presence of the Deaf man."

Others would seek to speak directly to the court:

> "I would ask if it was possible to say something on his behalf."
> "I would refer the magistrate to. . . . [Deaf organisations]"

The overriding question for an interpreter in this situation is, "is there justification for saying something to someone?" If it is agreed that the court system may be discriminating against the Deaf man by not being aware of the place the school has in the cultural life of such a person, then the interpreter may be the only one to see how this may affect the outcome. Therefore, the question needing to be asked is, is it ethically proper *not* to say anything? This is different to assuming that the Deaf man is either guilty as charged or not. Some respondents clearly do take a view about whether the man is guilty and use this as a reason for not saying anything:

> *"No way. He broke the law and it's up to justice to deal with him. I am not an advocate."*

Of course, this example is one in which the factors affecting any decision interact in complex ways. We do not wish to draw any over-simplistic conclusions from it. What does come across, however, is that there is an ethical dimension to interpreters' decision-making in such a context which is neither accounted for nor entirely guided by the predicted Code-model. Whatever their reasoning – in terms of legality, morality, professionalism and so forth – almost one third of respondents to the survey feel that they would take a non-mechanistic line.

Table 1   Summary of statistics.

Scenario	Non-mechanistic	Mechanistic
Tablet	99%	1%
Baby	77%	23%
Interview	68%	32%
Court	31%	69%

Conclusions

The summary above fundamentally shows that the dominant, mechanistic Code-model does not accord fully with interpreters' own views on their own professional practices: if it did, the left-hand column would (at the very least) consistently feature much smaller numbers than the right. Our key early response to the comments returned by practising interpreters to these questions was that there needed to be a fuller reworking of the Code which would guide interpreters more explicitly on how to respond in the face of dilemmas such as these. This view has shifted over time, so that we would now argue that it is not the *Code* which should change – though complacency is never healthy – so much as the professional *culture* which it is designed to reflect and engender. Pivotal to such change are (a) the educational processes by which practitioners are enculturated and (b) the articulation of the ethical values which underpin the wording of the published Code.

Facing up to any residual complacency, it is possible that the Code can still valuably be revised so that it guides interpreters into ethically *engaged* choices – such as they already make – instead of saying "it's not my responsibility to have an ethical view". They would thus be enabled to make their choices feeling humane, empowered and professional, instead of humane but disempowered and professionally negligent.

Nevertheless, the survey responses suggest to us that interpreters would welcome the availability of guidance on good practice when faced with such dilemmas. The establishment of a resource base which pooled information on strategies adopted in real situations – in other words, where experienced professionals' own interpretations of their Code guidelines were respected and could be accessed to inform future practice – might in itself be a positive step which would clearly acknowledge the inadequacy of any assumption that professional behaviour is unproblematic.

We would argue for the value of using interpreters' experiences in dealing with tricky situations to develop more comprehensive guidelines enabling practitioners to negotiate the complexities and unexpectedness of many real-life situations. When dilemmas occur, and people find good, solid, satisfactory solutions or strategies for dealing with them, then there ought to be an ongoing attempt to codify those strategies in some kind of annex to the basic Code (which represents core interpreter values or ethics). An ever-evolving form of the Code can then develop a kind of "case law". It would not provide all the answers but it would offer interpreters knowledge of how seemingly anomalous or ambiguous situations may be negotiated skilfully whilst still keeping in touch with those basic ethics.

Regulatory bodies for interpreting may declare that they want and encourage and even expect interpreters to use the Code "sensibly", by taking it as a guideline and letting "common sense" decide. The problem is that "common sense" is not common to all. Therefore our conclusion – supported, we would argue, by the variability in responses to our survey questions, and the comments made by interpreters in answering those questions – is that interpreters are looking for more fully articulated written guidelines and a more fully developed education in how to use the Code with sensitivity to context.

At present, our experience is that we face a situation where many interpreters actually expect the Code to guide them in some simple black-and-white fashion: they want the Code to tell them exactly what to do. If our perception is accurate (and we feel that this survey helps to confirm that it is), then it needs to be better established during the education of interpreters that grey goes with the territory, and that would-be professionals had better learn to live with it, and indeed to embrace it. Being able to act competently within the grey zone is an integral part of their professionalism. Enabling trainees to get to grips with this – including learning the underpinning values and reaching an understanding of the complexity and multi-dimensionality of their practical application – will take time and probably substantial periods of apprenticeship.

In conclusion, we would wish to reiterate the need for resistance of the conspiracy of silence. Within interpreting agencies and through interpreting associations, in particular, ways must be found to facilitate the proper exploration of professional dilemmas. (To take one instance, this study threw a harsh light upon the extent to which the notion of "cultural mediation" may presently be papering over cracks.) This can be done with consumers and fellow practitioners to the benefit of all parties.

Finally, once again (cf. Turner 1996), we feel that the study gives evidence for the view that interpreters are typically very ready to relate their actions to the Code – for better or worse. This in itself, we stress, is evidence of a real willingness to accept a fully regulated professional approach which in itself, in principle, gives a very solid foundation.

Note

1   There were a total of 103 replies to the questionnaire: 51 Registered Trainee interpreters and 48 Registered Qualified interpreters. There were 33 male and 70 female respondents. The study began as part of a larger questionnaire survey composed by a group of postgraduate students and supervised primarily by Mary Brennan, along with contributions from David Brien and Richard Brown (as members of the team of the Deaf Studies Research Unit, University of Durham).

References

Cooke, M. (1995) Review of K. Laster and V. Taylor (1994) *Interpreters and the Legal System*, Sidney: The Federation Press. *Forensic Linguistics* 2 (1): 126–32.

Roy C. B. (1993) "The Problem with Definitions, Descriptions and the Role Metaphors of Interpreters", *Journal of Interpretation* 6 (1): 127–54.

Scott Gibson, L. (1991) "Sign Language Interpreting: An Emerging Profession", in S. Gregory and G. M. Hartley (eds) *Constructing Deafness*, London: Pinter Press, in association with The Open University, pp. 253–8.

Tate, G. (1996) "Elements of a Model of the Community Interpreter: Dialogue Interpreting and a Code of Practice", unpublished MS, DSRU, University of Durham.

Turner, G. H. (1995) "Rights and Responsibilities: The Relationship Between Deaf People and Interpreters", *Deafness* 11 (3): 4–8.

—— (1996) "Regulation and Responsibility: The Relationship Between Interpreters and Deaf People", *Deaf Worlds* 12 (1): 1–7.

Looking Ahead

THIS PAPER PROVIDES a felicitous ending to a volume which began by tracing the role of interpreting in Antiquity. While drawing our attention to the marginalization of orality throughout history and to the Eurocentricity of the interpreting profession, Michael Cronin also points to the many historical, political and sociological implications which have yet to be explored. The paper is an abridged version of an essay that first appeared in *Translation and Power* (Tymoczko and Gentzler 2002).

Cronin's interest in interpreting – he teaches interpreting theory on the MA program in conference interpreting at Dublin City University – is part of a much broader agenda. As he notes in *Across the Lines: Travel, Language and Translation*, "Interpreters are valuable not only because of what they do but because of who they are. They are generally part of the host community and as such are conduits for privileged 'inside' information on the society and culture. They confer authenticity and verisimilitude on the account" (Cronin 2000: 72).

Michael Cronin is the Director of the Centre for Translation Studies at Dublin City University as well as a Professional Member (translation/interpreting) and former Chairperson of the Irish Translators' Association. In addition to the book cited above, he is also the author of *Translating Ireland: Translation, Languages, Identities* (Cork University Press, 1996) and a co-editor of *Unity in Diversity: Current Trends in Translation Studies*, the proceedings volume of an international conference held in 1996 at Dublin City University.

Further reading: Cronin 2000; Tymoczko 1990.

Michael Cronin

THE EMPIRE TALKS BACK: ORALITY, HETERONOMY AND THE CULTURAL TURN IN INTERPRETING STUDIES

[. . .] **DESPITE ITS HISTORICAL** antiquity and geographical spread, interpreting studies still remain very much a minority interest in Translation Studies. [. . .] And yet interpreting as an activity that goes on in courts, police stations, social welfare offices, conferences, coach tours, factory floors, journalism assignments, airports, is arguably the most widespread form of translation activity in the world today and has been for tens of thousands of years. Why then this "minoritization" of interpretation? In a world of globalization, increased refugee and immigrant flows, and exponential growth in tourism, interpreting should be a leading area in cultural investigations of language contact, yet this is largely not the case. In addition, power is everywhere in the definition, context and practice of interpreting, yet there has often been a reluctance to reflect on the consequences of power for knowledge in interpreting studies.

In this essay, I will begin by exploring the fundamentally oral nature of interpreting and the neglect by interpreting scholars of precious insights from literacy/orality studies. It will then be argued that interpreting studies are characterised by a signal bias towards prestigious forms of interpreting practice in developed countries and that this geopolitical partiality has to be challenged by a new "cultural turn" in interpreting studies. Similar to what has already occurred in translation studies, this turn would encourage scholars to explicitly address questions of power and issues such as class, gender, race in interpreting situations. Examples are taken from colonial history and the development of tourism to illustrate areas that could be usefully investigated by a more explicitly material history of interpreting, guided by the "cultural turn" paradigm. Particular attention is paid to ambivalent perceptions of the interpreter, to the particular role of the interpreter as returned native, to the shift from heteronomous to autonomous interpreting and to the part played by interpreting in occasioning the emergence of the native as a hermeneutic subject. It is the contention of this essay that a more materialist, politically self-aware approach to interpreting studies would unlock the enormous research potential of this area of translation enquiry and highlight the importance of interpreting and interpreters in any assessment of the impact of translation on humanity, past and present.

Interpreting and orality

[. . .] The overwhelming fact of human language has been its orality. Walter J. Ong, in *Orality and Literacy* (1982), describes the momentous changes brought about in our understanding of the world through the invention of the technologies of writing and printing. The changes are all the more powerful for being unnoticed and he argues that, "Freeing ourselves of chirographic and typographic bias in our under-standing of language is probably more difficult than any of us can imagine" (Ong 1988: 77). Ong bemoans the fact that philosophy and intellectual history have largely neglected orality studies, but his indictment could be extended to translation studies. [. . .]

The neglect of orality in interpreting studies is equally disturbing. Comments on differences between translating and interpreting in translation history are largely confined to the observation that speech is ephemeral and that evidence for interpret-ing must be sought indirectly through written sources. The authors of "Interpreters and the Making of History" in *Translators through History*, edited by Jean Delisle and Judith Woodsworth, note the following:

> The spoken word is evanescent. Our knowledge of the past performance of interpreters tends to be derived from such sources as letters, diaries, memoirs and biographies of interpreters themselves, along with a variety of other documents, many of which were only marginally or incidentally concerned with interpreting.
>
> (Bowen *et al.* 1995: 245)

The observation, while self-evidently true, tends to miss a more fundamental point about translation and orality. [. . .] Any examination of the role of interpret-ing in translation history cannot examine an oral practice through the explicative apparatus of chirographic and typographic translation. It is not simply a question of the words vanishing once spoken. The context of primary orality means that the meaning of the exchange will be strikingly different from a similar exchange in the context of literacy. If we do not recognise the specific psychodynamics of orality, then our analyses of interpreting encounters will repeat assumptions that underlie depictions of unsophisticated and dissembling natives. The fact that an oral culture may not deal in items such as geometrical figures, abstract characterisation, the reasoning processes of formal logic, comprehensive descriptions and explicitly articulated self-analysis often leads to the biased conclusion by external commenta-tors that non-literate persons are, at best, naive and, at worst, confused and

dishonest. Literates have generally failed to recognise the specificity and sophistica-
tion of oral thinking, and historians of translation have also so far failed to fully
appreciate the importance of orality studies for their subject area. Indeed, it might
be argued that the hold of literacy on our analytical worldview means that we tend
to exaggerate the importance of textual translation and ignore the far-reaching
historical and political effects of interpreting encounters.

[. . .] The impact of writing and print technology has been such that few
areas on the planet have escaped the influence of the literate mind. The penetra-
tion of literacy has, however, been uneven, and many areas from rural Ireland to
North Africa to inner-city ghettoes in the United States have cultures with a
significant oral base. In a discipline like translation studies dominated by the
typographic cultures of highly-literate Western elites who speak majority languages, the danger is that whole areas of translation practice, informed by residual
orality in many different regions of the world, will be either misunderstood or
simply ignored.

It might be thought that anthropology and ethnography would have addressed
the problem ignored by translation studies, the role of translation in largely oral
cultures. However, as Kate Sturge (1997) has pointed out, anthropology and ethnography have, on the whole, been strangely indifferent to the activity of translation,
even though translation would appear to be central to the concerns of these disciplines. [. . .] The problems of ethnographic translation scholars are the problems
faced by interpreters in many parts of the world. A chief question is how to properly
understand illocutionary and perlocutionary acts in interlingual exchange. Moreover, no adequate account of the role of the interpreter in many cultures can be
given if the *entre-deux* is not also seen to include mediation (successful or unsuccessful) between the different mindsets of orality and literacy. Furthermore, if interpreting studies as the study of an oral practice were to take orality seriously, then it
would contribute greatly to expanding areas of translation studies such as screen
translation and the possibilities of multilingual print–speech conversion in Web
development. Secondary orality, the orality of the telephone, radio, television – as
distinct from the primary orality of non-literate cultures – has expanded exponen-
tially in our age. Therefore, interpreting as an area of translation studies that in
theory deals with the phenomenon of human speech in language transfer ought
ideally to be able to make a major contribution to the understanding of the interaction between translation and secondary orality. This, however, by and large has not
happened.

The geopolitics of Interpreting Studies

[. . .] Research in interpreting is still strikingly under the sway of the conference
interpreting paradigm. As Mona Baker noted with respect to interpreting in politically sensitive contexts, "Although some work has recently been done on consecutive
interpreting (especially as performed in the conference setting) and on liaison interpreting (in community and court settings), research on interpreting is still heavily
influenced by the priority which has traditionally been given to simultaneous conference interpreting" (Baker 1997: 111). One reason for the primacy of this paradigm is

undoubtedly geopolitical. Gile declares that most conference interpreters, "ont leur domicile professionnel dans les pays européens, surtout en France, en Suisse, en Belgique et dans d'autres pays d'Europe occidentale" (1995: 13). The largest conference interpreting markets are Paris, Brussels, Geneva and Tokyo, and almost all the research centres mentioned by Gile are to be found in the developed world. [. . .]

The professional concerns of the First World thus become the theoretical concerns of humanity and the theoretic paradigm of interpreting is restricted to reflect the market and institutional realities of wealthier nations. The relative neglect of other forms of interpreting that are much more extensively practised, such as community/bilateral/dialogue interpreting (which even Gile admits is "la forme d'interprétation la plus générale" (1995: 12)), is arguably grounded in material inequalities that universalize First World experience. The minoritizing effect of this ideological sleight of hand is threefold:

1   The breadth of the activity is ignored by concentrating on what is a minority sector in the overall field of interpreting, thus weakening the impact of interpreting theory on translation studies as a discipline.
2   Interpreting practice in developing countries that is not covered by the conference interpreting paradigm is largely ignored.
3   Minority groups in developed countries (refugees, immigrants, ethnic minorities) can themselves be victims of this theoretical exclusion as they often only merit "conference" status when it is not they who speak but others (social workers, government officials, academics, the police) who speak for them.

In his critique of postmodern approaches to ethnography, P. Steven Sangren argues that the "anthropological analysis of the authority of ethnography must specify the conditions of ethnography's production and reproduction in society, especially academic institutions, not just in texts" (Sangren 1992: 279). Little critical attention has been paid to the conditions of production (and reproduction) of the theory of interpreting, including the siting of interpreting research centres in academic institutions in the developed world.

One further effect of the recurrent emphasis on conference interpreting is the privileging of positivism in research. Gile laments the prevalence of speculative, reflexive approaches to interpreting theory that were not superseded until the mid-1980s. He argues for a systematic, rigorous empiricism, based on facts that will earn for interpreting studies legitimacy in the scientific community. Conference interpreting offers ideal conditions for observing input and output. The problem of course, as he is forced to admit, is that analysing the actual process of interpreting is much more difficult, and given the complexity of the phenomenon, it is not always easy to isolate separate components for analysis (Gile 1995: 215, 220). The obvious theoretical danger is that the approach will privilege further depoliticized, minimally contextualized experiments, carefully controlled by a researcher who assumes objectivity, and that these experiments will be carried out almost invariably in conference interpreting on the grounds that the booth is the nearest thing we have in interpreting to a cage.

A cultural turn, boundary crossings and monsters

As mentioned above, there is valuable, ideologically sensitive work being done in areas of interpreting other than conference interpreting. However, this type of research is still significantly under-represented in interpreting research. In addition, for understandable pedagogic and professional reasons, work in the area of community interpreting, for example, has largely been concerned with issues of training, certification, and the practical difficulties facing community interpreters in their everyday work. For these reasons, I want to argue here for the development of a "cultural turn" in interpreting studies. The work of Susan Bassnett, André Lefevere, José Lambert, Theo Hermans, and, more recently, Sherry Simon and Lawrence Venuti has radically altered the focus of research in translation, opening up a whole range of questions and issues linked to race, class, gender, and ideology that had previously been peripheral, if not simply ignored, in translation studies. Studies of interpreting in this sense have not moved on and have remained largely unaffected by the exciting theoretical developments elsewhere in translation studies. There is a need for a material history of interpreting that would examine all forms of interpreting as they are grounded in the economic, political, and cultural conditions of people's lives. A possible cultural turn had been anticipated for interpreting by the sociologist R. Bruce W. Anderson in his essay "Perspectives on the Role of the Interpreter" (1976). [. . .] In investigating the role of the interpreter in different situations, he suggested exploring the variables of social class, education, gender, age, and situational factors, such as arena of interaction (political, military, academic, religious) and level of tension. Anderson also noted the importance of the relative prestige of the national or ethnic groups involved in the interpreting transaction and attitudes towards the languages spoken. Despite Anderson's acuteness, his work did not lead to any significant shift in interpreting studies, and the need for material/cultural/manipulation perspectives on interpreting is as urgent as when he wrote. Such an approach would not only greatly broaden the scope for research on contemporary situations but would also provide an impetus for historical work in interpreting to move from the descriptive to the analytical.

The areas that might be explored by a material history of interpreting are legion, but the focus in what follows will be on issues related to colonial history and travel writing. Interpreters are, by definition, those that cross linguistic and cultural boundaries; depending on the identity of the interpreter and the nature of the context, interpreters cross boundaries of gender, class, nationality, or ethnicity. The interpreter's situation is one of dialogue, but dialogue as defined by more recent ethnography. James Clifford and George Marcus, in *Writing Culture: The Poetics and Politics of Ethnography* (1986), claim that the new ethnographical use of dialogue:

> locates cultural interpretations in many sorts of reciprocal contexts, and it obliges writers to find diverse ways of negotiating realities as multi-subjective, power-laden, and incongruent. In this view, "culture" is always relational, an inscription of communicative processes that exist, historically, between subjects in relation to power.
>
> (Clifford and Marcus 1986: 15)

[. . .]

The Swedish anthropologist Göran Aijmer points out the political and epistemological problems that beset the use of informants although he does not (typically) mention the question of language:

> Informants' insights into their own society are interesting, but generally the interest lies in the extent to which the informant grasps his own social environment. There are also other issues, such as the way in which an informant's account forms a conscious strategy for self-presentation and the anthropologist's refutation of indigenous explanations, which have an obvious place in anthropological discourse.
>
> (Aijmer 1992: 296)

A conscious strategy for self-presentation can also be a covert strategy for self-preservation. Neither strategy has endeared interpreters to their compatriots, and it is possible to argue that interpreters are fit subjects for a new cultural teratology. Rosa Braidotti, in *Nomadic Subjects* (1994), defines monsters as follows:

> Monsters are human beings who are born with congenital malformations of their bodily organism. They also represent the in between, the mixed, the ambivalent as implied in the ancient Greek root of the word monsters, teras, which means both horrible and wonderful, object of aberration and adoration.
>
> (Braidotti 1994: 77)

An example of ambivalent responses to the interpreter can be seen in the *Lienzo de Tlaxacala*, an Indian picture history dating from around 1550. The history shows Doña Marina, Cortés's interpreter, looming over the other figures in the illustrations including Cortés himself. Doña Marina spoke Mayan because she had lived among the Tabascans, and she spoke the language of the Aztecs as she was of Aztec descent. After she had been given to the Spaniards, she is said to have learned their language quickly (Díaz del Castillo 1926). For some cultural commentators in post-independence Mexico, Doña Marina was monstrous, "mother of a bastard race of *mestizos* and a traitress to her country" (Mirandé and Enríquez 1979: 24). For others, her resourcefulness and cultural flexibility have excited admiration and she has been presented as a "herald of the culturally hybrid societies of the future" (Bowen *et al.* 1995: 262). Interpreters thus become recurring objects of ambivalence, in-between figures, loathed and admired, privileged and despised. Like the monstrous, they inspire awe and alienation.

The central problem of translation in general and interpreting in particular, is the problem of control. Anderson says of the interpreter that, "his position in the middle has the advantage of power inherent in all positions which control scarce resources" (Anderson 1976: 218). Proximity is both desirable, the desire to manipulate, and dreaded. The dread comes from the fear of being misled either by the native interpreter or by the non-native interpreter going native. The difficulty for the imperial agent is dealing with this monstrous doubleness, the potential duplicity of interpreters. William Jones, in his *Grammar of the Persian Language* (1771), stated that for British officials, "It was found highly dangerous to employ the natives as interpreters, upon whose fidelity they could not depend" (Niranjana 1992: 16). [. . .]

The choice for the architects of empire was between what might be termed *autonomous* and *heteronomous* systems of interpreting. An autonomous system is one where colonizers train their own subjects in the language or languages of the colonized. A heteronomous system involves the recruitment of local interpreters and teaching them the imperial language. The interpreters may be recruited either by force or through inducements. [. . .] The dilemma for interpreters in colonial contexts is whether they can return as *native*. If they do, the risk, of course, is that they *go native*. In 1830 Captain Fitzroy, later captain of the *Beagle*, abducted a number of Fuegians on his first trip to Tierra del Fuego. His crew gave them nicknames that stuck, Jemmy Button (exchanged for a mother-of-pearl button), York Minister, and Fuegia Basket. Jemmy Button was a huge success in England and became noted for his fastidiousness about cleanliness and dress. He learned English and was presented along with Fuegia Basket to Queen Adelaide. Button's English sojourn did not last indefinitely, and in 1833 he was back in Tierra del Fuego along with York Minister and Fuegia Basket. They had travelled there on the Beagle with a young English naturalist, Charles Darwin (Beer 1996:38–40). One reason for the repatriation of the Fuegians to Tierra del Fuego was the belief that their knowledge of English language and culture would facilitate trade in the area. Years later, W. Parker Snow, in his *A Two Year's Cruise off Tierra del Fuego, the Falkland Islands, Patagonia and the River Plate: a Narrative of Life in the Southern Seas*, gives an account of meeting Jemmy Button, "quite naked, having his hair long and matted at the sides, cropped in front, and his eyes affected by smoke" (Beer 1996: 69). Parker Snow goes on to note that Jemmy's tribe were the least reliable – they had learnt a double language and behaviour. Not only did Jemmy speak the indigenous language but he also spoke English, the language of the imperial trader. As a result, the English found that Jemmy's tribe was considerably more adroit in its dealings with them than other tribes and more likely to manipulate than be manipulated. The returned native had indeed gone native, but because he was not wholly native he was even more dangerous as a native. [. . .]

The shift to autonomous modes of interpreting is notable in Champlain's decision to set up the institution of *interprètes-résidents*, where young French adventurers went and lived among the tribes with whom the French traded and learned the language of the indigenous peoples. Later in the century, as a result of a decree drawn up by Colbert, the French Court in 1669 arranged to train French-born children known as "enfants de langue" in Turkish, Arabic, and Persian (St-Pierre 1995: 16–7). These trainee interpreters were assigned to French ambassadors and consuls abroad, where they learned and perfected their knowledge of different foreign languages. Any material history of interpreting would need to investigate the growth of foreign-language instruction in imperial countries and the move towards autonomous modes of interpreting.

The shift towards language autonomy should not be viewed, however, as solely the concern of Empire. Developments in tourism in the nineteenth century show similar preoccupations with the pitfalls of language heteronomy. [. . .] The *drogman* is a familiar figure in Orientalist literature, but the presence of the guide/interpreter was not always welcome. Karl Baedeker, indeed, saw the advent of the guide book as a step on the road to freedom from interpreting. In his preface to the eighth edition of the guide to Germany (1858), Baedeker speaks of releasing the traveller from the

> unpleasant, and often wholly invisible, tutelage of hired servants and guides (and in part from the aid of coachmen and hotelkeepers), to assist him in standing on his own feet, to render him *independent*, and to place him in a position from which he may receive his own impressions with clear eyes and lively heart.
>
> (Mendelson 1985: 387–8, his emphasis).

[. . .] The guide book translated the foreign culture into the mother tongue of the traveller. The traveller no longer had to rely on the oral translation of the guide/interpreter as the guide book provided the written translation. The Murray and Baedeker guides thus facilitated the transition from heteronomous dependency on the oral interpreter to an autonomous mode of travelling grounded in literacy.

Jemmy Button's shift in allegiance has many other historical parallels, and what they point out is that ethics in interpreting cannot be considered in a universal, ahistorical fashion, in isolation from hierarchical relationships of power. When Margareta Bowen, David Bowen, Ingrid Kurz and Francine Kaufmann, in their chapter on interpreting in *Translators through History*, claim that interpreting has a "history of problems" they attribute this history to intimate contact between people who often have strong personalities. The "problems" are defined as "issues of loyalty (interpreters jumping ship or changing sides), along with breaches of etiquette or even ethics" (Bowen *et al.* 1995: 273). To describe these issues as "problems" seems strangely naive in view of the evidence adduced in the chapter, which points to the strongly political nature of many interpreting transactions. The understatement completely obscures questions of ideology and power. In *The Imaginary Canadian*, Anthony Wilden has described the phenomenon of "symmetrization", which he defines as "the ideological and unreal 'flattening out' of a hierarchical relationship as it exists" (Wilden 1980: 77). [. . .] The role of interpreters throughout history has been crucially determined by the prevailing hierarchical constitution of power and their position in it. In this respect, if you or your people are seriously disadvantaged by the hierarchy, the most ethical position can be to be utterly "unfaithful" in interpreting in the name of another fidelity, a fidelity of resistance. This is not a "problem". It is a strategy for survival. Adopting a strategy of "symmetrization" therefore in interpreting history can lead to strongly decontextualized readings of historical encounters and inappropriate judgements of motives and practices.

Hermeneutic subjects

In her discussion of Mungo Park's *Travels in the Interior of Africa* (1860), Mary Louise Pratt describes "arrival scenes" as "particularly potent sites for framing relations of contact and setting the terms of its representation" (Pratt 1992: 78–80). Park's desire for communication with native Africans is consistently frustrated, and he becomes mainly an object of curious scrutiny for the indigenous peoples in these arrival scenes. However, Pratt at no point mentions language, though it would appear obvious that at first, in the absence of a common language, the Europeans and Africans could do little else but stare at each other. Moreover, Pratt misses the link between visual apprehension of reality and the collapse of language-based systems of communication. In the absence of language, the arrival scene is a tableau, a spectacle where the native other becomes an object of consumption. It is in this context that the full significance of the interpreting transaction must be understood.

[. . .] If language differentiates the animal from the human, then denying the utterances of others the status of language-that-can-be-translated is to reduce them to the condition of animals. Charles Darwin made the following observation on the language of the Fuegians:

> The language of these people, according to our notions, scarcely deserves to be called articulate. Captain Cook has compared it to a man clearing his throat, but certainly no European ever cleared his throat with so many hoarse, guttural, and clicking sounds.
>
> (Darwin 1986: 17)

Edward Tylor, in *Primitive Culture: Researches into the Development of Mythology, Philosophy, Religion, Language, Art and Custom* (1871), noted that the hunting down and killing of indigenous peoples of Tasmania was possible because colonists heard the languages of the aboriginal peoples as grunts and squeals. Deprived of language and therefore of culture, the Tasmanians were dehumanised and treated as prey for imperial hunters.

If a central problem of nineteenth century anthropology is whether human beings are the positivistic objects of a natural science or the human subjects of a hermeneutic inquiry, then it is arguable that the presence of the interpreter, the emergence of language mediation, is a crucial moment in the shift from the positivistic object to the human subject. [. . .] One could argue that the moment of translation is a shift from an encounter scene as a site of consumption to an encounter scene as a site of interaction. The traveller through translation is no longer an observer but part of what is observed. The shift from non-human to human status that is implicit in accession to language and, by association, to culture does not mean, of course, that there are no other means of exclusion. The other language can be described as inferior, the speakers as lazy, malevolent, treacherous. Nonetheless, once understanding is admitted through the possibility of translation, then the way of dealing with or describing the other must be fundamentally reorganised, if only because liberal elements in the imperial centres will accord full, hermeneutic status to the subjectivity of the colonial other on the basis of the evidence of translated language. It is precisely because Montaigne wants to challenge the pseudo-objectivity of Eurocentrism that he is intensely frustrated when the interpreting proves inadequate, as he relates in his famous essay on "Des Cannibales": "Je parlay à l'un d'eux fort long temps; mais j'avois un truchement qui me suyvoit si mal, et qui estoit si empesché à recevoir mes imaginations par sa bestise, que je n'en peus tirer guiere de plaisir" (de Montaigne 1988: 214).[1]

There are many other substantive areas that might be explored in a material/cultural theory of interpreting. One obvious area is interpreting and gender that has had many ramifications from the colonial period to the present. Here are questions that might be legitimately explored by philosophy, history, and psychoanalysis, where control of the speaking subject often implies control of the body. The control is rendered problematic, however, by the difficulty in controlling/monitoring the translation flow. It was a practice, for example, for certain Crown informers in the period of the Tudor conquest of Ireland to take Irish-speaking wives so as to enhance their intelligence-gathering activities. The problem was that the women on occasion would change sides and act as double-agents, supplying the Gaelic Irish with valuable information on troop movements (Jackson 1973). Hence, there was the repeated conflation of notions of personal fidelity and politico-linguistic fidelity. Fidelity to the colonizer becomes infidelity to the colonized, and the colonizer's fidelity, of course, is often purely instrumental. [. . .]

The gender status of droids is uncertain but their obedience is usually unquestioned. C-3PO is a dutiful droid until its transfiguration at the end of *The Return of the Jedi*, the third and last film in the original *Star Wars* trilogy. The droid is deified by the Ewoks on account of his ability to speak their language. C-3PO is a protocol droid, responsible for etiquette and interpreting, and masters a modest six million forms of communication. The elevation to deity embarrasses C-3PO on two counts. First, the droid has to inform Hans Solo that Solo is the main course for that evening's banquet, and, second, it confesses that impersonating a deity is against its programming. C-3PO, the rebel's interpreter, offers a heroic if humorous figure for interpreting theory, in the droid's struggle against empire and its scepticism regarding divine omnipotence. But interpreting does not have to be programmed for theoretical powerlessness. The antiquity of interpreting, the continued importance of orality as a feature of everyday life in a multilingual world, the crucial importance of the interpreting transaction in countless situations where questions of power and control are to the fore, show that there is a more urgent need than ever to bring a new materialist perspective to bear on interpreting studies to illuminate our translation past, present and future.

Acknowledgement

The author gratefully acknowledges the assistance of Barbara Godard and Mona Baker in sourcing some of the material that has been used in the preparation of this essay.

Note

1   "I talked to one of them for some time; but I had an interpreter who followed my meaning so badly, and was so hindered by stupidity from grasping my ideas, that I could hardly get any satisfaction from him." Translation by J. M. Cohen in Michel de Montaigne, *Essays*, Harmondsworth, Penguin, 1978, p. 119.

References

Aijmer, Göran (1992) "Comment on article by P. Steven Sangren," *Current Anthropology* 33: 296–7.

Anderson, R. Bruce W. (1976) "Perspectives on the Role of Interpreter," in Richard W. Brislin (ed.) *Translation: Applications and Research*, New York: Gardner Press, 208–28.

Baker, Mona (1997) "Non-Cognitive Constraints and Interpreter Strategies in Political Interviews," in Karl Simms (ed.) *Translating Sensitive Texts: Linguistic Aspects*, Amsterdam: Rodopi, pp. 111–29.

Beer, Gillian (1996) *Open Fields: Science in Cultural Encounter*, Oxford: Clarendon Press.

Bowen, Margareta, Bowen, David, Kaufmann, Francine and Kurz, Ingrid (1995) "Interpreters and the Making of History," in Jean Delisle and Judith Woodsworth (eds) *Translators through History*, Amsterdam: John Benjamins, pp. 245–73.

Braidotti, Rosa (1994) *Nomadic Subjects: Embodiment and Sexual Difference in Contemporary Feminist Theory*, New York: Columbia University Press.

Clifford, James and Marcus, George E. (eds) (1986) *Writing Culture: The Poetics and Politics of Ethnography*, Berkeley: University of California Press.

Darwin, Charles (1986) *Journal of Researches into the Geology and Natural History of the Various Countries visited by the H.M.S. "Beagle"*, Part I, in Paul Barrett and R. B. Freeman (eds) *The Works of Charles Darwin*, vol 2, London.

de Montaigne, Michel (1988) *Les essais*, vol. 1, Paris: Quadrige/PUF.

Díaz del Castillo, Bernal (1926) *The True History of the Conquest of New Spain*, London: Hakluyt Society.

Gile, Daniel (1995) *Regards sur la recherche en interprétation de conférence*, Lille: Presses Universitaires de Lille.

Jackson, Donald (1973) "The Irish Language and Tudor Government," *Éire-Ireland* 8 (1): 21–8.

Mendelson, Edward (1985) "Baedeker's Universe," *Yale Review*, Spring: 387–8.

Mirandé, Alfredo and Enríquez, Evangelina (1979) *La Chicana. The Mexican-American Woman*, Chicago: University of Chicago Press.

Niranjana, Tejaswini (1992) *Siting Translation: History, Poststructuralism and the Colonial Context*, Berkeley: University of California Press.

Ong, Walter J. (1988) *Orality and Literacy: The Technologizing of the Word*, London: Routledge.

Pratt, Mary Louise (1992) *Imperial Eyes: Travel Writing and Transculturation*, London: Routledge.

Sangren, P. Steven (1992) "Rhetoric and the Authority of Ethnography: 'Postmodernism' and the Social Reproduction of Texts," *Current Anthropology* 33: 277–96.

St-Pierre, Paul (1995) "Etre jeune de langue à l'âge classique," *Circuit*, printemps: 16–17.

Sturge, Kate (1997) "Translation Strategies in Ethnography," *The Translator* 3 (1): 21–38.

Tylor, Edward (1871) *Primitive Culture: Researches into the Development of Mythology, Philosophy, Religion, Language, Art and Custom*, London.

Wilden, Anthony (1980) *The Imaginary Canadian*, Vancouver: Pulp Press.

BIBLIOGRAPHY

Adamowicz, A. (1989) "The Role of Anticipation in Discourse: Text Processing in Simultaneous Interpreting," *Polish Psychological Bulletin* 20 (2): 153–60.

Ahrens, B. (1998) "Nonverbale Phänomene und Belastung beim Konsekutivdolmetschen," *TexTconTexT* 12 (= NF 2): 213–34.

Alexieva, B. (1983) "Compression as a Means of Realisation of the Communicative Act in Simultaneous Interpreting," *Fremdsprachen* 27 (4): 233–8.

—— (1985) "Semantic Analysis of the Text in Simultaneous Interpreting," in H. Bühler (ed.) *Xth World Congress of FIT. Proceedings*, Wien: Wilhelm Braumüller, pp. 195–8.

—— (1988) "Analysis of the Simultaneous Interpreter's Output," in P. Nekeman (ed.) *XIth World Congress of FIT. Proceedings: Translation, our future*, Maastricht: Euroterm, pp. 484–8.

—— (1992) "The Optimum Text in Simultaneous Interpreting: A Cognitive Approach to Interpreter Training," in C. Dollerup and A. Loddegaard (eds) *Teaching Translation and Interpreting: Training, Talent and Experience*, Amsterdam and Philadelphia: John Benjamins, pp. 221–9.

—— (1994) "Types of Texts and Intertextuality in Simultaneous Interpreting," in M. Snell-Hornby, F. Pöchhacker and K. Kaindl (eds) *Translation Studies – An Interdiscipline*, Amsterdam and Philadelphia: John Benjamins, pp. 179–87.

—— (1997) "A Typology of Interpreter-Mediated Events," *The Translator: Studies in Intercultural Communication* 3 (2): 153–74.

—— (1998) "Consecutive Interpreting as a Decision Process," in A. Beylard-Ozeroff, J. Králová and B. Moser-Mercer (eds) *Translators' Strategies and Creativity*, Amsterdam and Philadelphia: John Benjamins, pp. 181–8.

—— (1999) "Understanding the Source Language Text in Simultaneous Interpreting," *The Interpreters' Newsletter* no. 9: 45–59.

Allioni, S. (1989) "Towards a Grammar of Consecutive Interpretation," in L. Gran and J. Dodds (eds) *The Theoretical and Practical Aspects of Teaching Conference Interpretation*, Udine: Campanotto Editore, pp. 191–7.

Alonso Bacigalupe, L. (1999) "Visual Contact in Simultaneous Interpretation: Results of an Experimental Study," in A. Álvarez Lugrís and A. Fernández Ocampo (eds) *Anovar/Anosar estudios de traducción e interpretación*, Vigo: Universidade de Vigo, vol. 1, pp. 123–37.

Altman, J. (1994) "Error Analysis in the Teaching of Simultaneous Interpreting: A Pilot Study," in S. Lambert and B. Moser-Mercer (eds) *Bridging the Gap:*

Empirical Research in Simultaneous Interpretation, Amsterdam and Philadelphia: John Benjamins, pp. 25–38.

Amoser, J. (1969) "Versuch einer Analyse des Prozesses des Konsekutiv- und des Simultandolmetschens," unpublished diploma thesis, University of Heidelberg.

Anderson, L. (1994) "Simultaneous Interpretation: Contextual and Translation Aspects," in S. Lambert and B. Moser-Mercer (eds) *Bridging the Gap: Empirical Research in Simultaneous Interpretation*, Amsterdam and Philadelphia: John Benjamins, pp. 101–20.

Anderson, R. B. W. (1976) "Perspectives on the Role of Interpreter," in R. W. Brislin (ed.) *Translation: Applications and Research*, New York: Gardner Press, pp. 208–28.

—— (1978) "Interpreter Roles and Interpretation Situations: Cross-Cutting Typologies," in D. Gerver and H. W. Sinaiko (eds) *Language Interpretation and Communication*, New York and London: Plenum Press, pp. 217–30.

Andres, D. (2000) "Konsekutivdolmetschen und Notation. Empirische Untersuchung mentaler Prozesse bei Anfängern in der Dolmetscherausbildung und professionellen Dolmetschern," unpublished doctoral dissertation, University of Vienna.

Apfelbaum, B. (1999) "Aspekte der Sprecherwechselorganisation in Dolmetschinteraktionen – Eine konversationsanalytische Fallstudie am Beispiel von deutsch–französischen Fachschulungen," in H. Gerzymisch-Arbogast, D. Gile, J. House and A. Rothkegel (eds) *Wege der Übersetzungs- und Dolmetschforschung*, Tübingen: Gunter Narr, pp. 209–40.

—— and Wadensjö, C. (1997) "How Does a Verbmobil Affect Conversation? Discourse Analysis and Machine-supported Translatory Interaction," in C. Hauenschild and S. Heizmann (eds) *Machine Translation and Translation Theory*, Berlin and New York: Mouton de Gruyter, pp. 93–122.

Armstrong, S. (1997) "Corpus-based Methods for NLP and Translation Studies," *Interpreting: International Journal of Research and Practice in Interpreting* 2 (1/2): 141–62.

Baker, M. (1997) "Non-Cognitive Constraints and Interpreter Strategies," in K. Simms (ed.) *Translating Sensitive Texts: Linguistic Aspects*, Amsterdam and Atlanta: Rodopi, pp. 111–29.

Balzani, M. (1990) "Le contact visuel en interprétation simultanée: resultats d'une expérience (Français–Italien)," in L. Gran and C. Taylor (eds) *Aspects of Applied and Experimental Research on Conference Interpretation*, Udine: Campanotto Editore, pp. 93–100.

Barik, H. C. (1969) "A Study of Simultaneous Interpretation," unpublished doctoral dissertation, University of North Carolina, Chapel Hill.

—— (1971) "A Description of Various Types of Omissions, Additions and Errors of Translation Encountered in Simultaneous Interpretation," *Meta* 16 (4): 199–210.

—— (1972) "Interpreters Talk a Lot, Among Other Things," *Babel* 18 (1): 3–10.

—— (1973) "Simultaneous Interpretation: Temporal and Quantitative Data," *Language and Speech* 16 (3): 237–70.

—— (1975) "Simultaneous Interpretation: Qualitative and Linguistic Data," *Language and Speech* 18 (2): 272–98.

Barik, H. C. (1994) "A Description of Various Types of Omissions, Additions and Errors of Translation Encountered in Simultaneous Interpretation," in S. Lambert and B. Moser-Mercer (eds) *Bridging the Gap: Empirical Research in Simultaneous Interpretation*, Amsterdam and Philadelphia: John Benjamins, pp. 121–37.

Barsky, R. (1996) "The Interpreter as Intercultural Agent in Convention Refugee Hearings," *The Translator: Studies in Intercultural Communication* 2 (1): 45–63.

Beaugrande, R. de (1980) *Text, Discourse and Process*. London: Longman.

—— and Dressler, W. U. (1981) *Introduction to Text Linguistics*, London: Longman.

Bendik, J. (1996). "On Suprasegmentals in Simultaneous Interpreting," in K. Klaudy, J. Lambert and A. Sohár (eds) *Translation Studies in Hungary*, Budapest: Scholastica, pp. 176–90.

Berk-Seligson, S. (1988) "The Impact of Politeness in Witness Testimony: The Influence of the Court Interpreter," *Multilingua. Journal of Cross-cultural and Interlanguage Communication* 7 (4): 411–39.

—— (1989) "The Role of Register in the Bilingual Courtroom: Evaluative Reactions to Interpreted Testimony," in I. Wherritt and O. García (eds) *US Spanish: The Language of Latinos*, special issue of the *International Journal of the Sociology of Language* 79 (5): 79–91.

—— (1990a) *The Bilingual Courtroom: Court Interpreters in the Judicial Process*. Chicago and London: The University of Chicago Press.

—— (1990b) "Bilingual Court Proceedings: The Role of the Court Interpreter," in J. N. Levi and A. G. Walker (eds) *Language in the Judicial Process*, New York: Plenum, pp. 155–201.

—— (1999) "The Impact of Court Interpreting on the Coerciveness of Leading Questions," *Forensic Linguistics: The International Journal of Speech, Language and the Law* 6 (1): 30–56.

—— (2000) "Interpreting for the Police: Issues in the Pre-Trial Phases of the Judicial Process," *Forensic Linguistics: The International Journal of Speech, Language and the Law* 7 (1): 213–38.

Bowen, M., Bowen, D., Kaufmann, F. and Kurz, I. (1995) "Interpreters and the Making of History," in J. Delisle and J. Woodsworth (eds) *Translators through History*, Amsterdam and Philadelphia: John Benjamins, pp. 245–73.

Brennan, M. and Brown, R. K. (1997) *Equality Before the Law: Deaf People's Access to Justice*, Durham: Deaf Studies Research Unit, University of Durham.

Brien, D. (ed.) (1992) *Dictionary of British Sign Language/English*, London: Faber.

Brislin, R. W. (ed.) (1976a) *Translation: Applications and Research*, New York: Gardner Press.

—— (1976b) "Introduction," in R. W. Brislin (ed.) *Translation: Applications and Research*, New York: Gardner Press, pp. 1–43.

Broadbent, D. E. (1952) "Speaking and Listening Simultaneously," *Journal of Experimental Psychology* 43: 267–73.

Bros-Brann, E. (1975) "Critical Comments on H. C. Barik's Article 'Interpreters Talk a Lot, Among Other Things,' Babel, no. 1, 1972, Vol. XVIII," *Babel* 21 (2): 93–4.

Brown, P. and Yule, G. (1983) *Discourse Analysis*, Cambridge: Cambridge University Press.

Bühler, H. (1980) "Translation und nonverbale Kommunikation," in W. Wilss (ed.) *Semiotik und Übersetzen*, Tübingen: Gunter Narr, pp. 43–53.

—— (1985) "Conference Interpreting – a Multichannel Communication Phenomenon," *Meta* 30 (1): 49–54.

—— (1986) "Linguistic (Semantic) and Extra-linguistic (Pragmatic) Criteria for the Evaluation of Conference Interpretation and Interpreters," *Multilingua* 5 (4): 231–5.

—— (1989) "Discourse Analysis and the Spoken Text – a Critical Analysis of the Performance of Advanced Interpretation Students," in L. Gran and J. Dodds (eds) *The Theoretical and Practical Aspects of Teaching Conference Interpretation*, Udine: Campanotto Editore, pp. 131–5.

—— (1990) "Orality and Literacy – Theoretical and Didactic Considerations in the Context of Translation Studies," in R. Arntz and G. Thome (eds) *Übersetzungswissenschaft: Ergebnisse und Perspektiven*, Tübingen: Gunter Narr, pp. 536–44.

Cairncross, L. (1989) *Cultural Interpreter Training Manual*, Toronto, Ontario: Ministry of Citizenship.

Carlet, L. (1998) "G. V. Chernov's Psycholinguistic Model in Simultaneous Interpretation: An Experimental Contribution," *The Interpreters' Newsletter* no. 8: 75–92.

Carr, S. E., Roberts, R., Dufour, A. and Steyn, D. (eds) (1997) *The Critical Link: Interpreters in the Community. Papers from the First International Conference on Interpreting in Legal, Health, and Social Service Settings (Geneva Park, Canada, June 1–4, 1995)*, Amsterdam and Philadelphia: John Benjamins.

Cartellieri, C. (1983) "The Inescapable Dilemma: Quality and/or Quantity in Interpreting," *Babel* 29 (4): 209–13.

Chernov, G. V. (1973) "K postroeniyu psikholingvisticheskoy modeli sinkhronnogo perevoda [Towards a Psycholinguistic Model of Simultaneous Interpretation]," *Linguistische Arbeitsberichte* 7: 225–60.

—— (1977) "Kumulative dynamische semantische Analyse des Eingangstextes beim Simultandolmetschen," in O. Kade (ed.) *Vermittelte Kommunikation, Sprachmittlung, Translation*, Leipzig: Verlag Enzyklopädie, pp. 93–104.

—— (1978) *Teoriya i praktika sinkhronnogo perevoda* [Theory and Practice of Simultaneous Interpretation], Moscow: Mezhdunarodnyye otnosheniya.

—— (1979) "Semantic Aspects of Psycholinguistic Research in Simultaneous Interpretation," *Language and Speech* 22 (3): 277–95.

—— (1985) "Interpretation Research in the Soviet Union: Results and Prospects," in H. Bühler (ed.) *Xth World Congress of FIT. Proceedings*, Wien: Wilhelm Braumüller, pp. 169–77.

—— (1987) *Osnovy sinkhronnogo perevoda* [Fundamentals of Simultaneous Interpretation], Moscow: Vysshaya Shkola.

—— (1992) "Conference Interpretation in the USSR: History, Theory, New Frontiers," *Meta* 37 (1): 149–62.

—— (1994) "Message Redundancy and Message Anticipation in Simultaneous Interpretation," in S. Lambert and B. Moser-Mercer (eds) *Bridging the Gap:*

Empirical Research in Simultaneous Interpretation, Amsterdam and Philadelphia: John Benjamins, pp. 139–53.

Chernov, G. V. (1999) "Simultaneous Interpretation in Russia: Development of Research and Training," *Interpreting: International Journal of Research and Practice in Interpreting* 4 (1): 41–54.

Chesterman, A. (1993) "From 'Is' to 'Ought': Laws, Norms and Strategies in Translation Studies," *Target: International Journal of Translation Studies* 5 (1): 1–20.

Cokely, D. (1985) "Towards a Sociolinguistic Model of the Interpreting Process: Focus on ASL and English," unpublished doctoral dissertation, Georgetown University, Washington DC.

—— (1986) "The Effects of Lag Time on Interpreter Errors," *Sign Language Studies* 53: 341–76.

—— (1992) *Interpretation: A Sociolinguistic Model*, Burtonsville, Maryland: Linstok Press.

Collados Aís, A. (1994) "La comunicación no verbal y la didáctica de la interpretación," *TexTconTexT* 9 (1): 23–53.

—— (1998) *La evaluación de la calidad en interpretación simultánea: La importancia de la comunicación no verbal*, Peligros, Granada: Editorial Comares.

Cronin, M. (2000) *Across the Lines: Travel, Language and Translation*, Cork: Cork University Press.

Dalitz, G. (1973) "Zur Beschreibung typischer Vorgriffsfälle beim Simultandolmetschen," in A. Neubert and O. Kade (eds) *Neue Beiträge zu Grundfragen der Übersetzungswissenschaft*, Leipzig: Verlag Enzyklopädie, pp. 123–8.

Dam, H. V. (1993) "Text Condensing in Consecutive Interpreting," in Y. Gambier and J. Tommola (eds) *Translation and Knowledge: SSOTT IV*, Turku: University of Turku, Centre for Translation and Interpreting, pp. 297–313.

—— (1996) "Text Condensation in Consecutive Interpreting. Summary of a PhD dissertation," *Hermes. Journal of Linguistics* no. 17: 273–81.

—— (1998) "Lexical Similarity vs Lexical Dissimilarity in Consecutive Interpreting," *The Translator: Studies in Intercultural Communication* 4 (1): 49–68.

Danks, J. H., Shreve, G. M., Fountain, S. B. and McBeath, M. K. (eds) (1997) *Cognitive Processes in Translation and Interpreting*, Thousand Oaks, London and New Delhi: Sage.

Darò, V. (1990) "Speaking Speed During Simultaneous Interpretation: A Discussion on its Neuropsychological Aspects and Possible Contributions to Teaching," in L. Gran and C. Taylor (eds) *Aspects of Applied and Experimental Research on Conference Interpretation*, Udine: Campanotto Editore, pp. 83–92.

—— (1995) "Attentional, Auditory, and Memory Indexes as Prerequisites for Simultaneous Interpreting," in J. Tommola (ed.) *Topics in Interpreting Research*, Turku: University of Turku, Centre for Translation and Interpreting, pp. 3–10.

—— and Fabbro, F. (1994) "Verbal Memory during Simultaneous Interpretation: Effects of Phonological Interference," *Applied Linguistics* 15 (4): 365–81.

—— Lambert, S. and Fabbro, F. (1996) "Conscious Monitoring of Attention during Simultaneous Interpretation," *Interpreting: International Journal of Research and Practice in Interpreting* 1 (1): 101–24.

Dawrant, A. (1996) "Word-order in Chinese–English Simultaneous Interpretation:

An Initial Exploration," unpublished MA thesis, Graduate Institute of Translation and Interpretation Studies, Fujen Catholic University, Taipei.

Déjean le Féal, K. (1978) "Lectures et improvisations: Incidences de la forme de l'énonciation sur la traduction simultanée," unpublished doctoral dissertation, Université de la Sorbonne Nouvelle, Paris III.

—— (1982) "Why Impromptu Speech Is Easy to Understand," in N. E. Enkvist (ed.) *Impromptu Speech: A Symposium*, Åbo: Åbo Akademi, pp. 221–39.

Diriker, E. (1999) "Problematizing the Discourse on Interpreting – A Quest for Norms in Simultaneous Interpreting," *TEXTCONTEXT* 13 (= NF 3): 73–90.

Dodds, J. M. and Katan, D. [*et al.*] (1997) "The Interaction between Research and Training," in Y. Gambier, D. Gile and C. Taylor (eds) *Conference Interpreting: Current Trends in Research*, Amsterdam and Philadelphia: John Benjamins, pp. 89–107.

Dollerup, C. and Loddegaard, A. (eds) (1992) *Teaching Translation and Interpreting: Training, Talent and Experience*, Amsterdam and Philadelphia: John Benjamins.

Donovan, Clare (1990) "La fidélité en interprétation," unpublished doctoral dissertation, Université de la Sorbonne Nouvelle, Paris III.

Dressler, W. (1974) "Der Beitrag der Textlinguistik zur Übersetzungswissenschaft," in V. Kapp (ed.) *Übersetzer und Dolmetscher. Theoretische Grundlagen, Ausbildung, Berufspraxis*, Heidelberg: Quelle & Meyer, pp. 61–71.

Driesen, C. J. (1985) "L'interprétation auprès des tribunaux pénaux de la RFA (français–allemand)," unpublished doctoral dissertation, Université de la Sorbonne Nouvelle, Paris III.

Edwards, A. B. (1995) *The Practice of Court Interpreting*, Amsterdam and Philadelphia: John Benjamins.

Enkvist, N. E. (ed.) (1982) *Impromptu Speech: A Symposium*, Åbo: Åbo Akademi.

ESIT (2001) "Interpretation," available HTTP: http://www.esit.univ-paris3.fr/interpretation.html (14 April 2001).

Ezrachi, J., Roziner, I., Lewin, I., Pardo, A. and Melamed, S. (2002) "A Study of Workload and Burnout in Simultaneous Interpreting: Integrative Summary Report," Tel Aviv: Mertens-Hoffman, Inc.; Geneva: AIIC.

Fabbro, F. and Darò, V. (1995) "Delayed Auditory Feedback in Polyglot Simultaneous Interpreters," *Brain and Language* 48: 309–19.

Falbo, C. (1993) "L'interprète: recepteur et producteur textuel," *The Interpreters' Newsletter* no. 5: 101–6.

—— (1998) "Analyse des erreurs en interprétation simultanée," *The Interpreters' Newsletter* no. 8: 107–20.

Feldweg, E. (1996) *Der Konferenzdolmetscher im internationalen Kommunikationsprozeß*, Heidelberg: Groos.

Fenton, S. (1997) "The Role of the Interpreter in the Adversarial Courtroom," in S. E. Carr, R. Roberts, A. Dufour and D. Steyn (eds) *The Critical Link: Interpreters in the Community*, Amsterdam and Philadelphia: John Benjamins, pp. 29–34.

Frey, R., Roberts-Smith, L. and Bessell-Browne, S. (1990) *Working with Interpreters in Law, Health and Social Work*, Perth: State Advisory Panel for Translating and Interpreting in Western Australia, for the National Accreditation Authority for Translators and Interpreters (NAATI).

Frishberg, N. (1990) *Interpreting: An Introduction*, 2nd edn, Silver Spring, Maryland: Registry of Interpreters for the Deaf.

Gallina, S. (1992) "Cohesion and the Systemic-Functional Approach to Text: Applications to Political Speeches and Significance for Simultaneous Interpretation," *The Interpreters' Newsletter* no. 5: 62–71.

Gambier, Y., Gile, D. and Taylor, C. (eds) (1997) *Conference Interpreting: Current Trends in Research*, Amsterdam and Philadelphia: John Benjamins.

Garber, N. and Mauffette-Leenders, L. A. (1997) "Obtaining Feedback from Non-English Speakers," in S. E. Carr, R. Roberts, A. Dufour and D. Steyn (eds) *The Critical Link: Interpreters in the Community*, Amsterdam and Philadelphia: John Benjamins, pp. 131–43.

García-Landa, M. (1978) "Les déviations délibérées de la littéralité en interprétation de conférence," unpublished doctoral dissertation, Université de la Sorbonne Nouvelle, Paris III.

—— (1981) "La 'théorie du sens', théorie de la traduction et base de son enseignement," in J. Delisle (ed.) *L'enseignement de l'interprétation et de la traduction: de la théorie à la pédagogie*, Ottawa: University of Ottawa Press, pp. 113–32.

—— (1995) "Notes on the epistemology of translation theory," *Meta* 40 (3): 388–405.

Gerver, D. (1969) "The Effects of Source Language Presentation Rate on the Performance of Simultaneous Conference Interpreters," in E. Foulke (ed.) *Proceedings of the Second Louisville Conference on Rate and/or Frequency-Controlled Speech*, Louisville, Kentucky: Center for Rate-Controlled Recordings, University of Louisville, pp. 162–84.

—— (1971) "Aspects of Simultaneous Interpretation and Human Information Processing," unpublished D. Phil. thesis, Oxford University.

—— (1972) "Simultaneous and Consecutive Interpretation and Human Information Processing," London: Social Science Research Council, Research Report HR 566/1.

—— (1974a) "The Effects of Noise on the Performance of Simultaneous Interpreters: Accuracy of Performance," *Acta Psychologica* 38 (3): 159–67.

—— (1974b) "Simultaneous Listening and Speaking and Retention of Prose," *Quarterly Journal of Experimental Psychology* 26 (3): 337–41.

—— (1975) "A Psychological Approach to Simultaneous Interpretation," *Meta* 20 (2): 119–28.

—— (1976) "Empirical Studies of Simultaneous Interpretation: A Review and a Model," in R. W. Brislin (ed.) *Translation: Applications and Research*, New York: Gardner Press, pp. 165–207.

—— (1981) "Frames for Interpreting," in A. Kopczyński (ed.) *Proceedings of the IXth World Congress of FIT*, Warsaw: Interpress, pp. 371–80.

—— and Sinaiko, H. W. (eds) (1978) *Language Interpretation and Communication. Proceedings of the NATO Symposium, Venice, Italy, September 26–October 1, 1977*, New York and London: Plenum Press.

—— Longley, P., Long, J. and Lambert, S. (1984) "Selecting Trainee Conference Interpreters: A Preliminary Study," *Journal of Occupational Psychology* 57: 17–31.

Gile, D. (1983) "Aspects méthodologiques de l'évaluation de qualité du travail en interprétation simultanée," *Meta* 28 (3): 236–43.

—— (1984) "Les noms propres en interprétation simultanée," *Multilingua* 3 (2): 79–85.

—— (1985a) "Le modèle d'efforts et l'équilibre en interprétation simultanée," *Meta* 30 (1): 44–8.

—— (1985b) "La sensibilité aux écarts de langue et la sélection d'informateurs dans l'analyse d'erreurs: une expérience," *The Incorporated Linguist* 24 (1): 29–32.

—— (1987) "La terminotique en interprétation de conférence, un potentiel à exploiter," *Meta* 32 (2): 164–9.

—— (1989a) "Les flux d'information dans les réunions interlinguistiques et l'interprétation de conférence: premières observations," *Meta* 34 (4): 649–60.

—— (1989b) "La communication linguistique en réunion multilingue – Les difficultés de la transmission informationnelle en interprétation simultanée," unpublished doctoral dissertation, Université de la Sorbonne Nouvelle, Paris III.

—— (1990a) "Scientific Research vs. Personal Theories in the Investigation of Interpretation," in L. Gran and C. Taylor (eds) *Aspects of Applied and Experimental Research on Conference Interpretation*, Udine: Campanotto Editore, pp. 28–41.

—— (1990b) "L'évaluation de la qualité de l'interprétation par les délégués: une étude de cas," *The Interpreters' Newsletter* no. 3: 66–71.

—— (1991a) "Methodological Aspects of Interpretation (and Translation) Research," *Target: International Journal of Translation Studies* 3 (2): 153–74.

—— (1991b) "A Communication-Oriented Analysis of Quality in Nonliterary Translation and Interpretation," in M. L. Larson (ed.) *Translation: Theory and Practice. Tension and Interdependence*, Binghamton, New York: SUNY, pp. 188–200.

—— (1992) "Predictable Sentence Endings in Japanese and Conference Interpretation," *The Interpreters' Newsletter*, Special Issue 1: 12–23.

—— (1994) "Opening Up in Interpretation Studies," in M. Snell-Hornby, F. Pöchhacker and K. Kaindl (eds) *Translation Studies – An Interdiscipline*, Amsterdam and Philadelphia: John Benjamins, pp. 149–58.

—— (1995a) *Regards sur la recherche en interprétation de conférence*, Lille: Presses Universitaires de Lille.

—— (1995b) "Interpretation Research: A New Impetus?," *Hermes. Journal of Linguistics* no. 14: 15–29.

—— (1995c) *Basic Concepts and Models for Interpreter and Translator Training*, Amsterdam and Philadelphia: John Benjamins.

—— (1995d) "Fidelity Assessment in Consecutive Interpretation: An Experiment," *Target: International Journal of Translation Studies* 7 (1): 151–64.

—— (1997) "Conference Interpreting as a Cognitive Management Problem," in J. H. Danks, G. M. Shreve, S. B. Fountain and M. K. McBeath (eds) *Cognitive Processes in Translation and Interpreting*, Thousand Oaks, London and New Delhi: Sage, pp. 196–214.

—— [*et al.*] (1997) "Methodology," in Y. Gambier, D. Gile and C. Taylor (eds) *Conference Interpreting: Current Trends in Research*, Amsterdam and Philadelphia: John Benjamins, pp. 109–22.

Gile, D. (1998) "Observational Studies and Experimental Studies in the Investigation of Conference Interpreting," *Target: International Journal of Translation Studies* 10 (1): 69–93.

—— (1999a) "Doorstep Interdisciplinarity in Conference Interpreting Research," in A. Álvarez Lugrís and A. Fernández Ocampo (eds) *Anovar/Anosar estudios de traducción e interpretación*, Vigo: Universidade de Vigo, vol. 1, pp. 41–52.

—— (1999b) "Testing the Effort Models' Tightrope Hypothesis in Simultaneous Interpreting – A Contribution," *Hermes. Journal of Linguistics* no. 23: 153–72.

—— (1999c) "Variability in the Perception of Fidelity in Simultaneous Interpretation," *Hermes. Journal of Linguistics* no. 22: 51–79.

—— (2000) "Issues in Interdisciplinary Research into Conference Interpreting," in B. Englund Dimitrova and K. Hyltenstam (eds) *Language Processing and Simultaneous Interpreting: Interdisciplinary Perspectives*, Amsterdam and Philadelphia: John Benjamins, pp. 89–106.

Goldman-Eisler, F. (1967) "Sequential Temporal Patterns and Cognitive Processes in Speech," *Language and Speech* 10 (3): 122–32.

—— (1968) *Psycholinguistics: Experiments in Spontaneous Speech*, London and New York: Academic Press.

—— (1972) "Segmentation of Input in Simultaneous Translation," *Journal of Psycholinguistic Research* 1 (2): 127–40.

—— (1980) "Psychological Mechanisms of Speech Production as Studied Through the Analysis of Simultaneous Translation," in B. Butterworth (ed.) *Language Production. Vol. 1: Speech and Talk*, London: Academic Press, pp. 143–53.

—— and Cohen, M. (1974) "An Experimental Study of Interference between Receptive and Productive Processes Relating to Simultaneous Translation," *Language and Speech* 17 (1): 1–10.

González, R. D., Vásquez, V. F. and Mikkelson, H. (1991) *Fundamentals of Court Interpretation: Theory, Policy, and Practice*, Durham, North Carolina: Carolina Academic Press.

Gran, L. and Dodds, J. (eds) (1989) *The Theoretical and Practical Aspects of Teaching Conference Interpretation*, Udine: Campanotto Editore.

Hale, S. (1997a) "The Treatment of Register Variation in Court Interpreting," *The Translator: Studies in Intercultural Communication* 3 (1): 39–54.

—— (1997b) "The Interpreter on Trial: Pragmatics in Court Interpreting," in S. E. Carr, R. Roberts, A. Dufour and D. Steyn (eds) *The Critical Link: Interpreters in the Community*, Amsterdam and Philadelphia: John Benjamins, pp. 201–11.

—— (1999) "Interpreters' Treatment of Discourse Markers in Courtroom Questions," *Forensic Linguistics: The International Journal of Speech, Language and the Law* 6 (1): 57–82.

Halliday, M. A. K. (1978) *Language as Social Semiotic*, London: Edward Arnold.

—— (1985) *An Introduction to Functional Grammar*, London: Edward Arnold.

—— (1989) *Spoken and Written Language*, Oxford: Oxford University Press.

—— and Hasan, R. (1976) *Cohesion in English*, London: Longman.

Harris, B. (1981) "Observations on a Cause Célèbre: Court Interpreting at the Lischka Trial," in R. Roberts (ed.) *L'interprétation auprès des tribunaux*, Ottawa: University of Ottawa Press, pp. 189–202.

—— (1990) "Norms in Interpretation," *Target: International Journal of Translation Studies* 2 (1): 215–19.

—— and Sherwood, B. (1978) "Translating as an Innate Skill," in D. Gerver and H. W. Sinaiko (eds) *Language Interpretation and Communication*, New York and London: Plenum Press, pp. 155–70.

Hatim, B. (1997) *Communication Across Cultures: Translation Theory and Contrastive Text Linguistics*, Exeter: University of Exeter Press.

—— and Mason, I. (1990) *Discourse and the Translator*, London: Longman.

—— and Mason, I. (1997) *The Translator as Communicator*, London and New York: Routledge.

Herbert, J. (1952) *The Interpreter's Handbook: How to Become a Conference Interpreter*, Genève: Librairie de l'Université Georg.

Hermann, A. (1956) "Dolmetschen im Altertum. Ein Beitrag zur antiken Kulturgeschichte," in K. Thieme, A. Hermann and E. Glässer, *Beiträge zur Geschichte des Dolmetschens*, München: Isar Verlag, pp. 25–59.

Heynold, C. (1995) "La visioconférence multilingue: Premières expériences à la Commission Européenne," *Translatio. Nouvelles de la FIT – FIT Newsletter* N.s. 14 (3/4): 337–42.

Holmes, J. S ([1972]/1988) "The Name and Nature of Translation Studies," in J. S Holmes, *Translated! Papers on Literary Translation and Translation Studies*, Amsterdam: Rodopi, pp. 67–80.

Hornberger, J. (1997) "Evaluating the Costs of Bridging Language Barriers in Health Care," *Journal of Health Care for the Poor and Underserved* 9 (Suppl.): 26–39.

—— Gibson, C. D., Wood, W., Degueldre, C., Corso, I., Palla B. and Bloch, D. A. (1996) "Eliminating Language Barriers for Non-English-Speaking Patients," *Medical Care* 34 (8): 845–56.

Hu, G. (1990) "An Exploration into Sci-Tech Interpretations: Abstract Interpreting Approach," *Babel* 36 (2): 85–96.

Ingram, R. (1974) "A Communication Model for the Interpreting Process," *Journal of Rehabilitation of the Deaf* 7 (3): 3–9.

Isham, W. P. (2000) "Phonological Interference in Interpreters of Spoken Languages: An Issue of Storage or Process?" in B. Englund Dimitrova and K. Hyltenstam (eds) *Language Processing and Simultaneous Interpreting: Interdisciplinary Perspectives*, Amsterdam and Philadelphia: John Benjamins, pp. 133–49.

Ivanova, A. (1996) "Intertextuality in Conference Discourse: Processing Issues in Simultaneous Interpreting," *Working Papers in English and Applied Linguistics*, vol. 3, Cambridge: RCEAL, University of Cambridge, pp. 85–99.

Jansen, P. (1995a) "The Role of the Interpreter in Dutch Courtroom Interaction: The Impact of the Situation on Translational Norms," in J. Tommola (ed.) *Topics in Interpreting Research*, Turku: University of Turku, Centre for Translation and Interpreting, pp. 11–36.

—— (ed.) (1995b) *Translation and the Manipulation of Discourse: Selected Papers of the CERA Research Seminars in Translation Studies 1992–1993*, Leuven: The Leuven Research Centre for Translation, Communication and Culture.

Jekat, S. (1997) "Automatic Interpreting of Dialogue Acts," in C. Hauenschild and S. Heizmann (eds) *Machine Translation and Translation Theory*, Berlin and New York: Mouton de Gruyter, pp. 145–55.

Jekat, S. and Klein, A. (1996) "Machine Interpretation: Open Problems and Some Solutions," *Interpreting: International Journal of Research and Practice in Interpreting* 1 (1): 7–20.

Jessnitzer, K. (1982) *Dolmetscher. Ein Handbuch für die Praxis der Dolmetscher, Übersetzer und ihrer Auftraggeber im Gerichts-, Beurkundungs- und Verwaltungsverfahren*, Köln: Carl Heymanns Verlag.

Jörg, U. (1995) "Verb Anticipation in German–English Simultaneous Interpreting: An Empirical Study," unpublished MA dissertation, Department of Modern Languages, University of Bradford.

—— (1997) "Bridging the Gap: Verb Anticipation in German–English Simultaneous Interpreting," in M. Snell-Hornby, Z. Jettmarová and K. Kaindl (eds) *Translation as Intercultural Communication*, Amsterdam and Philadelphia: John Benjamins, pp. 217–28.

Jones, R. (1998) *Conference Interpreting Explained*, Manchester: St. Jerome Publishing.

Kade, O. (1963) "Der Dolmetschvorgang und die Notation. Bedeutung und Aufgaben der Notiertechnik und des Notiersystems beim konsekutiven Dolmetschen," *Fremdsprachen* 7 (1): 12–20.

—— (1967) "Zu einigen Besonderheiten des Simultandolmetschens," *Fremdsprachen* 11 (1): 8–17.

—— (1968) *Zufall und Gesetzmäßigkeit in der Übersetzung*, Leipzig: Verlag Enzyklopädie.

—— and Cartellieri, C. (1971) "Some Methodological Aspects of Simultaneous Interpreting," *Babel* 17 (2): 12–16.

Kadric, M. (2000) "Interpreting in the Austrian Courtroom," in R. P. Roberts, S. E. Carr, D. Abraham and A. Dufour (eds) *The Critical Link 2: Interpreters in the Community*, Amsterdam and Philadelphia: John Benjamins, pp. 153–64.

—— (2001) *Dolmetschen bei Gericht. Erwartungen, Anforderungen, Kompetenzen*, Wien: WUV-Universitätsverlag.

Kalina, S. (1998) *Strategische Prozesse beim Dolmetschen: Theoretische Grundlagen, empirische Fallstudien, didaktische Konsequenzen*, Tübingen: Gunter Narr.

Karttunen, F. (1994) *Between Worlds: Interpreters, Guides, and Survivors*, New Brunswick, New Jersey: Rutgers University Press.

Kaufert, J. M. and Koolage, W. W. (1984) "Role Conflict among 'Culture Brokers': The Experience of Native Canadian Medical Interpreters," *Social Science & Medicine* 18 (3): 283–6.

Kaufert, J. M. and Putsch, R. W. (1997) "Communication through Interpreters in Healthcare: Ethical Dilemmas Arising from Differences in Class, Culture, Language, and Power," *Journal of Clinical Ethics* 8 (1): 71–87.

Kintsch, W. and van Dijk, T. A. (1978) "Toward a Model of Text Comprehension and Production," *Psychological Review* 85 (5): 363–94.

Kirchhoff, H. (1976a) "Das Simultandolmetschen: Interdependenz der Variablen im Dolmetschprozeß, Dolmetschmodelle und Dolmetschstrategien," in H. W. Drescher and S. Scheffzek (eds) *Theorie und Praxis des Übersetzens und Dolmetschens*, Frankfurt am Main: Peter Lang, pp. 59–71.

—— (1976b) "Das dreigliedrige, zweisprachige Kommunikationssystem Dolmetschen," *Le Langage et l'Homme* 31: 21–7.

Kitano, H. (1993) "La traduction de la langue parlée," in A. Clas and P. Bouillon (eds) *La traductique: Études et recherches de traduction par ordinateur*, Montréal: Presses de l'Université de Montréal, pp. 408–22.

Klonowicz, T. (1994) "Putting One's Heart into Simultaneous Interpretation," in S. Lambert and B. Moser-Mercer (eds) *Bridging the Gap: Empirical Research in Simultaneous Interpretation*, Amsterdam and Philadelphia: John Benjamins, pp. 213–24.

Knapp, K. and Knapp-Potthoff, A. (1985) "Sprachmittlertätigkeit in interkultureller Kommunikation," in J. Rehbein (ed.) *Interkulturelle Kommunikation*, Tübingen: Gunter Narr, pp. 450–63.

Knapp-Potthoff, A. and Knapp, K. (1986) "Interweaving Two Discourses – The Difficult Task of the Non-Professional Interpreter," in J. House and S. Blum-Kulka (eds) *Interlingual and Intercultural Communication. Discourse and Cognition in Translation and Second Language Acquisition Studies*, Tübingen: Gunter Narr, pp. 151–68.

—— (1987) "The Man (or Woman) in the Middle: Discoursal Aspects of Non-Professional Interpreting," in K. Knapp and W. Enninger (eds) *Analyzing Intercultural Communication*, The Hague: Mouton, pp. 181–211.

Kohn, K. and Kalina, S. (1996) "The Strategic Dimension of Interpreting," *Meta* 41 (1): 118–38.

Kondo, M. (1990) "What Conference Interpreters Should Not Be Expected To Do," *The Interpreters' Newsletter* no. 3: 59–65.

—— and Tebble, H. [*et al.*] (1997) "Intercultural Communication, Negotiation, and Interpreting," in Y. Gambier, D. Gile and C. Taylor (eds) *Conference Interpreting: Current Trends in Research*, Amsterdam and Philadelphia: John Benjamins, pp. 149–66.

Kopczyński, A. (1980) *Conference Interpreting: Some Linguistic and Communicative Problems*, Poznań: A. Mickiewicz University Press.

—— (1982) "Effects of Some Characteristics of Impromptu Speech on Simultaneous Interpreting," in N. E. Enkvist (ed.) *Imprompu Speech: A Symposium*, Åbo: Åbo Akademi, pp. 255–66.

—— (1994) "Quality in Conference Interpreting: Some Pragmatic Problems," in M. Snell-Hornby, F. Pöchhacker and K. Kaindl (eds) *Translation Studies – An Interdiscipline*, Amsterdam and Philadelphia: John Benjamins, pp. 189–98.

Kurz, I. (1983) "'Der von uns . . . ': Schwierigkeiten des Simultandolmetschens Deutsch–Englisch," in *Festschrift zum 40jährigen Bestehen des Instituts fur Übersetzer- und Dolmetscherausbildung der Universität Wien*, Tulln: Dr. Ott-Verlag, pp. 91–8.

—— (1985) "The Rock Tombs of the Princes of Elephantine. Earliest references to interpretation in Pharaonic Egypt," *Babel* 31 (4): 213–18.

—— (1986a) "Das Dolmetscher-Relief aus dem Grab des Haremhab in Memphis. Ein Beitrag zur Geschichte des Dolmetschens im alten Ägypten," *Babel* 32 (2): 73–7.

—— (1986b) "Dolmetschen im alten Rom," *Babel* 32 (4): 215–20.

—— (1989) "Conference Interpreting: User Expectations," in D. L. Hammond (ed.) *Coming of Age: Proceedings of the 30th Annual Conference of the American Translators Association*, Medford, New Jersey: Learned Information, pp. 143–8.

Kurz, I. (1993) "Conference Interpretation: Expectations of Different User Groups," *The Interpreters' Newsletter* no. 5: 13–21.

—— (1995) "Watching the Brain at Work – An Exploratory Study of EEG Changes During Simultaneous Interpreting (SI)," *The Interpreters' Newsletter* no. 6: 3–16.

—— (1996a) *Simultandolmetschen als Gegenstand der interdisziplinären Forschung*, Wien: WUV-Universitätsverlag.

—— (1996b) "Special Features of Media Interpreting as Seen by Interpreters and Users," *XIV World Congress of the Fédération Internationale des Traducteurs (FIT). Proceedings*, vol. 2, n.p.: AUSIT, The Australian Institute of Interpreters and Translators, pp. 957–65.

—— (2000) "Tagungsort Genf/Nairobi/Wien: Zu einigen Aspekten des Teledolmetschens," in M. Kadric, K. Kaindl and F. Pöchhacker (eds) *Translationswissenschaft. Festschrift für Mary Snell-Hornby zum 60. Geburtstag*, Tübingen: Stauffenburg, pp. 291–302.

—— (2001a) "Überwindung von Sprach- und Glaubensgrenzen – Translation im frühchristlichen Alltag und bei den Konzilien," in G. Hebenstreit (ed.) *Grenzen erfahren – sichtbar machen – überschreiten. Festschrift zum 60. Geburtstag von Erich Prunč*, Frankfurt: Peter Lang, pp. 207–18.

—— (2001b) "Conference Interpreting: Quality in the Ears of the User," *Meta* 46 (2): 394–409.

—— and Pöchhacker, F. (1995) "Quality in TV Interpreting," *Translatio. Nouvelles de la FIT – FIT Newsletter* N.s. 14 (3/4): 350–8.

Kusztor, M. (2000) "Darstellung von Kohärenz in Original und Verdolmetschung," in S. Kalina, S. Buhl and H. Gerzymisch-Arbogast (eds) *Dolmetschen: Theorie – Praxis – Didaktik, mit ausgewählten Beiträgen der Saarbrücker Symposien*, St. Ingbert: Röhrig Universitätsverlag, pp. 19–44.

Kutz, W. (1990) "Zum Kompressionszwang beim Simultandolmetschen," *Fremdsprachen* 34 (4): 229–34.

Lamberger-Felber, H. (1998) "Der Einfluß kontextueller Faktoren auf das Simultandolmetschen. Eine Fallstudie am Beispiel gelesener Reden," unpublished doctoral dissertation, University of Graz.

—— (1999) "Lexikalische Variabilität beim Simultandolmetschen: Ein textstatistisches Experiment," in H. Gerzymisch-Arbogast, D. Gile, J. House and A. Rothkegel (eds) *Wege der Übersetzungs- und Dolmetschforschung*, Tübingen: Gunter Narr, pp. 179–94.

Lambert, S. M. (1983) "Recall and Recognition among Conference Interpreters," unpublished PhD dissertation, University of Stirling.

—— (1988) "Information Processing Among Conference Interpreters: A Test of the Depth of Processing Hypothesis," *Meta* 33 (3): 377–87.

—— and Moser-Mercer, B. (eds) (1994) *Bridging the Gap: Empirical Research in Simultaneous Interpretation*, Amsterdam and Philadelphia: John Benjamins.

Lang, R. (1978) "Behavioral Aspects of Liaison Interpreters in Papua New Guinea: Some Preliminary Observations," in D. Gerver and H. W. Sinaiko (eds) *Language Interpretation and Communication*, New York and London: Plenum Press, pp. 231–44.

Laplace, C. (1994) *Théorie du langage et théorie de la traduction. Les concepts-clefs de trois auteurs: Kade (Leipzig), Coseriu (Tübingen), Seleskovitch (Paris)*, Paris: Didier Érudition.

Laster, K. (1990) "Legal Interpreters: Conduits to Social Justice?" *Journal of Intercultural Studies* 11 (2): 16–32.

——— and Taylor, V. (1994) *Interpreters and the Legal System*, New South Wales: The Federation Press.

Lebhar Politi, M. (1989) "A propos du signal non verbal en interprétation simultanée," *The Interpreters' Newsletter* no. 2: 6–10.

Lederer, M. (1978a) "La traduction simultanée – Fondements théoriques," doctoral dissertation, Université de Paris IV.

——— (1978b) "Simultaneous Interpretation–Units of Meaning and Other Features," in D. Gerver and H. W. Sinaiko (eds) *Language Interpretation and Communication*, New York and London: Plenum Press, pp. 323–32.

——— (1981) *La traduction simultanée – Expérience et théorie*, Paris: Minard Lettres Modernes.

——— (1982) "Le processus de la traduction simultanée," *Multilingua* 1 (3): 149–58.

——— (ed.) (1990) *Études traductologiques – en hommage à Danica Seleskovitch*, Paris: Minard Lettres Modernes.

——— (1994) *La traduction aujourd'hui – Le modèle interprétatif*, Paris: Hachette.

Lee, T. (1999a) "Speech Proportion and Accuracy in Simultaneous Interpretation from English into Korean," *Meta* 44 (2): 260–7.

——— (1999b) "Simultaneous Listening and Speaking in English into Korean Simultaneous Interpretation," *Meta* 44 (4): 560–72.

Levý, J. (1967) "Translation as a Decision Process," in *To Honor Roman Jakobson, II*, The Hague: Mouton, pp. 1171–82.

Linell, P., Wadensjö, C. and Jönsson, L. (1992) "Establishing Communicative Contact through a Dialogue Interpreter," in A. Grindsted and J. Wagner (eds) *Communication for Specific Purposes / Fachsprachliche Kommunikation*, Tübingen: Gunter Narr, pp. 125–42.

Livingston, S., Singer, B. and Abrahamson, T. (1994) "Effectiveness Compared: ASL Interpretation vs. Transliteration," *Sign Language Studies* 82: 1–53.

Lonsdale, D. (1996) "Modeling SI: A Cognitive Approach," *Interpreting: International Journal of Research and Practice in Interpreting* 1 (2): 223–60.

——— (1997) "Modeling Cognition in SI: Methodological Issues," *Interpreting: International Journal of Research and Practice in Interpreting* 2 (1/2): 91–117.

LuperFoy, S. (1996) "Machine Interpretation of Bilingual Dialogue," *Interpreting: International Journal of Research and Practice in Interpreting* 1 (2): 213–33.

——— (1997) "Discourse Processing for Voice-to-Voice Machine Translation," in C. Hauenschild and S. Heizmann (eds) *Machine Translation and Translation Theory*, Berlin and New York: Mouton de Gruyter, pp. 223–50.

Mack, G. and Cattaruzza, L. (1995) "User Surveys in SI: A Means of Learning about Quality and/or Raising Some Reasonable Doubts," in J. Tommola (ed.) *Topics in Interpreting Research*, Turku: University of Turku, Centre for Translation and Interpreting, pp. 37–49.

Mackintosh, J. (1983) "Relay Interpretation: An Exploratory Study," unpublished MA dissertation, Birkbeck College, University of London.

Mackintosh, J. (1985) "The Kintsch and van Dijk Model of Discourse Comprehension and Production Applied to the Interpretation Process," *Meta* 30 (1): 37–43.

—— (1995) "A Review of Conference Interpretation: Practice and Training," *Target: International Journal of Translation Studies* 7 (1): 119–133.

—— (1999) "Interpreters Are Made Not Born," *Interpreting: International Journal of Research and Practice in Interpreting* 4 (1): 67–80.

Marrone, S. (1993) "Quality: A Shared Objective," *The Interpreters' Newsletter* no. 5: 35–41.

Mason, I. (ed.) (1999) *Dialogue Interpreting*, Special Issue of *The Translator: Studies in Intercultural Communication* 5 (2).

—— (2000) "Models and Methods in Dialogue Interpreting Research," in M. Olohan (ed.) *Intercultural Faultlines*, Manchester: St. Jerome Publishing, pp. 215–31.

—— (ed.) (2001) *Triadic Exchanges. Studies in Dialogue Interpreting*, Manchester: St. Jerome Publishing.

Massaro, D. (1975) *Experimental Psychology and Information Processing*, Chicago: Rand McNally.

Mattern, N. (1974) "Anticipation in German–English Simultaneous Interpreting," unpublished diploma thesis, University of the Saar, Saarbrücken.

Mazzetti, A. (1999) "The Influence of Segmental and Prosodic Deviations on Source-Text Comprehension in Simultaneous Interpretation," *The Interpreters' Newsletter* no. 9: 125–47.

Mead, P. (1999) "Interpreting: The Lexicographers' View," *The Interpreters' Newsletter* no. 9: 199–209.

Mesa, A.-M. (2000) "The Cultural Interpreter: An Appreciated Professional. Results of a Study on Interpreting Services: Client, Health Care Worker and Interpreter Points of View," in R. P. Roberts, S. E. Carr, D. Abraham and A. Dufour (eds) *The Critical Link 2: Interpreters in the Community*, Amsterdam and Philadelphia: John Benjamins, pp. 67–79.

Metzger, M. (1999) *Sign Language Interpreting: Deconstructing the Myth of Neutrality*, Washington, DC: Gallaudet University Press.

Meyer, B. (1998) "What Transcriptions of Authentic Discourse Can Reveal about Interpreting," *Interpreting: International Journal of Research and Practice in Interpreting* 3 (1): 65–83.

Mikkelson, H. (1996a) "The Professionalization of Community Interpreting," in M. Jérôme-O'Keeffe (ed.) *Global Vision. Proceedings of the 37th Annual Conference of the American Translators Association*, Alexandria, Virginia: American Translators Association, pp. 77–89.

—— (1996b) "Community Interpreting: An Emerging Profession," *Interpreting: International Journal of Research and Practice in Interpreting* 1 (1): 125–9.

—— (1998) "Towards a Redefinition of the Role of the Court Interpreter," *Interpreting: International Journal of Research and Practice in Interpreting* 3 (1): 21–46.

—— (1999) "Interpreting Is Interpreting – or Is It?" Paper presented at the 30th Anniversary Conference of the MIIS Graduate School of Translation and Interpretation, Monterey, California, 11–13 January 1999. Available HTTP: http://www.acebo.com/papers/interp1.html (9 August 2000).

Mizuno, A. (1999) "Shifts of Cohesion and Coherence in Simultaneous Interpretation from English into Japanese," *Interpreting Research: Journal of the Interpreting Research Association of Japan*, AILA '99 Tokyo Special Issue, 8 (2): 31–41.

MMIA (1996) *Medical Interpreting Standards of Practice*, Boston, Massachusetts: Massachusetts Medical Interpreters Association, and Education Development Center, Inc.

Morris, R. (1993) "Images of the Interpreter: A Study of Language-Switching in the Legal Process," unpublished doctoral dissertation, Department of Law, Lancaster University.

—— (1995) "The Moral Dilemmas of Court Interpreting," *The Translator: Studies in Intercultural Communication* 1 (1): 25–46.

—— (1999) "The Gum Syndrome: Predicaments in Court Interpreting," *Forensic Linguistics: The International Journal of Speech, Language and the Law* 6 (1): 6–29.

Moser, B. (1976) "Simultaneous Translation: Linguistic, Psycholinguistic and Human Information Processing Aspects," unpublished doctoral dissertation, University of Innsbruck.

—— (1978) "Simultaneous Interpretation: A Hypothetical Model and its Practical Application," in D. Gerver and H. W. Sinaiko (eds) *Language Interpretation and Communication*, New York and London: Plenum Press, pp. 353–68.

Moser, P. (1995) "Simultanes Konferenzdolmetschen. Anforderungen und Erwartungen der Benutzer. Endbericht, im Auftrag von AIIC," Wien: SRZ Stadt- und Regionalforschung.

—— (1996) "Expectations of Users of Conference Interpretation," *Interpreting: International Journal of Research and Practice in Interpreting* 1 (2): 145–78.

Moser-Mercer, B. (1984) "Testing Interpreting Aptitude," in W. Wilss and G. Thome (eds) *Translation Theory and its Implementation in the Teaching of Translating and Interpreting*, Tübingen: Gunter Narr, pp. 318–25.

—— (1985) "Screening Potential Interpreters," *Meta* 30 (1): 97–100.

—— (1992) "Terminology Documentation in Conference Interpretation," *Terminologie et Traduction* no. 2/3: 285–303.

—— (1994a) "Training and Research: The Foundation for Conference Interpretation," *ATA Chronicle* 23 (6): 14–15.

—— (1994b) "Aptitude Testing for Conference Interpreting: Why, When and How," in S. Lambert and B. Moser-Mercer (eds) *Bridging the Gap: Empirical Research in Simultaneous Interpretation*, Amsterdam and Philadelphia: John Benjamins, pp. 57–68.

—— (1997a) "Process Models in Simultaneous Interpretation," in C. Hauenschild and S. Heizmann (eds) *Machine Translation and Translation Theory*, Berlin and New York: Mouton de Gruyter, pp. 3–17.

—— (1997b) "Beyond Curiosity: Can Interpreting Research Meet the Challenge?," in J. H. Danks, G. M. Shreve, S. B. Fountain and M. K. McBeath (eds) *Cognitive Processes in Translation and Interpreting*, Thousand Oaks, London and New Delhi: Sage, pp. 176–205.

—— Künzli, A. and Korac, M. (1998) "Prolonged Turns in Interpreting: Effects on Quality, Physiological and Psychological Stress (Pilot Study)," *Interpreting: International Journal of Research and Practice in Interpreting* 3 (1): 47–64.

—— Frauenfelder, U. H., Casado, B. and Künzli, A. (2000) "Searching to Define Expertise in Interpreting," in B. Englund Dimitrova and K. Hyltenstam (eds) *Language Processing and Simultaneous Interpretation: Interdisciplinary Perspectives*, Amsterdam and Philadelphia: John Benjamins, pp. 107–31.

Mouzourakis, P. (1996) "Videoconferencing: Techniques and Challenges," *Interpreting: International Journal of Research and Practice in Interpreting* 1 (1): 21–38.

Namy, C. (1978) "Reflections on the Training of Simultaneous Interpreters: A Metalinguistic Approach," in D. Gerver and H. W. Sinaiko (eds) *Language Interpretation and Communication*, New York and London: Plenum Press, pp. 25–33.

Niska, H. (1995) "Just Interpreting: Role Conflicts and Discourse Types in Court Interpreting," in M. Morris (ed.) *Translation and the Law*, Amsterdam and Philadelphia: John Benjamins, pp. 293–316.

—— [*et al.*] (1999) "Quality Issues in Remote Interpreting," in A. Álvarez Lugrís and A. Fernández Ocampo (eds) *Anovar/Anosar estudios de traducción e interpretación*, Vigo: Universidade de Vigo, vol. 1, pp. 109–21.

Oléron, P. (1992) "Autobiographie," in F. Parot and M. Richelle (eds) *Psychologues de langue française. Autobiographies*, Paris: Presses Universitaires de France, pp. 135–59.

—— and Nanpon, H. (1965) "Récherches sur la traduction simultanée," *Journal de Psychologie Normale et Pathologique* 62 (1): 73–94.

Ong, W. J. (1982) *Orality and Literacy: The Technologizing of the Word*, London and New York: Methuen.

Padilla, P., Bajo, M. T., Cañas, J. J. and Padilla, F. (1995) "Cognitive Processes of Memory in Simultaneous Interpretation," in J. Tommola (ed.) *Topics in Interpreting Research*, Turku: University of Turku, Centre for Translation and Interpreting, pp. 61–71.

Paneth, E. (1957) "An Investigation into Conference Interpreting (with Special Reference to the Training of Interpreters)," unpublished MA thesis, University of London.

—— (1962) "The Interpreter's Task and Training," *The Incorporated Linguist* 1 (4): 102–9.

—— (1984) "Training in Note-Taking (for interpreting)," in W. Wilss and G. Thome (eds) *Translation Theory and its Implementation in the Teaching of Translating and Interpreting*, Tübingen: Gunter Narr, pp. 326–32.

Paradis, M. (1994) "Toward a Neurolinguistic Theory of Simultaneous Translation: The Framework," *International Journal of Psycholinguistics* 9 (3): 319–35.

Pearl, S. (1995) "Lacuna, Myth and Shibboleth in the Teaching of Simultaneous Interpreting," *Perspectives: Studies in Translatology* 3 (1): 161–90.

Pinter, I. (1969) "Der Einfluß der Übung und Konzentration auf simultanes Sprechen und Hören," unpublished doctoral dissertation, University of Vienna.

Pöchhacker, F. (1992) "The Role of Theory in Simultaneous Interpreting," in C. Dollerup and A. Loddegaard (eds) *Teaching Translation and Interpreting: Training, Talent and Experience*, Amsterdam and Philadelphia: John Benjamins, pp. 211–20.

—— (1993) "From Knowledge to Text: Coherence in Simultaneous Interpreting," in Y. Gambier and J. Tommola (eds) *Translation and Knowledge: SSOTT IV*, Turku: University of Turku, Centre for Translation and Interpreting, pp. 87–100.

—— (1994a) *Simultandolmetschen als komplexes Handeln*, Tübingen: Gunter Narr.

—— (1994b) "Simultaneous Interpretation: 'Cultural Transfer' or 'Voice-over

Text'?," in M. Snell-Hornby, F. Pöchhacker and K. Kaindl (eds) *Translation Studies – An Interdiscipline*, Amsterdam and Philadelphia: John Benjamins, pp. 169–78.

—— (1995a) "Simultaneous Interpreting: A Functionalist Perspective," *Hermes. Journal of Linguistics* no. 14: 31–53.

—— (1995b) "Slips and Shifts in Simultaneous Interpretation," in J. Tommola (ed.) *Topics in Interpreting Research*, Turku: University of Turku, Centre for Translation and Interpreting, pp. 73–90.

—— (1999a) Review of Collados Aís (1998), *Interpreting: International Journal of Research and Practice in Interpreting* 4 (2): 219–23.

—— (1999b) "'Getting Organized': The Evolution of Community Interpreting," *Interpreting: International Journal of Research and Practice in Interpreting* 4 (1): 125–40.

—— (2000a) "The Community Interpreter's Task: Self-Perception and Provider Views," in R. P. Roberts, S. E. Carr, D. Abraham and A. Dufour (eds) *The Critical Link 2: Interpreters in the Community*, Amsterdam and Philadelphia: John Benjamins, pp. 49–65.

—— (2000b) *Dolmetschen. Konzeptuelle Grundlagen und deskriptive Untersuchungen*, Tübingen: Stauffenburg.

—— (2001) "Quality Assessment in Conference and Community Interpreting," *Meta* 46 (2): 410–25.

Poyatos, F. (1983) *New Perspectives in Nonverbal Communication Studies: Cultural Anthropology, Social Psychology, Linguistics, Literature and Semiotics*. Oxford: Pergamon Press.

—— (1987) "Nonverbal Communication in Simultaneous and Consecutive Interpretation: A Theoretical Model and New Perspectives," *TexTconTexT* 2 (2/3): 73–108.

—— (1993) *Paralanguage: A Linguistic and Interdisciplinary Approach to Interactive Speech and Sounds*. Amsterdam and Philadelphia: John Benjamins.

—— (ed.) (1997a) *Nonverbal Communication and Translation. New Perspectives and Challenges in Literature, Interpretation and the Media*, Amsterdam and Philadelphia: John Benjamins.

—— (1997b) "The Reality of Multichannel Verbal–Nonverbal Communication in Simultaneous and Consecutive Interpretation," in F. Poyatos (ed.) *Nonverbal Communication and Translation*, Amsterdam and Philadelphia: John Benjamins, pp. 249–82.

Quigley, S. P. and Youngs, J. P. (eds) (1965) *Interpreting for Deaf People*, Washington, DC: US Department of Health, Education and Welfare.

Rehbein, J. (1985) "Ein ungleiches Paar – Verfahren des Sprachmittelns in der medizinischen Beratung," in J. Rehbein (ed.) *Interkulturelle Kommunikation*, Tübingen: Gunter Narr, pp. 420–48.

Riccardi, A. (1998) "Interpreting Strategies and Creativity," in A. Beylard-Ozeroff, J. Králová and B. Moser-Mercer (eds) *Translators' Strategies and Creativity*, Amsterdam and Philadelphia: John Benjamins, pp. 171–9.

Roberts, R. P. (1997) "Community Interpreting Today and Tomorrow," in S. E. Carr, R. Roberts, A. Dufour and D. Steyn (eds) *The Critical Link: Interpreters in the Community*, Amsterdam and Philadelphia: John Benjamins, pp. 7–26.

Römer, L. (1968) "Einige syntaktische Gesetzmäßigkeiten beim Simultandol-metschen," in A. Neubert (ed.) *Grundfragen der Übersetzungswissenschaft*, Leipzig: Verlag Enzyklopädie, pp. 65–72.

Roothaer, R. (1978) "Ein Modell für das Simultandolmetschen," *Mitteilungsblatt für Dolmetscher und Übersetzer* 24 (4): 2–7.

Roy, C. (1989) "A Sociolinguistic Analysis of the Interpreter's Role in the Turn Exchanges of an Interpreted Event," unpublished doctoral dissertation, Georgetown University.

—— (1993) "The Problem with Definitions, Descriptions and the Role Metaphors of Interpreters," *Journal of Interpretation* 6 (1): 127–54.

—— (1996) "An Interactional Sociolinguistic Analysis of Turntaking in an Interpreted Event," *Interpreting: International Journal of Research and Practice in Interpreting* 1 (1): 39–67.

—— (2000) *Interpreting as a Discourse Process*, Oxford: Oxford University Press.

Salevsky, H. (1982) "Teoreticheskie problemi klassifikatzii vidov perevoda [Theoretical Problems of the Classification of Types of Translation]," *Fremdsprachen* 26 (2): 80–6.

—— (1987) *Probleme des Simultandolmetschens. Eine Studie zur Handlungsspezifik*, Berlin: Akademie der Wissenschaften der DDR.

—— (1992) "Dolmetschen – Objekt der Übersetzungs – oder Dolmetsch-wissenschaft?" in H. Salevsky (ed.) *Wissenschaftliche Grundlagen der Sprachmitt-lung*, Frankfurt am Main: Peter Lang, pp. 85–117.

—— (1993a) "The Distinctive Nature of Interpreting Studies," *Target: International Journal of Translation Studies* 5 (2): 149–67.

—— (1993b) "What Is Meant by Interpreting Studies and What Is their Purpose?" in J. Králová and Z. Jettmarová (eds) *Translation Strategies and Effects in Cross-Cultural Value Transfer and Shifts. The 8th International Conference on Transla-tion and Interpreting held in Prague, 20–22 October 1992*, Prague: Charles University, pp. 115–25.

—— (1994) "Möglichkeiten und Grenzen eines Interaktionsmodells des Dol-metschens," in M. Snell-Hornby, F. Pöchhacker and K. Kaindl (eds) *Translation Studies – An Interdiscipline*, Amsterdam and Philadelphia: John Benjamins, pp. 159–68.

Sanz, J. (1931) "Le travail et les aptitudes des interprètes parlementaires," *Anals d'Orientació Professional* 4: 303–18.

Sauvêtre, M. (2000) "De l'interprétariat au dialogue à trois. Pratiques européennes de l'interprétariat en milieu social," in R. P. Roberts, S. E. Carr, D. Abraham and A. Dufour (eds) *The Critical Link 2: Interpreters in the Community*, Amsterdam and Philadelphia: John Benjamins, pp. 35–45.

Schjoldager, A. (1995a) "An Exploratory Study of Translational Norms in Simul-taneous Interpreting: Methodological Reflections," *Hermes. Journal of Linguistics* no. 14: 65–87.

—— (1995b) "Interpreting Research and the 'Manipulation School' of Translation Studies," *Target: International Journal of Translation Studies* 7 (1): 29–45.

—— (1996) "Simultaneous Interpreting: Empirical Investigation into Target-text/Source-text Relations," unpublished PhD dissertation, Aarhus School of Business.

Séguinot, C. (1989) "The Translation Process: An Experimental Study," in C. Séguinot (ed.) *The Translation Process*, Toronto: H. G. Publications, pp. 21–53.

Seleskovitch, D. (1962) "L'Interprétation de Conférence," *Babel* 8 (1): 13–8.

—— (1968) *L'interprète dans les conférences internationales: problèmes de langage et de communication*, Paris: Minard Lettres Modernes.

—— (1975) *Langage, langues et mémoire. Étude de la prise de notes en interprétation consécutive*, Paris: Minard Lettres Modernes.

—— (1976) "Interpretation, A Psychological Approach to Translating," in R. W. Brislin (ed.) *Translation: Applications and Research*, New York: Gardner Press, pp. 92–116.

—— (1978) "Language and Cognition," in D. Gerver and H. W. Sinaiko (eds) *Language Interpretation and Communication*, New York and London: Plenum Press, pp. 333–41.

—— (1982) "Impromptu Speech and Oral Translation," in N. E. Enkvist (ed.) *Impromptu Speech: A Symposium*, Åbo: Åbo Akademi, pp. 241–53.

—— (1999) "The Teaching of Simultaneous Interpretation in the Course of the Last 50 Years," *Interpreting: International Journal of Research and Practice in Interpreting* 4 (1): 55–66.

—— and Lederer, M. (1984) *Interpréter pour Traduire*, Paris: Didier Érudition.

—— and Lederer, M. (1989) *Pédagogie raisonnée de l'interprétation*, Paris: Didier Érudition. [English translation by J. Harmer (1995) *A Systematic Approach to Teaching Interpretation*, Registry of Interpreters for the Deaf.]

Setton, R. (1993) "Is Non-Intra-IE Interpretation Different? European Models and Chinese–English Realities," *Meta* 38 (2): 238–56.

—— (1994) "Experiments in the Application of Discourse Studies to Interpreter Training," in C. Dollerup and A. Lindegaard (eds) *Teaching Translation and Interpreting 2: Aims, Insights, Visions*, Amsterdam and Philadelphia: John Benjamins, pp. 183–98.

—— (1998) "Meaning Assembly in Simultaneous Interpretation," *Interpreting: International Journal of Research and Practice in Interpreting* 3 (2): 163–99.

—— (1999a) *Simultaneous Interpretation: A Cognitive-Pragmatic Analysis*, Amsterdam and Philadelphia: John Benjamins.

—— (1999b) "Cognitive Pragmatics in T & I Research," in A. Álvarez Lugrís and A. Fernández Ocampo (eds) *Anovar/Anosar estudios de traducción e interpretación*, Vigo: Universidade de Vigo, vol. 1, pp. 307–15.

Shackman, J. (1984) *The Right to Be Understood: A Handbook on Working with, Employing and Training Community Interpreters*, Cambridge, England: National Extension College.

Shiryayev, A. (1979) *Sinkhronniy perevod. Deyatelnost sinkhronnogo perevodchika i metodika prepodavaniya sinkhronnogo perevoda* [Simultaneous Interpretation: The Activity of a Simultaneous Interpreter and Methods of Teaching Simultaneous Interpretation], Moscow: Voyenizdat.

Shlesinger, M. (1989a) "Simultaneous Interpretation as a Factor in Effecting Shifts in the Position of Texts on the Oral–Literate Continuum," unpublished MA Thesis, Tel Aviv University.

—— (1989b) "Extending the Theory of Translation to Interpretation: Norms as a Case in Point," *Target: International Journal of Translation Studies* 1 (1): 111–16.

Shlesinger, M. (1994) "Intonation in the Production and Perception of Simultaneous Interpretation," in S. Lambert and B. Moser-Mercer (eds) *Bridging the Gap: Empirical Research in Simultaneous Interpretation*, Amsterdam and Philadelphia: John Benjamins, pp. 225–36.

—— (1995) "Stranger in Paradigms: What Lies Ahead for Simultaneous Interpreting Research?," *Target: International Journal of Translation Studies* 7 (1): 7–28.

—— [*et al.*] (1997) "Quality in Simultaneous Interpreting," in Y. Gambier, D. Gile and C. Taylor (eds) *Conference Interpreting: Current Trends in Research*, Amsterdam and Philadelphia: John Benjamins, pp. 123–31.

—— (1998) "Corpus-based Interpreting Studies as an Offshoot of Corpus-based Translation Studies," *Meta* 43 (4): 486–93.

—— (1999) "Norms, Strategies and Constraints: How Do We Tell Them Apart?," in A. Álvarez Lugrís and A. Fernández Ocampo (eds) *Anovar/Anosar estudios de traducción e interpretación*, Vigo: Universidade de Vigo, vol. 1, pp. 65–77.

—— (2000a) "Strategic Allocation of Working Memory and Other Attentional Resources," unpublished PhD dissertation, Bar-Ilan University.

—— (2000b) "Interpreting as a Cognitive Process: How Can we Know What Really Happens?," in S. Tirkkonen-Condit and R. Jääskeläinen (eds) *Tapping and Mapping the Processes of Translation and Interpreting. Outlooks on Empirical Research*, Amsterdam and Philadelphia: John Benjamins, pp. 3–15.

Sia, Gion Sing (1954) *Manual for Interpreters and Clerks of Courts*, Federation of Malaya: Government Printer.

Snell-Hornby, M., Pöchhacker, F. and Kaindl, K. (eds) (1994) *Translation Studies – An Interdiscipline*, Amsterdam and Philadelphia: John Benjamins.

Steiner, B. (1998) "Signs from the Void: The Comprehension and Production of Sign Language on Television," *Interpreting: International Journal of Research and Practice in Interpreting* 3 (2): 99–146.

Stenzl, C. (1983) "Simultaneous Interpretation: Groundwork Towards a Comprehensive Model," unpublished MA thesis, Birkbeck College, University of London.

Strong M. and Fritsch-Rudser, S. (1992) "The Subjective Assessment of Sign Language Interpreters," in D. Cokely (ed.) *Sign Language Interpreters and Interpreting*, Burtonsville, Maryland: Linstok Press, pp. 1–14.

Sturge, K. (1997) "Translation Strategies in Ethnography," *The Translator: Studies in Intercultural Communication* 3 (1): 21–38.

Sunnari, M. (1995) "Processing Strategies in Simultaneous Interpreting: 'Saying It All' vs. Synthesis," in J. Tommola (ed.) *Topics in Interpreting Research*, Turku: University of Turku, Centre for Translation and Interpreting, pp. 109–19.

Tannen, D. (1982) "The Oral/Literate Continuum in Discourse," in D. Tannen (ed.) *Spoken and Written Language: Exploring Quality and Literacy*, Norwood, New Jersey: Ablex, pp. 1–16.

Taylor, C. (1989) "Primary and Secondary Orality in Teaching Interpreting Technique," in J. M. Dodds (ed.) *Aspects of English. Miscellaneous Papers for English Teachers and Specialists*, Udine: Campanotto Editore, pp. 93–102.

Taylor Torsello, C. (1996) "Theme as the Interpreter's Path Indicator through the Unfolding Text," *The Interpreters' Newsletter* no. 7: 113–49.

—— [*et al.*] (1997) "Linguistics, Discourse Analysis and Interpretation," in Y. Gambier, D. Gile and C. Taylor (eds) *Conference Interpreting: Current Trends in Research*, Amsterdam and Philadelphia: John Benjamins, pp. 167–86.

Tebble, H. (1999) "The Tenor of Consultant Physicians: Implications for Medical Interpreting," *The Translator: Studies in Intercultural Communication* 5 (2): 179–200.

Teo, Say Eng (1983/4) "The Role of Interpreters in the Malaysian Courts," unpublished thesis, Faculty of Law, University of Malaya, Kuala Lumpur.

Thiéry, C. (1975) "Le bilinguisme chez les interprètes de conférence professionnels," unpublished doctoral dissertation, Université Paris III.

Tommola, J. (ed.) (1995) *Topics in Interpreting Research*, Turku: University of Turku, Centre for Translation and Interpreting.

—— (1999) "New Trends in Interpreting Research: Going Psycho – or Neuro?," in A. Álvarez Lugrís and A. Fernández Ocampo (eds) *Anovar/Anosar estudios de traducción e interpretación*, Vigo: Universidade de Vigo, vol. 1, pp. 321–30.

—— and Hyönä, J. (1990) "Mental Load in Listening, Speech Shadowing and Simultaneous Interpreting: A Pupillometric Study," in J. Tommola (ed.) *Foreign Language Comprehension and Production*, Turku: AFinLA, pp. 179–88.

—— and Laakso, T. (1997) "Source Text Segmentation, Speech Rate and Language Direction: Effects on Trainee Simultaneous Interpreting," in K. Klaudy and J. Kohn (eds) *Transferre Necesse Est: Proceedings of the 2nd International Conference on Current Trends in Studies of Translation and Interpreting, 5–7 September, 1996, Budapest, Hungary*, Budapest: Scholastica, pp. 186–91.

—— and Lindholm, J. (1995) "Experimental Research on Interpreting: Which Dependent Variable?" in J. Tommola (ed.) *Topics in Interpreting Research*, Turku: University of Turku, Centre for Translation and Interpreting, pp. 121–33.

Toury, G. (1980) *In Search of a Theory of Translation*, Tel Aviv: The Porter Institute for Poetics and Semiotics, Tel Aviv University.

—— (1991) "What Are Descriptive Studies into Translation Likely to Yield Apart from Isolated Descriptions?," in K. van Leuven-Zwart and T. Naaijkens (eds) *Translation Studies: The State of the Art*, Amsterdam and Atlanta: Rodopi, pp. 179–92.

—— (1995) *Descriptive Translation Studies and Beyond*, Amsterdam and Philadelphia: John Benjamins.

Treisman, A. M. (1965) "The Effects of Redundancy and Familiarity on Translating and Repeating Back a Foreign and a Native Language," *British Journal of Psychology* 56: 369–79.

Turner, G. H. (1995) "Rights and Responsibilities: The Relationship between Deaf People and Interpreters," *Deafness* 11 (3): 4–8.

—— (1996) "Regulation and Responsibility: The Relationship between Interpreters and Deaf People," *Deaf Worlds* 12 (1): 1–7.

Tweney, R. D. and Hoemann, H. W. (1976) "Translation and Sign Languages," in R. W. Brislin (ed.) *Translation: Applications and Research*, New York: Gardner Press, pp. 138–61.

Tymoczko, M. (1990) "Translation in Oral Tradition as a Touchstone for Translation Theory and Practice," in S. Bassnett and A. Lefevere (eds) *Translation, History and Culture*, London: Pinter, pp. 46–55.

Tymoczko, M. and Gentzler, E. (eds) (2002) *Translation and Power*, Amherst, Massachusetts: University of Massachusetts Press.

Van Besien, F. (1999a) "Anticipation in Simultaneous Interpretation," *Meta* 44 (2): 250–9.

—— (1999b) "Strategies in Simultaneous Interpretation: Anticipation," *Interpreting Research: Journal of the Interpreting Research Association of Japan*, AILA '99 Tokyo Special Issue, 8 (2): 21–30.

Van Dam, I. M. (1989) "Strategies of Simultaneous Interpretation," in L. Gran and J. Dodds (eds) *The Theoretical and Practical Aspects of Teaching Conference Interpretation*, Udine: Campanotto Editore, 167–76.

Venuti, L. (ed.) (2000) *The Translation Studies Reader*, London and New York: Routledge.

Vermeer, H. J. (1978) "Ein Rahmen für eine allgemeine Translationstheorie," *Lebende Sprachen* 23: 99–102.

—— (1989) *Skopos und Translationsauftrag*, Heidelberg: Universität Heidelberg.

—— (1996) *A Skopos Theory of Translation (Some Arguments For and Against)*, Heidelberg: TexTconTexT Verlag.

Viaggio, Sergio (1992) "Teaching Beginners to Shut Up and Listen," *The Interpreters' Newsletter* no. 4: 45–58.

Viezzi, M. (1993) "Considerations on Interpretation Quality," in C. Picken (ed.) *Translation – The Vital Link: Proceedings of the XIIIth World Congress of FIT*, vol. 1, London: Institute of Translation and Interpreting, pp. 389–97.

—— (1996) *Aspetti della Qualità in Interpretazione*, Trieste: Scuola Superiore di Lingue Moderne per Interpreti e Traduttori.

Vuorikoski, A. (1993) "Simultaneous Interpretation – User Experience and Expectations," in C. Picken (ed.) *Translation – The Vital Link: Proceedings of the XIIIth World Congress of FIT*, vol. 1, London: Institute of Translation and Interpreting, pp. 317–27.

Wadensjö, C. (1992) *Interpreting as Interaction: On Dialogue Interpreting in Immigration Hearings and Medical Encounters*, Linköping: Linköping University, Department of Communication Studies.

—— (1993) "The Double Role of a Dialogue Interpreter," *Perspectives: Studies in Translatology* 1: 105–21.

—— (1995) "Dialogue Interpreting and the Distribution of Responsibility," *Hermes. Journal of Linguistics* no. 14: 111–29.

—— (1997) "Recycled Information as a Questioning Strategy: Pitfalls in Interpreter-Mediated Talk," in S. E. Carr, R. Roberts, A. Dufour and D. Steyn (eds) *The Critical Link: Interpreters in the Community*, Amsterdam and Philadelphia: John Benjamins, pp. 35–52.

—— (1998) *Interpreting as Interaction*, London and New York: Longman.

—— (1999) "Telephone Interpreting and the Synchronization of Talk in Social Interaction," *The Translator: Studies in Intercultural Communication* 5 (2): 247–64.

—— (2000) "Co-constructing Yeltsin – Explorations of an Interpreter-Mediated Political Interview," in M. Olohan (ed.) *Intercultural Faultlines: Research Models in Translation Studies I*, Manchester: St. Jerome Publishing, pp. 233–52.

Welford, A. T. (1968) *Fundamentals of Skill*, London: Methuen.

Williams, S. (1995) "Observations on Anomalous Stress in Interpreting," *The Translator: Studies in Intercultural Communication* 1 (1): 47–64.

Yaghi, H. M. (1994) "A Psycholinguistic Model for Simultaneous Translation, and Proficiency Assessment by Automated Acoustic Analysis of Discourse," unpublished doctoral dissertation, University of Auckland, New Zealand.

Yagi, S. M. (1999) "Computational Discourse Analysis for Interpretation," *Meta* 44 (2): 268–79.

Zimman, L. (1994) "Intervention as a Pedagogical Problem in Community Interpreting," in C. Dollerup and A. Lindegaard (eds) *Teaching Translation and Interpreting 2: Insights, Aims, Visions*, Amsterdam and Philadelphia: John Benjamins, pp. 217–24.

Zimnyaya, I. and Chernov, G. V. (1973) "Veroyatnostnoe prognozirovanie v protsesse sinkhronnogo pereovoda [Probability Prediction in the Process of Simultaneous Interpretation]," in A. Leontyev, N. Zhinkin and A. Shaknarovich (eds) *Predvaritelnyye materialy eksperimentalnych issledovaniy po psicholingvistike* [Preliminary Results of Experimental Studies in Psycholinguistics], Moscow: Institut Yazykoznaniya Akademii Nauk, pp. 110–77.

NAME INDEX

SUBJECT INDEX